THE WORLD OF BUSINESS

FIFTH EDITION

THE WORLD OF BUSINESS

FIFTH EDITION

Jack Wilson

David Notman

Lorie Guest

Terry G. Murphy

NELSON EDUCATION

NELSON / E D U C A T I O N

The World of Business
Fifth Edition

Authors
Jack Wilson, David Notman, Lorie Guest, Terry G. Murphy

NELSON EDUCATION

Director of Publishing
Beverley Buxton

General Manager, Social Studies, Business Studies, and Languages
Carol Stokes

Publisher,
Doug Panasis

Managing Editor, Development
Karin Fediw

Product Manager
Mary Jo Climie

Assistant Editor
Alisa Yampolsky

Editorial Assistant
Kimberly Murphy

Photo Research/Permissions
MRM Associates

Executive Director, Content and Media Production
Renate McCloy

Director, Content and Media Production
Lisa Dimson

Senior Content Production Manager
Sujata Singh

Production Manager
Cathy Deak

Production Coordinator
Kathrine Pummell

Design Director
Ken Phipps

Cover Design
Rocket Design

Cover Image
© 2007 JupiterImages and its Licensors. All Rights Reserved.

Printer
Transcontinental Printing Inc.

Reviewers
The authors and publisher gratefully acknowledge the contributions of the following educators:

John Pownall, York Region District School Board, ON

Michelle Presotto, Toronto Catholic Board, ON

Zenobia Omarali, Toronto District School Board, ON

Wendy Jo Hanninen, Toronto District School Board, ON

Lynda Anstett, Halton District School Board, ON

Terry G. Murphy, Limestone District School Board, ON (retired)

FIRST FOLIO RESOURCE GROUP, INC.

Project Supervisor
Fran Cohen

Project Manager
Paula Chabanais

Line Editors
Nancy Mucklow, Wendy Thomas

Production Editor
Shana Hayes

Art Direction/Interior Design
Tom Dart

Composition
Tom Dart, Kim Hutchinson, Cara Scime, Adam Wood

Copy Editors
Shana Hayes, Linda Pruessen

Proofreader
Cheryl Tiongson

Profile Writers and Researchers
Shannon Falconer, Catherine Shea

Index
Laurie Coulter

Illustration
leifpeng.com

Every effort has been made to trace ownership of all copyrighted material and to secure permission from copyright holders. In the event of any question arising as to the use of any material, we will be pleased to make the necessary corrections in future printings.

A Note from the Publisher:
The brand names and photos that appear in this book do not represent endorsements, but rather are business-related examples relevant to the content of the text.

Acknowledgments

The authors would like to recognize and applaud the contributions of several people who assisted in the production of the fifth edition of *The World of Business*. Doug Panasis was a driving force in getting our project approved and he continued to be involved each step of the way. Thanks for pushing all of us in the right direction. We were also very fortunate to have the support of Fran Cohen and her team at First Folio Resource Group during the reviewing and editing process. In particular, Paula Chabanais has to be given much credit for her efforts in pulling together all of the authors' text material, coordinating a team of development editors, and keeping everything on track and on time. Paula, you were amazing and we thank you most sincerely.

Carol Stokes directed the efforts of several Thomson Nelson personnel who were responsible for conducting market research and hosting focus group sessions around the province. It was this feedback from classroom practitioners and from the business community that resulted in a commitment to produce a fifth edition of *The World of Business*.

This one is for the "little people"—my nieces and nephews: Wendy, Steven, Neal, Shannon, David, Andy, Jennifer, Stacey, and Todd—JW

To friends and family, for their interest, encouragement, and support—DN

In memory of my mom and dad. They taught me to value education, writing and fostered my love of teaching. You are missed—LG

To my wife Katherine (Kit); Jamie and Laura; and to Karen, Russ, and our beautiful and wonderful granddaughters Macy and Ella; thanks for all your love and support—TGM

Preface

The fifth edition of *The World of Business* builds on the framework of previous editions while addressing curriculum changes mandated by the Ministry of Education (MOE). To that end, the fifth edition incorporates the five critical areas of learning as identified by the MOE: business skills, communication in a business environment, digital literacy, financial literacy, and ethical, moral, and legal considerations.

The authors chose to deal with ethical, moral, and legal considerations in two ways. First, Chapter 3 on Business Ethics and Social Responsibility is devoted to this subject and covers expectations that deal with ethical dilemmas and controversial business issues. Also you will find at least one feature box on ethical, moral, and legal considerations in each chapter, which will keep this critical area of learning at the forefront.

One of the major additions to this edition is the international profile at the end of each chapter. The authors feel strongly that students should learn about Canadian businesses. However, many of the companies students interact with are global. This is of significant importance when one considers the opportunities for Canadian businesses at an international level.

There are two activities in each chapter that can be considered as part of performance tasks: a Team Activity and a Portfolio assignment. The Team Activities require students to perform an actual task—such as marketing a school event—and can be a competitive project. The Portfolio assignments assist the students in compiling an industry profile that illustrates the student's understanding of most of the specific expectations associated with each of the chapters, and which teachers can use as a culminating task for assessment purposes.

The fifth edition has many other useful features, brief summaries of all of the features are listed below. New features for the fifth edition include: Keep in Mind; Oops!; In the News; Ethical, Moral, and Legal Considerations; Literacy Links; Team Activity; and International Profile.

Features of the Fifth Edition

Overall Expectations
At the beginning of each unit, the *overall expectations* for each strand in the Ontario curriculum are listed.

Student Expectations

At the beginning of each chapter, the specific *student expectations* for each strand in the Ontario curriculum are listed.

Chapter Opening Profiles

These profiles highlight a *Canadian* company whose business activities reflect the main ideas of the chapter. For example, Chapter 3 on Business Ethics features the Kicking Horse Coffee Co., a company whose founders have ethical beliefs about organic food and fair trade. (Please note: all companies included in these profiles were Canadian owned when the book was written.)

Before You Begin

Questions or activities open each chapter and are designed to pique students' interest, build on prior knowledge, and engage them in discussion about what they will be reading. This feature, combined with the *Reflect on Your Learning* feature, provides a wraparound approach to each chapter.

Keep in Mind

These summary features are designed to act as a student organizer by pulling together concept headings presented in the chapter. This mind map is a *new* feature and will help students as they first read the chapter, as well as provide them with a reference check when they review.

Oops!

Businesses learn from their mistakes if they wish to survive. This *new* feature identifies some classic mistakes made by businesses. An understanding of these mistakes can be used effectively as a discussion starter in the classroom.

Business Facts

Two or three *Business Facts* are provided in each chapter and offer interesting information and statistical data about the world of business.

In the News

The *In the News* features provide a brief look at business stories that are making the news. This information is designed to complement and extend the chapter text material for a further understanding of business concepts.

Ethical, Moral, and Legal Considerations

This *new* feature introduces brief scenarios which question whether a business made a right or wrong decision. Sometimes business decisions push the limits of acceptability and legality and many business decisions do not always favour employees, consumers, other businesses, or the environment. By examining such scenarios, students will gain insight into another aspect of business decision making.

Literacy Links

This *new* feature provides hints to improve the students' reading, writing, and comprehension of the material.

Cartoons

At least one *cartoon* per chapter is used to link a humorous situation to the concepts that are being introduced. Cartoons can stimulate thought and discussion in the classroom and provide a springboard for teachers to engage students in further study.

Stretch Your Thinking

This feature is designed to help students develop critical and creative thinking and inquiry skills. It extends the knowledge that is presented in the chapter content.

DVD Links

DVD icons appear throughout the chapters and link to a *new* DVD program series. The DVD program can be used to introduce, illustrate, and/or summarize concepts presented in the chapters. Plus, each DVD program comes with a print support package designed to assist the teacher when using this *new* feature.

E-activity Links

E-activity icons appear throughout each chapter and link to the Thomson Nelson Learning website. These activities will help you use the Internet effectively to research business topics. The notes at the Thomson Nelson website connect the Internet research activity with chapter topics, concepts, and skills, and contain references to relevant sections of the chapter and its features.

Review Questions

Review questions are spread throughout the text material to allow students to help understand the concepts introduced. The questions are based on the knowledge presented in the chapter.

End of Chapter Questions

The end of chapter questions are organized according to the Ministry of Education's Achievement Chart categories, namely Knowledge, Thinking, Communication, and Application.

Team Activity

Working as a team is a critical skill in any business environment and this *new* feature will help students work with colleagues in problem-solving situations. The team activity is loosely based on the television show *The Apprentice*, and teachers may wish to introduce some light-hearted competitiveness to this assignment.

Reflect on Your Learning

These questions appear at the end of the chapter and often link back to the *Before You Begin* feature that appeared at the beginning. This feature is designed to enable students and teachers to help assess what knowledge has been acquired and what attitudes have changed through working with the chapter.

Portfolio

A portfolio is a collection of a student's best work on a specific topic and this feature is designed to help students accomplish that task. In Chapter 1, a student selects an industry to study, profiles that industry, and, in subsequent chapters, builds his or her portfolio around the industry by adding information relevant to the ministry expectations for each chapter. This collection of work will help illustrate the student's understanding of the ministry expectations. This portfolio can be used as a summative assessment for the course.

International Profile

This feature highlights *international* businesses that operate around the world. By using a case study approach, students will learn more about these businesses, many of which they deal with on a daily basis. This *new* feature is similar to the domestic profiles but will offer a sense of international companies and their scope.

TABLE OF CONTENTS

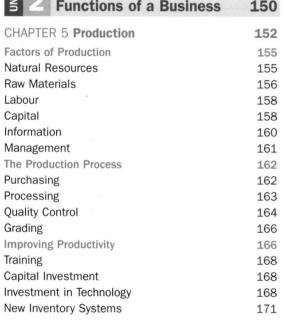

UNIT 1

Business Fundamentals

"An organization's ability to learn, and translate that learning into action rapidly, is the ultimate competitive advantage."

Jack Welch, former CEO of General Electric

OVERALL EXPECTATIONS

- demonstrate an understanding of how businesses respond to needs, wants, supply, and demand
- compare types of businesses
- demonstrate an understanding of ethics and social responsibility in business
- demonstrate an understanding of the benefits and challenges for Canada in the field of international business

Economic Basics

SPECIFIC EXPECTATIONS

After completing this chapter, you will be able to

- explain how needs and wants create opportunities for business

- describe the concepts of supply and demand and the conditions that affect them

- compare the ways in which different industries, sectors, and competitors address similar consumer needs and wants

Pita Pit

Can fast food be healthy? John Sotiriadis and Nelson Lang, the founders of Pita Pit, thought so and saw a need in the market for a healthy fast-food outlet. Pita Pit puts a fresh twist on fast food and is an alternative to traditional burger and pizza places. Pita Pit opened its first store in Kingston, Ontario, in 1995. In 1997, the Pita Pit franchise expanded across Canada and in 1999 expanded into the United States. Today there are 220 stores worldwide, with two to four new locations opening monthly.

Pita Pit's success is built around understanding their customers. Pita Pit has a loyal following of students and health-conscious individuals who want a healthy meal. Yet their customer base has broadened as students become professionals and as healthy eating is emphasized in society.

Pita Pit aims to please their customers on five dimensions: convenience, accessibility, service, atmosphere, and taste. Pita Pit tries to be accessible and convenient by locating its stores close to its customers, usually on or around college campuses and social hubs. Pita Pit also maintains extended hours, usually until 3 a.m. or 4 a.m., in order to satisfy hungry bar-goers after a night out or students studying late. Pita Pit also delivers. Often the delivery person arrives on a bicycle, reflecting Pita Pit's health-conscious image.

The atmosphere, service, and taste are consistent across locations. Stores are decorated in bright colours with familiar Pita Pit cartoon characters on the menu. Service is standardized as franchise owners receive training at national training centres. Pitas are made to order to the customer's exact specifications on the spot from a wide variety of fillings.

Pita Pit has faced increased competition from established fast-food chains. Most fast-food restaurants now have healthier meals and salads on their menu. However, Pita Pit feels that by specializing in pitas they have an advantage. Pita Pit feels they make one item extremely well as opposed to many items unimpressively. And they also understand their customers do not want to see fries and burgers on their menu. Pita Pit is distinctively healthy and that is why customers love it.

A hungry student chooses to go to the Pita Pit for her lunch break.

QUESTIONS

1. How has Pita Pit been successful in matching its understanding of customers with the needs and wants of its customers?

2. Businesses always try to gain a competitive edge on their competition. Explain how Pita Pit has been successful in this regard.

Keep in Mind

1. profit or non-profit
2. large or small
3. forms of business ownership
4. goods or services
5. channels of distribution
6. role in the community
7. jobs

Before You Begin

Oprah Winfrey once said, "I feel that luck is preparation meeting opportunity." What do you think she meant by this statement? What connection does this statement have with the business world?

What Is a Business?

Is a Saturday-morning garage sale a business? Yes, it is. What about a corporation such as Telus Mobility that employs thousands of people? Yes, as well. Businesses come in all sizes and shapes. Some are local, some are regional, some are national, and some are global. And some are a combination of one or more of these forms.

There are many different ways to describe or classify a business, depending on characteristics such as the purpose of the business, its size, its structure, and the role it plays in a community.

Profit or Non-profit?

Some businesses are run for profit. A definition of a business run for profit is "an organization that produces or sells goods or services to satisfy the needs, wants, and demands of consumers for the purposes of making a profit." While most businesses are run for profit, others, such as charities, are organized strictly to help people in a community. These community-help organizations are called non-profit or not-for-profit organizations.

A For-profit Business

The goal of most businesses is to make a profit by supplying goods and services to meet consumer demands. **Profit** is the income that is left after all costs and expenses are paid. **Expenses** are those expenditures that are involved in running a business, such as wages, as well as those assets that get "used up" in the process, such as paper and toner. **Costs** are the amount of money required for each stage of production, such as the cost of raw materials. To be successful, a for-profit business must earn profit while keeping both expenses and costs down.

For example, if a store sells gym equipment for $500, and costs and expenses for that gym equipment total $350, the profit on the sale is $150. As costs and expenses increase, the owner's profit gets smaller. For this reason, businesses try to keep costs and expenses as low as possible by being efficient and well organized. One of the largest expenses for any business is its payroll—the wages it pays its employees. If a business decreases its staff to save on expenses, profits may increase. However, if there are not enough employees to do the work, sales could decrease and profits could actually decline. (See Chapters 9 and 11 for more information on increasing profit and controlling costs and expenses.)

Revenue – Expenses = Profit (or Loss)

Making a profit enables a business to put more money back into the operation for expansion and growth. Some businesses might choose to use profits to provide better goods or improved services. Profit also gives the owner money to spend on personal needs and wants. If a business does not make a profit but the owner is still able to pay all debts, the business is considered solvent. **Solvency** means having the ability to pay your debts and meet financial obligations. But over time, a business's failure to make a profit will eventually force an owner to close the operation. In 1999, insolvency led to the closure of Eaton's department stores all across Canada.

Businesses are always looking for ways to produce new and better goods and to provide better services to customers so they can increase their profits. Successful businesses anticipate and prepare for the changing wants and needs of consumers.

Non-profit and Not-for-profit Organizations

A **non-profit organization** is one that does not seek profit as its primary motive, but instead raises funds for a specific goal. In fact, only charities and charitable organizations can truly be called non-profit. They operate for the good of the community and the people they serve. For example, the Canadian Breast Cancer Foundation exists to advance cancer research, education, diagnosis, and treatment. It does this through donations and through fundraising events such as the CIBC Run for the Cure.

Not-for-profit organizations, such as housing or child-care co-operatives, also do not seek profit. Any surplus funds that they have are used to improve the services offered to members; they do not distribute profits to their members. Unlike for-profit businesses, the purpose of the organization is to meet specific needs of its members. Not all co-operatives are not-for-profit, however. Some do generate profits, which are shared among members or are used to expand the organization. A **co-operative** can be defined as an independent association of persons who come together to meet their economic, social, and cultural needs and goals. They accomplish this objective by creating a jointly owned and democratically controlled business.

A crowd of supporters run by Toronto's Queen's Park during the 2006 CIBC Run for the Cure.

Large or Small

Are most businesses large or small? Despite what advertising makes us believe, most businesses are either small- or medium-sized. A **small-** or **medium-sized business** (SMB) is defined as any business that employs fewer than 500 people. There are over one million SMBs in Canada, employing more than 60 percent of the Canadian workforce.

Forms of Business Ownership

A business can also be described informally by how it is owned. For example, a business owned by one person is called a sole proprietorship. A business that is owned by its workers or by members who buy from the business is called a co-operative. (See Chapter 2 for more detail about the different forms of business ownership.)

Goods or Services

A business can be classified by the **goods** that it produces or **services** that it offers. Best Buy sells electronic goods, while a local food bank provides a service to the community. Canadian businesses provide a wide range of products and services to consumers.

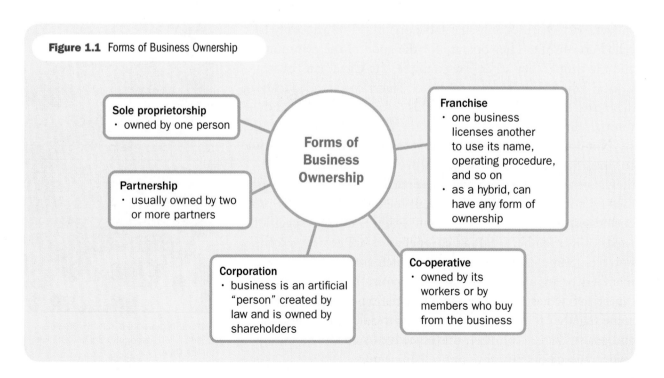

Figure 1.1 Forms of Business Ownership

Sole proprietorship
· owned by one person

Partnership
· usually owned by two or more partners

Forms of Business Ownership

Franchise
· one business licenses another to use its name, operating procedure, and so on
· as a hybrid, can have any form of ownership

Corporation
· business is an artificial "person" created by law and is owned by shareholders

Co-operative
· owned by its workers or by members who buy from the business

This hotdog stand is an example of a small business.

Table 1.1

Top 10 Business Opportunities for 2006

1. alternative health products
2. biometrics or high-tech security
3. diet/exercise expert
4. eco-goods
5. medical tourism
6. financial advisor/ retirement planner
7. organic or specialty foods
8. recycling technology
9. education services/ products
10. home improvement contractor

Channels of Distribution

A business can also be classified by *how* it delivers goods or services to its customers. Some businesses, such as retail stores and fitness clubs are "bricks and mortar" businesses. Customers go to a building to buy a product or use a service. Other businesses are less visible. They distribute their products and services through channels such as telephone marketing, catalogues, or e-commerce. (See Chapter 8 for more information about channels of distribution.)

Can you name a business that exists only on the Internet? Is it a successful business? With thousands of websites to access through search engines such as Google, Internet businesses can provide services and goods to consumers all over the world with the click of a mouse.

Role in the Community

A business can be classified by the different functions that it performs in its community. For example, the Canadian Diabetes Association offers support and raises funds to help people in need.

Jobs

Finally, a business can be classified by the types of jobs that it provides. For example, a health club provides jobs to personal trainers, front desk workers, office workers, maintenance workers, and possibly food service personnel.

Business Fact

In a recent survey, 78% of Internet users reported that they use the Internet to research a product or service before buying it.

⊕ E-ACTIVITY

Visit www.nelson.com/WOB and follow the links to learn more about Strategis, the Industry Canada website that provides valuable consumer and business information.

The Role of the Consumer

Most businesses provide goods or services designed to satisfy consumer needs and wants. **Producers** are the businesses that make goods or provide services. For example, a computer manufacturer is a producer of a good, while a computer-repair shop is a provider of a service. **Consumers** are the people who buy computers, along with those who have their computers serviced at computer-repair shops. Companies that can attract more consumers to their business will have more opportunities to generate sales and make a profit.

Producers and consumers operate together to create a marketplace. A **marketplace** is any location where producers and consumers come together to engage in the buying or selling of goods and services, such as a mall, a farmer's market, or a fast-food restaurant.

The consuming habits of Canadians tell businesses what goods and services consumers want, when they want them, where they want them, and how much they are willing to pay for them. Businesses use this information, along with their own research, to provide goods and services in sufficient quantities to satisfy consumer demands. However, businesses can only respond to the demands of consumers and consumer groups if it is possible and profitable for them to do so. Businesses need you and you need businesses.

Stew Leonard's, a chain of American supermarkets, has this message etched in stone in front of each store:

Rule #1: The customer is always right.

Rule #2: If the customer is wrong, re-read Rule #1.

Do you agree? These two rules suggest that the customer is in control of business.

Do businesses really function this way? Think of some examples where you have noticed businesses following these rules. Can you think of businesses that don't follow these rules?

When businesses produce whatever they want, we say that businesses are in control of the market. But when consumers influence what businesses produce, we say that consumers are in control of the market. In today's business climate, the consumer plays a vital role in influencing what businesses produce and how they deliver their products and services.

Consumer Influence on Products

Years ago, businesses used to dictate what was produced, when it was produced, and in what quantities. In other words, businesses controlled the business environment. For example, when cars were first produced, you could choose to buy or not buy a car, but that was where your choices ended. In fact, to quote automaker Henry Ford, "People can have the Model T in any colour—so long as it's black." Imagine if car-buyers today were told they could only choose one colour of car!

Over time, customers told car producers what they wanted, and eventually, the car industry provided more options. They had to—more car producers were entering the market as **competition**, and customers were choosing to go to the car producers who made the kinds of cars they wanted to buy. In other words, they were going to businesses that met their needs and wants.

In 1940, Bantam made family cars and the first successful "Jeep" for the U.S. military. Unfortunately, the military contract went to Ford, and Bantam stopped car production a year later.

Think about everything you bought over the past month. Did it matter to you whether you could choose the colour, style, size, or other options? When you bought clothes, did you ever notice that certain colours or styles stayed on the rack, while others sold out quickly? What information do clothing producers get from your choices and decisions as a consumer? In what ways can businesses use this information to make business decisions? (See the decision-making model on page 21.)

This shift from businesses controlling the marketplace to consumers having more influence in controlling the marketplace took place during the 1950s and has continued since that time. Demand, supply, and price concepts, which helped influence this shift, will be discussed later in this chapter.

When Products Become Obsolete

Consumer choices not only determine which products will be successful, they also determine which ones will fail. If all Canadians decided that they no longer wanted or needed a good, such as an all-terrain vehicle, then all-terrain vehicles would no longer be produced.

Over time, goods can become **obsolete**, meaning that people no longer want them or that new or improved goods replace them. Treadle sewing machines, steam-powered locomotives, wringer washing machines, manual typewriters, Beta cassette recorders, and 8-track cassettes are just a few of the goods that have become obsolete in Canada.

Services can also become obsolete. In the early 1900s, all street lamps were gaslights. Each night, a lamplighter would light each lamp by hand. Coal and ice were delivered to homes so that people could heat their houses and keep their food cold. These services are no longer provided because they are no longer needed or wanted.

This manual typewriter is an example of a product that has become largely obsolete.

Consumer Influence on Price

What happens when businesses are in control? They have **pricing power**: they can charge high prices and raise prices when costs go up. But when consumers are in control, they make choices that snatch that power away. Today's consumers want access to a wide variety of cheap, reliable goods and services. What happens if businesses do not give them the prices they want? Simple. They will go elsewhere. In other words, they "vote with their feet."

In the 1950s, when businesses had pricing power, there were a limited number of breakfast cereals. Today there are dozens of brands, with prices ranging from very low to very high. To determine the prices, cereal producers must consider not only the cost of producing a brand of cereal, but also the amount they think customers will be willing to pay for it. Still, cereal prices for different brands tend to fall into similar ranges. An inexpensive brand of cereal from one company will cost about the same as an inexpensive brand from another company. This is because the cereal price is determined, in part, by how much the consumer is willing to pay.

The same thing is true of cars. Have you ever wondered why the price of a new car from any manufacturer begins at about $14 000? The answer lies in competition. If only one company offered cars for sale, then that company could set the price and consumers would have to pay it if they wanted a car. Since many companies in today's market sell cars, they have to compete for the dollars of car-buying consumers. If their prices are too high, the consumers will take their business elsewhere. This encourages dealers to offer the best prices they can. If the cost of producing a starting-model car is about the same for any car company, then the base price different car dealers charge for their least expensive car will be approximately equal as well.

Consumer Influence on Service

Competition in business has given power to the consumer. Instead of simply being **customers**—people who always patronize a particular store or business—consumers have the power to choose where they will buy goods and services, and how much they will pay for them. This power is called **consumer purchasing power**. This power not only influences the types of product a business offers and how much it charges for them, but also its level of service.

For example, today's consumers can shop for DVDs at specialty stores like Rogers Video or Blockbuster, or at department stores, or they can choose to rent DVDs online and have them delivered directly to their home. A website called zip.ca allows consumers to rent DVDs online by following a four-step process. First, they create a wish list by choosing from over 50 000 titles; next, they receive the DVDs by first-class mail, which also includes a postage paid return envelope; next, they watch the DVDs at their leisure because there are no late fees or due dates; and lastly, they exchange these DVDs and have new ones delivered automatically.

An increasing range of choice for consumers encourages businesses to continually improve their services to compete for consumer dollars. Who's in charge of business today? You are!

Review Questions

5. Do you agree with the two rules for dealing with customers? (See page 11.) Give a reason to support your opinion.

6. How can consumers influence what businesses produce?

7. Provide an example of an obsolete good or service (one not already used in this chapter). Have DVD players made VCR players obsolete? Are digital cameras making film cameras obsolete? Explain.

8. Why is competition good for both consumers and businesses?

9. In your own words, explain what the expression "vote with their feet" means.

Starting a Business

So you want to start a business! As your business begins to take shape in your mind, there are several factors you need to consider. First, think about your own characteristics and interests. Do you feel you have the characteristics needed to become an entrepreneur? If so, what kind of business would you be interested in starting?

Now think about the people who are going to buy your products and services. Who are your potential customers? What do they want or need? How can you convince them that your business is the best one to provide these things for them?

Characteristics of Entrepreneurs

What type of person starts a business? What kind of personality traits do you need? Among other things, you need

- self-confidence
- a flair for innovation
- the ability to work alone
- an aptitude for managing others

Artists work in a home studio, creating pottery that will later be sold to interested customers.

Sure, being your own boss sounds like fun—driving expensive cars, having flexible hours, and going on business trips! But being your own boss is also about long hours, stress, and risk. You have to become an expert in all aspects of your business, including purchasing, marketing, and accounting.

The risk-taking, problem-solving, opportunity-aware people who start businesses are called **entrepreneurs**.

Do you think you have what it takes to start a business? Chapters 10 and 11 can help you decide.

Consumer Needs and Wants

Why do businesses provide goods and services to consumers? On the most basic level, it is to help satisfy the consumer needs and wants while making a profit or providing a service to the community.

Customer Needs

Sometimes, entrepreneurs start businesses to satisfy new customer **needs**. They recognize that an unsatisfied need is an opportunity for a business venture. Needs are things that are necessary for survival. Basic needs include food, basic clothing, and shelter.

In a country as prosperous as Canada, the majority of Canadians have met their basic needs. However, people often desire things that go beyond the basic needs for survival. Do you really *need* a car? Not likely. But that does not mean that you would not still want a car. On the other hand, if you were a delivery person for a pizza outlet on weekends, would you need a car? Absolutely.

Customer Wants

In contrast to needs, **wants** are things that are not necessary for survival, but that add comfort and pleasure to our lives. Sometimes a situation or a set of circumstances dictates how we view needs and wants for ourselves and for others. When we talk about needs and wants, we often lump them together and just call them wants.

Wants never end. How many wants do you have at any given time? Your wants are only limited by your imagination. Many people want to win a lottery, which may make it much easier to satisfy those other wants. Wants can be somewhat controlling because they can build on one another. That is, one want can lead to many other wants. For example, Jasmine wanted to learn how to speedskate. All she needed was good skates and proper clothing along with a place to practise. But Jasmine decided she wanted to try out for the regional championship in her first season. To do so, she would need better skates and some professional training. So one set of wants can lead to other wants.

When an entrepreneur is starting a business, it's important to consider the needs and wants of potential customers. The entrepreneur who figures out how to address these needs and wants has a great head start on a successful business!

Attracting Consumer Interest

Identifying the needs and wants of consumers is only the first step in planning a business. The next step is identifying the competition and figuring out how you will attract customers to your business and away from competitors. At this stage, it's important to think about how consumers will make their buying decisions.

Figuring out how your customers will answer these questions will help you plan everything from what goods and services you will offer to how you will distribute and market your products.

According to a survey conducted by a radio station, the number one gift requested for Father's Day in 2006 was a flat-screen television. Fathers did not want another tie. Surveys, even informal ones such as this one, give businesses clues about consumer wants, needs, and preferences. Should entrepreneurs pay attention to this type of feedback?

Stretch Your Thinking

Nobody wanted or needed a microwave oven until after it was created and promoted. But once it was ready for sale, the inventors had to create recipe books and cooking methods to prompt customers to buy microwaves. Have businesses learned to bypass consumer needs and wants? Are they first developing the products they want to sell, then convincing customers to buy them?

Yes, if they feel that the information is legitimate. For example, retail service businesses could make sure that there are more flat-screen televisions available in the marketplace, while apparel businesses could try to change consumer opinions about ties as gifts.

What strategies do businesses employ to research and respond to the wants and needs of consumers? Let's briefly examine the food and beverage business in Canada.

It has been said that the food and beverage industry is the only business that wakes up every morning with thousands of new potential customers, whether it does anything or not. What did you have for breakfast this morning? If you had cereal, what brand did you choose? Did Kellogg's make your cereal list? Or did Post, General Mills, or some other brand make it? If you had orange juice, did you consume Tropicana, Old South, a no-name brand, or did you choose something else? Since you had a choice of brands, there were many businesses competing for your breakfast food dollar.

How did your favourite brand win you over? Was it because of price, taste preference, promotion, health concerns, or some other factor? These are some of the strategies that businesses use to compete for consumers and also to compete with one another. New businesses offer products that they think are better than the ones competitors are offering. Existing businesses come up with "new and improved" goods through testing and research. Breakthroughs can give a business an advantage over competitors that translates into profits.

Oops!

In the 1990s, General Mills introduced a product under the Wheaties name called Wheaties Dunk-A-Balls cereal. The sweetened corn-and-wheat puffs cereal was shaped like basketballs. The target market—children—might have been satisfied with the product; however, parents or guardians buy food products, not children. Since adults tend to dislike kids playing with their food, which this product seemed to promote, the cereal failed in the marketplace. Is there any way that General Mills could have avoided this costly mistake?

A selection of product brands means competition between companies in order to win the customer's business.

Businesses don't always respond to customer feedback by creating new products. Sometimes they try to court consumer approval by promoting existing products or creating and promoting trends. For example, a company might use advertising or product placement in a popular movie to try to convince customers that its brand of bottled water is more desirable than any other brand.

Similar businesses compete with one another in addressing consumer needs and wants. For example, how much of your food dollar do you spend on fast-food outlets, restaurant services, grocery stores, catering businesses, home-delivery services, farmer's markets, and franchise businesses? For any one of these businesses to succeed, they must find a way to attract enough consumers to generate a profit and remain in business.

A business typically studies the needs and wants of consumers to figure out how to help consumers satisfy those needs and wants with the business's products and services. Is fulfilling these consumer needs and wants just a matter of making a good or a service available at the right time and at an appropriate price? Or does the business have to do much more research to come up with an improved product or a new way of doing things? Many opportunities for business ventures have been built on addressing and successfully answering such questions.

The World of Business **DVD**

"Remote Control: Advertising in Crisis" from *The World of Business DVD*

Making Good Business Decisions

Making good business decisions is more than a matter of good fortune, although even the most successful businessperson welcomes a bit of luck from time to time. One important business decision is determining how much inventory a business must carry to satisfy the needs and wants of consumers. **Inventory**, sometimes called stock, is the quantity of goods and materials kept on hand. If a business keeps too much inventory, a lot of financial resources are tied up. As a result, that money is no longer available to generate income for a business. If the inventory consists of bubble gum and soft drinks, stocking up on inventory would probably not be a major investment. However, if the business is a car dealership, there could easily be millions of dollars invested in inventory. A car dealership could have four versions of the same model car in four different colour combinations available for sale. If the dealership had to pay for these cars in advance, and if they did not sell quickly, a lot of the dealership's money would not be available for other purposes. A decision-making model could help the owner with this problem.

To make these decisions, businesses can use the five-step **decision-making model** that follows. (The same model can be used for personal decisions, such as which career to pursue or which post-secondary institution to attend.)

Suppose a car dealership has to decide how many cars to keep on the lot. They know it's important to have at least one of each model, so customers can compare and test different vehicles. But should they have more than one of some models on hand?

Here's how the five-step decision-making model could be used in this business situation:

1. **Determine what decision has to be made.** How many vehicles of each type should a car dealer keep on the lot to satisfy consumer demand?

2. **Identify the alternatives.** One alternative would be to have several models of each type of vehicle. A second alternative would be to have only one model of each type of vehicle available. A third alternative would be to have several models of some vehicles, and only one model of others.

Figure 1.2 The Decision-Making Process

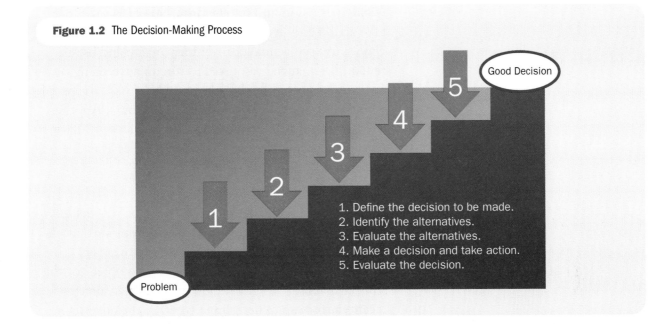

1. Define the decision to be made.
2. Identify the alternatives.
3. Evaluate the alternatives.
4. Make a decision and take action.
5. Evaluate the decision.

3. **Evaluate the advantages and disadvantages of each alternative.**

Several of each: One advantage of having many vehicles available is that it gives consumers a number of choices. Consumers can choose from a variety of in-stock models and colours. Possible disadvantages include the cost of purchasing many vehicles and finding space to display and store them.

One of each: An advantage of having only one model on hand is that the smaller inventory will not tie up a lot of financial resources. As a result, the dealer may be able to afford to spend more money on advertising. On the other hand, if competitors have larger inventories, consumers may decide to make their purchases at dealerships that offer more immediate choices.

Several of some and one of others: This alternative will cost more than having one of each model, but less than having multiple models of each vehicle. The advantage offered is that if there are several models of a popular vehicle, customers may be more likely to buy if they can drive their cars off the lot instead of waiting for delivery. Also, customers will be able to see some models in a range of colours and with different features.

Literacy Link

Checking your understanding
As you read a long passage of text, stop after each paragraph, and think about what you have read by
- asking a question
- clarifying something
- making a comment or a connection
Thinking aloud as you read helps you check your understanding of the text.

4. **Make a decision and take action.** Now it is time to take action and live with the decision. One dealer might choose to keep a smaller inventory on site and use the remaining financial resources to run an advertising campaign to promote a made-to-order service for people who would like different models and colours. Another, with greater financial resources, might choose to have several models of the most popular vehicles available on the lot.

5. **Evaluate the decision.** After some time has passed, it is wise to review the decision. If a mistake was made, reconsider the alternatives and take appropriate action. As you review your decision, new alternatives may surface. For example, the auto dealer who opted for the smaller inventory might decide to conduct a survey of recent customers to determine whether the advertising paid off in terms of increased sales.

Review Questions

10. Define the term entrepreneur. Identify three characteristics of entrepreneurs.

11. What is the difference between a need and a want? Identify one need and one want that you had two years ago. Explain how each has or has not been met over the past two years.

12. Give an example of a good or service that is currently being promoted as "new and improved."

13. Explain why a business might ignore the fifth step in the decision-making model. Explain whether you think it's acceptable to skip this step. What could be some of the consequences of not evaluating your decision?

Keep in Mind

1. natural resources
2. human resources
3. capital resources
4. interdependence
5. economic systems

Economic Resources

Where do goods and services originate? Goods and services do not just suddenly appear in the marketplace. Someone has to create them from basic components. Providing services requires skill and effort. **Economic resources**, also known as factors of production, are the means through which goods and services are made available to consumers. There are three kinds of economic resources: natural resources, human resources, and capital resources. Most products require a combination of all three economic resources. Because economic resources are limited, governments and businesses often work together to develop **economic systems** to ensure that a country's resources will not be overstretched.

Wheat, a natural resource, is harvested by a farmer in Manitoba.

Natural Resources

Natural resources are materials that come from the earth, water, and air. Soil, iron ore, gold, oil, trees, wildlife, agricultural goods, fish, and oxygen are all examples of natural resources used in the production of goods and services.

Unfortunately, most natural resources are non-renewable and are therefore limited. Others, such as forests, take decades to replenish. This means that businesses are limited in what they can build and produce. What actions can businesses take to ensure a long-term supply of non-renewable resources? What can they do before they face a shortage of resources?

Human Resources

Human resources (sometimes referred to as labour) are the people who work to create the goods and services. Some examples are farmers, factory workers, construction workers, website designers, investment bankers, teachers, nurses, and pilots. The human component is so important that many businesses have established a human resources department to manage their employees. (See Chapter 6 for more information on human resources.)

Capital Resources

Capital resources are the third factor of production. They include buildings, equipment, tools, trucks, and factories. Capital resources usually last for a long period of time and often require a substantial investment on the part of a business. In addition to purchasing buildings and equipment, businesses also require money—another capital resource—to buy the raw materials and services they use to produce their own good or service.

Stretch Your Thinking

What are the negative and positive considerations for choosing an alternative energy source over oil?

Interdependence

Our society is **interdependent**, which means it relies on the goods and services provided by thousands of different businesses to satisfy consumer needs and wants. Businesses are also highly interdependent. A clothing manufacturer, for example, buys the goods and services of many other businesses to produce a final good. To make a pair of jeans, the manufacturer relies on other businesses to provide the denim, thread, zippers, buttons, rivets, and sewing and cutting machines that it requires.

Ethical, Moral & Legal Considerations

In 2005, Canada was second only to Saudi Arabia in crude oil reserves, but almost 97 percent of Canada's reserve is in tar sands. The Athabasca Oil Sands development in northern Alberta currently produces 1.2 million barrels of oil per day and it is expected that increased production capabilities will add 2.4 million barrels per day by the year 2016. But removing that oil from the tar sands requires a lot of energy. Currently the tar sands project burns natural gas to heat the steam that removes the oil. The tar sands project is the largest single producer of greenhouse gases in North America. What are some of the harmful effects of greenhouse gases? Should businesses and consumers be concerned about the effects?

Alberta's oil sands represent the world's largest petroleum resource basin.

Business interdependence is illustrated by the relationship between logging and paper production. a) A cedar tree is cut down. b) Logs are transported to a pulp and paper mill. c) A pulp and paper mill. d) Sheets of paper are manufactured at the mill. e) A tree nursery, where saplings are planted so that the land can be reforested.

Interdependence means that one business can depend on another for its economic resources. For example, the shopping list for a large manufacturing company might include lumber (a natural resource) from one company, machinery and replacement parts (capital resources) from another, and accounting services (human resources) from yet another company. A supermarket relies on food from farms (natural resources), equipment at food-processing facilities (capital resources), and drivers who transport the food to the store (human resources). Because businesses are interdependent, economic systems are needed to ensure that businesses can depend on getting the support they need from other businesses.

Economic Systems

What happens if a country runs short of one or more economic resources? A shortage of economic resources means trouble for business. For example, oil is a natural resource whose supply seems to fluctuate. From time to time, oil-producing countries use oil as a political tool and cut back their oil production. This causes the world price of oil to go up.

In the News

Have you ever heard of a video game that simulates an economic system by trading in virtual goods? EverQuest, launched in 1999, is a game that allows players to sell off their characters or virtual possessions and in the process gain wealth.

Trying to understand economics has always been confusing because in the real world, there is no level playing field. If people behaved as economists predicted they would, then there would be a fair marketplace in which to operate and everything would be equal. However, this just does not happen. Some people are born into wealth and are provided with many opportunities, while others are born into situations characterized by poverty and have great challenges to overcome in order to become successful. Is that fair? Some people argue that people prefer a free market, even if it results in wealth for some people and poverty for others; while other people argue that capitalism is unfair and that those in power abuse it.

So the EverQuest video game levels the playing field that is not level in real life. According to experts who play the game, EverQuest is strangely similar to a modern free-market society. All players begin the game with nothing. They start with zero skills, no money, and only the clothes on their backs. Wealth comes only from working hard, honing skills, and clever trading, not from relatives, luck, deviousness, or social connections. Playing this game approximates real-life experience, but one that exists only in a virtual world. Some people suggest that the best way to save the real world from government intervention is to make it more like EverQuest. Do you think that by playing a video game a person could simulate an experience that may have a direct connection to a real-life experience? How much do luck, deviousness, family wealth, and social connections affect success in real life?

In addition, the world's oil reserves are slowly running out. The oil consumption of Western nations such as Canada has been steadily increasing over the past 30 years. Meanwhile, economies in India and China are growing, and their demand for oil is increasing. These two pressures on the world's oil supplies may reduce the supply of oil for businesses in Canada.

Businesses that rely on oil need to find alternative forms of energy. This is where **economic systems** come into play. An economic system is a way of dealing with the selection, production, distribution, and consumption of goods and services in society. Government and business work together to foster activity and growth in the marketplace.

In the case of an oil shortage, business and government work together to look for ways to share the existing oil in a fair way, and also to develop other forms of energy, such as nuclear, hydro, solar, and wind.

Economic systems have to answer three major economic questions:

1. What goods and services should be produced within the system?

2. For whom should these goods and services be produced?

3. How should these goods and services be produced?

Many economic systems operate in the world today. Each has advantages and disadvantages, and each is designed to deal with problems created by limitations. For example, a furniture manufacturing plant can produce only a certain number of tables and chairs because it has only a certain number of workers, factories, pieces of equipment, and lumber. In the same way, a country has limited economic resources and so there are limits on the types and amounts of goods and services that a country's businesses can produce. Economic systems are designed to allow countries and businesses to make the most of the resources they have, and sometimes, as in the case of alternative energy sources, to develop new resources that will allow them to expand economically.

Keep in Mind

1. law of demand
2. law of supply
3. relating price to supply and demand

Demand, Supply, and Price

The amount of a good or service that consumers demand, the amount that suppliers can supply, and the price all affect one another. Let's examine the relationship between demand, supply, and price.

Law of Demand

Demand is the quantity of a good or service that consumers are willing and able to buy at a particular price. Since each of us has different needs and wants and different levels of ability to pay for things, we each have different demands. When we buy a particular good or use a particular service, we are expressing a demand for it. Usually, consumers buy more (increase demand) as prices decrease. As prices increase, consumers buy less (decrease demand). This relationship is called the **law of demand**.

Conditions That Create Demand

Several conditions create a demand. First, the consumer must be aware of, or interested in, the good or service. Businesses usually address this condition by advertising or marketing their good or service. Other conditions involve having an ample supply of the good or service available and establishing prices that are reasonable and competitive. Finally, the good or service must be

Table 1.2

Factors That Can Increase or Decrease Demand	
Factor	**Influence on Demand**
Changing consumer income	Generally speaking, as incomes increase, people tend to buy more than before. For example, a pay raise may result in someone buying a new flat-screen TV, renting a cottage for a holiday, or buying new living-room furniture. However, for some types of goods, the opposite can be true. For example, an increase in income may result in the purchase of fewer grocery items because people are buying more restaurant meals.
Changing consumer tastes	Changes in consumer tastes over time can cause an increase in demand for fashionable items and a decrease in demand for what is perceived as unfashionable. For example, certain styles of jeans come into fashion, go out of fashion, and come back into fashion.
Changing expectations for the future	If consumers expect that either prices or income will increase in the future, they will often purchase more in anticipation of the change. An upward change in expectations results in an increase in demand. However, if consumers expect the prices or income to decrease, then demand will decrease as well.
Changes in population	An increase in population creates an increase in the need for housing, cars, roads, waterworks and sewers, schools, grocery stores, hospitals, clothes, and nearly every good and service imaginable. Also, as certain segments of the population increase, demand for goods associated with those segments increases as well. Presently in Canada, there is an increase in the population of people over the age of 55. As a result, demand is increasing for health care; certain sports activities, such as golf; and housing, in the form of adult lifestyle and retirement homes.

accessible—conveniently located for the consumer to purchase. For this reason, businesses, and especially retailers, must consider carefully where they will locate their business. Business owners often describe their top three priorities as "location, location, location," indicating the vital connection between location and demand.

In addition to the conditions that create demand for a particular product or service (customer awareness, supply, price, and accessibility) there are several factors that can increase or decrease demand. Table 1.2 summarizes these factors.

Law of Supply

If the goods and services consumers demand can be provided at prices they are willing to pay, businesses will supply them. **Supply** is the quantity of a good or service that businesses are willing and able to provide within a range of prices that people would be willing to pay. Businesspeople recognize consumers'

Oops!

Is it possible to turn silver into gold? In the 1970s, Texas billionaire Nelson Bunker Hunt and his brother managed to accumulate nearly a third of the world's silver supply, pushing the price to $50 an ounce. The brothers decided not to sell right away, knowing that increasing the supply without increasing the demand would drive prices down. When other silver investors found out what was happening, they began to panic—and sell. Prices quickly fell 80 percent, leaving the Hunts with a lot of silver worth less than what they had paid. After declaring bankruptcy, the brothers were convicted of conspiring to manipulate the New York Metals Market.

needs and wants and try to provide the goods and services to satisfy them—at a profit, of course. Some businesses are more efficient than others. Take, for example, a particular group of businesses that produce similar goods for the same market. Those businesses that are more efficient will produce more goods for a given price than businesses that are less efficient. Generally speaking, as prices increase, producers will be able to use the increased revenue to put more goods and services on the market. With higher prices, they can afford to pay overtime, expand their factories, hire another shift of employees, and buy more productive equipment. This relationship of increasing the quantity supplied as prices increase is called the **law of supply**.

Conditions That Affect Supply

The supply of a good or service is affected by the cost of producing it and, to some extent, by the price consumers are willing to pay for it. Occasionally, a business will try to create demand for a new good or service simply by supplying it for sale in the marketplace and marketing it as well. Although this strategy involves risk, it also produces an opportunity for enormous profits if a demand is created.

In addition to the conditions that determine supply for a particular product or service (the cost of production and the price consumers are willing to pay) there are several factors that can increase or decrease supply. Table 1.3 summarizes these factors.

Frank and Ernest

© 2004 Thaves. Reprinted with permission. Newspaper dist. by NEA, Inc.

In the News

Changing technology influences both demand and supply. For example, new technology has been developed that enables adults to monitor and control their children's telephone calls. Parent Patrol allows parents or guardians to set controls, such as the time of day their children can use their telephones, the numbers they can call or receive calls from, the number of minutes they're allowed, and the services they can access. The service can block numbers individually, or block all numbers that aren't in the system. Fine-tuning of the system could also turn off text messaging during school hours. Parent Patrol was launched in the fall of 2006. Its purpose is to help deal with huge telephone bills and help prevent predators from gaining access to the cell phones of young people. What do you think might have happened to the consumer demand for this product after it was introduced? If Parent Patrol becomes very successful, do you think the supply of this product, and other similar products, will increase or decrease? Why?

Table 1.3

Factors That Can Increase or Decrease Supply	
Factor	**Influence on Supply**
Change in the number of producers	If a particular good seems to provide attractive profits, new businesses will soon start to produce similar goods. The result is that supply will increase as more of these goods enter the market. When supply increases, if demand remains the same, prices will decrease because of the increased competition.
Changes in price	If the price of a good decreases, then people may stop producing it. For example, if the price of wheat decreases, farmers may shift production from wheat to corn or soybeans. The wheat supply will then decrease as the corn or soybean supply increases.
Changes in technology	Changes in technology can reduce the cost of production, encouraging more businesses to start producing a product. This will increase supply. For example, as computer-chip technology has improved, computers have become much more powerful, much cheaper to produce, and more affordable to many more consumers. This improvement has drastically increased the supply of PCs and laptop computers worldwide.
Changing expectations for the future	Producers must always plan ahead to forecast sales, production, financing, and marketing. Many producers try to predict economic conditions and consumer demand for two to five years in advance. As conditions change, they increase or decrease production accordingly, and this increases or decreases supply. Imagine the planning and forecasting that must take place before a new car rolls off the assembly line (for example, determining what colours consumers will want this season).
Changing production costs	If a local baker can find a lower cost source for sugar and flour, he or she can produce more goods for the same cost of production. In this case, the supply will increase because the baker wants to increase profit. If production becomes more expensive, then the supply will decrease.

Relating Price to Supply and Demand

Price is determined by many factors, including both demand and supply. And, as you have seen, both demand and supply change as the result of the actions of consumers and producers. If consumer demand for a good or service is high while the supply of that same good or service is low, prices will tend to be high. Conversely, if consumer demand for a good or service is low while the supply of that good or service is high, prices will tend to be low. Prices tend to fluctuate, sometimes rapidly, because demand and supply are constantly changing. For example, during autumn, businesses have a large supply of fall and winter goods for sale. Prices of these goods usually remain higher during this time period. But before winter comes to an end, businesses will put these goods on sale to clear them out and make room for spring and summer stock.

Price is also influenced by the cost of producing a good or service. For example, if the cost of producing the latest electronic gadgets were low enough that they could be sold for $50, many of us would be able to own one. Low prices tend to increase the quantity demanded by consumers. On the other hand, if ballpoint pens cost $50 each, most of us would be forced to use pencils. High prices tend to decrease the quantity of goods and services that consumers will buy. In other words, high prices usually decrease the quantity demanded.

Review Questions

18. How does a change in price affect the law of demand and the law of supply?

19. Identify two conditions that create a demand for, and two conditions that create an impact on, the supply of goods or services.

20. In your own words, explain what the expression "a change in expectations of future conditions" means.

21. How can the prices of related goods impact on the supply of another good? Use an example to explain your answer.

CHAPTER REVIEW

Knowledge

1. Identify one non-profit and one not-for-profit organization in your community or surrounding area. What service does each one offer?

2. Peter Drucker, a well-known business expert, once wrote: "A business exists to create a customer." What does this statement mean in relation to this chapter? Do you believe this statement? Support your ideas with an example or explanation.

3. List five natural resources in or near your community (e.g., a forest or a river). Are any of them environmentally at risk? Explain.

4. Give an example of a product whose price tends to fluctuate up and down. Do increases in price affect people's purchases? Do reductions in price encourage or allow them to buy more? Explain how price affects sales.

5. Give an example that shows how businesses are interdependent, and another example that shows how businesses and consumers are interdependent.

Thinking

6. "Businesses sometimes take advantage of consumers." Give an example that supports this statement. Prepare a brief argument supporting or criticizing the action taken by the business in your example.

7. "Consumers sometimes take advantage of businesses." Give an example that supports this statement. Prepare a brief argument supporting or criticizing the action taken by the consumer in your example.

8. How does supply of a product affect the price of that product in the marketplace? How does demand for a product affect its price? How do they both affect the willingness of businesses to produce products or offer services?

9. How can an entrepreneur who doesn't have any formal business training become an expert in areas such as purchasing, marketing, and accounting?

Communication

10. Work in a group of not more than four students to discuss and answer these two *What if* questions. Prepare a draft copy before writing the final report. Create a third *What if* question related to the content of this chapter and discuss that as well. Prepare a report that lists all three of the questions and the answers decided on by the group.
    a) *What* would happen *if* all consumers had unlimited amounts of money to spend?
    b) *What* would happen *if* all businesses shut down their operations for a two-week period?

11. Contact a local business to find out what three changes they would make in the way they conduct business in order to make a profit (a) during good economic times, and (b) during poor economic times. List what consequences you think might occur as a result of these changes.

	Good Times	Poor Times	Consequence
1			
2			
3			

12. Imagine that your town's or city's chamber of commerce and economic development council have persuaded a call centre to set up operations in your community. The company expects to employ 300 people. Acting as the communications coordinator for the call centre, write a letter to the editor of the local paper listing three ways that you think the city would benefit from your company establishing itself in the community.

Application

13. Select a product from the list below (or from a list provided by your teacher). What is its current price? List the names of two similar products, and note their current prices. What was the price of your selected product last year at this time? Explain why the price has or has not changed over that period of time.
    - one litre of gasoline
    - one dozen extra-large eggs
    - one ounce of gold
    - one round-trip fare on Air Canada (economy class) from Halifax to Vancouver
    - one fast-food hamburger

14. Do you think that you would be a successful businessperson? Why or why not? Prepare a one-page explanation that describes the qualities and skills you possess that would contribute (or not contribute) to your future success as a businessperson. Note: You may wish to make reference to the Ontario Skills Passport website as part of your research.

15. Select a business in your community. Write a report on the business that includes
    - the natural resources that it uses
    - the different types of labour (human resources) that it uses
    - the capital goods (capital resources) that it uses
    - how it combines these resources in its operations

Team Activity—You're Hired!

Team activities are problem-solving tasks designed to help group members develop their ability to work effectively together. You may have already participated in team activities in a work-training seminar or as a member of a school group or sports team. At the end of each chapter in this text, you will be presented with an opportunity to be a member of a team and your team will be placed in a problem-solving situation.

Your teacher will help you set up teams and determine how each competition will be judged. Once the teams are established, the competition begins. If possible, more than one person will assess the team competitions. The judge(s) will declare a winning team after each chapter's team activity. You and your team will want to hear "You're Hired" as it will signal that your team has won the competition.

Note: Your teacher may choose to keep a team together throughout the course or to mix up the team members for each activity. In either case, teams could choose a team name.

Team Goal: To make the most money from a "flea market" sale

Team Assignment: The Classroom Flea Market

- Each team member brings two or three items to sell.

- Each team will be assigned a space to display their items.

- To ensure that your team makes the most money, be sure to price each item competitively and bring in items that are in demand.

- No item should be worth more than ten dollars.

- The sale should be held within one classroom period.

- Some examples of items to consider for sale include: CDs, DVDs, video games, baked goods, books, stuffed animals, etc. Ask your teacher about any school restrictions on baked goods due to food allergies.

- The winning team is the team that makes the most money.

The Portfolio Page

A portfolio is a collection of your best work on a specific topic. For this course, your portfolio will focus on an industry of your choice, so you should choose an industry that interests you. Throughout the course, you will add items to your portfolio that relate to the specific industry you have selected.

Start your portfolio by profiling your industry. To look up your industry, search for "Strategis" at www.nelson.com/WOB. Strategis is the Industry Canada website that lists, classifies, and profiles all of the industries in Canada. Then look for your industry under "Business Information by Sector" on the left side of the home page.

For Chapter 1, your portfolio should include a definition of business that uses as an example one or more actual businesses that operate within your industry. For example, if you selected Fast Food as an industry, then you might describe how Harvey's, Wendy's, KFC, or your local pizza restaurant is a business. You could include a photo or menu, an interview with the owner, or an audio or visual component that explains or illustrates how your business functions (e.g., how it makes a profit by selling hamburgers for more than it costs to make them).

In what other ways could you connect the information in this chapter with your industry? Think about ways that this information could be useful to the owners and operators of businesses within your chosen area. Now think of methods you could use to present that information to them. Add those ideas to your portfolio.

Your portfolio is an ongoing activity. You may discover interesting articles or illustrations in newspapers and magazines that illustrate important points from the textbook. Feel free to add material to your portfolio.

You will have lots of opportunities to share your work with others, including your teacher. Be sure to take advice to improve your portfolio.

When the course is finished, you will select the best work from your portfolio and use it to illustrate what you have learned about your chosen industry throughout the course. Your teacher will instruct you how to present this work for your final assessment.

Reflect on Your Learning

After studying the material presented in this chapter, what new arguments could you use to support Oprah Winfrey's statement in 'Before You Begin' on page 6?

IKEA

Ikea has the world living in "Swedephilia," literally. Furniture and products from Ikea can be found in households around the world. Ikea's motto is "Affordable Solutions for Better Living." Quality, low-priced furniture combined with Swedish charm has been the formula for Ikea's success.

Founded in 1943 by Ingvar Kamprad, Ikea got its name from Kamprad's initials, plus the initials of the farm (Elmtaryd) and the village (Agunnaryd) where he grew up in Sweden. Originally a mail-order catalogue company selling fountain pens, wallets, and other home accessories, Ikea opened its first retail store in 1953. Since then the company has expanded into 34 countries, built 235 stores, hired more than 90 000 employees, and in 2005 had sales of more than US$18.3 billion.

Kamprad saw an opportunity in Sweden's post–World War II furniture market. The population boomed and created a soaring demand for furniture, which caused its price to rise 41 percent faster than other household items. Also, young Swedish couples wanted their own furniture—rather than taking furniture that had been passed down from generation to generation—but they had limited budgets. Kamprad set out to create affordable, yet stylish, furniture that would be accessible to the masses.

The company's stores are located on large plots of land outside the city, never

One of the many IKEA stores found worldwide

in the downtown core, which capitalizes on cheaper real estate prices. Ikea also profits from the customer's willingness to work. Not only do customers have to drive to the stores, which are often hours away, they get their own purchases from the warehouse, drive the furniture home, and assemble it themselves.

Ikea's showroom strategy, whereby customers move along a carefully charted path, ensuring that all products are viewed before anything can be purchased, is extremely successful. In recent years, Ikea has modified this charted path by providing "shortcuts" to other sections of the store. Salespeople only offer advice when asked.

In order to fend off increasing competition, Ikea has expanded its services in order to meet customers' changing needs. For example, Ikea now offers home delivery, online shopping, at-home assembly, and, in certain locations, shuttle services to their stores. In addition, the company provides in-store designers who will help customize a kitchen or a bathroom. All these services meet consumers' changing needs and expectations.

Ikea continues to maintain and market its Swedish charm. All products have Swedish names, and Ikea restaurants serve more than 150 million Swedish meatballs per year to hungry shoppers. Although Ikea now shares the market with other self-assembly furniture suppliers, the company has lost little of its appeal for both price and design.

QUESTIONS

1. How has Ikea used changes in their customers' preferences and lifestyles to their advantage?

2. Given that customers must put in a great amount of effort to get to Ikea stores and to assemble their furniture, why do you think Ikea became so successful?

SPECIFIC EXPECTATIONS

After completing this chapter, you will be able to

- compare forms of business ownership
- identify the different types of businesses

- explain why a person or group of people would choose to establish one type of business rather than another
- identify the different business structures adopted by international business ventures

Mountain Equipment Co-op (MEC)

Around certain campfires, having a low Mountain Equipment Co-op (MEC) number is a defining characteristic of wilderness chic. Sara Golling is Member 21 and one of the founding board members. In 1971, she borrowed $5 and bought her co-op membership. That $5 price remains the same today. Golling's $5 investment has not changed or grown. In a private company, her investment would have been worth millions of dollars, but at MEC, she's just like any of the other 2.3 million owners, making MEC Canada's largest retail co-operative. (A co-operative, sometimes called a co-op, is a business owned by the workers or by members who buy the products or use the services that the business offers.)

The idea of MEC began in a tent. In 1971, a group of students from the University of British Columbia varsity outdoors club decided to start a business. They were fed up with having to travel to the United States to buy decent climbing and outdoor gear, so they decided to do something about it. They opened an outdoor-goods co-op that would stock merchandise that no other retailer in Canada sold. In order to purchase anything at their store, customers would have to pay a one-time membership fee of $5, which gave them a co-op membership. MEC has grown to be wildly successful without ever advertising.

Today, MEC is Canada's leading supplier of outdoor clothing and equipment. The company has 11 stores across Canada, and customers can also shop by mail or online. In 2005, MEC's most successful year thus far, sales reached $194 million and debt was eliminated.

From the start, MEC's major objective has been to have a small environmental footprint. In order to do this, MEC runs some programs that do not make conventional business sense. MEC created OutdoorGearSwap.com, a group where MEC members can trade their MEC equipment as opposed to buying more from MEC. Although this means fewer sales and lower revenue for MEC, it means less waste for the environment, and it creates goodwill for the company. MEC stores are also environmentally friendly, built with recycled materials, and contain environmentally friendly features, such as composting toilets and roof-top gardens. People don't shop at MEC just because of their products, but also because they are endorsing a respectful corporate citizen.

Co-op members have unique privileges. Most importantly, members elect the nine-member board of directors that oversees all decisions made in the company. Members are encouraged to attend the annual general meetings, held in Vancouver, in order to cast their vote and have their voices heard. The co-op business model also has business benefits. Co-ops do not pay income taxes on earnings. All profits are fed back into the co-op leading to lower prices for members.

The question remains, how has MEC been able to remain relevant and be so successful across generations of Canadians without advertising? Besides the obvious quality and variety of products offered, many feel that it is the co-op aspect of MEC. The co-op model both encourages and enables MEC to hear and respond to all co-op members.

Customers looking to purchase outdoor gear, head into Mountain Equipment Co-op's Toronto store.

QUESTIONS

1. Why is the co-op model able to hear and respond to the needs and concerns of all co-op members? What special benefits do co-op members have that customers of a regular store do not have?

2. Why don't other companies take on the co-op business model? Identify a benefit that the co-op model provides when compared to a sole proprietorship, a partnership, and a corporation.

Forms of Business Ownership

If you have ever had a job working for someone else, did you know who owned that business? Was your boss also the owner? Who was the boss of your boss? Could you have become a part owner in that business? Forms of business ownership and types of businesses help describe how businesses are organized and run. This chapter explores why a person might choose to establish one type of business rather than another, examines online business opportunities, and briefly describes the structures of international business ventures.

There are four main forms of business ownership: sole proprietorships, partnerships, corporations, and co-operatives. (For a quick summary of these forms of business ownership, see the diagram on page 8 in Chapter 1.) Franchises are sometimes labelled as a form of business ownership. However, franchises generally are better described as a hybrid, meaning that franchises combine several features of some of the other forms of ownership. Let's examine these forms of business ownership, including franchising, in more detail.

Sole Proprietorships

A **sole proprietorship** is a business owned by one person, normally referred to as a proprietor. The proprietor has many different responsibilities within the business. For example, the owner of a bicycle store usually buys the merchandise, sells to customers, does the accounting, arranges displays, and cleans the store. The owner owns all the equipment in the store and might own the building. Money to run the business usually comes from the owner's savings, friends, family, or from a bank loan. If the business does well, the owner enjoys all the profits. If the business does poorly, the owner is responsible for all the losses. The owner may even lose his or her home and other personal belongings. This is called **unlimited liability,** and it is the biggest disadvantage of organizing in this way.

The advantage of setting up your business as a sole proprietorship is that starting and administering the business is easier and less expensive than other forms of business. For example, if you choose the sole proprietor form of business and operate it under your own name, you don't even have to register your business with the government. And as a sole proprietor, you declare your business income on your personal income tax

Keep in Mind

1. sole proprietorships
2. partnerships
3. corporations
4. co-operatives
5. franchises

Before You Begin

With a partner, speculate about the types of decisions businesspeople must make before opening a business. Record your ideas so that you can compare them with your answers to the questions you will complete at the end of the chapter.

form, rather than filing a separate business tax form. Hundreds of examples of sole proprietorships can be found in the Yellow Pages with names such as Debbie's Party Time Outlet, Rashid's Rentals, JJ Express, Millie's Messenger Service, and Longo's Plumbing.

Partnerships

A **partnership** is a business that's usually operated by two or more individuals who want to share the costs and responsibilities of running a business. For example, lawyers who specialize in different areas of law, such as civil, divorce, real estate, corporate, family, and wills and power of attorney, will form partnerships so that they can serve a wider client base. They record the terms of their partnership in a **partnership agreement**. Examples of some famous business partnerships, which became well-known corporations, are A&W, Baskin-Robbins, Black & Decker, M&M's, and Proctor & Gamble. Can you name any others?

There are different kinds of partnerships. A **general partnership** is the most common form. In a general partnership, all partners have unlimited liability for the firm's debts. Unlimited liability means that each partner could be held

Sole proprietors sell their wares from individual booths at this farmers' market.

responsible for the other partner's business-related debts. In a **limited partnership**, on the other hand, partners have **limited liability**, which means they are only responsible for paying back the amount that they invested in the partnership. Even if the business fails, their personal savings and other assets cannot be used to pay the partnership's debts.

The main advantage of the partnership is the working relationship between the partners, rather than in the legal structure of the company. One partner could be the sales expert, while the other partner could handle the books and order inventory. The most successful partnerships are those where the partners have complementary talents and are comfortable sharing the decision making.

Corporations

A **corporation** is a business that has been granted legal status with rights, privileges, and liabilities that are distinct from those of the people who work for the business. Corporations can be as small as one person or as large as a **multinational**, also known as a transnational. While many people believe that all corporations are enormous, most corporations are owned entirely by individuals, families, and small groups.

However, large corporations usually cannot be managed well if they are owned and funded by only one or two people. For this reason, the ownership of these corporations is divided into many small parts, called **shares** or stock, which the original owners sell through a stock exchange (such as the Toronto Stock Exchange, or TSX). Once shares have sold, the corporation becomes a publicly traded (or publicly owned) corporation.

Stretch Your Thinking

John D. Rockefeller once said, "It's better to have a friendship based on a business partnership than a business partnership based on a friendship." Do you agree? Explain the position that you take.

Business Fact

Where can you find information on over 50 000 Canadian businesses? Check out Strategis, the Industry Canada website.

In the News

In this corner, we have golfer Tiger Woods, Tour de France master Lance Armstrong, and women's tennis star Serena Williams. In the opposite corner, we have hockey superstar Sidney Crosby, pitching ace Curt Schilling, and soccer idol David Beckham. What is this fight all about? Team Nike versus Team Adidas-Reebok. Up until Adidas decided to buy Reebok International Ltd., Team Nike had a far greater share of the market. But when Adidas teamed up with Reebok in 2005, Adidas-Reebok's market share of athletic footwear rose to 28 percent, almost catching up to Nike's 31 percent. There are many ways to market big-name brands, and competition at this level is ruthless. That is why companies spend millions of dollars acquiring celebrity endorsements to sell and market these brands. In competitive marketing, the name of the game is the *name* of the product. Team Adidas decided that getting bigger by partnering with another competitor was a good strategy for competing with Nike. Do you think that Team Adidas made a wise move? Explain.

Stockholder's share certificates

Individuals who buy shares become owners of the company and are called **shareholders.** The more shares a shareholder owns, the greater the control he or she has. Because there are so many owners, a **board of directors** is put into place to run the corporation.

Shareholders have limited liability, which means they cannot be held legally responsible for the debts of the corporation. This limited liability is an advantage because it encourages people to buy shares. If the corporation fails, the owners or shareholders lose only the amount that they've invested in shares. If the business earns a profit, some of it may be used to expand the company. A publicly traded corporation may pay out the rest to shareholders in the form of a **dividend**. The amount of the dividend paid for each share is calculated by dividing the total profit paid out by the total number of shares owned by shareholders. For example, if you held 100 shares in Canadian Tire Corporation (CTC), and if CTC declared a $2.00 dividend at the end of the year, you would receive a dividend cheque for $200.00.

Types of Corporations

There are different types of corporations. In a **private corporation** (e.g., Krispy Kernels), only a few people control all the shares, or stock, and, therefore, the business. Shares in the company are not listed for sale on a stock exchange, a trading market where shares are bought and sold. On the other hand, a **public corporation** (e.g., Research In Motion) raises money by making shares available to thousands of people through selling shares on the stock exchange. These individuals become the owners of the business. People with only a few shares of a stock have little influence on a company's policies. Major shareholders, on the other hand, can have a considerable impact because each share gives them one vote. Often, the founders, presidents, and major shareholders in large public corporations become very wealthy (see list on page 45).

A **Crown corporation** is a business operated by the provincial or federal government. Some examples of Crown corporations are the Business Development Bank of Canada (BDC), VIA Rail, Atomic Energy of Canada Limited, Canada Post, and the Canadian Broadcasting Corporation (CBC). Towns and cities can also be incorporated. They are organized as businesses, or as **municipal corporations** (e.g., the City of Halifax), to provide services to the local citizens.

A VIA train carries passengers through Canadian snow-covered terrain.

Table 2.1

Top 10 Most Wealthy Canadian Individuals and Families

1. The Thomson Family (Thomson Corp. is a world leader in information services): $22.16 billion

2. Galen Weston (The Weston family owns or controls over 200 companies, including George Weston Bakeries as well as stores such as Loblaws and Holt Renfrew): $9.28 billion

3. James (J. K.), Arthur, and John (Jack) Irving (Irving Oil, an oil company that owns Canada's largest oil refinery): $5.36 billion

4. Jeff Skoll (eBay's first employee and first president): $5.07 billion

5. James (Jimmy) Pattison (Jim Pattison Group is involved in transportation, communications, food products, packaging, and financial services): $4.5 billion

6. Paul Desmarais Sr. (Power Corporation, which has holdings in media, pulp and paper, and financial services): $4.25 billion

7. Edward (Ted) Rogers Jr. (Rogers Communications, a telecommunications giant): $3.65 billion

8. Saputo Family (Saputo Inc., a leader in the Canadian dairy industry): $3 billion

9. Bernard (Barry) Sherman (Barr Laboratories and Apotex, generic drug makers): $2.59 billion

10. David Azrieli (Canpro Investments Ltd., a designer and developer of skyscrapers and office towers): $2.37 billion

Co-operatives

A **co-operative** is a business owned by the workers or by members who buy the products or use the services that the business offers. The motive for operating a co-operative is service, not profit.

Like a corporation, boards of directors, who are members of the co-operative, own shares and run the co-operative. Unlike a corporation, however, each member has only one vote, regardless of the number of shares owned. Another major difference is that the profits of a co-operative are distributed according to how much each member spends at the co-operative. For example, a member who buys $5000 worth of goods or services will receive a dividend five times as large as someone who buys $1000 worth of goods or services.

The co-operative model has been adapted to almost every form of business in Canada. Consumer co-operatives, retail co-operatives, and worker co-operatives are three such adaptations. A local credit union where members pool their savings so that they can provide themselves with financial services at a reasonable cost is an example of a consumer co-operative. Retail co-operatives, such as IGA (Independent Grocers Alliance) and I.D.A. (Independent Druggists' Association), act as buying organizations for individual members. A worker co-operative is created to provide work for its members. Neechi Foods in Winnipeg, Manitoba, is an example of a worker co-operative.

Ethical, Moral & Legal Considerations

How does a mining corporation convince government officials to allow them to set up operations in their country? One way is to promise work for 85 percent of a town's population! During the late 1990s, a Canadian mining company set up operations in Chile. Since Canada and Chile had signed a trade agreement in 1997, this type of partnership seemed to make sense, partially because that trade agreement had a section dealing with environmental regulations. However, even those regulations failed to safeguard the community surrounding the town in Chile from having its environment contaminated. Not long after getting operations underway, the work at the mine generated acid rain and suspended dust, which contaminated the air, destroyed the plant life in the region, and also had a negative effect on livestock in the area. Because the mining company had convinced the authorities that the best regulation was self-regulation, it was almost impossible to point fingers at the guilty party. Were the mining company's promises worth the price that was paid?

In Canada, many co-operatives in the health care (Saskatchewan is the best provincial example), child-care (The Canadian Child Care Federation), and housing (Co-operative Housing Federation of Canada) sectors are not-for-profit co-operatives.

Franchises

In a franchise operation, one business, the **franchiser**, licenses the rights to its name, operating procedure, designs, and business expertise to another business, the **franchisee**. In this way, a franchisee buys a licence to operate a ready-made business and is often provided with a fully operational facility. The franchiser and the franchisee are independent businesses affiliated for this agreement only. This is why franchises can be thought of as a hybrid form of business ownership.

Franchise businesses are very popular in the business community. They offer brand recognition that consumers find more and more appealing. Hotels, motels, fast-food restaurants, and automobile dealerships are a few examples of franchise operations.

McDonald's is the number one company when it comes to having the greatest number of franchises worldwide. There are over 30 000 McDonald's franchises in 100 countries around the world with approximately 5000 of those franchises that are company owned.

E-ACTIVITY

Visit www.nelson.com/WOB and follow the links to learn more about franchises.

Table 2.2

Top 10 Franchises for 2006 (as listed in *Entrepreneur* magazine)	
1. Subway	6. Dunkin' Donuts
2. Quiznos Sub	7. Jani-King
3. Curves	8. RE/MAX International
4. UPS Store, The	9. 7-Eleven
5. Jackson Hewitt Tax Service	10. Liberty Tax Service

Notes: (1) Judging was based on such things as financial strength and stability, growth rate and size, number of years in business, start-up costs, but not on franchisee satisfaction. (2) McDonald's was ranked #16.

Before a franchise is awarded, the franchisee must meet many requirements. The most basic of these is payment of the franchise fee to the franchiser. These fees can range from thousands to millions of dollars. The more successful the franchise—the higher the franchise fee. Imagine having to pay $450 000 for a well-known coffee franchise before you even sell your first cup of coffee!

In addition to the initial franchise fee, the franchisee pays a monthly fee for being part of the franchise family. This franchise fee might be 5 percent of total monthly sales. The franchisee also has to pay the franchiser for national and local advertising (roughly 1 percent of monthly sales). Moreover, all supplies for the business often have to be purchased centrally through the franchiser. This type of quantity buying should work to the benefit of the franchisee by reducing the cost of supplies and providing uniform quality.

Some franchisers require the franchisee to go through a training period to learn how to do business according to their standards. In this way, brand recognition and quality is guaranteed. For example, a visit to Canadian Tire anywhere in Canada means an opportunity to save using Canadian Tire "money" while experiencing friendly service. Despite high franchise fees and monthly costs, franchise operations are often very successful.

In the News

Did you know that since Tim Hortons began, it has been a sole proprietorship, a partnership, a corporation, and a franchise operation? Tim Horton opened his first doughnut shop, originally called Tim Horton Donut Shop, in 1964. The store struggled for survival, and in 1965, Ronald V. Joyce took it over. Since it was the first one opened, that meant that Ron Joyce became the original franchisee of Store #1, located in Hamilton, Ontario.

Ron Joyce subsequently opened two more stores; and by 1967, Ron and Tim Horton became full partners in the company. After Tim's tragic death in a car accident in February of 1974, Ron Joyce became the sole owner. Tim Hortons then started selling franchises operating in Canada and later in the United States. In 1995, Tim Hortons merged with Wendy's International, Inc., so that it could expand further into the U.S. market. In 2006, Tim

Hortons became a publicly traded company, selling 17.25 percent of the company as shares. Wendy's still owned the other 82.75 percent of the company. In late 2006, Wendy's sold the remaining interest that they had in Tim Hortons to generate funds for other parts of its operations. Why has the Tim Hortons franchise been so popular in Canada? Will it succeed in the United States?

Some familiar Canadian franchises!

Table 2.3

Comparing Forms of Business Ownership					
	Sole Proprietorship	**Partnership**	**Corporation**	**Co-operative**	**Franchise**
Features	• one owner	• two or more owners • written partnership agreement	• many shareholders • one vote per share • board of directors	• owned by members • each member has only one vote regardless of number of shares • board of directors	• hybrid type of ownership
Advantages	• be your own boss • easy to start and end • profits to owner	• more capital and financing • shared responsibilities	• limited liability • transfer of ownership is simple	• less expensive goods/services • easily set up	• brand recognition • shared marketing • corporate training and support
Disadvantages	• unlimited liability • financing may be difficult • owner may not be familiar with all aspects of business	• unlimited liability in general partnerships • partner disagreements	• timely and costly startup • people who own only a few shares don't have a lot of influence on how the company is run	• decision-making process could be difficult	• franchise fee • monthly fee • requirement to buy from franchiser

Going into Business

Starting and running a business takes motivation, commitment, and talent. Before deciding to go into business, you have to do a lot of research and planning. What types of businesses are most likely to succeed for your business idea? Should you start an e-business or a traditional "bricks and mortar" business? Because the business environment is so complex, everything that you need to know before starting a business can't be explained here. As you do your research and planning, you can locate many other sources that provide useful information. Chapters 10 and 11, which focus on entrepreneurship, will also help you.

Frank and Ernest

© 2003 Thaves. Reprinted with permission. Newspaper dist. by NEA, Inc.

Why Start Your Own Business?

Have you ever worked for someone else and thought that you could do a better job if you were in charge? While many people spend their entire lives working for someone else and enjoy it, others hope to advance in the organization until they become the boss. That way, they can be the ones responsible for making final business decisions. A faster way to become the boss is to start your own business.

Many people go into business to achieve financial independence. In the beginning, having your own business is usually financially difficult—you need to spend quite a bit of money to get a new business off the ground. This money usually comes from your personal savings as well as from others who have loaned you money to help with start-up costs. But once the business begins to generate a profit, you are the primary beneficiary. If your business is successful, you will likely earn more money than you would working for someone else's company.

Starting your own business gives you the opportunity to use your skills and knowledge and to be creative. Some businesses are launched by an innovative idea for a product or service. For example, when magnetic tape (the kind used in cassette tapes) appeared in the marketplace as a device to store information, no one imagined that CDs and DVDs would come along later to replace it.

Stretch Your Thinking

Business ideas come from sources such as hobbies, interests, books, magazines, newspapers, and television programs. Ask yourself: What do I do well? What do others say I do well? Can I interest others in what I have to offer? Use your answers to identify business opportunities for yourself.

What Different Types of Businesses Are There?

Once you decide to go into business, you have to decide what type of business you want to own. Do you want to offer a service? Do you want to sell something? Or do you want to produce something?

Businesses are classified into types based on what they do.

What Are Your Skills and Interests?

Your experiences in school, in your private life, and possibly on the job have provided you with ideas, skills, and knowledge. Starting your own business gives you the opportunity to pursue these ideas and employ these capabilities. For example, if you enjoy doing small renovation projects, you might want to start a summer business building patio decks, fixing or erecting fences, or doing painting or staining jobs. If you would like the opportunity to be creative and achieve financial independence, then you should consider what business would be just right for you.

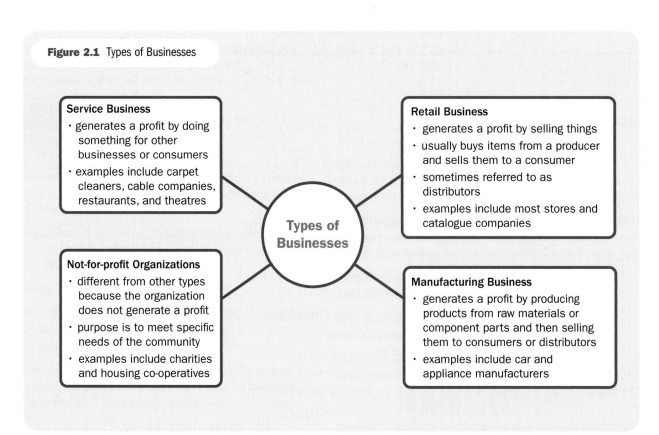

Figure 2.1 Types of Businesses

Service Business
- generates a profit by doing something for other businesses or consumers
- examples include carpet cleaners, cable companies, restaurants, and theatres

Retail Business
- generates a profit by selling things
- usually buys items from a producer and sells them to a consumer
- sometimes referred to as distributors
- examples include most stores and catalogue companies

Types of Businesses

Not-for-profit Organizations
- different from other types because the organization does not generate a profit
- purpose is to meet specific needs of the community
- examples include charities and housing co-operatives

Manufacturing Business
- generates a profit by producing products from raw materials or component parts and then selling them to consumers or distributors
- examples include car and appliance manufacturers

Paramount Imax is an example of a service business, Chapters represents a retail business.

Should Your Business Be Home-based?

Home-based businesses—sometimes called **SOHO** (short for "small office, home office")—are not a new idea. However, technological advances over the past two decades have changed how these businesses operate. Computers, scanners, video equipment, camcorders, and access to the Internet have transformed the home office into a "virtual" office.

Working out of the home may mean fewer meetings to attend, no office politics, and less time spent on the telephone or running from office to office. Running your business from home also means you can wear casual clothes—who's to know that you're sitting at your desk in jeans and a T-shirt!—and save on clothing and dry-cleaning costs. Not everyone, however, would enjoy working from home. Some people need personal contact or the discipline of a traditional work environment.

Today, many types of online businesses are home-based. For example, many cartoonists who work from home have their own websites. At these sites, customers can view samples of the cartoonist's work and purchase copies. Customers may also be able to submit online requests for customized illustrations and cartoons.

Stretch Your Thinking

Would a home-based business suit your personality? Why or why not?

This woman works from her home-based business.

In the News

Peter and Frank Zuuring, a father-and-son team, are now ready to commercially launch a new board game named Antarctica in an attempt to capture a share of the market for board games, which is estimated to exceed 90 million board games sold worldwide each year. The team has invested over four years and $200 000 in an effort to make the game ready for sale. The Zuurings have patented their idea as their own invention, but they realize that the same design could be used in other science fiction–like games that are designed in the future.

So far, they have already sold their business plan to investors who could help manufacture and distribute the product while the father-and-son duo are concentrating on getting the word out. To this end, they have launched a business, Savita Games, with a website. What other strategies could the father-and-son team use to get the word out?

Should Your Business Be Web-based?

Chapter 1 briefly examined what it would take to set up an online business. Perhaps this type of business is right for you! In today's electronic marketplace, consumers and sellers can conduct business without ever meeting face to face. This is known as **e-commerce**, which stands for "electronic commerce." To go shopping, all your customers need is Internet access. Most traditional businesses may be open 12 hours a day for six days a week. E-businesses are generally "24/7"—they are open 24 hours a day, seven days a week.

To conduct e-commerce, a business needs an actual physical space in which to operate. Electronically, the first thing the business needs is a **website** to conduct e-commerce transactions. It also needs a **domain name**—a catchy and simple Internet address—if it wants to present the business professionally to potential customers. This Internet address lets potential customers connect with the business **online**. Once a business website is created, **web pages** are necessary to advertise the goods or services that are for sale. Some small businesses do this design work themselves, but larger businesses usually hire professional Internet service businesses to do this work. E-businesses also need a method of processing payments. If it is more convenient for them, online businesses may hire other businesses to assist them with their payment process.

Once all this is accomplished, e-businesses can measure their success in different ways. Sales and profits are a critical indicator, but e-businesses can also gauge the popularity of their website by keeping track of the website hits. **Website hits** represent the number of people who visit the website. They are a reflection of whether the business's online presence has become well known and popular.

How big are online businesses? The following graph will give you an idea of how this marketplace has grown since the introduction of the World Wide Web in 1991.

⊕ E-ACTIVITY

Visit www.nelson.com/WOB and follow the links to learn more about web-based businesses.

Figure 2.2 Growth in the Total Number of Websites

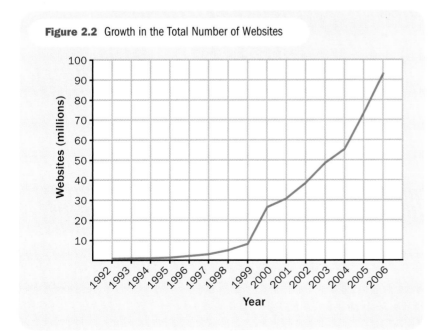

Deciding What to Sell Online

Many goods and services are selling well on the Internet, and the volume of sales is increasing rapidly. Some products that sell particularly well online include CDs, health products, books, software, downloaded music, and hardware. Clothes, jewellery, toys, and gift items are also gaining popularity online. Frequently used online services include car insurance shopping, banking and investing, distance education, airline bookings, and travel planning. Of course, the Internet has also created a market for many new types of services, such as web page design and Internet security services.

As more businesses go online, consumers are faced with a staggering number of goods and services. In the "real world," consumers can touch the goods they are considering buying. They can meet the people offering services. In contrast, e-commerce takes place in cyberspace, where nothing is tangible. As a result, some consumers are cautious about

In addition to selling merchandise from store locations, Apple products are also available for purchase online from Apple's website.

placing their trust in e-businesses. Research indicates that many consumers make buying decisions online but then buy offline. Many surveys have been done over the past several years in an attempt to find out about consumer reluctance to buy online. One survey cited the top reason for consumers hesitating to buy online was because they worried about unreliable or dishonest retailers. A more recent survey found that consumers were more worried about privacy issues, such as their information being stolen or misused.

Where Can You Find Information about a Business?

Imagine that you're thinking about going into business. Where can you find information that will help you make a good decision? It's important that your information be accurate and current. Libraries, existing businesses, trade associations, government resources, and the Internet are all sources of free information.

Industry Canada, a department of the federal government, provides a comprehensive Internet site called Strategis for Canadian businesses and consumers. Strategis gives Canadians direct access to valuable business and consumer information sources, timesaving interactive tools, and a large number of online and e-commerce services. A businessperson can use Strategis to find new markets, business partners, and technologies, or to learn about risk factors that may apply to the business venture. Strategis offers information on business opportunities and market analysis, promoting and improving your business, and contacts and events. This information is organized according to business categories or sectors. Strategis also gives advice on doing business both in and outside Canada.

Another source of information for businesspeople is Statistics Canada, which collects statistical information. For example, if you are interested in starting a business related to environmental affairs, you can see whether this area is growing. You might find out how much the environmental affairs sector contributes to Canada's total **gross domestic product (GDP)**. The gross domestic product is the total dollar value of all goods and services produced in a country during one year. It measures how a country's economy is performing.

Statistical information for business people is made available online by the federal government of Canada.

Ethical, Moral & Legal Considerations

The GDP is the most popular statistical tool for measuring the health of a country's economy. However, many people believe the GDP has serious shortcomings. For example, it measures every transaction as a gain. An oil spill off the west coast that causes an expensive clean-up effort would be recorded as a gain in the GDP because it generated employment and purchases. The GDP doesn't measure the loss of wildlife, natural resources, underground oil, water quality, and fisheries, nor does it measure human health or quality of life. What might be the long-term effects of measuring a country's economic health using only the GDP? Can you think of any other ways, besides the GDP, to measure a country's economic health?

What Are the Start-up Costs?

Where will you get the money to start a business? In Chapter 1, money was identified as one of the economic capital resources needed to run a business. You will need money to pay the rent or mortgage, to pay for other expenses such as salaries and advertising, and to buy equipment and goods. You will also need money for day-to-day operations.

Start-up money is available through two kinds of sources—debt financing and equity financing. **Debt financing** means borrowing money to run the business. **Equity financing** means using your savings or investor savings to run your business. Each method of financing has advantages and disadvantages. If you borrow a large sum from a bank, you may have difficulty repaying it on time. With equity financing, on the other hand, you must risk your own savings or be willing to risk the funds of others through a partnership or corporation. Equity financing often means giving up part of the ownership of the business.

Where Can You Find Financing?

Debt financing isn't automatically available. Financial institutions, such as banks, trust companies, and credit unions, lend money to businesses, but not until they have assessed several factors. They check the applicant's past credit history and review the company's business plan. They also try to judge whether the owner has the skills necessary to achieve the company's objectives. This information helps the lending institution predict how successful the business will be and whether the applicant will be able to repay the loan. Using all of that information helps the financial institution establish interest rates that will be charged for the loan. Higher interest rates are charged for higher risks, even though the applicant may not feel that they are a risk factor. (See Chapter 12 on Income Management for more information on financing a business.)

What Level of Risk Can You Expect?

Starting and operating a business can be a risky undertaking, even if you've done preliminary research and planning. Let's say you wanted to start a lawn-care and snow-clearing business. Here are some situations that you might encounter:

- A homeowner might be dissatisfied with the quality of your lawn-care service and refuse to pay you.

- Your business partner might make a deal with a customer that is unacceptable to you.

- You might hire an employee who fails to do the job properly. Terminating this employee might lead to legal action for wrongful dismissal.

This young entrepreneur speaks with a bank manager about debt financing.

This student cannot afford to start a business that has high financial risks, and so instead chose to start a small lawn-mowing company.

- A supplier might be late delivering the snowblower that you ordered, preventing you from fulfilling your commitments.

- You might use a product that kills your customer's lawn and results in a lawsuit for damages.

These types of risks could put you in financial difficulty. For example, the loss of customers or their failure to pay might mean that you are unable to repay a loan or pay for the snowblower and other supplies. Eventually, you may lose the capital that you invested and be forced out of business. Earlier this chapter pointed out that banks charge higher interest rates when they deal with a situation that could involve more risk. Individuals who establish businesses can use the same approach by charging more for services to guard against possible losses such as those described above.

What Steps Are Involved in Running This Business?

Some types of businesses are more complex than others. Usually, a complex business requires people with a variety of skills to start and run it successfully—especially when operating the business involves many different steps. In a manufacturing company, for example, someone has to determine what raw materials are necessary to make the finished product. Someone needs to ensure that those raw materials are available when needed; otherwise, production comes to a halt. Someone has to determine how many employees are required for the various stages of production. Having too many employees is costly; having too few employees slows production. And on it goes. In a complex operation, "someone" may in fact be several people.

What Resources Will You Need?

Cash, inventory, supplies, furniture and fixtures, computer hardware and software, equipment, tools, vehicles, and buildings are some resources that you may require to set up and run a business. As the owner, you must determine what resources you require and how much financing you will need to acquire them. This process is called **forecasting**.

Every three months or so, you will also need to figure out how much projected revenue you will have. Projected revenue is the amount of money that you think the business will generate over a period of time. **Revenue** is the amount of money you will gain from the sale of the product or service. Comparing this sales revenue with your total expenses and costs will help you determine profits or losses. If, for example, you project that the business will generate $8000 in sales revenue over the next three months and the costs and expenses should not exceed $5000, then your profit should be $3000. It's very important to accurately monitor the business over the three-month period to detect any problems that should be considered in the next forecast. If, for some reason, the sales revenue was lower than expected, or the expenses were higher than expected, the profits may evaporate. It is important to find out why this happened and then make another forecast. Chapter 9 on Accounting will explore the notion of forecasting in more detail.

Review Questions

10. Identify the three most common types of businesses.

11. Why would a business establish itself as a not-for-profit operation?

12. Identify a business start-up possibility for a person who is skilled as a musician or as a technician.

13. Define e-commerce. Why are consumers reluctant to buy online?

14. How has the introduction of PayPal helped online businesses?

15. Name the federal government website that provides valuable business and consumer information. How is that website organized?

16. What is the difference between debt financing and equity financing?

17. Why is forecasting a critical step in the process of running a business?

1. joint ventures
2. international franchises
3. strategic alliances
4. mergers
5. offshoring
6. multinational corporations

Business Fact

China is Canada's second-largest single-nation trading partner after the United States. The population of China now exceeds 1.3 billion people.

International Business Structures

If you had just started a software business, and you had a product to sell that appealed to consumers all over the world, where would it make sense to market and sell your product? In your local town or city? Across Canada? In the United States? In China?

Reaching the greatest number of customers is what usually drives businesses to expand internationally. If you sell to the people who live in a small town, you may reach a few thousand consumers. If you market your product across Canada, you could potentially reach millions of consumers. If you sell to people not only in Canada, but also in the United States or in China, you can potentially reach hundreds of millions of potential customers. The rest of this chapter deals with some of the different business structures that allow businesses to expand into international markets.

The name Lamborghini is recognized around the world as a business that manufactures high-end sports cars.

Joint Ventures

Joint ventures are excellent opportunities to market your products or services to a wider audience. You can establish more contacts, get more leads, and increase your customer base using this business structure. Producers typically are experts in producing products or services but these same producers may lack sufficient and efficient marketing tactics or techniques. Therefore, in spite of a useful and productive product or service, they are unable to generate revenue from the sale of a product or service. If the producer can find an efficient marketer, both could gain from sharing each other's expertise.

Freight containers from all over the world at a Halifax port

Joint ventures can be adopted for a trial period of a few weeks or months and should be continued only if they work to the advantage of both parties. A joint venture essentially matches the skills and expertise of two different individuals or businesses and, in the process, generates benefits for both parties. There is no legislation that specifically regulates joint ventures in Ontario, and there is no precise legal definition or status for a joint venture.

For example, Pacific Northern Gas Ltd. and Kitimat LNG Inc. are participating in a joint venture to build a $1.2 billion natural gas pipeline in northern British Columbia. The joint-venture partners are confident that they can overcome their biggest challenge—to find a long-term supply of natural gas to feed the pipeline. Part of this partnership agreement will be to build a pipeline system that will connect to a liquefied natural gas receiving terminal on the coast of northern British Columbia.

International Franchises

Franchises are also a way to achieve an international presence by authorizing a group or an individual to sell its goods or services. The franchisee (the one who buys the rights) pays for being able to ride on the success of the franchiser (the one who sells the rights). For example, when the Richmond, British Columbia–based company Boston Pizza expanded into the United States, it was able to quickly set up franchises across North America, supplying franchisees with real estate, construction, start-up procedures, fixtures, operating systems, signage, equipment, marketing programs, training, and menus, because it had developed the concept in Canada. In fact, the only change that was made for the U.S. market was a modification of the name

Stretch Your Thinking

Why would a joint venture make more sense than a partnership for an international business idea?

to Boston's, The Gourmet Pizza. The name change was designed to communicate the superior product offering—this wasn't just any pizza, it was "gourmet pizza" with a crust, seasonings, and flavours unlike any other.

Strategic Alliances

Strategic alliances are agreements between businesses in which each business commits resources to achieve a common set of objectives. Typically, a strategic alliance is used to help co-develop, co-produce, and co-market the products or services of the two businesses. Businesses may form strategic alliances with a wide variety of players: customers, suppliers, competitors, universities, or divisions of government. This type of agreement can help businesses improve competitive positioning, gain entry to new markets, supplement critical skills, and share the risk or cost of major development projects. While partners in the alliance, each business remains separate and entirely independent of the other partner. An example of a "made-in-

A sign for a McDonald's Drive Thru in Amman, Jordan

Canada" strategic alliance involves the Canadian Broadcasting Corporation (CBC). CBC-Radio Canada has developed alliances with other media businesses such as the *Toronto Star*, the *National Post, Maclean's Magazine* and *La Presse*. Combined efforts have resulted in joint coverage of major stories like health care and education. Another example of a strategic alliance, which reaches beyond the borders of Canada, is one between the Citizens Bank of Canada and Amnesty International. These two players have partnered together to help raise money for campaigns to protect fundamental human rights around the world. When people use their Amnesty International Visa card, Citizens Bank donates 10 cents to Amnesty International.

Businesses from the United States considering a strategic alliance find that Canadian businesses have a lot to offer. Canadian businesses have world-class technologies, are export-oriented, operate in a similar culture, and operate under government regulations that are not a disadvantage when compared to other countries.

Mergers

If the strategic alliance is successful, the two businesses may agree to a merger. A **merger** occurs when two or more companies join together, either because one has purchased a controlling interest in the other(s) or because the companies have combined their interests. A merger can help both companies strengthen their operations, enter new markets, and acquire new technologies, resources, and skills. If a smaller company merges with a larger one, the small company may also gain access to more capital or to a larger sales force. Companies will tend to consider a merger if that partnership allows them to increase market share, become a more efficient operation, or gain a competitive advantage. One of Canada's most famous merger attempts occurred in the Canadian banking system. In 1998, the Royal Bank and the Bank of Montreal announced a $40 billion proposal to merge. Within a few months, Canadian Imperial Bank of Commerce (CIBC) and the Toronto Dominion Bank (TD Bank) announced a $47 billion proposal to merge. But the federal government of Canada ultimately turned down the mergers because they wanted the banking system to remain as competitive as possible and, in the process, protect the interest of the public. The concern of the public was that too few banks could place too much power in the hands of not enough people!

> ### Business Fact
>
> In Canada in 2004, there were 859 announced merger and acquisition transactions valued at $115 billion.

In 2004, Molson, a Canadian brewery, announced a merger with an American brewery, Adolph Coors. Shareholders approved the $4.5 billion deal in 2005.

Offshoring

Offshoring is the relocation of some of a company's operations to another country. Typically, the new location takes advantage of much lower labour costs. For example, many Canadian manufacturing companies have moved to China and Mexico. In fact, few manufacturing companies remain in Canada. But more recently other factors have influenced companies' decisions to move offshore. For example, proximity to large, emerging buyer markets (such as China and India) and access to growing pools of skilled labour with low wages entice companies to consider moving elsewhere. Would it make sense for a Canadian manufacturer like Research In Motion (RIM) (manufacturers of the Blackberry) to set up an offshore branch in Japan or China? If RIM could reduce their costs of production and if the Asian market represented one of their major customers, it may make sense to establish an offshore operation. Other technology manufacturers, such as IBM and Hewlett-Packard, have already set up shop overseas. They are taking advantage of employees in India and China who have relatively high education levels but work for low pay relative to Canadian wages.

However, offshoring presents a public relations risk if it eliminates jobs in a company's home country. Firms must carefully weigh all the risks of offshoring before making a move. For example, if an offshore country's political climate is uncertain, or if the currency of that country is unstable,

In the News

In the summer of 2006, Google and eBay, two of the Internet's most prominent players, formed a strategic alliance that will see Google advertising used on eBay websites outside of the United States. Previously, in the spring of 2006, eBay had announced a similar deal with Yahoo to serve all of its advertising within the United States.

The advantage of combining forces is to introduce "click and call" website technology to more people. "Clicking" a link on a website will allow consumers to be able to "call" eBay merchants or Google advertisers. The goal is to develop a whole new way for buyers and sellers to connect online, which will financially benefit both Google and eBay. Above all, this partnership alliance is about speed. It is about having a service available that can make an instant connection with someone who wants to buy something now. Maybe even before they can change their mind!

an offshore move could prove more costly than beneficial. Trade barriers could also be a stumbling block in a move, a topic that will be discussed more fully in Chapter 4 on International Business.

Multinational Corporations

A **multinational corporation** is a business enterprise that conducts business in several different countries. These corporations operate as if there aren't any borders, so the global marketplace becomes their place of business. Why do they do business in this fashion? In the long run, it could save money. A multinational corporation could have its corporate headquarters located in Canada, its raw material sources in South Africa, its production plant in Germany, and some of its retail stores in Japan. The reason for doing this is to take advantage of what each country has to offer. In the process of doing business, these corporations observe national regulations, rules, and policies in the countries in which they operate. However, many multinationals are powerful enough to pressure governments to give in to their demands.

A call centre in India answers calls made from customers in North America.

Ethical, Moral & Legal Considerations

Were you aware that Canada has a *Corruption of Foreign Public Officials Act*? This Act, passed in 1998, makes it a criminal offence punishable by up to five years in jail for a Canadian businessperson to pay a bribe to a foreign public official to gain a business advantage. Before the Act was passed, such behaviour was considered only an ethical issue; but with the passing of the Act it has become a legal issue. The Act covers loans, awards, and advantages of any other kind made directly or indirectly to a government official to obtain a business advantage. For example, paying an agent to assist in obtaining a government contract or allowing that agent to use some of the funds to influence government officials is considered illegal.

The most common threat is to close offices and lay off thousands of workers and take the employment elsewhere.

When a multinational corporation invests in another country, that country can benefit in several ways. Extra jobs, new technology, and training are the positive benefits of the arrival of a multinational corporation. However, there could also be a downside to the arrival. Some multinational corporations have been known to take advantage of the fact that workers in the new country will work for less money. This cheap labour helps keep costs of production lower but it does not benefit the citizens of those countries. See Chapter 4 for more information on International Businesses.

Review Questions

18. Why might a manufacturer seek out a business with which to form a joint venture?

19. Identify five players that could form a strategic alliance with a business.

20. What is the difference between a strategic alliance and a merger?

21. What are some possible drawbacks to an offshore move for a business?

22. What benefits can a multinational corporation bring to a community when they decide to set up operations? Identify a possible drawback to the community.

CHAPTER REVIEW

Knowledge

1. Identify two skills that you now possess that could help you when working in a business environment.

2. Owning one share in a co-operative is different from owning one share in a public corporation. What difference does it make for voting or for sharing the company profits?

3. Make a list of financial institutions in your community where you could borrow money if you were to start a business.

4. List the domain names of ten online businesses with which you are familiar. What good or service does each website provide?

Thinking

5. Prepare a partnership agreement for a lawn-care or snow-removal business.

6. If you had the choice to finance your business using either debt or equity financing, which one would you select? Explain your choice.

7. Debbi Fields of Mrs. Fields Cookies said "You should be the best at what you do." What does she mean by this statement? How would being the best at what you do be good for a business?

8. Explain what is meant by the following expression: "In cyberspace nothing is tangible."

9. Explain the difference between a joint venture, a strategic alliance, and offshoring.

10. In a group, discuss why Tim Hortons reorganized and changed its type of ownership several times. Have a spokesperson report back to the class with your ideas.

11. What factors do you think might contribute to a customer visiting or revisiting a website? What factors might discourage a customer from visiting or revisiting a website?

Communication

12. Invite to your class two or more representatives from a sole proprietorship, a partnership, a corporation, or a co-operative. Ask each representative to talk about his or her type of business ownership and to provide an overview of its advantages and disadvantages. Introduce each representative to your class, giving some information about the types of products or services that the business offers. Class members should be prepared to ask the businesspeople questions.

13. Choose one of the Crown corporations mentioned on page 44. Prepare an advertisement that tells what services the corporation provides.

14. Return to the list of potential risks involved in the lawn-care and snow-clearing business (page 59). Work with a partner to discuss how you would respond to each situation.

Application

15. Working with a partner, select two businesses in your community that have the same type of ownership (e.g., two sole proprietorships). Gather as much information as you can about each business. Try to acquire data that deals with the business's start-up costs, the availability of financing, the complexity of production, and the business's resource requirements. Which of these businesses would you prefer to own? Record your findings in a chart and briefly summarize the reasons for your choice.

16. Find out the start-up cost for each of the following franchises: Burger King, Merry Maids, and Tim Hortons. What do you get for your investment? Use the Internet, advertisements, and personal contacts. Make a list of all of the advantages and disadvantages of becoming a potential franchisee. (Note: If you have difficulty finding one of these, substitute another franchise.)

17. Select one person or family from Table 2.1 on page 45. Using research tools, such as the Internet, magazines, and libraries, find more about that person or family. How was the fortune attained? What business or businesses were involved in amassing this huge amount of money? Provide some financial details on the history of the person or the family.

18. Lower labour costs in other countries may attract Canadian international businesses, but the wages paid to workers in those countries may not be enough for them to live on. It also is virtually impossible for workers in some countries to establish a union to ensure fair wages, safe working conditions, and job security. In small groups discuss what you think Canadians should do about these complex human rights issues? Report your group's findings back to the class.

Team Activity

Team Goal: To identify types of businesses found in your community

Team Assignment: Neighbourhood Businesses

Your team should find two specific examples of each of the following types of businesses within your community:

- service—non-retail
- retail
- franchise
- manufacturing
- not-for-profit
- public corporations
- crown corporations

The winning team will be the first team to provide a list of fourteen local businesses.

Portfolio

If possible, identify at least one of each of the business types (sole proprietorship, partnership, corporation, co-operative, or franchise) for businesses within your selected industry. Describe their organization in detail from information you collected on their website. If you cannot find examples of one or more of the business types, explain why you think your specific industry is not ideal for this type of business.

For your corporate example, obtain the company's annual report and comment on the success of the firm. Track the company's share price over the rest of the course. Compare the beginning price with the final price and account for any discrepancies.

What is the most popular form of business ownership in your industry? Why is this so?

Reflect on Your Learning

Review your answers to the Before You Begin question on page 41. How would you answer this question now that you've read this chapter?

Southwest Airlines

Rollin King had been on too many costly and inconvenient business trips. As he complained about this to his lawyer Herb Kelleher, they came up with a great idea. King and Kelleher imagined an airline that would make it less expensive to fly than to drive between two points in Texas. At the time this idea was outlandish, but in 1967, they founded Air Southwest, later renamed Southwest Airlines in 1971.

The competition fought to keep Southwest on the ground. However in 1971, Southwest won an intense legal battle and the right to fly in Texas. Initially, Southwest flew three planes to locations in the state of Texas. Today the company flies 80 million passengers a year to 62 cities all across the United States more than 3100 times a day.

The company turned its first annual profit in 1973 and has been profitable every year since, including the years following September 11, 2001. This profit record is unmatched by any other company in the commercial airline industry. How can Southwest be so successful in such a turbulent industry?

Southwest is the world's premiere low-cost, no frills airline—and is often unsuccessfully imitated by competitors. Although its structure can be easily imitated, its culture cannot. All employees are paid with stock options and participate in profit sharing, and since they are technically Southwest owners, they are more motivated to work to improve their company.

Southwest invented the "10 minute turn." That is, Southwest can land a plane, unload, clean the cabin, board new passengers, and take off again in 10 minutes. All employees help clean the cabin and check tickets, including the pilots. Southwest also keeps expenses low by flying out of secondary airports, not using travel agents to sell tickets, and serving minimal food on board. The success of Southwest even created a new business concept—the Southwest Effect—which states that when an aggressive and innovative company enters a market, the market itself changes, and usually grows dramatically.

To fight off competitors, Southwest has developed frequent flyer programs, offered free drink promotions, and moved into more airports. Customers are still the top priority. "I tell my employees that we're in the service business, and it's incidental that we fly airplanes," says Kelleher.

Luggage is unloaded from a Southwest Airlines plane.

QUESTIONS

1. Define the word "culture." How is Southwest Airlines culture different from its competition?

2. In what way does Southwest Airlines qualify as a "service" business?

3 Business Ethics and Social Responsibility

SPECIFIC EXPECTATIONS

After completing this chapter, you will be able to

- explain the concepts of ethics and social responsibility as they apply to business

- assess ethical dilemmas in the workplace

- explain controversial business issues from a local, national, and international perspective

- describe the impact of business on a local community

Kicking Horse Coffee Co.

Leo Johnson and Elana Rosenfeld are the husband and wife team responsible for the creation and production of Canada's number one organic and fair-trade coffee company, Kicking Horse Coffee Co. Founded in 1996 and located in the Canadian Rockies in the British Columbia town of Invermere (population 3600), the company employs fifteen people. Even though the location is remote, and the number of staff is small, Kicking Horse Coffee Co. manages to sell more than 10 000 kg of coffee each week to grocery stores throughout Canada, the United States, and Holland. Revenue projections for 2006 are $10 million from the company's sales of thirty different blends of organic and fair-trade coffee, organic and fair-trade teas, and organic chocolate. (Organic products are produced naturally, without pesticides or additives. Fair-trade products come from farmers in disadvantaged countries. These products are brought to European and North American markets through aid organizations or co-operatives, not middlemen, ensuring that the farmers do not have to accept unfair prices in order to sell their products internationally.)

In 2003, the couple was awarded the Young Entrepreneurship Award for British Columbia by the Business Development Bank of Canada in recognition of the success of Kicking Horse Coffee Co. So, what is the secret to (and story of) the Kicking Horse Coffee Co.'s success?

Elana (born in Toronto) and Leo (born in Fredericton) first met in British Columbia. Together and separately, they had worked in restaurants, opened a fruit stand, and purchased and operated a café. In fact, the idea of Kicking Horse Coffee Co. came about because the couple had difficulties obtaining organic coffee, which they wanted to serve in their café. Specifically, Elana and Leo wanted to remain true to their ethical principles while providing coffee to their customers.

So began the Kicking Horse Coffee Co., a company founded on ethical beliefs that included promoting market interest in organic and fair-trade coffee.

The fair-trade feature means that Kicking Horse Coffee Co. purchases their organic coffee beans from small business co-operatives (co-ops). As explained in previous chapters, co-ops are businesses that are both owned and operated by the individuals who supply the product. Members of the co-ops (such as the coffee-bean farmers) are able to negotiate for prices that give them a higher standard of living. In addition to providing individuals with a better standard of living, the fair-trade requirements for coffee production state that certain environmental standards, which include restricting the use of potentially harmful agrochemicals, must be followed. Elana and Leo not only import their raw, organic coffee beans from countries such as Sumatra, Nicaragua, and Cuba, they also visit their producers' plantations to see for themselves the benefits that fair trade can bring to farmers.

In choosing to operate in the organic fair-trade coffee market, the founders were able to both uphold their ethical beliefs without compromise and select a market niche that had yet to be saturated with competing entrepreneurs. Indeed, the couple spotted an opportunity for organic and fair-trade coffee in the grocery-store market and pursued it. Now, they are represented in distribution outlets including Thrifty Foods, Canada Safeway Ltd., IGA, Save-On Foods, Urban Fare, and Loblaws. In addition to grocery stores, Kicking Horse coffee is also available for online purchase directly from the Kicking Horse Coffee Co. website.

Two of Kicking Horse's fair-trade coffees

QUESTIONS

1. How is Kicking Horse Coffee Co. different from its competitors? Why is it important to Elana and Leo that these differences be incorporated into their business operation?

2. What benefits has Kicking Horse Coffee Co. gained from its decision to sell organic and fair-trade products? Who else benefits from this decision? How?

Business Ethics

What would you do in each of the following situations?

1. Your friend asks you to add a few extra hours to a work time sheet for him, but you know that he did not put in the time.

2. A salesperson in an electronics store offers to sell you an iPod after hours at a discounted price.

3. You are aware that the teller gave you back too much money when completing a banking transaction.

Ethics are the rules that help us tell the difference between right and wrong and encourage us to do the right thing. They can help people decide on the best course of action in situations where they aren't sure what to do.

What Is Ethical Behaviour?

Ethical behaviour is behaviour that conforms to ethics—individual beliefs and social standards about what is right and good. Ethics are important for getting along with others, living with yourself, and having a good character. Ethical behaviour is based on values such as trustworthiness, respect, responsibility, caring, justice, and good citizenship, and on adherence to moral rules. Our **values** tell us what we think is important and this, in turn, helps us make decisions about right and wrong. For example, a person who values trustworthiness is unlikely to betray a friend. **Morals** are the rules we use to decide what's good and what's bad. For example, one moral rule might be that stealing is bad because it harms the person you steal from.

As a society, we tend to judge people more on their morals than their values. In fact, some of the most difficult decisions to make are the ones in which our personal values conflict with our moral rules. When we make decisions that run counter to our values and morals, and do things that our individual beliefs and social standards define as being bad or wrong, we are demonstrating unethical behaviour.

Let's examine the first situation described earlier—adding a few extra hours to your friend's time sheet. In this situation, there are two choices—either to add the extra hours or not to add them. If you add a few hours to a time sheet, your friend will get paid for work that he did not perform. Who wins and who loses with this choice? Would a decision like that bother you?

Keep in Mind

1. What is ethical behaviour?
2. What role should ethics play in business?
3. How can businesses resolve ethical dilemmas?
4. What happens when people don't behave ethically?

Before You Begin

What do the terms values, morals, and ethics mean to you? Share your thoughts with a partner and record your opinions so that you can reflect on them later.

Stretch Your Thinking

Author Isaac Asimov once stated, "Never let your sense of morals get in the way of doing what's right." State in your own words what you think Asimov meant.

A shopper reads nutrition information in order to decide on the best product.

What happens if your friend asks you to do the same thing again in the future?

On the other hand, if you don't add the hours to the time sheet, your friend may be angry with you. Is that important to you? What are the possible consequences?

Your values and morals both tell you that dishonesty is wrong. Consider the amount of harm that could result from your decision. If you add the hours, the company will be harmed because it has to pay money without receiving any benefit in return. There will also be harm to you or your friend if someone finds out what you did. You could lose your jobs! Is it worth the risk? Ethical behaviour is all about doing the right thing.

What Role Should Ethics Play in Business?

Ethics are based on both individual beliefs and standards in society. They vary from person to person, situation to situation, and culture to culture. Society's ethics are usually minimum standards for decency and respect of others. Individual ethics are personal beliefs about what is good and bad. Business ethics are tied to both society's ethics and the ethics of the individuals who work for, and buy products from, the company. For example, suppose you work for a company that makes cyanide gas. You know this gas can be harmful to people. Is it unethical that you make this gas? After all, you aren't using it to poison people. Should you do it because it will help the company make a profit? Should you be concerned that workers might be exposed to toxic effects from working with the gas? In this situation, you must decide whether this work is unethical and whether you are willing to expose yourself to trouble with your boss by opposing it.

How do you apply your personal beliefs in a business environment? Shouldn't you just do exactly what you are told to do? After all, the employer is paying you. Shouldn't the employer get to decide what you do? Would guidelines be helpful for making these decisions?

Stretch Your Thinking

What are some products that could be considered unethical and morally wrong? Select one of these products and give reasons why you think this product is unethical.

A Code of Ethics

Businesses face ethical questions every day concerning the products or services they sell and the way they deal with people inside and outside the company. Many companies choose to operate according to a **code of ethics**—a document that explains specifically how employees should respond in different situations.

A code of ethics is especially useful when problems arise. For example, in the Chicago area in 1982, someone contaminated several bottles of Tylenol with poison, and seven people died as a result. This was the first case of product tampering of its kind. Johnson & Johnson, the manufacturer of Tylenol, followed its code of ethics and immediately pulled every package of the product off the shelves throughout North America, even though this was very expensive for the company. Johnson & Johnson also changed its packaging so it would be much more difficult for someone to contaminate the product in the future. The recall and repackaging effort cost the corporation about US$100 million, but it also showed customers that the company cared about their safety.

A code of ethics helps different people approach problems in the same way. Many companies have gone beyond simply writing a code and have established educational programs to help employees learn to behave more ethically. Program topics range from making personal calls during business hours to handling employee layoffs.

The World of Business DVD

"Raging Bull"
from The World of Business DVD

Frank and Ernest

THE QUESTION OF RIGHT AND WRONG IS VERY CLEAR. I WANT YOU TO CLOUD IT UP FOR ME.

THAVES

The problem with creating and applying a code of ethics is that drawing a line between right and wrong isn't always easy. Is it wrong for a businessperson to give a client a gift because that client has been a valued customer over the past year? Or is this bribery? Is it wrong for a politician to make a phone call to a bank manager to help a friend obtain a business loan? Is this using political influence for personal purposes?

Rogers Communications Inc. Code of Ethics and Conduct

The Board of Directors (the "Board") of Rogers Communications Inc. (the "Company", which for the purpose of this Code includes its subsidiaries) has adopted this code of conduct and ethics for directors and officers of the Company (the "Code") to:

1. endorse and promote the Company's commitment to honest and ethical conduct, including fair dealing and ethical handling of conflicts of interest;

2. promote full, fair, accurate, timely, and understandable disclosure;

3. promote compliance with applicable laws and governmental rules and regulations;

4. ensure the protection of the Company's legitimate business interests, including corporate opportunities, assets, and confidential information;

5. deter wrongdoing.

All directors and officers of the Company are expected to be familiar with the Code and to adhere to those principles and procedures set forth in the Code that apply to them. The Company's more detailed policies and procedures that apply to all employees of the Company set forth in the Company's Business Conduct Guidelines are separate requirements and are not part of this Code.

For purposes of this Code, the "Code of Ethics Contact Person" will be the Chair of the Corporate Governance Committee of the Board.

A group of colleagues trying to work through a dilemma

Instead of referring to a written guideline, you can ask yourself, "If I take this action, will anyone suffer as a result?" For example, if a salesperson knowingly sells an item that does not have a return guarantee without informing the customer, the customer (and the business) could suffer. You don't need a code of ethics to decide if it is wrong.

In Canada, the law details acceptable business behaviour, but companies can still behave unethically without actually breaking the law. Like the law, no code of ethics can provide guidance for every possible situation. Although codes of ethics sometimes help people make decisions, they are not conclusive guides to distinguishing between right and wrong, and they are not necessary for every company. As a result, some would say that people should rely on their own judgment first.

How Can Businesses Resolve Ethical Dilemmas?

A **dilemma** is a situation where there is a difficult choice between two or more options. Dilemmas have good points and bad points on both sides. But not all dilemmas are right-versus-wrong scenarios. For example, a business decision about where to locate is a decision and may even be a dilemma if there are a lot of issues to consider. But it is not an ethical dilemma because it is not a right-versus-wrong decision.

Stretch Your Thinking

How can businesses end up with a bad reputation? Are bad reputations always the business's fault? What can a company do to change a negative public image?

This police officer is "blowing the whistle."

An **ethical dilemma** is a moral problem with potential right or wrong answers. It occurs in business when a business has a decision to make that weighs values and morals against profitability and competitiveness. Suppose you are the manager of a business that has no really good place to dispose of its toxic waste, so the company has been simply dumping it. If you stop dumping it, you will hold up production until you find a proper place to dispose of it. But what if that turns out to be very expensive? Should you inform the business owners that the company is violating an environmental code? Or should you just ignore the problem?

Some ethical dilemmas facing society and business include downsizing of staff, pollution control, disposal of toxic waste, depletion and allocation of scarce resources, cost containment, changes in law and technology, employee rights, discrimination against women and minorities, and product safety.

Resolving ethical dilemmas requires honesty, the ability to work co-operatively, respect for others, pride in one's work, willingness to learn, dependability, responsibility for one's actions, integrity, and loyalty. It may help to respond to the following questions when seeking a resolution:

1. Who will be helped by what you do?
2. Who will be hurt?
3. What are the benefits and problems of such a decision?
4. Will the decision survive the test of time?

The types of ethical dilemmas people encounter in business, and the approaches used to resolve them, are continually changing and developing. This timeline (Figure 3.1) shows some of the changes that have occurred over the last 50 years.

Whistle-blowing

Whistle-blowing is the decision of an employee to inform officials or the public about a legal or ethical violation. The employee discovers unethical, immoral, or illegal actions at the workplace and has to make a decision about what to do. Is it the right thing to inform someone else about these actions and, if so, how should that be done? Will the whistle-blower be rewarded or punished?

In the United States, the year 2002 became known as the "Year of the Whistle-blower," and *Time Magazine* named three female whistle-blowers as their "Persons of the Year."

Figure 3.1 Ethical Dilemmas and Developments Over Time

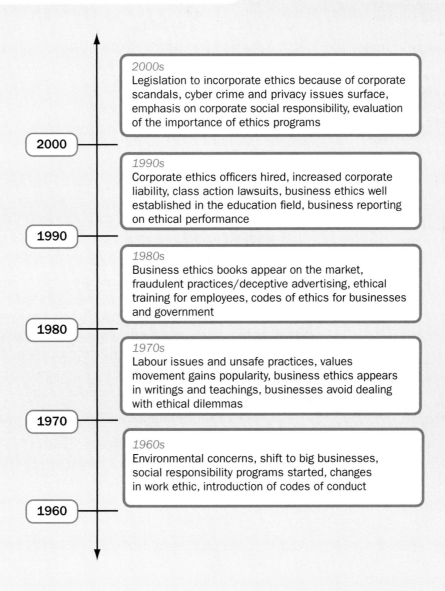

Examples of issues that a whistle-blower might report include
- someone submitting false information on an expense report
- a business that's ignoring hiring procedures for minorities
- a business that's knowingly ignoring workplace safety codes
- a business that's not observing mandated health codes

What Happens When People Don't Behave Ethically?

Imagine that you handle the bookkeeping for your company. Sounds boring? For day-to-day activities, it's probably not too exciting. But what if your boss asks you to alter some of the accounts to hide sums of money that seem to have disappeared? Or what if you come across some interesting figures about the company's future plans, and you decide to buy some shares in the company as a result of seeing these figures? Suddenly, you are dealing with important ethical issues—and not simply ethical issues either! These types of actions can land you in jail.

Table 3.1 shows some examples of situations in which people don't behave in an ethical way, and others are harmed as a result.

Fraud, accounting scandals, and insider trading are some of the major ethical issues that have become associated with businesses.

Fraud

Fraud is the crime of lying or pretending. Some businesses mislead consumers and try to trick them into buying something in order to maximize their profits. The *Competition Act* 2002 bans these types of fraud and deceptive business practices:

1. false or misleading advertising
2. advertising a bargain price for merchandise that is unavailable for sale in a reasonable quantity ("bait and switch" selling)

In the News

Did you know that the film industry makes many movies about unethical practices? Movies that turn whistle-blowers into heroes have included the following:

1. *An Inconvenient Truth* (impact of global warming)
2. *The Insider* (secrets of the cigarette industry)
3. *Open Heart* (medical care in hospitals)
4. *Quiz Show* (ethical dilemma concerning cheating)
5. *Erin Brockovich* (industrial poisoning of a water supply)
6. *All the President's Men* (political cover-up)
7. *The China Syndrome* (nuclear accident)
8. *Silkwood* (safety concerns)
9. *Serpico* (police corruption)
10. *Roger & Me* and *The Big One* (corporate downsizing)

3. placing two different prices on a product and selling it to the consumer at the higher price (double ticketing)

Several types of fraud can involve consumers and businesses. Fraud offences are constantly changing and can vary in their level of sophistication. Here's an alphabetical list of the more common frauds with examples.

E-ACTIVITY

Visit www.nelson.com/WOB and follow the links to learn more about telemarketing scams and how consumers can protect themselves.

1. *Bank fraud*—A bank officer makes a fraudulent loan to a non-existent business and then pockets the money.

2. *Consumer fraud*—A business tricks customers into buying goods or services they don't really need through unethical advertising or false claims.

3. *Contract fraud*—A business or individual uses temptations, such as bribes or kickbacks, to create a contract.

4. *Insurance fraud*—A business or individual falsely claims lost, damaged, or stolen property in order to receive insurance settlements.

5. *Mail fraud*—An individual uses the postal service for fraudulent purposes, such as mailing phony job opportunities, chain letters, or inheritance scams.

6. *Pyramid scheme fraud*—A person participating in the scheme recruits others in order to receive more money than she or he invested in the scheme.

7. *Stock market fraud*—An individual uses insider trading or other techniques to buy and sell stocks at artificial values.

8. *Telemarketing fraud*—A company uses high-pressure phone calls to get customers to buy now or to donate funds to bogus charitable causes.

9. *Welfare fraud*—An individual receives benefits without being eligible.

Bre-X

One famous fraud case was the story of the Canadian mining company Bre-X. Bre-X came to the attention of the general public when it was reported that the company was sitting on an enormous gold deposit in Indonesia. In 1995, Bre-X announced that significant amounts of gold had been discovered and, as a result, its stock price went up. How much? Bre-X stock went from less than a dollar per share, known as a penny stock, to a high of $286.50 per share. If an owner or investor had bought in at the beginning and sold when the stock reached its peak, he or she would have made about $286.00 on each and every share. A thousand dollar investment could have turned into $286 000 for that investor! However, it was a massive fraud because there was no gold. Once doubt about the gold find started growing, people began selling off their shares. Bre-X went bankrupt in 2002, and the investors who still had stock lost every penny they had invested.

Table 3.1

Examples of Unethical Behaviour in Business	
Unethical Behaviour	**Consequence**
Fraud: A method used to deceive someone for personal gain	• harm to the person who is deceived • loss of job and/or jail time
Forgery: A form of fraud that could involve passing bad cheques by forging someone else's name	• harm to the people whose signatures are forged or who accept bad cheques • loss of job and/or jail time
Theft: Stealing someone's property	• harm to the victim • loss of job and/or jail time
Employer Theft: Could involve taking advantage of employees by not paying for overtime worked	• harm to the employees that could result in people quitting • loss of job and/or jail time
Embezzlement: A form of fraud where a person violates a trust by moving funds into their account instead of the correct account	• harm to the person or company whose funds are stolen • loss of job and/or jail time
Misuse of Funds: Moving monies from one account to another without permission or direction	• harm to the person or company whose funds are misused • loss of job and/or jail time
Discrimination: Not hiring a person because of an issue not related to the person's ability to do the job (e.g., race, religion, gender, or disability)	• harm to company because new employees aren't always the best people for the job • loss of job
Environmental Violations: A company ignoring laws and regulations that involve toxic waste	• harm to the environment and possibly to people and animals • fine and/or decrease in market value of stock
Concealing Information: Not disclosing data that should be shared, for example, about defective products	• harm to customers or employees, for example, because of unsafe products or working conditions • fine and/or decrease in market value of stock
Tampering with Records: A form of fraud where records are altered in some way to deceive other persons	• harm to the people who are being deceived • loss of job and/or fine and/or jail time

Bre-X Minerals Group in Indonesia

Ethical, Moral & Legal Considerations

"I consider my past immoral, unethical, and illegal. It is something I am not proud of," said Frank W. Abagnale Jr., the youngest person to ever make the FBI's most-wanted list. Beginning at the age of 16, Abagnale wrote bad cheques totalling $2.5 million over a six-year period in 26 countries. As a con artist, he impersonated a doctor, a lawyer, and an airline pilot. His career in crime lasted six years from 1963 to 1969. The 2002 movie *Catch Me If You Can* was based on Abagnale's life. After being caught and serving time in prison, Frank Abagnale became a consultant for the FBI where he worked on white-collar crime. How would a business take care of a bad cheque that they may have received from a con artist like Frank? What can a business employee do to detect a con artist? How can companies protect themselves from con artists and fraud artists?

Accounting Scandals

Willie Sutton, a famous bank robber whose crimes were committed in the 1920s, 30s, and 40s, was once asked why he robbed banks. His response was: "Because that's where the money is." Today, money exists in the form of currency and online transactions. Accounting is the process of identifying, measuring, and communicating financial information about a business so that informed judgments and decisions can be made based on that information. An **accounting scandal** is a publicly exposed crime involving accountants or senior executives who alter accounting records for personal benefit. Accounting scandals typically take place in large corporations. Chapter 9 deals with the subject of accounting and provides more details about accounting procedures. When an accounting scandal is uncovered in a business, outside accountants are appointed to find out what happened. A **forensic accountant** is an accountant who investigates legal and financial documents, looking for evidence of tampering. (See Chapter 9 for more information on forensic accounting.)

In small businesses, accounting crimes often involve embezzlement. **Embezzlement** is a type of accounting fraud in which an accountant or senior executive invents phony accounts and redirects company money into them for personal gain. Business owners sometimes do not pick up on embezzlement activities until they have gone on for a long time.

In large businesses, fraud often involves "cooking the books" regarding assets and liabilities. **Assets** are items that a business owns, such as buildings, land, equipment, cash, and receivables. **Liabilities**, on the other hand, are debts that a business owes. Corporate fraud often involves misusing or misdirecting funds, overstating revenues, understating expenses, overstating the value of corporate assets to the public shareholders, or under-reporting liabilities. **Auditors** are outside accountants who check the financial records of companies. The owners and shareholders rely on auditors to make sure that these frauds do not occur. But if a highly experienced accountant is committing the fraud, even an auditor may have difficulty detecting it. Enron is an example of a public corporation that was involved in an accounting scandal.

Fraud exposed!

Enron

The biggest accounting scandal that has ever taken place involved an American energy company called Enron. In the late 1990s, Enron was considered one of the world's leading electricity, natural gas, and communications companies. It also had the label of being "America's Most Innovative Company" for six consecutive years. But in 2001, Enron went bankrupt. An audit revealed that the assets and the profits of Enron had been grossly inflated and in some cases were even non-existent. Enron was accused of inflating its income figures by US$586 million over a four-year period. The collapse of the company had a tremendous impact on employees and investors. Over 20 000 people lost their jobs, and at the same time, millions of investors lost US$60 billion dollars. Moreover, the accounting company that had been auditing Enron's books for decades—Arthur Andersen Inc.—also went bankrupt. Several senior executives of both companies faced criminal charges and jail sentences.

Insider Trading

Wouldn't it be great to have access to the winning lottery numbers before they are drawn? In business, corporate executives normally do have access to winning lottery numbers—in the form of confidential information about the business and its future plans. A quick investment in the right company could make you a lot of quick money! But buying or selling shares in a company based on this type of confidential information is known as **insider trading**, and it's illegal. For example, if you are an executive and you learned in a meeting that an accounting scandal about the company is going to hit the newspapers tomorrow, you also know that the price of the company's shares will drop as the wary public sells off their shares. You might decide to quietly sell your shares now, before the price drops. However, authorities at the stock exchange watch for these timing issues and will likely discover that you have committed the crime of insider trading. Stock markets operate on the premise that everyone learns about the same information at the same time and therefore no one gets an unfair advantage. Insider trading occurs when someone makes an investment decision based on confidential information that is not available to the general public.

For example, Martha Stewart of Martha Stewart Living Omnimedia Inc. allegedly received insider information from someone about the company ImClone, and she dumped her stock in ImClone before the price dropped, thus saving a potential loss. However, there is some debate whether Stewart was given confidential information or simply an insider's best guess at what was going to happen. But because she tried to hide the truth about what she had done, and because she wanted to prevent further scandal, Martha Stewart went to jail all the same.

But not all insider trading is illegal. It is perfectly legal for people who work for a company to buy and sell stock in that company, as long as they inform the stock exchange that they are doing it. Insider trading only becomes illegal if someone purchases or sells stock based on information that has not yet been made public, thereby giving themselves an advantage over all other investors. For example, having prior knowledge of an upcoming takeover of a company could give a person an unfair advantage when buying or selling shares of a corporation.

It is not easy to detect insider-trading practices, so regulators use sophisticated computer programs to search for abnormal patterns of the sale of stocks. This unethical and illegal practice, when noticed, is prosecuted by **provincial securities commissions**. Even though the penalties vary from province to province, those guilty of insider trading could face fines of up to $1 million, be forced to turn over their profits, face jail sentences for up to two years, and could be banned from future trading in securities.

Traders working the floor of the New York Stock Exchange

Review Questions

1. What does the term ethics mean?

2. Do most people practise good ethical behaviour? Should they?

3. How can a business convey its ethics and values to its employees, customers, and owners?

4. Use an example to describe what is meant by "ethical dilemma."

5. a) Define whistle-blowing.

   b) Describe a hypothetical job situation in which you might be a whistle-blower.

6. What is an accounting scandal?

7. Is insider trading always illegal? Explain.

Keep in Mind

1. CSR principles
2. duty to report
3. laws that govern corporate ethics (i.e., workplace safety, antidiscrimination issues, accessibility issues, environmental responsibility, labour practices)
4. fair trade

Business Fact

According to a GlobeScan study, 56% of shareholders believe that socially responsible companies are more profitable and 18% say they have bought or sold shares because of the company's social or environmental performance.

Ethics and Corporate Social Responsibility

Businesses exhibit **corporate social responsibility** (CSR) through their values, their ethics, and the contributions that they make to their communities. In other words, CSR has to do with "What you do, how you do it, and when and what you say."

A socially responsible business provides goods and services in line with society's values. Socially responsible businesses are concerned about how they protect customers and treat employees and shareholders. For example, a business may discover that it can make a higher profit by closing a plant in one town and opening a new plant one hundred kilometres away. What should the people who run the business consider as they decide whether or not to open the new plant? What obligations do they have to their employees, to their shareholders, or to the community where their old plant is located? Will the new plant result in harm or benefit to people in the community where it is going to be built?

Training employees to work safely is very important.

CSR Principles

CSR companies believe that it is important for businesses to be socially responsible to their employees, their customers, and their communities. These are the companies that actively support community projects, that provide money for children's sports teams, or that develop innovative programs to keep their employees happy and healthy.

Businesses that practise CSR make every effort to support their beliefs by adhering to the following CSR principles.

Business ethics and corporate social responsibility concepts have been around for some time. So haven't most, if not all, businesses already adopted these guidelines? No. The news is filled with examples of unethical and illegal business practices. The sad truth is that too many businesspeople believe that normal business procedures mean dealing with ethics only when necessary, or not dealing with ethics at all.

Figure 3.2 CSR Principles

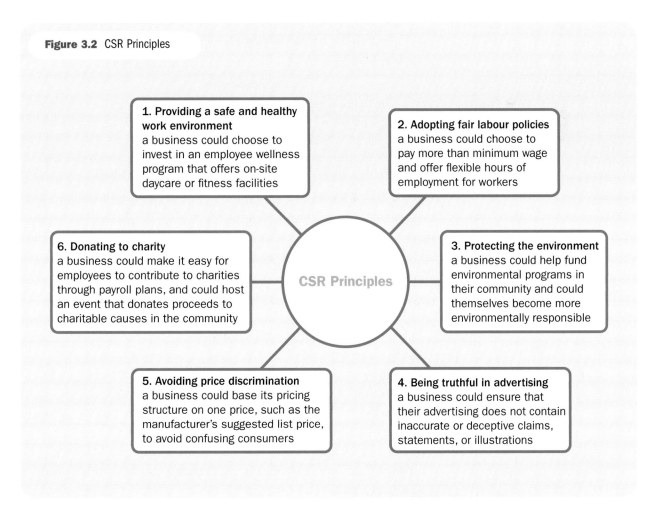

1. **Providing a safe and healthy work environment**
a business could choose to invest in an employee wellness program that offers on-site daycare or fitness facilities

2. **Adopting fair labour policies**
a business could choose to pay more than minimum wage and offer flexible hours of employment for workers

3. **Protecting the environment**
a business could help fund environmental programs in their community and could themselves become more environmentally responsible

4. **Being truthful in advertising**
a business could ensure that their advertising does not contain inaccurate or deceptive claims, statements, or illustrations

5. **Avoiding price discrimination**
a business could base its pricing structure on one price, such as the manufacturer's suggested list price, to avoid confusing consumers

6. **Donating to charity**
a business could make it easy for employees to contribute to charities through payroll plans, and could host an event that donates proceeds to charitable causes in the community

CSR Principles

Keeping our environment clean is healthy for humans, plants and animals.

Ironically, the same people who cheat in their financial dealings or steal office supplies want the corporations that they invest in to be straightforward, honest, and truthful in its dealings with them. But ethics have to apply at all levels of business, from the lowest-paid employee to the president and shareholders.

Why should businesses practise business ethics and engage in corporate social responsibility? Here is a top-10 list of reasons why they may choose to do so.

Table 3.2

Top 10 Reasons for Business Ethics
1. satisfy shareholder expectations
2. protect the reputation of the business
3. build trust with those groups with which they work
4. guard against unethical employees and competitors
5. establish a working environment that matches their core values
6. ensure that the business is an equal opportunity employer
7. maintain a safe working environment for employees
8. engage actively with local communities as a partner
9. maintain high standards of integrity
10. adhere to the practice of full disclosure on the quality of goods and services

An Example of Corporate Social Responsibility

The City of Kitchener, Ontario, is a large employer with about 1200 employees. In other words, the City is a corporation. It has to practise its own corporate social responsibility. The City offers several workplace health and safety programs for its employees, including training and personal development opportunities, an employee assistance program for staff to access free counselling and workshop services, career counselling, and a wellness program. The City also has a diversity committee that looks into fair hiring practices, retention and recruitment strategies, and accessibility and accommodation issues for employees with disabilities.

In addition, the City also promotes environmental responsibility through recommendations from its environmental advisory committee, its use of Smart cars in its fleet, and its power consumption reduction strategies in summer (turning off fountains, dimming lights, and raising the air-conditioning temperatures in City offices).

Duty to Report

Should a business develop and follow their own business ethics, or should they simply follow the laws that apply to the business? As businesses get larger and larger, ethical dilemmas become even more difficult because many groups have to be satisfied. For example, corporations have a **duty to report**, which means they must disclose all important information to shareholders, business partners, lenders, insurers, communities, regulators, consumers, employees, and investors. Employees who have knowledge that a law, regulation, policy, or ethical guideline has been, or may be, violated must promptly report such information. This is not always an easy task.

Laws that Govern Corporate Ethics

In Canada, we have many different laws that govern ethical behaviour in business. Some of these have to do with the actions of individuals. (Earlier in this chapter you read about some of the crimes, such as fraud, that employees and business owners can commit.) However, there are also laws that govern the way a business as a whole can interact with its employees, its customers, and the community in which it operates. These laws relate to six major areas: workplace safety, antidiscrimination issues, harassment, accessibility issues for people with disabilities, environmental responsibility, and labour practices.

Literacy Link

Vocabulary in context
If you want to increase your reading speed and expand your vocabulary, try to determine the meaning of words from the context of the sentence rather than relying on your dictionary.

E-ACTIVITY

Visit www.nelson.com/WOB and follow the links to learn more about laws that govern ethical behaviour in business.

Randy Eresman, president and CEO of EnCana—one of North America's leading gas producers—speaks to shareholders at the company's annual general meeting.

Workplace Safety

The workplace used to be a place where people often died. When the Canadian Pacific railroad was built across Canada in the 1880s, more than 1000 Chinese workers imported to work on the project died on the job. These workers had been assigned all the most dangerous jobs, such as working with explosives. Around the same time, mining jobs weren't much safer because methane gas caused explosions, and mines had no safety features. Workers had no right to a safe workplace. But even well into the 1900s, mine work still wasn't safe. Miners developed diseases from inhaling silica dust, asbestos, or chemicals, and from being exposed to radiation. More recent mine disasters include: Westray Mine, Plymouth, Nova Scotia (1992) and Sago Coal Mine, West Virginia, United States (2006).

Today, many office workers get sick from poor air quality, stress-related injuries, and equipment-related injuries such as carpal tunnel syndrome. Unfortunately, too many companies get caught up in the drive for higher profits and tend to allow workplace safety to become an afterthought.

However, the majority of businesses practise sound business ethics and obey ever-improving workplace safety laws. How can a business respond to some of these workplace problems? One way is to provide a safe and healthy work environment for their employees. For example, a business may initiate an employee wellness program. Such a program might offer employees flexible hours, professional development opportunities, and on-site daycare or fitness facilities.

In Ontario, the *Occupational Health and Safety Act* (OHSA) was instituted to ensure workplace safety and health. This act defines the rights and responsibilities of workers. Workers have three basic rights in the workplace: the right to refuse unsafe work, the right to participate in the workplace health and safety activities, and the right to know about the actual hazards in the workplace. As a result, worker safety is now a priority for almost all employers. (Chapter 6 outlines a variety of employee wellness programs and discusses workplace safety as well.)

Antidiscrimination Issues

Discrimination is incompatible with standards of professional ethics and with ethical behaviour. Some people argue that **gender discrimination** is irrelevant in today's workplace because important changes have removed gender discrimination. Women

A firefighter puts on a protective uniform before attending a call.

Business Fact

According to the Ontario Workplace Safety and Insurance Board, in 2002, the average lost-time injury in Ontario cost $59 000. In 2006, the cost was approximately $98 000.

Ethical, Moral & Legal Considerations

Workers have rights in the workplace, but not all new employees are given enough training when working in dangerous environments. A 16-year-old in British Columbia was given 20 minutes of training on how to operate a forklift truck. This instruction amounted to learning how to use the levers and how to lift heavy pallets high off the ground. One morning, because the forklift was blocking traffic, the young worker pushed the reverse lever while standing beside the forklift, which is something he had seen other workers do. The forklift shifted his way, and while trying to get out of its way, he slipped on hydraulic fluid that was on the floor. After being crushed by the machine, he woke up three days later in the hospital. He had 65 staples in his body, two metal rods and six screws in his back, one missing kidney, paralyzed legs, and little hope of ever walking again.

Was it right to allow this worker to operate a forklift after 20 minutes of training? Who is at fault? What should teenage workers do if they are asked to perform jobs they don't believe are safe?

have successfully lobbied for changes that have improved their status in the business world, and they are now able to compete on an equal basis for management and high-level positions. Employees have the right to work in an environment where their individual values are respected. In general, this means that an employee is not singled out or treated differently because of his or her race, religion, gender, or sexual orientation.

Companies may not even be aware that they are discriminating. For example, many women and minority or disabled workers face a glass ceiling in the workplace. A **glass ceiling** describes the invisible barriers to senior leadership positions.

Companies with glass ceilings don't have official policies of appointing only white, able-bodied males to these positions; yet procedures, expectations, selection and recruitment practices, job assignments, performance evaluations, decisions about salaries, and the working environment all may work together to prevent women, minorities, and disabled people from obtaining promotions.

Some businesses have established educational programs or hired an antidiscrimination officer to help prevent incidents of discrimination. McMaster University is an example of an institution that has hired an antidiscrimination officer. The job of that officer at McMaster is to uphold academic freedom and freedom of expression and association.

Harassment

Many businesses also recognize the legal and moral responsibility to protect all of their workers from harassment and to take action if such behaviour does occur. **Harassment** refers to those behaviours that are found to be threatening or disturbing, and these behaviours are not acceptable in society. Many businesses have policies and procedures for dealing with harassment complaints. Examples include bullying, stalking, and other forms of harassment that deal with sexual, racial, sexual orientation, or disability issues. Racial harassment is hurtful or offensive behaviour based on race, ethnic, or national origin. It includes written or verbal threats or insults based on race, ethnicity, or skin colour; abusive comments about racial origins; ridicule based on cultural grounds; derogatory name calling; racist jokes; damage to property; the display of offensive graffiti; and encouragement of others to commit any of the above.

Accessibility Issues

Many people who have some kind of disability need and want to work, but businesses sometimes have difficulty accommodating

This female manager works hard to overcome gender discrimination in the workplace.

disabled workers because there are so many different kinds of disabilities. As a result, laws help guide businesses by balancing the rights of the disabled individual to work and the rights of businesses to limit how much they need to do for disabled workers. Many businesses have built ramps and purchased alternative equipment to help accommodate disabled workers. Meanwhile, the law enforces the rights of the individual to a fair job interview that does not discriminate based on disability.

Today, businesses have a duty to accommodate people with disabilities to help eliminate discrimination in the workplace. The **duty to accommodate** refers to an employer's obligation to take appropriate steps to eliminate discrimination against employees. This duty to accommodate is written into Sections 2 and 15 of the *Canadian Human Rights Act*. The act stipulates that accommodation is required, short of undue hardship for the business. An employee who has been denied accommodation can file a complaint under the act. Failure to provide accommodation, short of undue hardship for the business, may result in legal action against the business.

Most businesses practise sound business ethics by finding ways to help accommodate workers who are disabled. These accommodations include changing the job tasks that a worker does, allowing guide dogs in a work environment, making the work space more user friendly, providing sign-language support, and training other workers who work with disabled workers.

More and more companies are adapting the work environment so that people with different physical abilities can work comfortably and productively.

Business Fact

It is estimated that there are 610 million disabled people worldwide. Disability affects 20% of the working population.

Environmental Responsibility

Who is responsible for the environment? What role should businesses play in dealing with environmental issues? Does the fact that temperatures seem to be rising over time have anything to do with business?

The good news is that both individuals and businesses are making positive strides to help deal with the environment. The not-so-good news is that it has taken media attention to get environmental issues high on the list of priorities with many businesses. Why have businesses avoided this issue? They would argue that they have a corporate responsibility first to owners, then to customers, then to employees, and then to partners. All these responsibilities are higher on the list of priorities than the responsibility that deals with the environment, that is, to society. However, if businesses keep taking from the environment without putting anything back, the resources will become depleted.

Environmentalists tell us that the clock is ticking and we can no longer assume that someone else will fix the problem.

Typically, environmental concerns are categorized under air, land, and water, as illustrated by the following examples.

The government of Canada has responded to environmental challenges by passing environmental protection laws and by working with international organizations formed to protect Earth's air, land, and water. However, environmental strategies can be controversial since people disagree about what needs to be done and how to do it, and since businesses are sometimes asked to make sacrifices. For example, in order to reduce the amount of pollution a factory puts into the air, it may be required to buy expensive new equipment, radically change its production procedures, or limit the hours during which it operates.

Environmental Protection Act

During the growth period of the 1980s and 1990s, Canada experienced some large-scale environmental disasters, such as the Exxon Valdez oil spill off the west coast of Canada. In response, the government introduced laws and regulations to help prevent future environmental disasters. One of these laws was the *Canadian Environmental Protection Act* 1999, which is administered by Environment Canada.

Figure 3.3 Areas of Environmental Concern in Canada

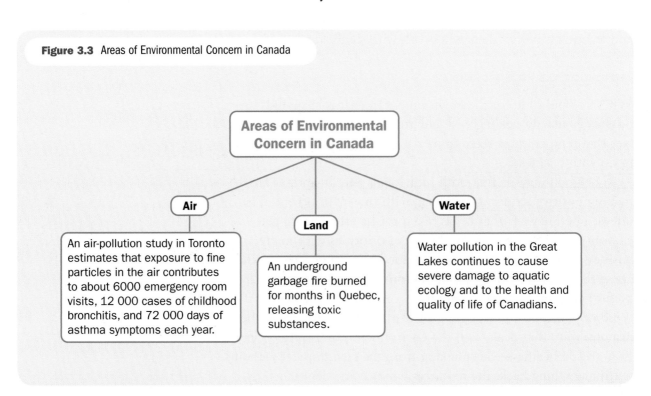

Areas of Environmental Concern in Canada

Air

An air-pollution study in Toronto estimates that exposure to fine particles in the air contributes to about 6000 emergency room visits, 12 000 cases of childhood bronchitis, and 72 000 days of asthma symptoms each year.

Land

An underground garbage fire burned for months in Quebec, releasing toxic substances.

Water

Water pollution in the Great Lakes continues to cause severe damage to aquatic ecology and to the health and quality of life of Canadians.

Figure 3.4 Highlights of the *Canadian Environmental Protection Act* (CEPA)

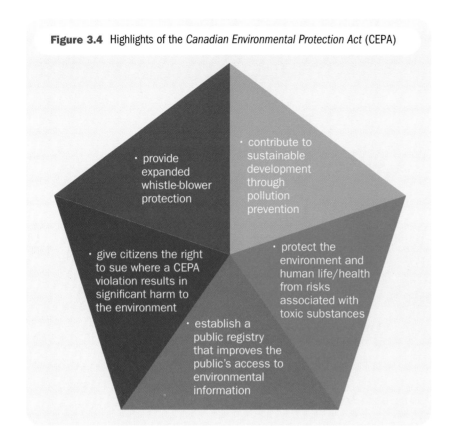

- provide expanded whistle-blower protection
- contribute to sustainable development through pollution prevention
- give citizens the right to sue where a CEPA violation results in significant harm to the environment
- protect the environment and human life/health from risks associated with toxic substances
- establish a public registry that improves the public's access to environmental information

However, even with legislation in place, some businesses ignore the laws. Why? Because it may be more costly for businesses to comply, and this added expense could have an impact on their profitability.

Kyoto Protocol

In 1997, representatives from around the world met in Kyoto, Japan, and reached an agreement on targets to combat global warming. Global warming is the gradual increase of the temperature of the earth's lower atmosphere as a result of increased greenhouse gases in the atmosphere. The agreement is known as the **Kyoto Protocol** (sometimes referred to as the *Kyoto Accord*). Canada signed the agreement in 1998, and the Canadian Parliament ratified the agreement in 2002. The Kyoto Protocol required countries to reduce carbon dioxide emissions so, by 2012, they will be about 5 percent less than they were in 1990. However, Canada's progress has been much slower than anticipated because reducing emissions has proved more difficult and costly for both businesses and individuals than was initially expected.

All wildlife deserve protection from oil spills and other environmental hazards caused by humans.

Business and the Environment

How businesses respond to environmental concerns tells us about their ethics, that is, how they feel about doing what is right. Many businesses have contributed to environmental problems but, at the same time, many have committed resources to pursue solutions. For example, in May of 2005 General Electric announced the beginning of an environmentally friendly initiative. Part of this initiative is dedicated to focus on clean technologies, and the company will commit US$1.5 million per year.

How important are environmental concerns to business? Businesses have been described from time to time as appearing to resemble a three-legged stool. Each leg of the stool stands for a different goal of that business and these "legs," or goals, are financial, environmental, and social.

However, the problem with this image is that the amount of corporate resources spent on environmental and social goals is never equal to what is spent trying to generate profits (financial goals).

This imbalance, in large part, is due to the obligation of managers to please owners and shareholders. The pursuit of profitability can put pressure on businesses to cut costs, for example, by moving production to locations where environmental regulations are less restrictive.

In too many cases, dealing with environmental concerns has only come about because of constant scrutiny of business practices by different levels of government, the media, pressure groups, and consumers. When a company's reputation is at stake, the company is likely to invest more to achieve environmental and social goals, that is, to try to balance the three-legged stool. The good news is that initiatives that benefit the environment can also increase profits. For example, energy efficiencies and waste reduction may reduce costs, while the use of modern, cleaner technologies may increase productivity. And it's also important to remember that responding to environmental and social concerns can attract customers, enhancing a business's competitive advantage in the marketplace.

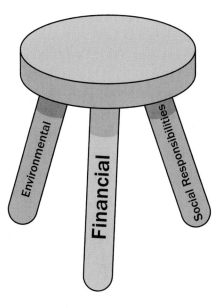

Thousands of people march through the streets on December 3, 2005, in support of a worldwide day of protest against global warming.

Stretch Your Thinking

After the federal election in January 2006, the new Canadian government decided that, rather than spending money on international programs they saw as unrealistic and unachievable, they would focus on developing "made-in-Canada" solutions to the problem of carbon dioxide emissions and place a new emphasis on the development and deployment of clean technology. If you were in charge of the Canadian government, what would you do to reduce Canada's carbon dioxide emissions?

Labour Practices

In Ontario, the *Employment Standards Act* sets out certain mandatory minimum conditions of employment. It governs areas such as hours of work, overtime pay, minimum wage, holidays, vacations, equal pay for male and female employees, employee benefit plans, pregnancy, parental leave and other leaves of absence, notice of termination of employment, and severance and termination pay.

To complicate the issue for a business employer, certain categories of employees may be exempt from some of these employment standards, depending on the jurisdiction. For example, supervisors and managers are often exempted from hours of work and overtime pay provisions. Also, changes in labour law can occur. For example, in 2000, the Ontario Conservative government raised the maximum permitted hours of work to 60 per week, so long as the employee agreed. However, in 2004, the new Ontario Liberal government cut back the maximum number of hours that employees can work.

Pay Equity

Pay equity legislation has been around since 1978, but it has seen a lot of changes over the years, and it still doesn't always deliver in terms of equal pay for work of equal value. The legislation is designed to prohibit an employer from paying employees of one sex differently than employees of the other sex who perform the same or substantially the same work. Substantially the same work is judged by assessing the skill, effort, and responsibility required and the conditions under which the work is performed.

Ethical, Moral & Legal Considerations

In 2004, employees of the City of Kitchener who were performing routine maintenance at a park uncovered discoloured soil and debris beneath the surface. Experts concluded that there was no evidence that anyone had been exposed to the materials in the soil. The City could have kept the cleanup quiet and low-key, simply stating that work was being done on the park without elaborating on the cause. Instead, the City closed the park as a precaution while the soil was being tested. Tests revealed slightly elevated levels of lead and zinc in the soil, and the City proceeded with an environmental clean-up program.

Notices were sent out regularly to residents and the media, providing the results of the soil sampling and the clean-up plan. Public meetings were held, and information phone lines were established. At every stage, the public was informed about what exactly was found in the soil, and what was being done to address it.

Then why, according to the Canadian Human Rights Commission, do women who work full time make an average of only 72 cents for every dollar earned by men? Some would argue that the wage gap has to do with differences in education, experience, and hours of work. However, Canadian economists estimate that 20 to 30 percent of the gap is due to discriminatory attitudes towards women in the workplace.

Privacy Laws

Like pay-equity legislation, privacy laws can affect how businesses work. The *Personal Information Protection and Electronic Documents Act* came into full effect on January 1, 2004. The law requires all provincially regulated businesses to fully explain what personal information they require from employees or customers, and why they need it, before they can obtain it. The law gives individuals the right to demand full disclosure of any personal information a company holds on them, and people can challenge the accuracy or use of their personal information. This means that businesses such as your local video store have to be accountable for any personal information they collect about their customers.

> **The World of Business DVD**
> "Under the Radar"
> from *The World of Business DVD*

Fair Trade

While some types of ethical behaviour in business are required by law in Canada, there are other types that are voluntary. One example is **fair trade**, the practice of helping producers in developing countries bypass expensive middlemen so they can sell their goods in other countries for a fair profit.

For centuries, farmers in less-developed countries have struggled to make a decent living. To add to their problems, unscrupulous corporations and middlemen sometimes pay farmers poorly for their crops and then sell these crops on the international market at much higher prices. Sometimes the farmers starve on the money they earn, but they have no other way to sell their crops internationally. Fair trade began about 50 years ago as a grassroots movement to help farmers get a fair price for their goods. A **grassroots movement** is one that develops from the bottom up, not from the top down. In this case, the fair-trade initiative began with a partnership between farmers and aid organizations that help them reach markets in Europe and North America.

Ethical, Moral & Legal Considerations

Many countries do not respect labour laws and allow child labour to take place. An estimated 246 million children are engaged in child labour around the world—a number that is roughly nine times the population of Canada. Child labour refers to children under the age of 12 working in activities that, for the most part, are very harmful to them. According to UNICEF, 70 percent of child labourers work in agriculture. Many work in mines, or with chemicals and pesticides, or with dangerous machinery in agriculture. Others work as domestic servants or in workshops, more accurately labelled sweatshops, and are paid little or no wages for this work.

Exploiters tend to justify their involvement by claiming that these children are helping out at home, need to work, and get to keep the money that they earn. However, those children should be in a school, not in a field or factory. What companies are you aware of that have been accused of exploiting child labour?

Fair-trade goods, such as fair-trade coffee, tend to cost a little more than the grocery-store brands. However, some consumers insist on buying nothing else, which helps to grow the fair-trade market. Consumers know that when they support fair trade, they are not exploiting poor farmers in distant countries. Fair-trade products are always marked with a fair-trade logo, such as the **TransFair Canada** symbol. TransFair Canada is one **non-profit organization** that assures consumers that the goods are certified and that the purchases are benefiting the producers and workers. The TransFair symbol is a certified trademark, but it applies to the product, not to the company that sells it.

Fair trade is a type of ethical trading in which consumers decide to do what is right. Ethical trading means using trade to help ensure that the basic labour rights of employees in other countries are respected. For example, many religious organizations, trade unions, and clubs have policies of buying only fair-trade coffee and tea for events and meetings. But companies can also participate in ethical trading by enforcing fair-trade practices on their suppliers. Today, close to a million farmers in 44 developing countries work with and benefit from the sale of fair-trade certified products. Some of these certified products include coffee, tea, rice, bananas, cocoa, sugar, honey, and fruit juices.

FAIR TRADE CERTIFIED

CERTIFIÉ ÉQUITABLE

Business Fact

In the United Kingdom, the largest national fair-trade market by volume, sales of products bearing the FAIRTRADE mark are running at around £100 million per year (C$211 million).

Review Questions

8. Which is more important—doing the right thing or being perceived as having done the right thing? Explain.

9. To whom do corporations have a duty to report?

10. Define what the terms glass ceiling and gender discrimination mean.

11. What does a duty to accommodate mean for a business?

12. Why was pay equity legislation necessary in Canada? Has it accomplished its objective?

13. What law was passed by Parliament to help protect against environmental disasters, such as the Exxon Valdez oil spill?

14. Define global warming.

CHAPTER REVIEW

Knowledge

1. If your employer doesn't have a written code of ethics, what key question can you ask yourself when you find yourself in an ethical dilemma at work? Suggest a second question to ask yourself as well.

2. Why is the *Competition Act* important for consumers? for businesses?

3. What is the purpose of the *Occupational Health and Safety Act* (OHSA)? What three rights does it guarantee for workers?

4. What kind of wrongdoing would most likely prompt you to become a whistle-blower? Are there certain kinds of wrongdoing that would not prompt you to become a whistle-blower? Explain.

5. Why is fair trade necessary? Who benefits when fair trade practices are in place?

Thinking

6. A person owns a non-profit agency that helps young people find jobs. A car dealership offers to donate a $20 000 van to the agency. But the dealership wants the agency to state in writing that the donated van is worth $40 000. This lie would allow the dealership to write off a $40 000 donation on its taxes, instead of a $20 000 donation. The agency really needs the van. What should the owner do in this case? Justify the position that you take.

7. Review your school's guidelines for student behaviour. How are these guidelines similar to the code of ethics a business might have? How are they different?

8. Working with a partner, visit the website of one of the organizations listed below. Find and summarize the organization's behaviour guidelines for one of the following groups: communities, employees, customers, suppliers, or owners. Present your findings to the rest of the class. Include in your presentation your view of the guidelines. Do you agree with them? How could they be improved?
   a) The International Chamber of Commerce
   b) Canadian Business for Social Responsibility
   c) Ethicscentre.ca
   d) The Institute for Global Ethics
   e) Businessethics.ca

Communication

9. Search through magazines and newspapers to find a current ethical issue that affects the business world. Discuss the issue with a partner. Write a summary that explains both sides of the issue (the points in favour and the points against).

10. A rich person and a poor person commit the same type of fraud crime. The rich person is fined $75 000 and the poor person is sent to jail for one year. Is this fair? Write a letter to the editor of your local newspaper outlining your opinions on this subject.

11. A public company wants to devote more of its resources to social responsibility. With a partner, role-play opposing views. One of you is the Chief Executive Officer (CEO) of the company. The other represents the shareholders who want to see a large return on their investment. Plan your argument before you begin.

12. "Our employees have worked 514 days without a workplace accident." This is a message that could appear on a company signboard in view of the passing public. Compose a similar signboard message that would inform the public about how the company is involved in one of the other CSR principles.

Application

13. Many people believe that practising ethical behaviour will limit their opportunities and profit. If being unethical means getting ahead, then people are sometimes willing to act unethically. Do you believe that unethical behaviour is ever justified? Divide into two groups, those who support unethical behaviour in some circumstances and those who think that unethical behaviour is always wrong. After sharing information within each group, debate the topic.

14. Research a company in your community that has a socially responsible program. How long has this company's program been in place? What impact has it had on your community?

15. Accounting scandals, insider trading, fraud, and environmental disasters are some of the major ethical issues associated with businesses. Select a Canadian event that relates to one of these ethical issues and research it further. How did this event cause problems for consumers and businesses? Did it create any benefits for consumers and businesses? Has anything been done to prevent similar events from occurring in the future?

16. Contact the Chamber of Commerce in your community. Compare the services offered in your community with those offered by the Chamber of Commerce in your community or region. Identify an ethical dilemma that your Chamber of Commerce has faced and explain what was done to solve that dilemma.

Team Activity

Team Goal: To devise a classroom code of ethics

Team Assignment: Classroom Conduct

- Your team should devise a top-10 list of rules for ethical behaviour for use in the classroom.

- Your team's list should be creative while still being practical.

- The team that is judged to have the best list will win this competition.

- Your teacher will determine the criteria for winning.

Portfolio

What major ethical issues have affected companies in your industry? Collect newspaper articles, Internet reports, or magazine features that comment on them and illustrate how one or two of these companies dealt with the ethical dilemmas they faced.

Report on the corporate social responsibility efforts of two of the companies in your selected industry.

Outline the impact of your industry on your community. Ask the question, "What would happen to my community if the industry I am studying disappeared?"

Reflect on Your Learning

Now that you understand more about ethics and ethical behaviour, why do you think that acting ethically is so difficult for some people and businesses? Can ethics be simplified into one rule?

Gap Inc.

In the late 1960s, when Don Fisher was unable to find a decent pair of jeans that fit, he and his wife, Doris, decided that it was time that shopping became easier.

The couple imagined a store that would cater to the individual by providing a far greater range of styles and sizes than most casual wear retailers (at that time) supplied. So in 1969, Don and Doris tackled the issue head on and founded a business that would eventually become one of the world's largest specialty retailers. The name that they chose for this new store was Gap.

Since the creation of its first San Francisco-based store, Gap Inc. has become responsible for the operation of more than 3000 stores located in cities around the globe, including the United States, Canada, the United Kingdom, France, and Japan, where employees collectively number in the range of 15 000.

The current president and CEO of Gap Inc. is Paul Pressier, who, in 2002, took over the positions from Millard Drexier, who became Donald Fisher's successor in 1995. Although Gap was the first clothing brand to be offered by Gap Inc., three additional brands have since been included in the company's roster: namely, Banana Republic,

Gap Inc. has stores throughout the world.

Old Navy, and Forth & Towne. The financial success of Gap Inc. was almost instant and has continued to grow. In 1970 sales were US$2 million and in 2005, revenue reached US$16 billion.

In addition to being widely recognized as a retailer of popular apparel, Gap Inc. has received much attention for its partnerships with various organizations promoting human rights for workers worldwide and supporting environmental and social causes, including the Social Accountability International's Corporate Involvement Program, the United Nations' Global Compact, and the Ethical Trading Initiative.

In fact, Gap Inc. was ranked by Business Ethics magazine in 2006 as among the "100 Best Corporate Citizens."

However, Gap Inc. has not always received such impeccable publicity in terms of its ethics reviews. In 1995, Mandarin International, a Taiwanese-owned factory located in El Salvador that manufactured Gap clothing, was exposed for labour code violations and poor working conditions. Although Gap Inc. denied having any knowledge of the human rights abuses, the company became the target of intense campaigning in Canada, the United States, and El Salvador, where labour organizations and solidarity groups called for Gap Inc. to improve the working conditions at Mandarin International. As a result, one year after the incident, Gap Inc. partnered with three independent organizations to form the Independent

Monitoring Working Group. It also developed its Code of Vendor Conduct, which is based on internationally accepted labour standards. Such initiatives marked the beginning of Gap Inc.'s solid commitment to creating long-term change in third-party garment factories.

In addition to the social responsibilities that Gap Inc. has taken upon itself, Gap Foundation, the non-profit charitable arm of the business, has been providing assistance to underserved communities around the world since 1977. In fact, between 2000 and 2004 alone, the foundation donated a total of US$60 million in cash grants, with the primary focus on supporting children and youth.

QUESTIONS

1. What was the response of Gap Inc. after the exposure of human rights abuses at Mandarin International in 1995?

2. How is Gap Inc. now involved in promoting safe environments for workers in third-party garment factories?

SPECIFIC EXPECTATIONS

After completing this chapter, you will be able to

- explain the potential benefits and social costs of international business for domestic and foreign partners
- explain the barriers and obstacles to conducting international business for domestic and foreign partners

- identify Canada's major imports and exports
- identify Canada's major trading partners and trade agreements
- describe the business etiquette and culture of other countries

Cirque du Soleil

Always wanted to run away to the circus? In 1984, a group of young street performers in Quebec known as *Le Club des Talons Hauts* (which translates as "The High-Heels Club") started *Cirque du Soleil* ("Circus of the Sun") so they could entertain and see the world. A small dream that turned into an international success: the initial troupe of 74 entertainers has since become an entertainment corporation employing more than 3000 individuals worldwide. Several members of the initial 1984 group are still active in Cirque's productions; the most notable is billionaire Guy Laliberté: a former fire-breather and stilt-walker, now Cirque's founding president and CEO.

Originally, the troupe toured only one show at a time, performing to an average audience size of 270 000 people per year from 1984 to 1989. Much has changed since then. In 2003, Cirque productions ran on three continents, with close to 7 million people attending a show. In fact, in the 22 years that the company has been operating, more than 37 million people have attended a Cirque production in at least one of the almost 100 cities in which Cirque has performed.

The first installment of money that enabled Cirque du Soleil to begin touring in 1984 came from the provincial government of Quebec. The grant was given when Laliberté approached the city of Quebec with a proposal for a show (called Cirque du Soleil) to be performed in honour of Canada's 450th anniversary. However, since 1992, Cirque has not received grants from either the government or the private sector. Clearly, lack of funding has not slowed the company down, since annual revenues for 2005 were estimated to be between US$550 million and US$600 million.

Cirque du Soleil's World Headquarters are located in Montreal, but the company's presence is international, with six shows touring cities across North and South America, Europe, Australia, and New Zealand. In December 1998, the company opened its first Cirque du Soleil store with a permanent theatre located at the Walt Disney World Resort, close to Orlando, Florida. Cirque du Soleil has a second resident show site in Las Vegas, Nevada, and is negotiating to set up another site in New York City's theatre district.

From the beginning, Cirque's productions were far from conventional. The shows have always featured unusual costumes, clever performances, and original music without the use of spoken dialogue, so as to appeal to a diverse audience. Cirque du Soleil does not include the costly and controversial animal acts that have been a tradition in most circuses.

Cirque du Soleil performers get "bent out of shape" during the company's opening performance of *Bellagio* in Las Vegas.

Additionally, Cirque shifted the focus of its shows away from children to adult audiences, which allowed for higher ticket prices.

Innovation and diversity are the hallmarks of a Cirque production. Consider, for example, *Ka*—their recent US$165 million martial-arts-themed production being performed at the MGM Grand in Las Vegas. The troupe for *Ka* consists of more than 700 artists, from 40 different countries, speaking 25 languages. Cirque has even had to hire translators for this production.

Although Cirque has so far focused its attention primarily on North American and European audiences, Cirque and Disney are collaborating on a permanent show to be launched in Tokyo, Japan, in 2008.

QUESTIONS

1. Why is Cirque du Soleil considered an international entertainment corporation and how does it try to appeal to an international audience?

2. There are five reasons for doing business internationally: product, price, proximity, preference, and promotion. How would each of these reasons apply to Cirque du Soleil?

What Is International Business?

Have you checked the labels on your clothes recently? How many of your clothing items were made in Canada? Probably not very many. In fact, probably none! That is because the manufacturing of clothing is no longer a very big industry in Canada. The Canadian clothing industry is composed almost entirely of distributors and retailers, rather than manufacturers. However, millions of business transactions that relate to the manufacturing of goods do take place in Canada every day.

A **domestic transaction** is the selling of items produced in the same country. For example, if you visit a local store and buy a bicycle that has been manufactured in Canada, you engage in a domestic transaction. An **international transaction** is the selling of items produced in other countries. For example, your local sportswear store may sell sports shoes made in Mexico. Even if you buy the shoes at a local store, the transaction is considered international because the goods were produced in one country and sold in another.

International transactions involve creating, shipping, and selling goods and services across national borders. Because these transactions usually involve exchanges of one type or another, they are often referred to as international trade or **foreign trade**. By participating in an international transaction, you are contributing to the **global economy**.

Keep in Mind

1. access to markets
2. cheaper labour
3. increased quality of goods
4. increased quantity
5. access to resources

Before You Begin

Name businesses in your community that are owned by companies outside Canada. Find out when and where one of these companies first began operating in Canada.

BMW is a German car manufacturer. This BMW X5 is assembled in South Carolina, United States.

> "Business is not financial science; it's about trading, buying, and selling. It's about creating a product or service so good that people will pay for it."
> **Anita Roddick**, owner of The Body Shop

Canadian businesses participate in the global economy because they trade in millions of dollars worth of manufactured items from all over the world.

Benefits for Business

International trade offers many benefits for businesses, including access to markets, cheaper labour, increased quality and/or quantity of goods, and access to resources that may not be available at home.

Access to Markets

Most countries rely on international trade for their economic survival. Trading abroad makes sense for Canadian businesses. Why? With a world population of over six and one-half billion people, the international market for Canadian products and services is roughly 200 times as large as the domestic market!

However, larger markets don't always translate into greater sales. Sometimes, Canadian companies have difficulty adapting their products to suit a foreign market. Consumers in other parts of the world have different wants and needs. A company must understand these wants and needs before it tries to sell its goods and services internationally. A **global product** is a standardized item that is offered in the same form in all the countries in which it is sold. Some examples of global products are pencils, soccer balls, and cameras.

Packaged food items are not global products. They are usually difficult to market as global products because people in different parts of the world have different tastes. For example, some people in Great Britain, Ireland, Scotland, and Atlantic Canada may enjoy blood sausage (sometimes called blood pudding). But this is not a meal that would go over well in many other countries. It would not be on everyone's menu!

A plate filled with pieces of blood pudding

Cheaper Labour

Why do Canadians buy items made in other countries? If you guessed that the prices are cheaper because of cheaper labour costs, you identified the number one reason. Canadian businesses attempt to reduce their costs of production and in the process maximize their profits. However, in doing so, other costs, which may affect the Canadian business, can surface when dealing in an international market. See page 119 for more information about the potential costs of relying on foreign labour to reduce prices.

Increased Quality of Goods

Doing business internationally can help producers improve the quality of the products they sell. For example, let's examine a luxury car to demonstrate how one car manufacturer improves quality by taking advantage of what other countries have to offer. The BMW X5 is an illustration of how goods manufactured in different countries can come together to form a final product. The X5's engine is assembled in Munich, Germany, and then it's shipped across the ocean in finished form to the production plant in South Carolina, United States. Magna Corporation, in Ontario, Canada, manufactures the rear-view mirror. The leather on the seats comes from South Africa. And the Michelin tires? They are manufactured in France. Automotive engineers at BMW search the world for parts that will help them create the best possible products for their customers. The BMW X5 was so popular when it was introduced that it resulted in another version, which was designed to expand the market for BMW, called the X3.

Increased Quantity

As access to international markets increases, so does the potential for increased sales (as long as the product has international appeal). As a result, companies may need to step up production to meet increased demand. Sometimes, the need for more products can be met by increased efficiency or longer hours of operation at existing production facilities. At other times, a company may decide to set up a new facility, perhaps in another country where goods are to be sold.

The majority of new businesses fail within the first year of operation. However, some businesses not only survive locally but thrive nationally and even internationally. Roots Canada Ltd. is an example of one Canadian business that started in 1973 as a footwear manufacturer and has become a leader in producing custom merchandise worldwide. How did they do it? Finding a way to appeal to people all over the world was the challenge, and Roots found their springboard with the Olympic movement in 1976 when they were invited to make footwear for the Canadian Olympic team. Since then Roots has been outfitting Olympic teams all over the world: the Olympic games in Calgary, in 1998, and in Salt Lake City, in 2002, when Roots apparel was worn by the U.S. President as he addressed 4 billion viewers during the opening ceremonies. Roots has also outfitted teams from Great Britain and Barbados and will be on hand for the 2010 games that will be hosted in Vancouver, British Columbia. Would you consider Roots apparel a global product?

Access to Resources

In Chapter 1, you read about three types of economic resources: natural resources, human resources, and capital resources. International connections can give a business access to all three types of resources. For example, a Canadian company that makes bamboo furniture likely imports some or all of its bamboo—a natural resource—from another country, since bamboo is scarce in Canada. A company that builds a new factory in China may do so, in part, to take advantage of China's cheaper labour cost (human resources). A company that buys specialized machinery (a capital resource) made in Japan for use in a new plant they're building in Ontario is also taking advantage of international resources.

The Five Ps of International Business

International business not only offers advantages to business, it also benefits consumers. Wouldn't it be nice to take advantage of what Paris, France, has to offer? Or how about seeing what Turtle Island in Fiji can sell us? Countries like France and Fiji offer goods and services that Canadians might want or need. If a country can produce all the goods and services that its domestic consumers need and want at prices consumers are willing to pay, why would they need to buy from other countries?

Let's look at fruits and vegetables, for example. Canada could probably produce enough fruit and vegetables for its domestic market on a year-round basis. But growing produce indoors is far more expensive than buying it from countries that have longer or different growing seasons. In addition, beaches in the winter months in Canada are significantly less appealing than those in Fiji. When each country is able to focus its efforts on what it can do best, everyone benefits. Consumers have access to a broader variety of goods and services, offered at a wider range of prices, and businesses can sell their goods and services to many more markets.

International business provides increased markets for businesses and a broader choice of products, services, and prices for consumers. As companies expand to serve new markets, they create jobs both at home and overseas. When Canadian and international businesses exchange goods and services, they also exchange knowledge. This exchange of knowledge results in new approaches to production, marketing, and selling that benefit Canadian consumers as well as producers. It may also bring political benefits. According to an old saying, "Countries that trade with one another seldom go to war with each other." Often, international business activities open a dialogue between nations that improves mutual understanding, builds lines of communication, and increases the level of respect people have for one another.

There are five major reasons for doing business internationally: product, price, proximity, preference, and promotion. These reasons are sometimes called the five Ps of international business, and they represent the benefits of getting involved with businesses outside of Canada.

Product

A country's resources determine what goods and services it can produce. Because Canada's climate isn't suited to growing citrus crops, Canadian grocery stores buy oranges and grapefruit from countries with warmer climates, such as the United States, Mexico, and Israel. Canada has an abundance of corn and strawberries in the summer months, but not in the winter. On the other hand, Canada has large forests and wheat fields that can provide lumber and grain for countries that don't have an abundance of these resources, such as England and Japan.

Price

The cost of producing a particular good or service varies from one country to another. If the cost of wages, taxes, and raw materials is lower in another country, it may be less expensive to produce some goods overseas and ship them to Canada than it would be to produce them domestically.

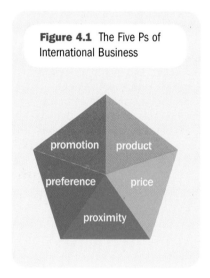

Figure 4.1 The Five Ps of International Business

If a business can produce items with lower costs, then it may be able to charge consumers a lower price and increase sales and profits by selling a greater number of units.

Proximity

In Canada, 80 percent of the population lives within 170 km of the American border. In fact, many small Canadian communities are closer to large American cities than they are to large Canadian cities. For example, the city of Windsor, Ontario, and nearby Essex County have a population of about 350 000 people. They are located just across a bridge from Detroit, Michigan, a city of several million people. As a result, Detroit has a great influence on businesses located in and near Windsor who supply Detroit's car manufacturing plants with parts and labour.

Preference

Some countries specialize in certain types of goods or services that have a reputation for quality all over the world. Even though similar goods can be made domestically, many people still prefer to buy foreign specialties, such as Belgian chocolates, Swiss watches, Australian wine, German cars, and Canadian wheat.

Promotion

Before the invention of global communications technology, such as satellite broadcasting and the Internet, businesses found it difficult to let people far away know about the goods and services they sold. Today, technology makes it simple for businesses to promote their products anywhere in the world. According to Interbrand Corporation's website, a business in today's market could develop a global brand name in three years by using the

Frank and Ernest

©1997 Thaves. Reprinted with permission. Newspaper dist. by NEA, Inc.

Internet. Before the Internet, it would have taken decades to accomplish the same objective. Some companies spend millions of dollars to translate their television or radio advertisements into many different languages and broadcast them around the globe. Others spend comparatively small amounts of money to set up websites that can be accessed from anywhere. Either way, ease of promotion is an incentive for companies to reach beyond their domestic market for customers.

Costs of International Trade

Doing business internationally can provide a wide range of benefits for both businesses and consumers, but it's important to realize that these benefits don't always come without costs. These costs, sometimes referred to as hidden costs or social costs, are very real to the countries involved in domestic or international trade. **Social costs** include offshore outsourcing, human rights or labour abuses, and environmental degradation.

Offshore Outsourcing

Offshore outsourcing is the practice of hiring service providers from countries where labour costs are lower to complete some or all of the steps in the production process. This process, also known as contracting out, is often defined as the assigning of jobs from *internal* production *within* a business to an *external* business that specializes in that operation.

Women in a garment factory in India check the stitching on the finished products.

In the News

In an attempt to find employees with strong communication skills, McDonald's has experimented with outsourcing their drive-thru functions. Customers may have assumed that they were talking to someone "inside" the restaurant but that someone could be at a call centre hundreds of kilometres away. The test market for this approach was the Pacific Northwest of the United States, and the remote call centres were staffed by professional order-takers. According to McDonald's executives, this outsourcing could increase order accuracy and speed up the drive-thru service. In fact, one McDonalds' restaurant owner claims that this new service saves up to 20 seconds per order. However, this trial experiment has not been adopted at all McDonald's and has generated some criticism.

Outsourcing is a business decision that is made to lower costs or to allow the business to focus on those tasks that it does better. Other potential advantages of outsourcing include being able to move production facilities closer to natural resources, take advantage of more efficient technologies, or profit from another country's innovations or tax structures. Many high-tech jobs and customer support services for businesses have been outsourced to emerging or new markets such as India, China, and Costa Rica. However, before a business decides to outsource some or all of its production, it usually considers other costs that are associated with that type of move, such as salaries, benefits, training, and recruiting. Service work can also be outsourced. Using the Internet, many North American companies outsource services such as bookkeeping and updating records to countries on the other side of the world. Because of the time difference, companies in those countries work through the North American night and return the completed work by morning.

In the future, the face of offshore outsourcing may change. Many companies will not outsource to a particular country at all. Instead, they will turn to large **transnational** corporations—companies that operate in several countries. These transnationals will have access to many resources and expertise and an ability to spread risk. Outsourcing will follow the lead of the retail big-box stores that create one-stop shopping venues for consumers. As these transnational one-stop "shops" grow in size, they will gain a significant competitive advantage over even the strongest individual outsourcing markets.

Human Rights Issues and Labour Abuses

Human rights issues and labour abuses are two ethical problems that result from offshore outsourcing. Workers in many poor

Stretch Your Thinking

According to a study done by PricewaterhouseCoopers, Canada employs approximately 150 000 workers devoted to outsourcing projects originating in the United States, with as many as 75 000 of these Canadian workers being call-centre employees. According to another PricewaterhouseCoopers study, more than 75 000 Canadian information technology jobs could be lost to offshore outsourcing by 2010. What are the implications of this outsourcing trade-off? Explain.

countries face a wide range of abuses in the workplace. These abuses could include labour exploitation, including physical and sexual abuse, forced confinement, non-payment of wages, denial of food and health care, and excessive working hours with no rest days. The Canadian business that is doing the outsourcing may not even be aware of this abuse and may have little or no control over the situation.

Child labour is another problem with outsourcing. Child labour is defined as regular employment for boys and girls under the age of 16. For example, in Indonesia alone, the International Labour Organization (ILO) estimates that there are nearly 700 000 child domestic workers, many working for foreign companies. The **International Labour Organization** is the UN specialized agency that seeks the promotion of social justice and internationally recognized human and labour rights. According to ILO, more girls under the age of 16 work in domestic service (doing housework and caring for children) than in any other category of child labour. Many countries have been known to ignore abuses that target children and women.

Consumer action groups seek to improve conditions for workers in other countries by exposing abusive situations to the media and by encouraging companies to become more aware of labour practices in their foreign operations. The companies can then take steps to ensure that Canadian workplace expectations are met in their facilities.

Business Fact

According to the Employment Standards Code of Alberta, children aged 15 are allowed to work outside of normal school hours. Children aged 12 to 14 can work for two hours per day outside of normal school hours, and eight hours on the weekend.

Ethical, Moral & Legal Considerations

Is it fair to use children as young as four to work for a living? If a 13-year-old child is paid 10 cents an hour, would you consider that earning a living? Children are used in parts of the world to work long hours, often in dangerous and unhealthy conditions. Many are exposed to chemicals and are not provided with gloves or masks to safeguard their bodies. Working at rug looms has left some children with eye damage and lung disease, and they may end up with arthritic conditions as they get older. Children making silk thread in India dip their hands into boiling water that burns and blisters them. They also can be exposed to smoke and fumes from machinery, handle dead worms that cause infections, and guide twisting threads that cut their fingers. Children have also been used to harvest sugar cane: they use machetes to cut cane for up to nine hours a day in blistering sun, and if injured on the job, no medical care is available to them. There are as many abuses as there are jobs. Human Rights Watch and Amnesty International are just two groups that try to make a difference in protecting children throughout the world.

Environmental Degradation

Sustainable development is a process of developing land, cities, businesses, and communities that meets the needs of the present without compromising the ability of future generations to meet their own needs. But businesses can sometimes play both sides of the sustainability development issue. On the one hand, they can have sound sustainable development policies. But on the other hand, they can push to meet their business goals, while ignoring the damage this growth causes. Some of these controversial issues were dealt with in Chapter 3 on business ethics and corporate social responsibility.

What would happen if businesses failed to pay attention to sustainable development when doing business in Canada and beyond? An example of a negative environmental impact is something known as environmental degradation. **Environmental degradation** occurs when nature's resources such as trees, habitat, earth, water, and air are being consumed faster than nature can replenish them. Businesses need to be aware of how their procedures and policies impact the environment and consider investing research and development funds to help find solutions.

Beneath the smog of a summer's day in Toronto, a kayaker paddles in Lake Ontario.

If a business is not part of the solution, it could be part of the problem. Research in car design, for example, could include holistic product design, technology for reduced fuel use, and new standards for the use of environmentally friendly materials, for product recycling, and for new materials and processes, such as those that increase the efficiency of engines. Each of these changes could impact in a positive way on the environment.

Barriers to International Business

The Canadian government uses barriers, sometimes referred to as roadblocks, to help protect domestic businesses and consumers. These barriers can be used to help assist a new business in getting started as well as to protect an existing industry struggling in a competitive global environment. Or they can protect consumers from problematic imports, such as automobiles that may not conform to Canadian safety standards. Some of these barriers and obstacles include tariffs or custom duties, tariff barriers and non-tariff barriers, increased costs, and excise taxes.

Some countries prohibit the entry of certain goods. For example, Canada prohibits the import of illegal narcotics, certain weapons, and products made from endangered animals. Print materials that have been ruled obscene or that promote hatred or treason may also be stopped at the border. The government allows some goods to enter the country only if they have been inspected, are accompanied by a valid permit, or have special packaging and labelling. For example, the Canadian Food Inspection Agency tests for antibiotic, drug, and hormone residues in meat, allergens and pesticide residues in food, and other threats to the safety of the food we eat. Also, product labelling must comply with Canada's official language policy.

Tariffs

If you were to go to the store to buy a jar of salsa, which one would you purchase? Would it be the cheapest one? Or would you buy the salsa that was made in Canada? Since the ingredients are basically the same, why don't they all cost the same amount? The price differential could have something to do with tariffs. **Tariffs**, also called **customs duties**, are a form of tax on certain types of imports. Tariffs are levied on a percentage-of-value basis (e.g., 6.1 percent of retail value) or on a specific basis (e.g., $6 per 100 kilograms).

> ### Keep in Mind
>
> 1. tariffs
> 2. non-tariff barriers
> 3. costs of importing and exporting
> 4. excise taxes
> 5. currency fluctuations

> ### The World of Business DVD
>
> **"Ben and Jerry's: A Frozen Empire"**
> from *The World of Business DVD*

According to Customs-Tariff Schedule 2006, the following are examples of tariff rates that apply to imported goods: men's or boys' overcoats made of wool (18%); prepared painting canvas (7%); and seats used in a motor vehicle (6%).

Tariffs represent one of the most important tools for any government in managing trade with other nations. This form of a tax could give a price advantage to Canadian businesses, which could allow them to compete with foreign competitors. Finished imported goods would cost more with the tariff added, and as a result, Canadian businesses might be able to sell those same goods for a lower price.

It is the duty of Finance Canada to monitor Canadian tariff policies and those of other nations and to develop new policies that will best serve the Canadian economy. One example of a change in Canada's tariff policy occurred effective January 1, 2005. At that time, the Government of Canada eliminated tariffs on fibre and yarn imports and on imports of textile inputs used by the apparel industry. That made it less expensive for Canadian textile and apparel companies to acquire goods that they use in the production of finished products, thus keeping their costs down. It has been estimated that this change in the tariff policy has saved the Canadian textile and apparel industry more than $90 million since the tariff was eliminated.

Table 4.1

Imported Goods That Require Permits, Inspection, or Special Packaging	
Imported Goods	Government Department
endangered animals and plants and products made from them	Environment Canada
agricultural and food products	Agriculture and Agri-food Canada
fish and fish products	Fisheries and Oceans Canada
non-food products and clothing, precious metals, and radio communications equipment	Industry Canada
food, drugs and medicines, pharmaceuticals, medical and radiation-emitting devices	Health Canada
hazardous waste, goods that may contain chlorofluorocarbons or leaded gas	Environment Canada
motor vehicles	Transport Canada

Each country sets its own rules for dealing with imports. These rules are generally in place to protect domestic industry. **Tariff barriers** are often the subject of international negotiations, and these trade barriers are gradually being reduced as countries create trade agreements.

Non-tariff Barriers

Tariffs are not the only barriers countries can use to protect domestic industry. **Non-tariff barriers** are standards for the quality of imported goods that are set so high that foreign competitors cannot enter the market. For example, if Canada set very high standards for safety and emission controls on imported automobiles, few existing imported vehicles would meet the standards. Foreign competitors would either have to withdraw from the Canadian market or spend a lot of money to engineer better vehicles. A country can also impose non-tariff barriers by requiring an international business to apply for a licence to sell goods in its market. If the licence is expensive, foreign businesses will be discouraged from exporting goods. Non-tariff barriers can also be imposed at the border, where goods have to pass a customs inspection in order to enter the country. For example, the European ban on hormone-treated beef products is a form of non-tariff barrier.

Transport trucks enter the United States from Canada after inspection by a customs official.

Costs of Importing and Exporting

Price is based on the cost of manufacturing, plus the costs of storage, marketing, shipping, advertising, overhead, and the profit margins of each business involved. Assume that a business in Nova Scotia wants to sell its goods to Japan. The shipping costs to Japan are much higher than shipping costs to Vancouver. Airfreight would cost much more than a cargo ship, but it would also get the goods to market faster. Would the cost of a translator have to be included in the price? How about interest costs if money had to be borrowed to finance the shipment? Are there any additional labelling costs? And, if the good has to be sold at a discount at a later date, who absorbs that cost? These are the extra costs associated with importing and exporting, all of which raise the cost of the traded item.

Shipping cost is one of the largest components of the landed cost. The **landed cost** is the actual cost for an imported purchased item, composed of the vendor cost, transportation charges, duties, taxes, broker fees, and any other charges. The total landed cost determines whether a foreign purchase is a better deal than a domestic purchase.

Excise Taxes

An **excise tax** is a tax on the manufacture, sale, or consumption of a particular product within a country. For example, the Canadian government charges an excise tax of 10 cents per litre on gasoline, raising about $4 billion per year, while provincial governments charge an average of 14.5 cents per litre. Not long ago, there was a 10 percent excise tax on jewellery, including diamonds and other precious stones. Excise taxes depend on the quantity or mass of an item. For example, Canada charges an excise tax on the mass of a passenger automobile that exceeds 2007 kg.

The government mainly uses excise taxes to raise money. However, it may apply an excise tax to some products (e.g., tobacco) to discourage people from engaging in a certain activity (e.g., smoking). With other products, such as imported wine and petroleum products, the government imposes excise taxes to increase the cost of these imported goods to encourage consumers to buy Canadian products.

Currency Fluctuations

If you were to purchase US$100 at a financial institution, how much would you have to pay in Canadian dollars? If you made that purchase today rather than one month from today, would you pay the same amount? Because currencies fluctuate on a daily basis, it is highly unlikely that these two purchases would result in the same cost for you. Why? One of several factors that influence the shifting currency exchange rates between countries has to do with the strength of the economies of the two countries in relation to one another. For example, in the year 2002 the currency exchange rate between the Canadian and American dollar significantly favoured the American consumer or businessperson. During that year, the American economy was strong in comparison to the Canadian economy, and purchasing US$100 would have cost C$157. However, the economies of countries do not remain stable, therefore in January 2007, the purchase of US$100 would have cost C$115. Now imagine the daily impact of completing hundreds, or even thousands, of transactions for a Canadian business with businesses south of the border. How much could that cost? Currency exchange rates have a very real impact on doing business internationally.

Review Questions

1. What is a domestic transaction? An international transaction?

2. Define global product and trade deficit.

3. List five reasons for doing business internationally.

4. What is the current exchange rate between Canada and the United States? How much would it cost a Canadian business to purchase US$100 today?

5. It's an old saying that "Countries that trade with one another seldom go to war with each other." Give a counter-example in which two countries went to war in spite of their trade relationship.

6. What does offshore outsourcing or contracting out mean?

7. What is the purpose of the International Labour Organization?

8. Define sustainable development.

9. What causes environmental degradation?

10. What is the difference between a tariff and a non-tariff barrier?

11. Why is it very important to accurately calculate the landed cost of imported goods?

12. Identify two reasons why governments use excise taxes.

Keep in Mind

1. balance of trade
2. imports
3. exports
4. Canada's major trading partners

Flow of Goods and Services

Goods and services flow into Canada as imports, and they flow out as exports. The imports coming into Canada include raw materials, processed materials, semi-finished goods, or manufactured products that are ready for sale. The less finished the imports are, the more jobs they create for Canadians. For example, an auto manufacturer might import windshields, tires, transmissions, and other parts for assembly at a Canadian plant. This situation provides jobs for workers at the assembly plant, but it doesn't provide as many jobs as there would be if the vehicles were assembled from scratch here in Canada. Even if the vehicles were manufactured overseas and imported in a finished state, there might still be jobs for Canadians in design, engineering, administrative, marketing, or sales positions.

The types of goods that are imported and exported by Canadians fit into several categories. Statistics for Canadian imports and exports in 2005 are shown in Figure 4.2.

Balance of Trade

Countries try to maintain a balance of trade between the value of the products they import and the value of the products they export. A **balance of trade** is the relationship between a country's total imports and total exports. If the country pays more for imports than it earns from exports, there is a **trade deficit**. If the country earns more from exports than it pays for imports, there is a **trade surplus**.

Governments usually try to reduce a high trade deficit because it means that money is flowing out of the country and fewer jobs are being provided. On the other hand, trade surpluses are beneficial to a country's economy, especially if the surplus is made up primarily of manufactured goods. Exporting manufactured goods means that many workers are required in the production process. In 2005, Canada had an overall trade surplus of just under $65 billion. This surplus was the direct result of an $85 billion trade surplus with the United States that helped balance the $20 billion trade deficit that resulted from all other international trading.

Stretch Your Thinking

Why are similar goods, like machinery and automobiles, both imported to and exported from Canada? One reason could be to take advantage of lower manufacturing costs in another country. For example, car parts could be imported, assembled, and the final product could then be shipped back to the same country. What other reasons could there be for this type of trade?

Imports

A business that wants to start importing goods for sale in Canada should consider the five main ways of offsetting the risks of importing in Figure 4.3.

Exports

The idea to export a good or service can come either from the company that produces it or from buyers in a foreign market who wish to purchase it. **Direct exporting** means the exporter deals directly with the importer and does not use an intermediary. **Indirect exporting** means the goods move from the exporter to an intermediary and then on to the importer.

Established companies usually export directly. These businesses often have the resources to set up offices and sales staff in a foreign country or to send a sales representative to the international market. Many new companies use indirect exporting because they don't have the resources to establish themselves abroad. They hire an intermediary who may be more familiar with regulations and restrictions than they are. The intermediary will handle all the paperwork and may help collect money. Direct exporting can be risky; with indirect exporting, the intermediary assumes some of the risk. In certain cases, even large, established businesses use indirect exporting since some countries, including those in the Middle East, Central America, and Asia, prohibit direct exporting—probably to create jobs for local intermediaries.

⊕ E-ACTIVITY

Visit www.nelson.com/WOB and follow the links to learn more about Canada's imports and exports.

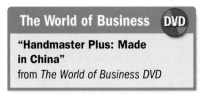

The World of Business DVD

"Handmaster Plus: Made in China"
from *The World of Business DVD*

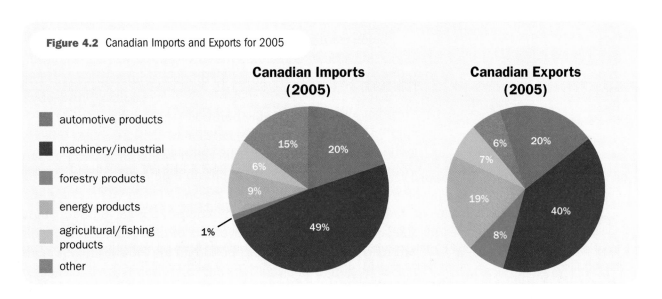

Figure 4.2 Canadian Imports and Exports for 2005

Canadian Imports (2005)

- automotive products
- machinery/industrial
- forestry products
- energy products
- agricultural/fishing products
- other

20%, 15%, 6%, 9%, 1%, 49%

Canadian Exports (2005)

20%, 6%, 7%, 19%, 8%, 40%

Figure 4.3 Five Ways to Offset the Risks of Importing

Five Ways to Offset the Risks of Importing

1. Before you fill your warehouse with imported goods, take the time to measure consumer interest in what you plan to sell. If no one wants to buy your goods, you will find yourself with large bills to pay and no way to pay them.

2. Choose foreign suppliers with care. You not only need a supplier who can provide the right goods; you also need one who can supply them at the right price and at the right time. Government agencies such as Foreign Affairs and International Trade Canada can help you find the best possible foreign suppliers for your business.

3. Make an effort to learn about the culture you will be dealing with. Cultural sensitivity can help you establish a positive relationship with your suppliers, while cultural clashes can quickly break a deal. (Read further in the chapter for more suggestions about dealing with other cultures.)

4. Give careful thought to the purchase agreement before you sign it and make sure to word the agreement so it covers every eventuality. Ask questions:
· Who pays the shipping costs?
· When do the goods have to be paid for?
· What happens if the goods are damaged during shipping?

5. When the goods arrive, make sure everything you ordered is there and in good condition. You will likely need to pay import or customs duties that are based either on the value of the goods or on other factors, such as quantity or weight.

Offsetting Risks

Exporters can offset risks through careful planning. If you plan to export a product to a foreign market, start by conducting market research to make sure there are consumers in the market who will buy your goods. Ask Foreign Affairs and International Trade Canada to help you locate potential customers. You may also find it helpful to use the Internet to contact agencies such as the Asia Pacific Foundation of Canada, Canadian Manufacturers and Exporters, and the Canadian Association of Importers and Exporters.

Canadian embassies are also good sources of advice and can help you get to know your potential customers. According

Currencies from different countries

to embassy staff, foreign clients often ask the following kinds of questions to find out about potential exporters of goods or services:

- What is unique or special about your company, product, or service? How do you market and sell your products?

- Who uses your product or service? To whom do you sell in Canada and abroad?

- Which countries or regional markets are you targeting, and why? What do you know about these markets?

- How do you plan to enter the market? Will you sell the products directly? license people to sell your products? set up a joint venture with another business? invest in a venture that already serves the market?

- How would you describe the typical buyer, distributor, agent, or partner you want to work with in this market?

- When do you plan to visit the market? How will you adapt your product-related literature to suit the needs of this market?

Canada's Major Trading Partners

In some ways, international trade is like collecting trading cards. You can use whatever you have in abundance to trade for whatever you need. The only difference is that countries don't usually trade goods directly. Instead, they buy and sell goods for money.

Canada has trade partners all over the world, and Canadian companies continue to seek out new partners all the time. However, without a doubt, Canada's number one trade partner is the United States (See Table 4.2). There are a number of reasons why it makes sense for Canadians to develop a solid trade relationship with their nearest neighbour. First, shipping costs are cheaper for nearby destinations. Second, Canadians and Americans share many of the same interests, so the same products and services will likely appeal to both groups. Canadians and Americans speak the same language, watch the same television programs, line up to see the same movies, and enjoy the same sports. Even though heightened security has changed many things, people from both countries still regularly travel back and forth across the border for business trips and vacations. Third, the United States population is approximately 10 times greater than Canada's. As a result, Canadian businesses can sell their products and services to a much larger market. A Canadian product that is successful in both Canada and the United States will likely be far more profitable for its manufacturer than one sold only in Canada.

In the News

How big is a billion? Imagine that you won $1 billion in a lottery. How long would it take you to count your winnings, loonie by loonie? Assume that you can count one loonie per second. You could count 60 loonies in one minute and 3600 loonies in one hour (60 × 60). Each day you could count 86 400 loonies (3600 × 24). Since there are 365 days in a year, you could count 31 536 000 in one year. Keep in mind: this is continuous counting and leaves no time to eat, sleep, shower, use your cell phone, or go to school.

So how many years does it take to count 1 000 000 000 loonies?

31 × 31 356 000 = 977 616 000 and 32 × 31 536 000 = 1 009 152 000. So the answer is between 31 and 32 years. And that leaves no time to spend your fortune!

Table 4.2

Canada's Top 10 Export Markets by Country, 2005	
Country	**% Share of Total Exports**
United States	84
Japan	2.1
United Kingdom	1.9
China	1.6
Germany	0.7
Mexico	0.7
France	0.6
South Korea	0.6
Belgium	0.5
Netherlands	0.5
Total of Top 10	93.2

Canada's Top 10 Import Markets by Country, 2005	
Country	**% Share of Total Imports**
United States	57
China	7.8
Japan	3.8
Mexico	3.8
Germany	2.7
United Kingdom	2.7
Norway	1.6
South Korea	1.4
France	1.3
Italy	1.2
Total of Top 10	83.8

Review Questions

13. Explain how imports and exports create jobs.

14. What is the difference between a trade deficit and a trade surplus?

15. How do exporters attempt to offset risks when dealing with foreign suppliers?

16. Canada imports crude oil but exports crude petroleum. Explain why this makes sense.

17. Canada's total exports for 2005 amounted to C$453 060 100 000 ($453 billion). Using percent share data from Table 4.2, calculate the total exports in dollars for the top four countries.

18. Canada's total imports for 2005 amounted to C$388 210 300 000 ($388 billion). Using percent share data from Table 4.2, calculate the total imports in dollars for the top four countries.

Canada and International Trade Agreements

You've already learned that countries often set up trade barriers, such as customs duties, tariffs, and embargoes, to protect domestic businesses. However, since World War II, many countries have taken part in negotiations to reduce or eliminate these barriers.

There are two main advantages to reducing trade barriers. The first is that domestic businesses are able to sell their products and services abroad at lower prices since customs duties are not added to the cost of domestic businesses' exports. If revenues from foreign sales are greater than the costs of shipping and marketing the product abroad, then profits increase and businesses grow. The second advantage is that consumers have access to new products, and existing domestic products must improve their quality or reduce their prices in order to compete with imported products.

Countries must come to a **trade agreement** in order to reduce trade barriers. If the countries are just beginning a trade relationship, this agreement usually deals mainly with importing and exporting products. The agreement states which tariff each country will drop or reduce and may include a process for resolving disputes. In today's economy, trade in services is just as important as trade in goods. Trade agreements need to include answers to questions such as when and why people will be permitted to work across international borders, what qualifications they will need, what standards will be applied to their work, and how businesses' trade secrets (also known as **intellectual property**) will be protected.

World Trade Organization (WTO)

The World Trade Organization developed out of a very important international trade agreement called the **General Agreement on Tariffs and Trade (GATT)**, which was signed in 1947 and came into effect in 1948. Countries that had been allies during World War II agreed on rules that would strengthen their trade relationships. Canada and 22 other nations signed this agreement. An international organization was set up to help the GATT member nations negotiate trade deals, resolve problems, and collect data about world trade.

Representatives from both emerging and developing countries meet during WTO talks held in Rio de Janeiro, Brazil, September 2006.

GATT endured for nearly 50 years and grew to include 115 member states. In 1995, the **World Trade Organization (WTO)** was established to replace the earlier GATT administration. With 139 member countries, the WTO is the principal international organization that deals with the rules of trade between nations. One important WTO agreement is the 1995 General Agreement on Trade in Services (GATS). The GATS sets guidelines for the trade of services (such as banking) across international borders. Currently, the WTO governs about 97 percent of all world trade.

North American Free Trade Agreement (NAFTA)

By 1986, Canada and the United States were ready to negotiate a free trade agreement. The agreement was intended to gradually phase out a number of tariff barriers that existed between the two countries. Canada hoped that the agreement would give Canadian businesses stable access to U.S. markets, clarify the rules about government assistance to industry, make it possible for Canadian companies to bid on U.S. government contracts, and allow Canada an equal say in the settlement of disputes. The United States wanted to clarify rules regarding services and intellectual property, reduce restrictions on American investment in Canadian industries, and increase their exports to Canada.

The **Canada–U.S. Free Trade Agreement (FTA)** came into effect in January 1989.

Table 4.3

Canada–U.S. Free Trade Agreement (FTA) (1989)		
Terms of the agreement: All products (other than exemptions) are duty-free if produced within the free-trade zone.		
	Canada	**United States**
Goals for the Agreement	• to be able to bid on U.S. government contracts • to clarify rules about government assistance to industry • to allow stable access to U.S. markets • to create a dispute settlement tribunal • to increase exports to U.S.	• to remove restrictions on U.S. investment in Canada • to clarify rules on intellectual property and service industries • to increase exports to Canada
Exemptions	dairy and poultry	sugar, dairy, peanuts, and cotton

Soon after the FTA came into effect, the United States announced a similar agreement with Mexico, and Canada asked to be included in the negotiations. The **North American Free Trade Agreement (NAFTA)**, which came into effect in 1994, joined all three countries in a continent-wide free-trade zone. All products can be traded across the three borders without tariffs as long as they were made within the free-trade zone.

Table 4.4

North American Free Trade Agreement (NAFTA) (1994)			
Terms of the agreement: All products are duty-free if produced within the free-trade zone. (Some exemptions for Canada and the United States are to be phased out in 2008.)			
	Canada	**United States**	**Mexico**
Economic Growth (1994–2003)	• Economic growth is up 30.9% since NAFTA. • Export sales to NAFTA partners increased by 104%. • Exports to the U.S. increased by 250% and now account for 87.2% of all Canadian exports.	• Economic growth is up 38% since NAFTA.	• Economic growth is up 30% since NAFTA.
Concerns Expressed about NAFTA	• The agreement gives the United States and Mexico too much access to Canada's natural resources, (e.g., minerals and timber) and this may lead to the gradual depletion of these resources. • Canada's cultural industries, including book and magazine publishing and television broadcasting, are gradually becoming Americanized.	• Canada and Mexico are perceived to be taking jobs away from Americans.	• Wealthier northern countries are perceived as exploiting Mexico for its low wages.
	• Trade agreements give businesses and transnationals power over elected governments, and, in time, these agreements will erode democracy.		

If a Canadian company manufactures shoes in Brazil and exports them to the United States, duties will apply, because the shoes were not made inside the free-trade zone. If a Brazilian company manufactures shoes in Canada and then exports them to the United States, the shoes will be duty free because they were made in Canada. Each day, NAFTA countries conduct nearly $1.7 billion in trilateral trade.

Other Free Trade Agreements

NAFTA is only one free trade agreement that Canada has with countries around the world. Some of Canada's trade agreements are regional (involving groups of countries), while others are **bilateral** (involving Canada and one other country or group).

In addition, Canada currently has bilateral free trade agreements with Chile and Israel, and is negotiating others with Costa Rica and a trading bloc made up of four Central American countries—Guatemala, El Salvador, Honduras, and Nicaragua. A **trading bloc** is a group of countries that share the same trade interests.

The Group of Eight

The **Group of Eight (G8)**, formerly known as the Group of Seven (G7), is an association of the world's most powerful industrialized democracies. Unlike other trading blocs, G8 countries are not located close together. Instead, countries from different parts of the world work together in the global economy.

> ### Stretch Your Thinking
>
> Some people argue that the G8 should expand by including other countries. If that were to happen, what countries should be invited to sit at the table?

In the News

Just because a trade agreement exists between countries doesn't mean that there won't be problems or issues. The biggest trade irritant between the United States and Canada is the softwood lumber industry. Over a three-year period, starting in 2002, the United States collected $5 billion in penalties on Canadian softwood lumber shipments to the United States. The purpose of these penalties was to protect the U.S. softwood lumber industry, even though a free-trade agreement made such penalties illegal. Canada contested the penalties in court and won several times, but the United States refused to co-operate. But in 2006, the United States and Canada signed an agreement to settle this issue. On September 12, 2006, the federal trade minister and his American counterpart formally signed the controversial agreement in Ottawa. A week later, the agreement passed its first parliamentary test in the House of Commons with a 172 to 116 vote. Legislation implementing the deal took effect November 1, 2006. Canada supplies about one-third of the softwood lumber used in the United States, mainly in housing construction and renovation. In 2005, Canada exported about $7.4 billion in softwood to the United States.

The original G7 consisted of four members from the European Union (Britain, France, Germany, and Italy), two from North America (Canada and the United States), and one from the Asia–Pacific region (Japan). The eighth member is Russia, which joined in 1998 and caused the group's name to change from G7 to G8.

Since 1975, the leaders of these countries have met at annual summits to deal with major economic and political issues facing their own countries and the broader international community. Topics dealt with at the summits include energy, employment, the environment, human rights, and arms control. G8 summits

Table 4.5

Other Free Trade Agreements		
	Description	**Canada's Interest**
Free Trade Area of the Americas (FTAA) (not yet signed into law)	• Expands NAFTA to include the countries of Central America, South America, and the Caribbean (except Cuba). • Many South American countries are opposed to FTAA because they believe powerful northern countries will exploit poor southern countries.	• Canada can increase trade with smaller nations.
Central American Free Trade Agreement (CAFTA) (2004)	• CAFTA is a trade agreement among Central American countries.	• Canada is not a member but supports CAFTA because it may lead to more support for FTAA.
European Free Trade Association (EFTA) (1960)	• EFTA links Norway, Switzerland, Iceland, and Liechtenstein. • Canada has a trade agreement with EFTA.	• Canada exports industrial goods such as aircraft and aircraft parts; natural resources such as gold, nickel, zinc, magnesium, and crude oil; and fisheries products to EFTA nations. • EFTA makes it easier to import agricultural products from EFTA countries into Canada.
Asia–Pacific Economic Cooperation (APEC) (1989)	• The original members were Australia, Brunei, Canada, Indonesia, Japan, South Korea, Malaysia, New Zealand, the Republic of the Philippines, Singapore, Thailand, and the United States. • Since 1991, China, Taiwan, Hong Kong, Mexico, Papua New Guinea, Chile, Peru, Russia, and Vietnam have joined.	• APEC links many countries for tariff-free trade.

set new priorities and directions and define new issues for the international community. In this way, the G8 provides guidance and support to established international organizations.

Review Questions

19. What kind of information is included in a trade agreement? Why are these agreements important?

20. Why does it make sense for Canada and the United States to be trading partners?

21. How do duty-free transactions work amongst the NAFTA partners?

22. Why do you think that Canada wanted to become part of EFTA and APEC?

23. What advantages are there for Canada in being one of the G8 members?

G-8 leaders (plus the Finnish Prime Minister and the EU Commission Chief) pose for a portrait in front of Konstantinovsky Palace, Russia, July 2006.

The Future of International Trade

During the first decade of the twenty-first century, the fastest growing trade group in the world will likely be the Asia–Pacific market. Countries in this region already form the largest trading bloc in the world. Like all trading blocs, APEC is protectionist by nature, meaning that it protects its own members' economic interests by imposing tariffs or quotas on imports from other countries. However, experts agree that continued economic prosperity requires that individual trading blocs lower their barriers and begin a period of global co-operation.

European Union (EU)

The **European Union** (EU) is the union of many European countries into a single market, a process that began after World War II and culminated in a single-currency market in 2002. The euro is the official currency of more than 300 million people in Europe. However, not all countries in the EU have adopted the euro, such as Denmark and the United Kingdom, but the hope is that all countries in the EU will adopt the euro as the official currency in due course. Unlike NAFTA, it is not simply a trading bloc. It has its own elected government and allows citizens to move freely from one country to another. EU membership could grow to as many as 28 countries by 2010, bringing the population of the EU from the current 370 million to more than 500 million.

Evolution of NAFTA

Like the EU, North America's NAFTA, or its FTAA successor, could gradually evolve from a trading bloc into a single market. Such a change would mean that Canadians could move freely

In the News

The European Union is a regional organization, a political union, and a common market of many countries in Europe. From a union of six countries (Belgium, France, Germany, Italy, Luxembourg, and the Netherlands) in the 1950s, it expanded to include Britain, Ireland, and Denmark in 1973.

Greece followed in 1981 and Spain and Portugal in 1986. By December 31, 1992, these 12 countries had dissolved their economic borders; agreed to the free exchange of goods, services, capital, and people among their member states; and became known as the European Union. Most members of the EU

adopted a single currency, the euro, in 1999. Since 1993, the EU has grown to 25 members with more European countries likely to join over the next few years. Collectively, the countries of the EU make it Canada's largest trading partner after the United States.

into the United States and Mexico. It would also mean that American and Mexican workers could compete with Canadian workers for jobs in Canada. A North American Union could even mean a single currency, similar to the euro.

Impact of Cultural Differences

The future of international trade depends, in part, on our ability to accept and respond to cultural differences. **Culture** is the sum of a country's way of life, beliefs, and customs. It influences how things are bought and sold. It sets the boundaries of what can and cannot be done, of what is acceptable or unacceptable. Culture is absorbed everywhere—at school, at home, and at work. Luckily, people who aren't born in a certain culture can still learn to operate within it.

Imagine for a moment the difficulties that might face a paint company in Mexico that wants to set up a branch plant in Canada. To begin with, the paint will need to be put into approved packages that are labelled in both French and English, with metric measurements. The language requirements mean that the Mexican company will have to invest in new packaging before the sales revenues begin to flow in.

Because of cultural differences, it may be difficult for the Mexican paint manufacturer to predict Canadian colour preferences or plan an advertising campaign that appeals to Canadians. To make choices, the manufacturer needs to do considerable market research in Canada, even though similar research may already have been done in Mexico. This research should include a study of social and environmental issues that are important to Canadians and demographic characteristics that shape the Canadian market.

Dealing with People

Doing business around the world not only means learning other languages and understanding other cultures; it also means learning the nuances of dealing with people and finding out what's important to them. Some key areas to find out about include punctuality, greetings, nonverbal communication, good manners, and decision-making processes.

Punctuality

In some cultures, such as North American cultures, people are expected to be on time for appointments. They rely on appointment books and calendars, and may even have to pay

Stretch Your Thinking

Choose a foreign country. What cultural differences must be considered by a Canadian paint company that wants to open a branch plant in that country?

A can of Mexican beans with the ingredients written in different languages

Japanese people believe that if they board a train it will arrive on time. This puts pressure on everyone to comply with this cultural norm. In April 2005, in an effort to make up 90 seconds of lost time, a 23-year-old train engineer was speeding so that the train he was driving would arrive precisely on time and commuters would not miss connecting trains. The excessive speed allowed the engineer to make up 30 seconds of lost time. However, it also resulted in loss of control by the engineer and the train jumped off the tracks and hurtled into a nine-storey apartment building. An obsession with "being on time" led to the deaths of 94 people.

Oops!

Music is enjoyed worldwide, but translating lyrics can be a challenge. The Japanese pop song "Ue O Muite Aruko" ("I Look Up When I Walk") became a hit in Britain and North America in the 1960s. Two versions were recorded—one by a Japanese artist and one by an American jazz singer—and both were sung in Japanese. However, the record company assumed that the title would be too difficult for an English audience, so they changed it to "Sukiyaki." The new title had nothing to do with the lyrics or meaning of the song and literally translated to "a sautéed beef dish!"

for missed appointments. In other cultures, time is considered to be flowing, flexible, and beyond people's control. What doesn't get done today can be done tomorrow. If you find out how important punctuality is in a country you plan to visit, you can set an acceptable pace, impress others with your good manners, and avoid long waits.

Greetings

In many countries, the way you greet someone is an important part of the impression you make. Handshakes are common in most countries, but not everyone shakes hands the same way. In France, for example, a single shake is all that's needed, and more may be considered rude. In most cultures, it's considered polite to make eye contact when you greet someone, but in others, averting your eyes is a sign of respect. These details are very important because the impression you create first is usually the one that stays with people over time.

Nonverbal Communication Signals

In many cultures, nonverbal signals tell far more than words. For example, in Asian cultures, refusing someone's request is considered rude, so Asian businesspeople may prefer not to give direct answers to questions asked during sales negotiations instead of saying "no." Businesspeople may have to rely on the body language of the person they're speaking with to tell them whether they have or have not made a sale.

Familiar gestures are not always a useful guide because they may have different meanings from one culture to another. To a Bulgarian, a nod of the head means "no," while shaking the head from side to side means "yes"—the opposite to the meaning of these gestures in North America. The "okay" sign commonly

In some cultures, shaking hands is both a greeting and a gesture that confirms a deal.

used in Canada (thumb and index finger touching to form a circle) is a symbol for money in Japan and is an offensive gesture in Brazil.

Cultural rules about touching other people also vary widely from one country to another. In one place, a pat on the back may be a friendly greeting; in another place, it may be an insult. In some places, standing too close to a person is considered an invasion of personal space. In other places, it is considered rude to stand far away. In a business situation, it's important to know these rules.

Good Manners

People in Canada, the United States, and some European countries like to do business quickly and efficiently. They tend to focus on the task at hand and try to get it done so they can move on to something else. Almost anywhere else in the world—particularly in Asian and Latin American countries—

it's considered polite to try to get to know the people you're doing business with before you discuss the business itself. The three Fs of business—family, friends, and favours—have a very strong influence on the business decisions people make. To be successful, it's essential to spend time establishing a relationship with customers and business associates before you proceed with your work.

Although good manners everywhere are based on the ideas of showing respect for others and making them feel comfortable, specific rules and expectations differ from one culture to the next. For example, in some countries, it's considered rude to use your left hand to give something to someone. In others, it's rude to ask about someone's spouse. Because it's hard to predict what people will expect from you, it's a good idea to do some research about etiquette before you travel to a foreign country.

Decision making

In North American business, decision making is typically a top-down process. People expect the president of a company to have much more say in an important decision than someone who works in a less senior position. Latin American cultures usually take a similar approach. However, in some other cultures, decisions are made from the bottom up. That means that before an important decision can be made, the person who makes the decision may need to consult everyone who will be affected by the outcome. As a result, decisions may sometimes take longer to make.

Global Dependency

The twentieth century was a time of almost unimaginable growth in the communications industry. People all around the world were drawn closer together by inventions such as the television, movies, satellite communications, and the Internet. This rapid growth has put us on the path to becoming a "global community."

If you walked down the streets of Taipei, Barcelona, Cairo, or Buenos Aires, you would likely see signs of home. You might see a Pizza Hut, an advertisement for a Will Smith movie, or a copy of *USA Today* newspaper. You'd see people wearing clothes with familiar logos. In a parking lot, you'd see familiar vehicles.

> **Business Fact**
>
> Triangular product logos aren't popular in some Asian countries, such as Hong Kong and Taiwan, because the triangle is associated with bad luck.

Why are consumers buying cars and clothing made in foreign countries? The simple answer is something called global dependency. **Global dependency** exists when customers in one country begin to demand items that are created in another country. These customers become aware of the products because of global communications. Over time, the products are incorporated into the culture of the people who buy them.

But the process doesn't always go smoothly. Awareness of different cultures and preferences is the key to success in a foreign market. A North American advertisement for a brand of laundry detergent might show dirty clothes on the left, the detergent in the middle, and clean clothes on the right. If this ad were introduced in a country where people read from right to left, such as Israel or Egypt, the result would be confusion and declining sales.

Since the pace of advances in communication technology seems to be speeding up, not slowing down, it's likely that global dependency will continue to increase as we move further into the twenty-first century. Despite the fact that the road to the future won't always be smooth, it seems likely that international business will play a vital role in determining what our "global community" will look like in the centuries to come.

A familiar North American computer product is advertised in Chinese in Beijing, China.

Review Questions

24. Describe several ways in which you could find out about the culture of another country.

25. Give an example of how each of the following is different in a non-Canadian culture: punctuality, greetings, nonverbal communication, good manners, and decision-making processes.

26. What is global dependency? How does it influence international business?

CHAPTER REVIEW

Knowledge

1. How does proximity encourage trade?

2. Use an example to show how a government can use a currency fluctuation as a barrier.

3. If a business plans to enter a foreign market, why would it be helpful to gather information about the discretionary incomes of potential customers?

4. Why is it important to watch body language when communicating with someone from another culture?

Thinking

5. If Canada did not buy and sell goods internationally, how would your community be affected?

6. Windsor, Ontario, benefits from being close to Detroit, Michigan. Name three other border cities across Canada that benefit from being close to large American cities. In what ways do the Canadian and American cities benefit?

7. Choose one country from Table 4.2 on Canada's export markets. Gather as much information as you can about that country's investment relationship with Canada. Create a visual display or multimedia presentation designed to help Canadian investors who might be interested in doing business with that country.

8. Do you think it's possible to have a world free-trade zone established at some point? Identify two benefits and two drawbacks of such a possibility.

Communication

9. If the Canadian government put stiffer controls on imports, it could increase the number of jobs for Canadians. Describe the advantages and disadvantages of this strategy. Then interview a businessperson in your community to get his or her opinion. Present your conclusions to the class in an oral report.

10. Using the Internet, the library, or another source, prepare an oral report on how important the market in China will be to your province or territory in the next 10 years.

11. Could Canada continue to exist as an independent nation inside a North American economic union? Research the potential impact of such a union on Canada's economy, environment, culture, and government. Then hold a class debate on this issue.

12. Culture has an influence on many aspects of people's everyday life, including music, clothing, and entertainment. Choose one of these areas. What can you learn about Canadian culture by examining this area? Then, choose another country and tell what you know about its culture by examining the same area.

Application

13. Select two products you use that are produced in Canada. Conduct research to find information that will help you determine whether these products are sold internationally and, if so, whether they are changed or repackaged for other markets. Write and illustrate a report to present your findings.

14. The BMW X5 was used as an example of a product that has component parts from around the world. Identify another product that relies on other countries for its component parts and write up your response using the X5 summary as a guideline.

15. A Canadian giftware manufacturer wants to sell products in the Mexican market and has come to you for advice. Consider what you have learned in this chapter and explain, in an oral report, the pros and cons of trying to enter this market. Conclude your report by making two recommendations to the Canadian manufacturer.

16. Find out how Canadian immigration patterns have changed in the past 40 years. What effect has this had on Canada's economic relationship with various countries?

Team Activity

Team Goal: To find examples of imports from the largest possible variety of countries

Team Assignment: Imported Goods

• Your team should bring to the classroom actual samples of imports from as many different countries as possible (pictures don't count).

• Your team's selection should consist of only one item per country. Each team will present their items to the class.

• The team that has examples of imports from the largest number of different countries will win this competition.

• In the case of a tie, the judge will use creativity or variety as a criteria for declaring a winner.

Portfolio

Select two businesses within your industry that export to different countries. Pick two of the countries that either (or both) of these businesses export to. Prepare a detailed profile of each of the countries including a discussion of its economy, political organization, language, climate, geography, population, trade agreements with Canada, culture, and infrastructure.

How do each of the businesses you selected trade with these nations? (Consider strategic alliances, company-owned stores or factories, distribution centres, and/or simple buy/sell arrangements.) Explain with pictures, diagrams, and specific examples where possible.

What products would these businesses import? List three or four items that one of the firms you selected as an exporter would need to import. What countries would supply the items?

Reflect on Your Learning

Would you like to work at a branch of a Canadian company set up in another country? Why or why not?

Google

Google is a global technology business that maintains the world's largest online index of websites and information by using an automated search technology that is made free to anyone with an Internet connection. As a result of their innovative web search technology, Google is among the world's most widely known brands and a top Internet destination. The company name is now a verb (to google) that's used everyday around the world.

So, how does Google earn a profit if users do not pay for web searches? The answer is: Simply by providing online advertising to businesses who pay for space on third-party websites that comprise the Google Network. Although the company doesn't disclose its financial results, annual revenue was estimated to be between US$700 million and US$1 billion for 2004, and the number of employees was more than 3000.

Google is the brainchild of Larry Page and Sergey Brin, both computer graduate students at Stanford University, who, in 1996, had started working together on designing a system to explore the Internet. Within a year, their new search engine, initially called BackRub, was causing a buzz on the Stanford campus. But, as Page explained, "We realized BackRub wasn't the world's greatest name." The search for a new name was on. When, finally, they came across a list of very large numbers, of which "google" was at the top, they knew they had found what they were looking for. A friend later informed them that the number is actually spelled "googol," but since the Google domain was still available, Page and Brin opted to keep the misspelling. A googol is the number one followed by 100 zeros and was

Larry Page and Sergey Brin are the founders of the popular Internet search engine Google.

chosen because it appropriately reflected the new search engine's objective: to organize the almost infinite amount of information worldwide and to make it universally accessible.

In September 1998, after two years of perfecting their new technology, the two former graduate students put their Ph.D. plans on hold and opened Google Inc. in Menlo Park, California. From the outset, Google was answering 10 000 search queries per day, and was named by *PC Magazine* as one of the Top 100 Websites and Search Engines for 1998.

By the end of 2000—despite Google's daily handling of more than 100 million searches —the company was looking for new ways to connect more people with more information worldwide. And so the company began to develop and extend its user interface. The result?

Users now have the opportunity to search sites written in 28 languages, including Arabic, Turkish, Korean, and Japanese. Furthermore, Google formed a partnership with the company Universo Online, making Google Latin America's number-one search engine. In 2004, the Google interface was available in more than 100 languages. Indeed, Google is so committed to providing global access to information that the company has extended versions of Google into many developing countries, from which they are unable to recover the costs, because they view the investment as an important social good rather than a market for profit.

In October 2006, Google purchased YouTube—the consumer media company for people to watch and share original videos through a Web experience—for US$1.65 billion

in stock. Founded in February 2005, YouTube allows people to easily upload and share video clips on and across the Internet through websites, blogs, and e-mail. YouTube currently delivers more than 100 million video views every day with 65 000 new videos uploaded daily. This acquisition by Google combines one of the largest and fastest-growing online video entertainment communities with Google's expertise in organizing information and creating new models for advertising on the Internet.

Because Google believes its primary competitive advantage to be surprise, Google does not like to talk much about future plans. However, just a quick look at the Google Labs web page will tell you that there is much more to come from this innovative and universal business.

QUESTIONS

1. What service does Google provide to its users? By what means are they able to obtain a profit?

2. Why is Google considered to be a *global* technology business? What is a user interface, and how has this enabled Google to increase information accessibility worldwide?

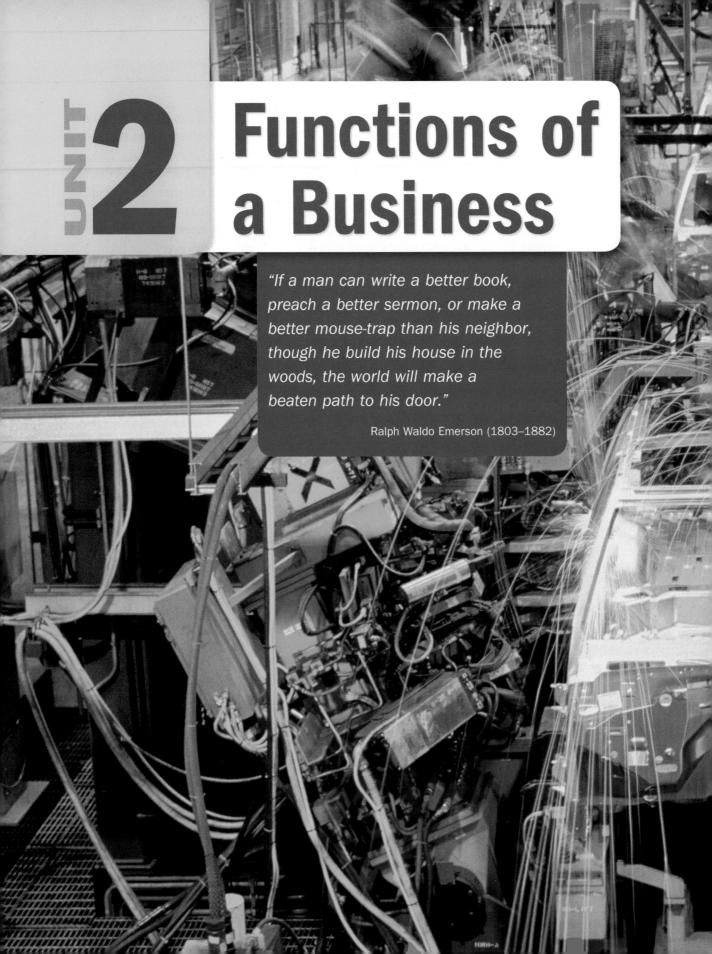

"If a man can write a better book,
preach a better sermon, or make a
better mouse-trap than his neighbor,
though he build his house in the
woods, the world will make a
beaten path to his door."

Ralph Waldo Emerson (1803–1882)

OVERALL EXPECTATIONS

- explain the role of production in business
- explain the role of human resources in business
- demonstrate an understanding of sound management practices in business
- demonstrate an understanding of the importance and role of marketing in business
- demonstrate an understanding of the importance and role of accounting in business
- demonstrate an understanding of the importance and role of information technology in business

5 Production

SPECIFIC EXPECTATIONS

After completing this chapter, you will be able to

- identify the factors involved in production
- explain the steps in the production process
- describe ways in which companies can improve productivity

- explain how information and communication technology affects the functions of a business
- use information and communication technology for a variety of business purposes

Ganong Bros. Limited

The history of Ganong Brothers chocolates stretches back to 1873, when James and Gilbert Ganong opened a grocery store in the small town of St. Stephen, New Brunswick. Initially, the purchasing and selling of candy comprised a small portion of their business. However, the brothers soon realized that there was great potential in the candy market. In 1884, they turned their grocery business into the candy company that is known today as Ganong Bros. Limited.

Ganong Bros. Limited is the oldest family-owned candy business in Canada, with an international reputation for quality products. Ganong introduced the world's first 5¢ chocolate nut bar, the all-day sucker, and the chicken bone—a satiny pink confection made of sugar, cinnamon, and chocolate. Ganong was also the first candy company to package chocolates in heart-shaped boxes—now the most popular Valentine's Day gift for romantic souls everywhere.

Ganong Brothers' method of producing fine chocolates hasn't changed much from when the company first started making candy more than one hundred years ago. It still purchases its cocoa, sugar, and nuts from countries around the world to ensure that the highest quality raw materials are used in Ganong chocolate.

This global sourcing of ingredients can present problems. Ganong Brothers must watch for events that can affect the supply and cost of such goods. For example, since the Ivory Coast is responsible for well over half the world's supply of cocoa, any civil unrest in this part of the world could greatly threaten both the harvest and shipment of cocoa beans. In turn, this would disrupt the world chocolate

Workers package boxes filled with chocolates.

supply and dramatically increase cocoa prices.

Sugar prices can also vary with supply and demand. In 2005, for example, Hurricane Katrina disabled a very large sugar refinery in New Orleans, resulting in much higher than normal sugar prices. The purchasing department at Ganong Brothers takes great care in obtaining these key ingredients in the right quantity, quality, and price.

The recipes for most Ganong Brothers chocolates date back many decades. All ingredients begin their journey to consumer products on the cook floor, where they are combined and cooked to specified temperatures and times. Depending on the type of chocolate being made, other key ingredients—such as rich cream or real butter— might also be added. Once the chocolate reaches the proper temperature, the liquid candy mixture is placed into a mould for the desired shape. When the individual candies have become firm, they travel under a waterfall of chocolate (an enrober) that smothers each piece in a blanket of either milk or dark chocolate. There are several quality checks conducted along the way, and any less-than-perfect pieces are removed from the line. Packers then place each perfect chocolate piece into the correct assortment box by hand, then send the box off to the cellophane wrapping machine. The finished boxes are shipped to the thousands of customers waiting for their orders.

Ganong Brothers has been manufacturing assorted boxed chocolates since the early 1900s. Throughout that time, technology has afforded many opportunities for change (for example, using more modern production techniques). However, Ganong Brothers takes great pride in continuing to use a process that is fundamentally no different than the one used to produce the first box of chocolate assortments almost a century ago. Tradition is a part of every candy they make.

QUESTIONS

1. How does Ganong Bros. Limited obtain the ingredients required to make their candies? What factors do they have to consider when deciding from where and when to make their purchase?

2. How is Ganong Bros. Limited different from other chocolate manufacturers?

Factors of Production

If you have ever made anything, you have been involved in production. If you have made a bowl of cereal, fried an egg, poured a glass of juice, or buttered a piece of toast, you have produced something that wasn't there before. You needed other items to make the toast—a toaster, bread, butter (or margarine), and a knife. Some peanut butter, honey, or jam would be nice, but not essential. And then, of course, there's your effort and skill.

Natural Resources

It may be hard to believe, but everything in the world is made from only six types of natural resources: agriculture, fishing and trapping, mining, water, fuel and energy, and logging and forestry. Think about your toast again. Agriculture provides the wheat for the flour used to make the bread. Mining supplies the bauxite that ends up as the aluminum that forms the toaster. Fuel and energy power the machines that manufacture the products.

Consider other products you use: your clothes, your phone, your pencil, your lunch. Make a list of the raw materials needed for them. You will discover that the origin of each product you name can be traced back to one of the six natural resource industries. These industries are known, collectively, as **primary industries**, because they are where all items start out.

Keep in Mind

1. natural resources
2. raw materials
3. labour
4. capital
5. information
6. management

Before You Begin

You are productive if you produce something—be it a product, a service, or even an idea. Some people are paid for being productive; others (such as students like you) are not. List five productive people you know and, in a sentence or two, describe what they produce. How are you productive?

A miner drills into the wall of a newly blasted tunnel, Hemlo Gold Mine, Ontario.

Figure 5.1 The Six Primary (or Extractive) Industries

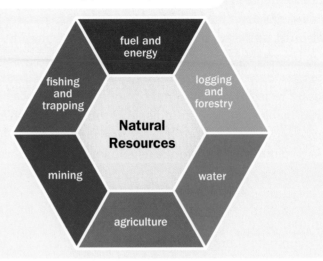

Since primary industries often require taking something out of the earth or the sea, they are also referred to as **extractive industries** ("to extract" something means to take it out, like a dentist would extract a wisdom tooth).

Raw Materials

Raw materials are any goods used in the manufacturing of other goods. Almost all the natural resources we consume were raw materials for other products or used to help make other products. Only rarely do we, as consumers, buy a natural resource (the exceptions are fish and fresh vegetables). Wheat, a natural resource, is the raw material that makes flour. Flour is the raw material that makes bread. Bread is the raw material that creates toast.

Frank and Ernest

© 2006 Thaves. Reprinted with permission. Newspaper dist. by NEA, Inc.

There are two main types of raw materials: ingredients and supplies.

Ingredients are the raw materials that go into a product. Notice that most of the ingredients in Dempster's Original 100% Whole Wheat bread are no longer natural resources. All the ingredients (except, perhaps, water) were taken from their original, natural states and converted into another product. This conversion is called **processing**. Flour mills process wheat into flour. Sugar refineries process sugar cane into sugar. Some chemical companies process minerals into chemicals, while others combine them into products most of us have never heard of—such as monoglycerides or sodium stearoyl-2-lactylate. Most people haven't heard of the thousands of businesses involved in processing natural resources into ingredients for familiar products. You will read more about processing later in the chapter.

Supplies are raw materials that *do not* become part of a new product, and in this way are different from ingredients. Ingredients are used in the product itself—peanuts are used in peanut butter, flour is used in making bread—but supplies are used in the running of the business. Supplies are used to maintain machinery and equipment, help in the administration of the offices, and keep the business clean. Oil, detergent, salt and pepper, paper towels, and envelopes are examples of typical business supplies. A service business—such as a doctor, accountant, or advertising agency—would use supplies instead of ingredients.

Dempster's bread and the ingredients required for its production

Business Fact

In 2001, there were 28 flour mills operating in Canada, employing 2000 people. About 80% of milling wheat is exported rather than milled in Canada.

Stretch Your Thinking

When can a natural resource also be a raw material?

Harvest

Store

Process

Canada Post's commemorative stamp celebrating the 50th anniversary of the establishment of the Canadian Labour Congress

Stretch Your Thinking

In a global economy, should Canadians support Canadian businesses that use foreign labour to reduce the cost of Canadian goods and services? Debate this issue.

This machine, for mixing dough, is an example of a bakery's capital goods.

Labour

Labour includes all the physical and mental work needed to produce goods or services. Most labour is a combination of mental and physical effort, although many jobs require more of one than the other. A computer systems training instructor would use mostly mental effort, while a construction worker would use primarily physical labour.

Labour is a very expensive cost of doing business, and many firms are constantly looking for ways to save money on labour. Numerous tasks once performed by people are now being **automated**—done by machines—or **consolidated**. Consolidation occurs when small manufacturing sites close down and centralize the work in one major site. Consolidation often makes it feasible to introduce even more automation. Tim Hortons, for example, consolidated its bakery operations after merging with the U.S. hamburger chain Wendy's in 1995. In 2003, Tim Hortons built a 230 000-square-foot plant in Brantford, Ontario, that has the capacity to make the baked goods for all the Tim Hortons' restaurants in Canada. The plant freezes semi-finished products and ships them to its locations across the country. The individual restaurants no longer need bakers on site, which saves the company a great deal of money.

Another way to save on labour costs is to **outsource**—hire another company to perform a task. With fast computers and secure websites, many outsourcing companies use inexpensive labour in India, Kenya, or Sri Lanka, for example, to manage other firms' payroll, human resources, health care plans, or financial services. Although outsourcing affects Canadian workers by taking away jobs, it does provide cheaper labour for Canadian companies.

Capital

Capital is the money invested in a business. Many people think of capital as money in all its forms: cash, stocks, bonds, accounts receivable, and so on. The owner of a business can use capital to purchase things the business needs to operate. If your business needs a new truck, for example, you can very easily exchange the money in your bank account—your monetary capital—for a new truck. This type of capital is called **liquid**, meaning a business can transform it into other things at any time, with minimum effort.

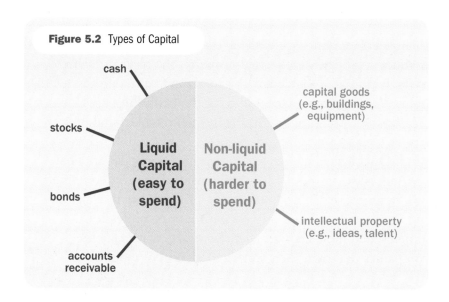

Figure 5.2 Types of Capital

cash

capital goods
(e.g., buildings,
equipment)

stocks

Liquid Capital (easy to spend)

Non-liquid Capital (harder to spend)

bonds

intellectual property
(e.g., ideas, talent)

accounts
receivable

Non-liquid capital consists of items a business owns that are part of the everyday operations and that cannot be easily converted into liquid capital. These items are called capital goods. For example, a bakery would need an industrial-size mixer to make its bread dough. Although the mixer is worth money, it is valuable only as a mixer in the bakery. If the bakery were to close and liquidate all the things it owns, the mixer would not be desirable to most buyers. If it did sell, it would sell for much less than it originally cost. You will learn more about liquidity in Chapter 9.

Ideas being shared between colleagues at the Canadian computer game design company Ubisoft

In the News

In June 2006, 76-year-old billionaire Warren Buffett unveiled plans to give away the bulk of his fortune—US$37.4 billion—to a foundation run by Bill and Melinda Gates. Gates is the founder of Microsoft Corporation. He and his wife run the world's largest charitable foundation, with assets of US$29 billion and an impressive track record of combatting HIV, tuberculosis, and malaria in Africa and southern Asia. Mr. Buffett, who founded Berkshire Hathaway Inc., a giant holding company, is the second richest man in the world. Bill Gates is the richest.

For some businesses, especially artistic or high-tech ones, the most important capital the company owns is not a tangible product at all. It is **intellectual property**, the ideas or talent of its workforce. Doubleday, the company that publishes books by Dan Brown (the author of the bestselling novel *The DaVinci Code*), has a fortune in intellectual capital in Brown's next book. Even though that book is still in Brown's head, Doubleday has a contract with him to publish it. That contract is worth hundreds of millions of dollars. A computer programmer with a brilliant gaming program has intellectual property worth millions as well. Movie stars, professional athletes, and rap stars sign talent contracts that make the companies that own their work a great deal of money.

Information

To produce goods and services competitively in a global economy requires information: information about new technology, customers, competition, political conditions, and sources of supply. Many businesses make extensive use of researchers who investigate all of the above and more. Although no business is failure proof, having access to accurate information certainly minimizes risk and enhances profitability.

Information itself has become a major commodity— a product for sale or for distribution. A business that has information or the means to acquire it can, in turn, charge

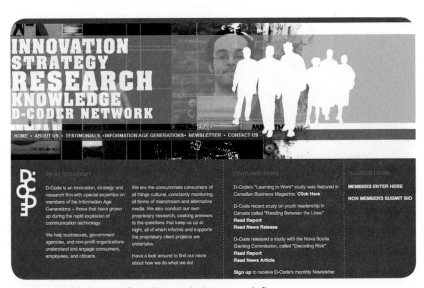

Home page of D-Code—a Canadian marketing research firm

to sell that information. An alternative is for a business to provide interesting data for free over the Internet and charge companies to advertise on its site. Industrial directories and databases, such as Frasers (Canadian) or the Thomas Register (American), list thousands of industrial businesses, allowing industrial buyers to find the right suppliers, distributors, and service companies. Marketing research companies, such as MarketQuest and D-Code, provide businesses with information about the latest trends and newest products, as well as monitoring advertising effectiveness, public opinions, and the competition. Financial companies, such as RBC Dominion Securities or BMO Financial Group, provide investment information.

Management

People who control the factors of production listed earlier are called **management**. Management allocates the company's resources, both capital and human, and decides what to purchase, what to make, whom to hire, where to sell, and so on. Higher-level managers also decide how a business's profits will be distributed: paying off debt, dividing it among the owners, reinvesting in the business through upgrades or expansion, or providing more employee benefits. A manager can be a single proprietor making all the decisions or the head of a huge organizational structure with a board of directors and a two-page organizational chart. Chapter 7 deals with management in much greater detail.

Oops!

In 1997, a group of Barbie doll collectors called Pink Anger organized a boycott of Barbie products. They accused Mattel (Barbie's manufacturer) of costly production errors. Poodle Parade Barbie, a supposedly exact replica of a 1965 doll, had a different haircut. The Francie doll, a replica of Barbie's friend, had shoes that didn't fit. Star Trek Barbie was shipped late, while other dolls were over-produced. The result was a drop in demand, which reduced the value of the collectible doll by at least half. Mattel responded to the boycott by promising to tighten up on production quality.

Review Questions

1. List and describe briefly the six factors of production.
2. What are the six primary industries? Name one finished product we get from each.
3. List five capital goods a wheat farmer might need.
4. Describe the role of management in an organization.
5. How can information be a product?

To prepare a hamburger, all four stages of the production process are required.

The Production Process

What process would you use, from start to finish, to make a hamburger? First, you would have to buy the meat—are you going to choose medium grade, which gives the most flavour, or lean, to avoid extra fat? You would also need to have buns, mustard, ketchup, relish, and pickles—and ensure that they were of the quality you wanted. Then you would have to cook the burger, which is a delicate procedure. Overcooking could ruin the meat, and undercooking could make you very sick. Finally, you would taste the burger itself to find out if you had made a high-quality product. If you cooked your burger following this system, you would have experienced all four stages of the production process: purchasing, grading, processing, and quality control.

Purchasing

In order to have enough raw materials on hand to produce the good or service a business needs to make, someone must be responsible for purchasing. In some firms, the purchasing task is large enough to merit an entire department. Other businesses outsource these duties to purchasing agents who know global markets and can negotiate lower prices. Retailers employ buyers, who search for products to sell in their stores. The retailer might be large enough to have a separate purchasing department to obtain supplies. (See Raw Materials at the beginning of the chapter.)

That is the main job of the purchasing department: to acquire the needed products at the best price. For example, a bread company packages its loaves in plastic bags, that cost 2¢ per bag. The company uses 4 million bags per year. What considerations must a purchaser take into account when buying more bags?

- The quality of the bag: If many bags tear, and bread becomes stale or contaminated, the company loses money and sales. The bags must be strong, not only to protect the bread, but also to survive the printing process, when the label is placed on it.

- The price of the bag: If a purchaser can negotiate a price of 1.5¢ per bag, the company saves 0.5¢ cent on every bag it uses. The total cost for the old bags was 4 million × 2¢ = \$80 000. The new price of bags is 4 million × 1.5¢ = \$60 000. The renegotiated price saved the company \$20 000, which is pure profit.

Table 5.1

Whose Bags Should We Buy?	
Questions to Ask	**Why We Need to Know**
How strong are your bags?	If the bags tear, bread will get stale or contaminated, and the company will lose sales. Cheaper bags won't save money if sales go down.
How much do the new bags cost?	We buy 4 million bags per year, so even a tiny difference in price can make a big difference. If we can buy bags for 1.5¢ instead of 2¢, we can save a lot of money. 4 million × 2¢ = $80 000 per year 4 million × 1.5¢ = $60 000 per year Difference: $20 000 per year
What are the hidden costs?	Hidden costs include shipping, taxes, and duties. If it costs an extra penny to bring each 1.5¢ bag to Canada, then the total cost of each bag is now 2.5¢. In this case, it's cheaper to stay with the old supplier for 2¢ per bag.

- The hidden costs of the bag: transportation costs, taxes, duties, etc. If the 1.5¢ bag was produced in Mexico, for example, and the extra costs worked out to 1 cent per bag, then the old deal is actually better. The total cost of each bag would be 2.5¢ cents and would therefore cost the company more money than before. A good purchasing agent or manager investigates all the possibilities.

Processing

Earlier in this chapter, you read that all non-service businesses convert one thing into another through processing. Consider aluminum, for example.

Aluminum comes from bauxite, an ore that contains aluminum oxide. Canada does not have bauxite mines, so aluminum producers must import the ore from countries such as Guinea, Australia, Brazil, Jamaica, and India. Processing bauxite into aluminum requires large amounts of energy. Canada's supply of cheap hydroelectric power has made it one of the world's leading producers of aluminum.

In the News

In October 2005, the Institute of Packaging Professionals honoured the best packages of the year. The institute judges consumer packages based on innovation, protection, economics, performance, and environmental impact. The top award was presented to the "Hercules," a 3.78 litres polyethylene terephthalate (PET) bottle, used for Hawaiian Punch and Mott's juice products manufactured by Cadbury Schweppes Americas Beverages.

The World of Business **DVD**

"The Iceland Experiment"
from *The World of Business DVD*

Refining is a processing step used by metal-producing firms, oil companies, and even sugar companies to convert a raw material into a semi-finished or finished product. Refining ore, for example, separates aluminum oxide from the rest of the mineral. It takes approximately 4 tonnes of bauxite to obtain 2 tonnes of aluminum oxide, which will become 1 tonne of aluminum metal.

The aluminum oxide goes through a smelting phase, in which it is heated to remove the aluminum from the refined ore. Smelting is a common process for metal extraction. The aluminum factory then processes the raw metal into bars, ingots, sheets, or wire. Other manufacturers purchase the metal to use in making cars, machinery, cables, and toasters (to name a very few of the thousands of products that use aluminum). As you can see, aluminum goes through a number of processing stages before it is ready for products you may use.

Quality Control

Quality control ensures that the product a company makes conforms to certain standards. In most cases, these standards are set by the company itself, but certain products, such as food,

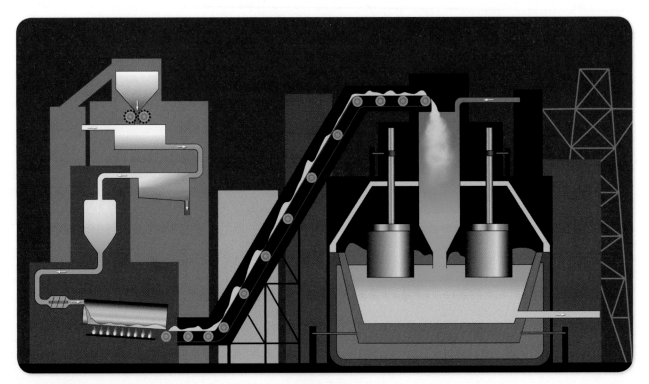

A schematic diagram that shows the stages of aluminum processing

medicine, and toys, must meet government standards as well. Large companies have quality control departments, which test samples of the finished product for defects. Rejected products are recycled, if possible. Even small firms must take quality control into account so that their customers can rely on them for consistency.

Quality standards are also set by the International Organization for Standardization, or ISO (the name is a short form of *isos*, the Greek word for "equal"). ISO is an organization that sets worldwide standards for numerous industries. Each of the 157 countries that belong to ISO can appoint one member to represent all the national standard institutes of its country. The Canadian member represents the Standards Council of Canada, which is the voice of the 15 000 Canadians who help set standards for Canadian products.

ISO helps businesses, consumers, customers, governments, and trade officials. All these people can be sure that an ISO-certified product meets international standards and expectations in such industries as aviation, automotive, construction, electronics, health care, medicine, telecommunications, and metals.

Ethical, Moral & Legal Considerations

Chicken is a very popular meat, but many feel the chicken production industry can be cruel to the birds. Broiler chickens are the most popular chicken on the market and fast-food menus. These chickens are raised in large, windowless buildings in flocks of between 20 000 and 50 000 birds. Feeding, watering, temperature, and ventilation are all automatically controlled. Most broiler chickens are slaughtered after just six or seven weeks (a chicken's natural lifespan is around seven years). The farm carefully controls the artificial lighting within the broiler sheds. When the chickens first arrive,

the lighting is bright so the chicks can find the food and water. This encourages eating and rapid growth. After a time, this lighting is dimmed in order to prevent fighting between chickens. The birds have little space in which to move. The space diminishes even further as the chickens grow.

Free-range chickens are raised in open pastures where they forage during the day for natural foods. They return to their nesting sheds at night. As a result of their daily exercise, the chickens develop good muscle tone and are much more meaty than the farmed chickens (it is the muscle tissue of the chicken

that we eat). The chickens are treated better, and the meat is tastier, but these birds are more expensive for the consumer.

If we impose free-range standards on all chicken production, the price of chicken will sky-rocket. How important is it to you how chickens are raised? Do you care more about the availability of inexpensive chicken from the supermarket or your favourite fast-food restaurant? What is your standard for the ethical treatment of chickens? Discuss your opinions with others in the class to obtain different points of view.

Products without certification may not meet these international standards. Would you fly on a plane that did not use ISO-certified parts?

Grading

Grading is related to quality control in that graded products are checked for size and quality against fixed standards for the product category. After the product is checked, it is assigned a specific grade: Grade A is better than Grade B, Prime is better than Choice, and so on. The grade is often prominently displayed on or near the product or on the packaging so the consumer can make informed judgments about a purchase. Eggs, fruit, and vegetables are graded (Grade A, Extra Large eggs, for example). So are gasoline, meat, grain, gemstones, and lumber.

Many other products are not formally graded, but the way they are advertised and sold can indicate that the product has not met the manufacturer's own standards. Manufactured products that have slight defects are sold as "seconds." Appliances that have surface damages are sold in "scratch and dent" sales. These products will be safe to use. Frequently, the flaws are cosmetic—that is, they affect only the way the way the product looks. Many consumers take advantage of the lower prices of less-than-perfect grades to save money.

Review Questions

6. What are two stages in metal processing?
7. Name five products that are graded.
8. What is the main role of the purchasing department?
9. Briefly describe the purpose of ISO.

Keep in Mind

1. training
2. capital investment
3. investment in technology
4. new inventory systems

Improving Productivity

Have you ever needed to get a report or essay done in a very short period of time? You have probably tried to speed up on the keyboard. Did you make mistakes that slowed you down because you were trying to go too fast? That's what often happens in businesses as well. Just because a production line moves faster, it does not mean an increase in productivity.

In the News

McDonald's Corporation trains its store managers in a very special way. It operates a Hamburger University. Each year 5000 to 7000 managers from any of the 118 countries where McDonald's operates receive training here. The major goal of the university is to be sure every McDonald's manager across the globe is getting the same message and using the same processes. The managers can train their staff, but McDonald's wants to train its managers.

To do this, the company operates a 130 000-square-foot building near the McDonald's corporate headquarters in Oak Brook, Illinois. Built in 1983, Hamburger U, as it's called, offers classes in 28 languages and has 19 trainers on site who teach the fundamentals of McDonald's management systems. McDonald's has also established six satellite universities around the world. Initial training is given to new employees at 139 regional training centres scattered about the globe. When it comes to training, few companies invest as much time and energy in the process as McDonald's does.

This machine increases productivity by filling hundreds of cans of paint very quickly.

The classic television sitcom *I Love Lucy* once aired an episode in which the heroine, Lucy, had to package chocolates from a moving belt. The belt speeds up, and she cannot package fast enough. She tries to solve the problem by eating the chocolates and stuffing them in her uniform and under her hat. Obviously, speeding up the belt did not increase her productivity.

Increasing productivity consists of maintaining quality while increasing speed, increasing quality while maintaining speed, or increasing both quality and speed. For example, if employee A in a local coffee shop serves 100 people per hour, and employee B serves only 50 people per hour, employee A could be considered twice as productive as employee B.

Productivity can always be improved. A faster machine, more employees, or an upgraded inventory system will produce things faster and maintain or improve quality. But improved productivity must also not decrease profitability. New machines, employees, and inventory systems cost money. The increase in productivity must result in more profit to be important in any business.

Training

Employees are productive when they know what they are doing. Training programs are essential for improving productivity. Good trainers, like good teachers, can help employees learn how to do their job better. There are four major types of training (see Table 5.2).

Capital Investment

A new computer, a new machine, a new office building: all these things require an investment of capital, and all of them could contribute to increased productivity. The cost/benefit comparison should be considered here, however. Will the cost of the new capital good increase productivity enough to pay for itself within a fixed period of time? If it takes too long to recoup the costs, the new item will not increase profitability even though it increases productivity.

Investment in Technology

What do the following have in common: accounting software that produces instant and up-to-date product sales data in any specific territory; import software that calculates taxes, duty, and currency conversions for shipments all over the

Stretch Your Thinking

Is it possible that employee B is actually as productive as employee A? Explain.

Lucy covered in melted chocolate.

Business Fact

Many businesses try to increase productivity by encouraging customers to "upsize": to order a larger amount than they had initially planned. For instance, it takes the same amount of time to sell a large drink as it does to sell a small drink, and the large drinks are much more profitable.

Table 5.2

Four Major Types of Training

1. Initial Training

New employees often receive paid training during their first few days on the job. Although some businesses try to minimize the training period so the employee will become productive more quickly, longer training can lead to increased productivity over the long run. If the training is too short, the employee may

- get frustrated and quit;
- make many mistakes, frustrating customers and co-workers; or
- damage expensive equipment.

2. Ongoing Training

When new systems or procedures become part of the business, training time must be allocated to help employees learn the new material. Management might also conduct refresher courses in customer relations, safety, and other important ongoing aspects of the job.

3. Retraining

When an employee transfers into a different job, retraining is often needed. The training manager may use techniques similar to those used in the initial training process.

4. Specialized Training

Training that helps workers upgrade their skills is called "professional development." Courses are offered away from the normal workplace and may be provided by specialists in a particular field, sometimes at a professional conference. Specialized training can be very expensive, but often pays off in terms of new ideas and enthusiasm that can greatly increase a person's productivity.

world; Research In Motion's BlackBerry: a phone, database, Internet, text-messaging centre, and appointment calendar all in one? These products are all examples of existing information and communication technology that increases productivity. Producers can communicate with suppliers, sales representatives can provide customer service or process orders, and purchasing managers can source cheaper products anywhere in the world, instantly. Retailers know how many size large sweatshirts are needed to replace inventory sold in a store in Flin Flon, Manitoba, within minutes of when they are needed. Technology allows companies to track shipments, research the competition, explore foreign markets, and arrange inventory

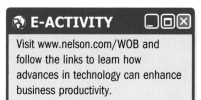

E-ACTIVITY

Visit www.nelson.com/WOB and follow the links to learn how advances in technology can enhance business productivity.

shipments to match the production schedule. Businesses that are not updating their technology are losing a major competitive edge in increased productivity.

Another way businesses can invest in applications of technology that will increase productivity is through robotics and automation. More and more production companies are using computer-controlled machinery to perform repetitive tasks. Robots require a major capital expenditure, but they provide a workforce that doesn't get sick or take vacation time, can work in conditions of extreme heat or cold, and work 24 hours a day, seven days a week, without pay.

The World of Business DVD

"Waterslides: Making a Splash"
from *The World of Business DVD*

Without the use of robotics and automation, assembly-line production of automobiles would be next to impossible.

New Inventory Systems

Several young entrepreneurs created a business based on a simple product called the Earth Buddy. The Earth Buddy was made of a leg from a pair of panty hose filled with some sawdust mixed with grass seed. The finished product had googly eyes and a painted nose and mouth. When you watered the Earth Buddy, the grass grew out of its head. It was a novelty product that was popular for a time. So popular, in fact, that the manufacturers kept running out of raw materials and had to stop production until they could get more sawdust, or panty hose, or even eyes. These entrepreneurs (who went on to found the toy company Spin Master Ltd.) learned a lesson: the importance of inventory management.

Production stops if all the raw materials are not there. Conversely, production speeds up if all the needed parts are there precisely when needed. **Just-in-time (JIT)** inventory systems coordinate suppliers, warehouse storage, and factory floor delivery so that no material is on the factory floor that won't be used up in a short space of time. Production statistics are fed from the factory's computer to the various suppliers who then know how much inventory they need to ship, and how much they must have on hand to prevent the type of inventory shortages that Earth Buddy experienced. This saves time, energy, waste, and factory space, and increases productivity a great deal. Factory workers no longer have to look for the inventory they need to make the product or their assigned portion of it. The just-in-time inventory system is all about having the right material, at the right time, at the right place, and in the right amount.

Review Questions

10. What are the four types of training?

11. State one way the following could improve productivity in a bakery:

    a) capital investment

    b) investment in new technology

    c) just-in-time inventory systems

CHAPTER REVIEW

Knowledge

1. List and describe briefly four ways to increase productivity.

2. Provide an example of each of the following:
   a) a capital good
   b) a product that's graded
   c) intellectual property
   d) professional development
   e) a primary industry

3. What is JIT?

Thinking

4. What would you need to consider if you were the purchaser of your company's office supplies?

5. Find on the Internet a "management seminar" for an industry that interests you. Describe it briefly.

6. Name five capital goods that every McDonald's has.

7. Using the Internet, research both a positive and a negative opinion about outsourcing. Write a report, summarizing each opinion briefly and providing your opinion. Be sure to cite your sources.

8. Describe two ways you could be more productive in your job or at school.

9. A large Ontario bakery uses 10 million kilograms of flour each year. The purchasing agent has two possible sources of supply. The first is nearby and sells flour at 87¢ per kilogram. The other supplier is in Alberta and sells flour for 75¢ cents per kilogram. It costs $80 per metric tonne to ship flour from Alberta. Which supplier should get the contract? What is the total savings to the bakery?

Communication

10. Create a mind map that traces the production of a pair of running shoes back to natural resources.

11. Visit Industry Canada online. Find *Company Directories Organized by Industry Sector.* Use this website to find a specific source for each of the following products:
    - dyes and pigments
    - dental equipment
    - stainless steel products

    Describe one of the specific sources you found using the following:
    - location
    - brief list of some of the company's products
    - short description of the company

Application

12. Using the same brand and container size for each product, find three separate prices for ketchup, cereal, and ice cream in local grocery stores. Which store had the overall best prices?

13. Visit and describe briefly two websites that provide information you could use in a soft drink bottling business. How would you use the information?

14. What's new at Research In Motion? Look up the company on the Internet, and describe briefly one of its new products.

15. Using a local business as an example, discuss in detail both the factors of production and production processes the business uses.

Team Activity

Team Goal: Manufacturing a product for profit

Team Assignment: Making Lunch

- Make a food product to sell at lunch in your school (pizza, fudge, popcorn, cookies, and so on). Be sure to check your school's policies and restrictions on food due to food allergies before you begin.

- Keep track of all the costs of the raw materials used in manufacturing your product. Assume a $25 cost for labour, rent, and equipment.

- Sell your product and record the revenue (money you collect). Be sure to sell out of your product, even if you have to sell it for a lot less at the end of lunch.

- Deduct the costs of labour, equipment, rent, and raw materials from the revenue to determine your profit.

The team that makes the most profit wins the competition for this round.

Portfolio

Illustrate what several of the businesses in your selected industry produce and how they do it. Many corporate sites allow you to contact the company, so you could e-mail them regarding your portfolio project. You could ask for annual reports and promotional material. These would make useful additions to your portfolio. You could also visit their corporate websites and download information.

Be sure to explain and illustrate all the factors of production and the production processes used in your industry. Which businesses in your industrial sector are most productive? Perhaps you could make suggestions as to how some businesses could increase productivity.

Reflect on Your Learning

Choose two of the people you named in the Before You Begin activity at the start of this chapter. Describe the factors of production and the production process they use to produce their product or service.

Nokia

If you own a cellular telephone made by Nokia, it might come as a surprise to learn that the roots of your wireless communication date back to 1865, when a mining engineer by the name of Fredrik Idestam founded a wood pulp mill in southwestern Finland. In fact, the evolution and foundation of Nokia Corporation extends beyond the lineage of just one business and is actually the result of a multi-industry merger that took place in 1967. So, how did such a high-tech mobile phone company arise from a simple forest industry business?

Nokia Corporation was formed when it partnered with two other Finnish companies, Finnish Rubber Works Ltd. and Finnish Cable Works. Nokia then gained its foothold in both the telecommunications and electronics market by purchasing other companies that were already well established in information technology. Although Nokia Corporation was initially involved in the production of computers, monitors, and televisions, the business has since diverged and has been focusing its attention primarily on telecommunications since the beginning of the 1990s.

Through its dedication and commitment to mobile communications, Nokia Corporation has become the world leader in the mobility industry. By the end of

Nokia has become the world leader in the mobility industry.

Nokia is able to quickly penetrate emerging markets.

2005, Nokia was operating 14 manufacturing facilities located in eight countries around the world, with research and development plants in 11 countries. The net sales generated by Nokia in 2005 were EUR 34 191 million, when employees of the company numbered more than 58 000.

Nokia's high-ranking position in global technology has been largely due to its joint ventures with various companies, which have provided Nokia with a competitive edge. Specifically, such multiple partnerships, especially in the areas of manufacturing, and research and development, have allowed Nokia to penetrate new and emerging markets more quickly, and have been effective in establishing innovative lines of production.

For example, in 2001 Nokia and the Finnish business Sampo together established Meridea Financial Software. Where Nokia's background is in the field of mobility, Sampo's expertise is in the realm of finance and banking. Together, the two companies work to share their knowledge. They now provide software to financial institutions, enabling customers to access financial services through mobile devices such as the Internet and telephones.

Nokia's products have won numerous awards, including the 2003 Frost & Sullivan Award for Product Innovation. The award is presented once a year to a company that has been innovative in launching a broad range of new products and technologies.

But not every product that Nokia produces is original. In 2006, Nokia launched, in Canada, a wireless BlackBerry-like device called the E62. The difference between the two products, however, is that the E62 is aimed to appeal to a wide audience, from "soccer moms to CEOs," says Paul Chapple, the general manager for Nokia Products Ltd. Canada. Although Nokia is clearly above its competitors in the realm of telecommunications, only time will tell whether the E62, or a version thereof, will be successful enough to give them the same lead in the wireless data market.

QUESTIONS

1. Provide one explanation for how Nokia Corporation has attained its leading position in the market of mobile telecommunications.

2. Explain the unique history and evolution of Nokia Corporation.

6 Human Resources

SPECIFIC EXPECTATIONS

After completing this chapter, you will be able to

- describe the functions of human resource management

- identify key employability skills
- describe a variety of business career paths
- identify the rights and responsibilities of employees and employers

KWA Partners (Rob Notman)

When you arrive for work, Rob Notman may be the last guy you want to see waiting in your office to meet you! That's because your company has probably just hired his firm, KWA Partners, to help you through a job loss. Even though that may not be the best news you get that day, the services being offered to you, commonly called outplacement services, may be one of the best employee benefits you have.

Outplacement services (also called career transition services) are designed to help individuals cope with the trauma of job loss and provide practical advice and techniques to move on to new careers. The services are paid for by the organization doing the downsizing and can include everything from career assessment to networking advice and interviewing practice.

Not all companies provide this service, but over the last 30 years, it has become a "best practice" in many sectors of the economy. Organizations that offer outplacement counselling can benefit substantially by being good corporate citizens and providing a benefit that decreases the stress somewhat for the remaining staff. Firms may also avoid high legal costs from lawsuits brought against them by angry ex-employees.

The true success of Rob's firm, however, is based on personal service: helping people make realistic and rewarding decisions regarding career paths in today's complex marketplace. Today, KWA Partners is part of a group of affiliated companies that is the largest Canadian-owned operation of its kind.

Rob Notman did not design this career based on his educational background (B.Sc. in Biology) or his first employment choices. This career just happened. His first 20 years in the workforce, however, allowed him to recognize the "perfect job" when it came along. "It really combined my desire to work with a variety of people, my proven strengths in this area, and the opportunity to motivate others, while making my mark," Rob says. Knowing your weaknesses and what you don't enjoy doing is as important as making the right career move, according to Rob.

The success of Rob Notman's business is based on personal service.

QUESTIONS

1. Why would you not want to see Rob Notman waiting for you at work?

2. What are "outplacement services"?

3. How did Rob Notman get into this career?

Keep in Mind

1. the labour market
2. determining the need for a new employee
3. looking for the right employee
4. the application process and the interview
5. job training
6. keeping good employees
7. departures, dismissals, and retirements
8. handling compensation
9. health and safety

Before You Begin

Make a list of the skills and abilities you would bring to a job. As you study this chapter, update your list as you discover more things to include.

A kitchen porter unloads a delivery.

The Functions of Human Resources Management

Have you ever applied for a job in a large firm like Wal-Mart or Loblaws? No doubt someone in the human resources department (HR) read your application. If you got a job interview, someone from HR interviewed you. If you got hired, the HR person hired you, set up your training program, and arranged for you to get paid (the important part!).

Managers of small businesses perform these human resources functions every day. Most large companies, however, have a **human resources department** that is responsible for coordinating all activities involving the company's employees. Human resources managers study the local labour market to discover where new employees will come from (for example, community colleges, local high schools, universities, business competitors), decide when a new employee is required, and determine what skills this employee should have. The human resources department searches for applicants, conducts interviews, and selects the best candidate. HR also sets up training programs for both new employees and employees who need new skills, administers payroll, creates programs that will help retain good employees, and handles worker transitions.

The Labour Market

The **labour market** is where employers (buyers of skills) meet employees (sellers of skills). Employers look at the labour market to determine what occupations and skills are available, what education and training is provided in the community, and what the economic conditions are in the area. Employees look at the labour market to find potential employers, determine the types of skills in demand, and find out what the employment rate is in the community. Both the employer and employee want to know what wage rates are offered to employees and what kinds of jobs will be popular in the future. Predictions about jobs are called **occupational forecasts**.

The following scenario demonstrates the labour market in action: The Bread Basket plans to open a bakery in a small New Brunswick city. It needs labour that falls into several categories. It needs dishwashers and kitchen help. These jobs are considered **unskilled labour** because little training is required.

It needs cashiers. A cashier position falls into the category of **semiskilled labour** because it requires some instruction. The bakery also needs cake decorators. Cake decorating is an example of **skilled labour** because employees require training from an educational institution or through previous employment. It must also hire **professional labour**—highly trained people with specific occupations, such as accountants and electricians. The most important professional that The Bread Basket needs, however, is a baker. The person hired must have work experience and be skilled at baking bread and desserts. Because the city's community college offers a program for bakers, there are likely trained bakers in the area. But bakeries are popular here, which may mean that the good bakers are already working.

A cashier at a café accepts payment from a customer.

When Emily Green graduates from the community college program, she notices a want ad for a baker in the local paper. She applies for the job. The interview goes well and The Bread Basket offers Emily the position, with a starting salary of $450 a week. Emily knows two other graduates—one works locally for $400 a week; the other works in a larger city and earns $600 a week. Emily, who was recognized by her college for her superior baking skills and who knows that good bakers are in short supply, asks for $500 a week. She also asks the bakery to develop a career plan that will provide for her promotion and growth. The bakery agrees and hires Emily.

In the News

In 2005, Statistics Canada noted that many labour market trends established in the 1990s had been reversed in the years since 2000. These changes included the growth and resurgence of construction and resource jobs, especially in rural areas. At the same time, more and more factory jobs disappeared, notably in the high-tech and auto industries found almost exclusively in large cities. In the service sector, the number of computer services remained about the same while jobs in public services, such as education and health care, were restored after cuts in the 1990s. Employment in multinational resource companies and in government grew. Meanwhile, older workers increasingly supplied these growing demands for labour.

Recent studies have found that the trends have remained the same. In particular, 2005 was a banner year for the resource sector and construction. These gains were reflected in stronger employment growth in rural areas and in large firms, with older workers continuing to fill the bulk of new jobs. Still, job growth outstripped the labour force, pushing joblessness to a 30-year low and boosting real wages. Another change was that full-time positions accounted for most of the job growth, especially in Alberta and British Columbia, where labour shortages emerged.

This cake decorator skillfully puts the ornamentation on a freshly baked cake.

The Importance of Productivity

What deal is made between the employer and employee? In the case of The Bread Basket, the employer offers to pay Emily to perform specific tasks—to bake bread, bagels, and pies. It agrees to pay her $500 a week to do these tasks. Although the deal does not state that Emily must produce a certain quantity and quality of goods, the bakery wants her to be a productive worker. If Emily makes 1000 items during a five-day week, the average labour cost for each item is 50¢ ($500 ÷ 1000). If she makes more items at the same salary, the average cost per item goes down and the bakery makes more profit. The Bread Basket, then, wants Emily to increase productivity.

But Emily feels she is already working very hard. The ovens are extremely hot, and she wants one more 15-minute break each day. This extra break could mean the number of items she bakes will decrease, and the cost of each item will increase. The bakery would make less profit. Clearly, the bakery and the baker need to come to an agreement about the number of items that can be expected, or find a way to use time more efficiently, in order to produce the same amount of items in less time.

The Importance of Skilled Labour

It is important for businesses to hire people who can do the job or be trained to do the job. The more skill an employee already has, the less a business has to invest in training. Skilled employees can mean savings for a business because they usually provide a better product or service. For example, if its bread is better than the competition's bread, The Bread Basket can charge more for its product. The bakery's reputation improves and the number of customers increases. A business must balance the quality of product or service it would like to provide with the amount of money needed to hire the skilled labour necessary to attain that quality.

The Importance of a Positive Attitude

Happy employees often make more or better products than unhappy ones. When Emily is grumpy and tired from the heat, her productivity declines. As she struggles to finish the day and get home to her air-conditioned apartment, she works at a slower pace and the quality of her baked goods suffers. Emily's mood also upsets other workers and affects the whole bakery. Giving her an extra break, air-conditioning the kitchen, and letting her go home early on particularly hot days are a few of the things the employer could do to keep Emily happy—and more productive.

> **The World of Business** DVD
>
> **"Unions Battle Wal-Mart Effect"**
> from *The World of Business DVD*

Determining the Need for a New Employee

One more thing The Bread Basket could do to keep Emily happy is to hire another kitchen staff member to assist her. The Bread Basket may not be able to afford another staff member, however, depending on its staffing budget. Most well-run businesses develop a staffing plan well in advance of actually needing the staff, to avoid hiring under pressure.

In medium-sized and large companies, the human resources managers predict their company's personnel needs. They determine how many employees will be needed when a company first opens and how many additional people will have to be hired if the company expands. They can forecast their company's **employee turnover**, the rate at which employees leave the firm voluntarily either for another job or to retire. They can also predict how their company's personnel needs will be affected by new technologies, changes in hiring practices, and shifts in economic conditions.

> **Stretch Your Thinking**
>
> What types of businesses do you think have the highest employee turnover? What factors might be responsible for this high turnover?

When a vacancy occurs, the human resources department tries to hire a qualified person from within the company to fill the position. This usually involves checking employee records. The records should show length of service, skill level, training received, and performance evaluations. If there are no suitable candidates within the company, the human resources department hires a person from outside. A business that is expanding or just starting out will also have to hire people from outside.

To better understand this process, imagine a local computer company with a staff of 20 people. The business grows rapidly, and it soon needs someone to head its new industrial sales division. One of its programmers knows the needs of the industrial market very well, and the company promotes her to head this division. But the new sales division also needs salespeople. No other employees can be moved from their current jobs without creating problems, so the company decides to hire from outside.

Looking for the Right Employee

The method a human resources manager uses to find an employee depends on the qualifications required for the job. A company may

- advertise in newspapers, journals, and magazines
- recruit on university and college campuses

Job opportunities advertised in a local newspaper

- post the job on Job Bank at the federal government's employment centre (**Human Resources Development Canada** [HRDC]) website
- post the job on an online recruiting site such as Workopolis
- post the job on the company website
- use high-school or university co-op programs
- hire an employee search firm (often called a **headhunter**)
- use an **employee referral program**
- search the files of recent job applicants

A computer company looking for a sales representative, for example, may place an advertisement in the classified ads section of local and national newspapers—most people looking for jobs check the newspapers for job opportunities. An ad in a computer-trade magazine will also reach the targeted labour market. A job posting on the business's website or an online recruiting site will attract people who regularly use the Internet. An employee referral program may be an effective way to find qualified workers. Many human resources managers feel current employees have the best connections to people working in similar jobs at other companies. It might make sense for the computer company to hire the services of an employee search firm that specializes in the computer industry. Campus recruiting is not the best option—although many university and college graduates possess the required computer skills, most lack sales experience. High-school co-op students also lack the needed experience. HRDC tends not to be a good source of highly qualified people in the computer industry. Because this is a new position within the company, applicants who recently applied for other positions probably aren't qualified for this one, so their applications won't be reconsidered.

The Application Process and the Interview

The human resources department receives submissions from hopeful applicants. These submissions often include a completed application form, a cover letter that asks for an interview, and a resumé listing the applicant's education, experience, interests, and abilities.

Ultimately, the business decides to hire or not hire an applicant based on an interview conducted by the human resources manager or another member of the human resources department. Usually, the manager of the department where the new employee will work also attends the interview. The interview team meets the applicant and asks questions to determine the applicant's personality, work habits, values, interests, and other qualities. After all the interviews have been conducted, the interview team rates each applicant. The team often conducts several rounds of interviews to narrow its choice. An applicant may be asked to come in for a second or even a third interview. The final step before hiring an employee is to conduct a reference check. The interviewer calls the applicant's references to verify the information in the application or to ask further questions.

Interview Tips

Here are several tips that can help whenever you have an interview for a job.

- Dress appropriately for the job. Don't be too formal or too casual.

- Go alone. Don't take friends or family with you.

Frank and Ernest

© 2004 Thaves. Reprinted with permission. Newspaper dist. by NEA, Inc.

A job interview being conducted by an employee from human resources

- Make sure you know when the interview will take place and how to find the location.

- Plan to arrive a few minutes early. Be sure to leave extra time in case you run into any problems with traffic or other delays on the way.

- When you arrive, take time to focus and calm down.

- When you meet the interviewer, give a firm handshake. Make eye contact and smile during the introduction.

- Be pleasant and enthusiastic, but avoid talking too much. Don't say more than you're asked to say.

- Listen carefully to each question and give a brief but complete answer.

- Try to be aware of your body language, facial expressions, and tone of voice.

- Remember to thank the interviewer at the end of the interview and to reaffirm your interest in the job.

Job Training

The human resources department coordinates orientation and training for all new employees. During **orientation**, new employees meet other employees and tour the workplace. The department introduces the business's policies on compensation, work hours, benefits, rules of behaviour, dress codes, health and safety procedures, and so on. New employees receive training on equipment they will use. Many companies also provide ongoing training, particularly in new technology, software, and equipment. Some arrange motivational presentations and provide training in stress management, increasing productivity, and management skills. These businesses believe in keeping employees happy, well qualified, and up to date in their skills.

Keeping Good Employees

Employers invest a great deal of time and expense to search for, hire, and train new employees. It makes sense, then, for employers to try to retain productive and valued employees. High employee turnover can result in costly problems. Not only must the search for new employees begin again, but employees are less productive during training because they are just learning how to do their jobs. As you've learned, lower productivity means significantly lower profit.

In a competitive labour market, businesses try to attract experienced employees, often from competitors. Some companies now go well beyond the usual compensation methods and offer special benefits, known as **perks**. Casual dress codes are more common. Some companies provide daycare services; others let employees set up playpens in their offices. Because fitness programs have positive effects on employee attitudes, more businesses offer on-site gym facilities. Companies arrange for massage therapists to make office calls. Special food is ordered for the staff kitchen. Reading rooms that look and feel like living rooms are arranged. And if you need a rest, some businesses even have nap rooms.

Colleagues take the company's private jet to a business meeting.

Departures, Dismissals, and Retirements

All employees eventually leave the business for which they work. The human resources department tries to make their transition easier, regardless of its cause. An employer who helps an employee make a smooth transition protects the reputation of the firm and maintains a good relationship with the employee.

Departures

Some employees leave their jobs voluntarily. Their departure could be based on personal or family needs, job dissatisfaction, or a better opportunity elsewhere. The employer can help in the transition by providing a letter of recommendation for the employee or by agreeing to act as a positive reference. The human resources department can arrange exit counselling. During the **exit interview**, an employee can discuss his or her future goals and make sure that leaving is the best way to achieve these goals. The employer should ensure that there is no ill will. The company may also ask departing employees for their opinions about how the work environment could be improved. Since the employees are leaving, they may be prepared to provide honest, valuable feedback.

Dismissals

Sometimes, employees leave a job involuntarily: A business decides that an employee is not fulfilling duties as required, and dismisses him or her. Prior to this point, however, employers record in an employee's personnel file any problems or concerns that might lead to dismissal: for example, lateness, absenteeism, or poor work habits. Many firms conduct corrective interviews. During a **corrective interview**, the employer discusses problems with the employee and, together, both parties make a plan for improvement. All conversations with the employee during the corrective interview should be summarized and signed as accurate by both the employer and the employee. After a set period of time, the employee must show improvement or face dismissal.

Companies also dismiss employees to cut back expenses. This type of dismissal is called **employee layoff**. Companies with unionized employees usually lay off workers in order of **seniority**. This means employees with fewer years of service are let go first. In non-unionized companies, the business usually lays off the employees who are least essential to its day-to-day operations.

Ethical, Moral & Legal Considerations

Which questions are allowed on an application form?

Can they ask about...
- gender
- religion
- race
- sexual orientation
- disability
- birthplace
- marital status
- ages of children
- number of children

Potential employers are not allowed, by law, to determine any of the above information before the interview except your name, nor are they allowed to ask about these points during an interview (although some characteristics would be obvious). The reason for this is to prevent discrimination in hiring.

Stretch Your Thinking

Why is it important for a business to document steps taken to improve an employee's performance?

Many companies provide a **severance package** to a dismissed employee. This package often contains a final payment, which usually depends on the amount of time the employee has worked for the business. For example, an employee might receive one week's salary for every year of service. The company may also provide **outplacement counselling** to ease the employee's transition by helping him or her search for a new job.

Retirement

Retirement normally occurs when an employee voluntarily withdraws from the labour market. Often, retirees have reached a certain age, sometimes as early as 55, when they qualify for a pension. A **pension** gives the employee income once he or she no longer works for the company. Throughout the employee's time at the company, both the employer and the employee contribute to the pension. Some people retire from one job and use their pension to start their own business. Because the Canadian population is living longer and remaining healthy, retirement may soon become just another career move for many people.

Handling Compensation

The most important consideration for employees is usually the amount of money they are paid, or **compensation**. The payroll office or department calculates the amount owing to the employees, after deductions for income tax, employment insurance, and other things, and makes sure the employee gets paid on the due date. Payroll is part of human resources.

Because the labour market is competitive, compensation is affected by supply and demand. For example, if many companies need staff with high-tech training but few people in the job market have this training, technology skills will be highly priced. The greater the demand for a particular skill, the higher the compensation. Compensation can take many forms.

Hourly Wages

One of the most common payment methods, especially for part-time employees, is the hourly wage. Rates range from the minimum wage paid to unskilled or semiskilled labour to hundreds of dollars an hour for skilled or professional labour. **Minimum wage** is the lowest hourly wage an employer can legally pay an employee. Hourly wage employees will receive an increased rate of pay if they work **overtime**, which means working more than regular work hours or on holidays.

Salary

A **salary** is a fixed amount of money that employees receive on a regular schedule, such as weekly or monthly. Often, it is expressed as a yearly amount. A business advertising for an accountant, for example, may offer $57 000 a year. Salaried jobs often do not specify how many hours employees will have to work, but if employees work more hours, no overtime is paid.

Salary plus Commission

In some sales jobs, especially retail, employers pay the employee a percentage of his or her sales. This **commission** is usually quite small, and is in addition to salary or hourly wages. Commission is an **incentive** that encourages employees to work harder. For example, an employee earning a 1 percent commission earns an extra $30 if he or she sells $3000 in goods. A higher commission usually means the salesperson is paid a lower salary or hourly wage.

Straight Commission

Straight commission is a form of compensation that is based solely on the employee's sales. Most often, people who sell to wholesale businesses or large industries, as well as people who sell high-priced items such as cars and houses, are paid straight commission. Employees can make a great deal of money from straight commission if they are talented salespeople, but if sales drop or if they have to take days off because of illness, they may earn little or no income.

Stretch Your Thinking

Check the classified ads in your local newspaper to find salaries for different kinds of jobs.

Figure 6.1 Forms of Compensation

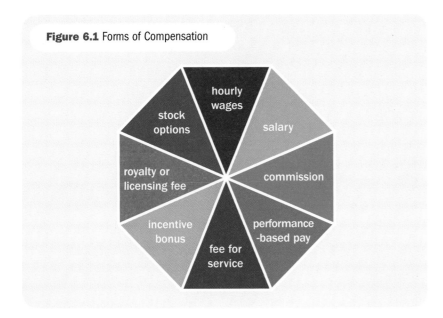

Incentive Bonus

Many businesses offer a **bonus**, or reward, for good performance. Sometimes, this type of reward is called variable pay. Companies set performance goals (also called **sales quotas** or targets) for each employee. If the employee meets the goal, he or she receives extra cash, a trip, a car, or something else of value.

Performance-based Pay

Performance-based pay is calculated on the amount of a particular product that an employee can make. Also known as **piecework**, this form of compensation is widely used in the clothing industry. Piecework rewards skill and speed: The more products employees can make for the business, the more money they can earn for themselves. However, performance-based pay can also lead to severe abuses. In parts of the world where poverty is widespread some employers offer very little compensation for piecework. In some cases, factories employ children, who will work for almost nothing. Some piecework factories become known as **sweatshops**. Not only are wages low, but employees are forced to work in unsafe and unhealthy conditions.

On the other hand, many reputable businesses use piecework. It allows employees to work at home with their own equipment—for example, a sewing machine, oven, or computer—and to set their own pace. It also allows people with family responsibilities to earn money at home.

The World of Business DVD

"Offshoring 'High Anxiety'"
from *The World of Business DVD*

Women in Asia at work in a sweatshop

Fee for Service

Construction, catering, and cleaning businesses often receive a fee-for-service form of compensation. They estimate how much it will cost in time and materials to do a job, and then build in an additional fee to ensure they earn a profit. With this estimate, the person who hires them—their employer—knows how much to expect to pay for the whole job. To prevent misunderstandings, the employer and employee sign a written contract. This contract usually offers some kind of guarantee and states the costs, time of completion, materials required, and so on.

Royalty or Licensing Fee

If you write a book, record a song, or have an idea you can sell, you may receive a **licensing fee** or **royalty**. Both terms refer to a payment for the use of ideas and creativity. For example, imagine you have created a successful cartoon character and that a T-shirt business wants to put your character on its product. You could rent your character to the company, and it could pay you a portion of the sale price from each T-shirt sold. Although the percentage is often small (between 1 percent and 5 percent), you don't risk losing any money if the T-shirts don't sell. The company that licenses your idea (**the licensee**) assumes that risk. In other cases, you might be paid a fixed licensing fee. You receive the same amount of money regardless of how many T-shirts the company sells. That would be to your advantage if the company does not sell a lot of T-shirts, but you might lose out if sales are high. In other cases, you might be paid a fixed licensing fee as well as a percentage of sales.

Stock Options

Businesses often offer shares as a form of compensation to attract desirable employees. The business gives employees an opportunity to buy company shares at a lower-than-market price. These shares are called **stock options**. Employees benefit from stock options because they can purchase the company's stock at a preset price for a given period of time, even if the stock's market price increases during that time. Companies benefit from issuing stock options because employees who own part of the company often work harder and stay longer than those who do not have an ownership stake.

Jessie's Catering is an example of a business that receives a fee-for-service form of compensation.

Stretch Your Thinking

If a company wanted to license one of your ideas or creations, would you prefer a fee based on percentage of sales or a fixed licensing fee? Explain your answer.

Health and Safety

Federal and provincial laws require businesses to provide and maintain a healthy and safe work environment. Besides their legal responsibility to do so, it makes sense for businesses to provide this kind of environment. A sick or injured employee has to take time off work and is unproductive during that period. An employee injured on the job may also take the employer to court. Businesses that focus on health and safety also create positive employee attitudes.

Health

Businesses suffer a double loss when an employee becomes ill. First of all, they lose the worker's skill and productivity. Second, many businesses provide **sick pay**: They continue to pay full wages to the employee while he or she is absent due to illness. Because businesses benefit from healthy employees, many companies offer **wellness programs**. These programs promote the physical and emotional well-being of employees and help reduce absenteeism. The more provisions an employer makes for employees' well-being, the more likely the employees will remain healthy and productive.

Table 6.1

Health and Wellness Programs	
Health Area	**Wellness Programs**
fitness programs	lunch-hour exercise programs; fitness-club memberships; fitness breaks instead of coffee breaks
antismoking programs	awareness campaigns; support for quitting; "quitting" or "terminating" bonuses
addiction treatment	paid time off for treatment; space and time for counselling programs; emotional support to addicted workers and their families
job stress	planned social activities and special events; relaxed dress code; flexible hours; working from home; job sharing (two or more employees share the same job and split the salary)
counselling	financial, marriage, and bereavement (loss of a loved one) counselling; job-related or extension courses; leave for further education; paid registration at conferences; professional development opportunities
other benefits	paid vacations; sick leave; bereavement and personal days (moving, errands, child or elder care, and so on); employee discounts; company car; health, dental, and optical plans; group life insurance, long-term disability, and accidental death benefits; daycare; profit sharing; expense accounts; free parking

Safety

Employers in Canada are legally required to maintain a safe workplace. Part Two of the *Canada Labour Code* and various provincial acts govern occupational health and safety. This legislation is intended to prevent accidents, injury, and disease related to employment activities. According to the legislation, employees have the right to

- be informed about known or foreseeable hazards in the workplace

- identify and resolve job-related problems in safety and health

- refuse dangerous work if they have reasonable cause to believe that a situation constitutes a danger

Some foreseeable hazards involve the use of equipment. The employer must ensure that all equipment is safe and that employees who use it have the proper training. The potential dangers of some types of equipment—table saws, for example—are obvious. But even office equipment can be harmful. Using a computer improperly can lead to a very painful injury called **carpal tunnel syndrome**. In its most severe form, this condition can cause crippling pain that shoots from the hand, up the arm, and as far as the shoulder.

Employers should also make certain that all dangerous chemicals and toxic waste are properly stored, and that employees know how to safely handle these substances. First-aid equipment must be available, and employees should be trained in first-aid procedures. The workplace should be free of hazards, such as unsafe electrical connections, slippery floors, and sharp edges. Employees should also be instructed in proper lifting techniques to avoid back injury. (Always bend at the knees and lift with the legs, rather than the back.) The workplace should be kept clean, with nothing left in the aisles or on the floor that might cause others to trip.

If an employee is injured on the job, a workers' compensation board pays the employee while he or she is recovering, provides additional medical coverage, and may arrange and pay for rehabilitation. The employer contributes premiums for this form of occupational insurance. If workers are injured on the job, it becomes very expensive for the business to hire and train replacement employees. The reputation of the business also suffers, making it hard for the company to attract good employees. If a particular business has a high number of injuries, the government may also investigate and lay charges if violations of safety rules are found.

Review Questions

1. What are the three purposes of a job interview?

2. List and give an example of the four types of labour in the labour market.

3. What are five functions of human resources management?

4. List and describe briefly five types of compensation. Ask several working people you know what type of compensation they receive. Which type is most typical, do you think?

5. Why do companies offer health and wellness programs to their employees?

6. What is the difference between a severance package and a pension?

Keep in Mind

1. academic skills
2. personal management skills
3. teamwork skills

Key Employability Skills

Are you employable? Would you hire you? What skills do you bring to an employer that he or she will pay for? The Conference Board of Canada has developed an employability skills checklist that outlines the academic skills, personal management skills, and teamwork skills that human resources managers across Canada have selected as the most important skills new employees can possess. With these skills, you are much more employable; without them you are much less so. How many of them do you have now?

Academic Skills

These skills provide the basic foundation to get, keep, and progress on a job and to achieve your best results. Canadian employers need a person who can communicate, think, and learn.

Communicate

To communicate well, you need to

- understand and speak the languages in which business is conducted

- listen to understand and to learn

- read, comprehend, and use written materials, including graphs, charts, and displays

- write effectively in the languages in which business is conducted

Think

Thinking involves a variety of mental skills. You need to know how to

- think critically and act logically to evaluate situations, solve problems, and make decisions

- understand and solve problems involving mathematics and use the results

- use technology, instruments, tools, and information systems effectively

- access and apply specialized knowledge from various fields (for example, skilled trades, technology, physical sciences, arts and social sciences)

Learn

Learning doesn't end the day you graduate from school. To succeed in your chosen line of work, you will need to continue to learn for the rest of your working life. You can do this by learning from others at your place of business, upgrading your skills and knowledge, and taking seminars offered by your employer. You might even return to school at some point!

Personal Management Skills

What are the skills, attitudes, and behaviours that will help you get a job, keep it, and achieve the best results of which you're capable? Canadian employers need a person who can demonstrate the following:

Positive Attitudes and Behaviours

- self-esteem and confidence

- honesty, integrity, and personal ethics

- a positive attitude toward learning, growth, and personal health

- initiative, energy, and persistence to get the job done

What language other than English can you speak? How will that help you in business?

Why did the language spoken by Chinese immigrants to Canada gradually shift from Cantonese to Mandarin?

If you were going to learn Chinese for business, would you learn Cantonese or Mandarin? Explain.

Responsibility

- the ability to set goals and priorities in work and personal life

- the ability to plan and manage time, money, and other resources to achieve goals

- accountability for actions taken

- adaptability

- a positive attitude toward change

- the ability to identify and suggest new ideas to get the job done—creativity

Teamwork Skills

Teamwork skills are those skills you need to work with others on a job and to achieve the best results. Almost all jobs require employees to work together, co-operate to achieve the firm's common goals, and get along with their co-workers. Canadian employers need a person who

- works well with others

- understands and contributes to the organization's goals

- understands and works within the culture of the group

- plans and makes decisions with others and supports the outcomes

In the News

Carson Hom's family has run a thriving fortune cookie and almond cookie company in Los Angeles County for 35 years. For much of that time, it was a business that required two languages: Cantonese, to communicate with employees and the Chinese restaurants that bought the cookies, and English, to deal with health inspectors, suppliers, and accountants.

But when Hom, 30, decided to start his own food-import company, he learned that this bilingualism wasn't enough anymore. He checked out the competition at a Chinese products fair in the San Gabriel Valley and found that he couldn't get much further than "hello" in conversing with vendors.

"I can't communicate," said Hom, whose parents are from Hong Kong. "Everyone around used to speak Cantonese. Now everyone is speaking Mandarin."

Cantonese, a sharp dialect full of slang and exaggerated expressions, was never the dominant language of China. But it came to dominate the Chinatowns of North America because the first immigrants came from the Cantonese-speaking southern province of Guangdong, where China first opened its ports to foreigners centuries ago.

It is also the chief language of Hong Kong, the vital trading and financial centre that became China's link to the West.

But over the last three decades, waves of Mandarin-speaking mainland Chinese and Taiwanese immigrants have diluted the influence of both the Cantonese language and the pioneering Cantonese families who ran Chinatowns for years.

- respects the thoughts and opinions of others in the group
- exercises "give and take" to achieve group results
- seeks a team approach as appropriate
- leads where appropriate, mobilizing the group for high performance

Review Questions

7. Name one employability skill you are sure you have. How would you demonstrate or prove that you have it during a job interview?

8. What is one employability skill you lack? What would you say about this skill gap if you were asked about it in a job interview?

Business Careers

So, what do you want to be when you grow up? Your answer today is likely quite different than the answer you gave when you first were asked this question as a six- or seven-year-old. Professional careers in medicine, law, or education provide good salaries and an exciting working environment. Home construction, plumbing, electrical work, and other trades are also popular career choices. But you have decided to take a business course (which is almost halfway over if you are reading Chapter 6). Perhaps you will select a career in business. There are lots from which to choose.

Keep in Mind

1. general business
2. accounting careers
3. consulting careers
4. entrepreneurship
5. financial careers
6. human resources careers
7. marketing careers
8. personal selling careers

General Business

You can start a career in business this week, if you wish. A high-school education is usually the minimum job requirement, but there are many entry-level jobs in businesses that can provide part-time work for you to do while still in school. General business careers provide a good living for hundreds of thousands of people who work as waiters, bartenders, secretaries, office clerks, drivers, and warehouse workers (to name a few). These entry-level jobs in business can lead to more responsible positions. However, many people enjoy the work they do and do not want the extra responsibility.

Accounting Careers

There are tax accountants, management accountants, even forensic accountants, all of whom work with income and expenses, assets and liabilities, and the financial records of businesses or individuals. All professional accountants must be certified (e.g., Certified Accountants [CA], Certified General Accountants [CGA], and Certified Management Accountants [CMA]), which means that after your four-year business degree, and two or three years working in an accountancy office, you get to write a very tough certification exam. If you pass, you can call yourself an accountant (see Chapter 9 for more information).

Consulting Careers

Consultants are people whom businesses and individuals pay for advice and expertise. Consultants know more than most people about a specific topic. Business consultants, for example, help people with management issues, marketing problems, public relations, and international trade, among other things. To become a consultant requires that clients believe you can solve a problem for them. You do not have to have any specific educational background, but you do need to have a great deal of knowledge. Consultants usually have had proven success in a business field as well as a good reputation in that field.

Entrepreneurship

You could always start your own business. Many people do, with varying degrees of success. Entrepreneurs need a lot of specific characteristics and skills (see Chapter 10) and a lot of capital. But if you're successful in this area, it can mean billions of dollars. The richest, most financially successful people in the entire world are entrepreneurs, many started out without much other than a really good idea and lots of intelligence. Neither Ray Kroc, who started the McDonald's restaurant chain, nor Dave Thomas, founder of Wendy's, completed high school.

Financial Careers

Bankers, stockbrokers, and money managers all make money looking after other people's assets. A financial career requires a business degree, and often an MBA. People in these financial industries work very hard under a great deal of pressure, but can make a great deal of money. You need to love working with figures and have nerves of steel to work in this sector.

When choosing a career, you can consider whether you prefer to work indoors, for example, in an accounting office...

...or outside like this environmental engineer who is taking samples for testing.

Bank tellers, loan officers, and financial planners also have careers in finance that are not as stressful. You can select many of these career paths right after completing a community college program or obtaining a university degree. The financial institution will train you on the job.

Human Resources Careers

This chapter has already outlined some of the positions required by a human resources department in a large corporation. You can take courses in human resources management at a community college or at some Canadian universities (York, Athabasca, and Royal Roads, for example).

Marketing Careers

Marketing provides some very exciting career paths. Advertising, promotions, publicity, packaging, and event planning all require special community college or university degrees and a great deal of creativity. You need an ability with words or a strong artistic sense to be able to create material that promotes products and services so they are noticed above the sights and sounds of all the other marketing efforts out there.

Retail marketing careers require a community college background and on-the-job training. Retail positions are an exciting way to learn about specific product lines. Management training programs provide chances for advancement. Retail entrepreneurs get to design their own store, decide on their product mix, write their own advertising, and basically perform all the functions of marketing at once. The buying side of retailing can take you abroad—to set up distribution networks, purchase foreign goods, or attend trade shows. You might travel the world in search of exotic products to sell in Canada or develop markets for your store in foreign lands.

Product development, marketing research, and logistics are marketing careers that do not have the same degree of creativity attached to them, but are interesting, well-paid careers nonetheless. Product development requires an academic background in design. You'll need a mathematics and statistical program for a marketing research career. Logistics—determining the cheapest, fastest, and safest way to transport goods from one place to another—requires a community college certificate and accreditation from the Canadian Institute of Traffic and Transportation (CITT).

Stockbrokers need nerves of steel and a good head for numbers.

Realtors have to be licensed before they can sell housing.

Personal Selling Careers

The type of sales task, the skills required to perform the task, and the income that can be earned vary widely among the salespeople (see Table 6.2).

Table 6.2

Types of Sales Positions			
Type of Sales Position	**Description**	**Skills Required**	**Remuneration**
retail clerk/ cashier	rings in the sales; provides some information to customers (e.g., Zellers)	must know store's layout and be pleasant at all times as he or she is last link between store and consumers	minimum wage
retail commissioned salesperson	sells big-ticket items, such as appliances and home furnishings (e.g., Leon's Furniture)	must have vast amount of product knowledge and sales ability	5–10% of his or her total sales
detail or route salesperson	delivery driver with sales responsibilities who monitors inventory levels, introduces new products, and creates merchandise displays (e.g., Weston's bread)	has knowledge of company's brands and the retail marketplace	salary plus commission; average to above-average wage
contact salesperson	does not sell the products; provides gatekeepers, such as doctors, teachers, and veterinarians with product information (e.g., pharmaceutical representative)	university-level product knowledge and knowledge of the targeted profession	good salary
sales representative	sells the products or services from a single manufacturer, importer, or distributor to other businesses (e.g., Innovation)	high degree of product knowledge and knowledge of the targeted industry	commission; potentially very high income
agent and broker	brings buyers and sellers together; agent usually acts for one side while broker acts for both (e.g., stockbroker, insurance agent)	must know a great deal about the market in which he or she operates	straight commission; among the highest paid professions in Canada
sales engineer	provides technical support for complex product installations, such as computers, production equipment, and industrial machinery (e.g., Alcan)	high level of expertise required for this work and often a university degree	very high salary
auctioneer	brings buyers together to bid on items presented at auction, such as cattle, grain, art, antiques, used cars, and estates (e.g., Sotheby's)	high degree of specific knowledge needed about the items up for auction	straight commission on the amount received from the bidding

Rights in the Workplace

Can your employer fire you anytime he or she wants? Do you get vacation pay if you have a part-time job? Can you be forced to work overtime? What rights do you have on the job? All employees and employers in Canada have certain rights. Many of these rights are based on the Universal Declaration of Human Rights, adopted by the General Assembly of the United Nations on December 10, 1948. The following articles, or sections of the declaration, are sometimes known as the Universal Employee Bill of Rights.

Keep in Mind

1. the rights of the employee
2. the rights of the employer

Universal Declaration of Human Rights

Article 4. No one shall be held in slavery or servitude; slavery and the slave trade shall be prohibited in all their forms.

Article 23. (1) Everyone has the right to work, to free choice of employment, to just and favourable conditions of work, and to protection against unemployment. **(2)** Everyone, without any discrimination, has the right to equal pay for equal work. **(3)** Everyone who works has the right to just and favourable remuneration, ensuring...an existence worthy of human dignity.... **(4)** Everyone has the right to form and to join trade unions....

Article 24. Everyone has the right to rest and leisure, including reasonable limitation of working hours and periodic holidays with pay.

Article 25. (1) Everyone has the right to a standard of living adequate for the health and well-being of himself and of his family, including food, clothing, housing, medical care, and necessary social services....

Article 26. Everyone has the right to job training. Job training shall be free, at least in the elementary and fundamental stages....

Flags of its member countries fly outside the United Nations building in New York City.

The Rights of the Employee

The provincial and federal governments have drafted legislation that sets out employment standards for workers in the private (Sears, Alcan, The Gap, etc.) and public sectors (Ontario Ministry of Education, Foreign Affairs and International Trade Canada, etc.). The legislation sets out provisions for the following:

- the minimum age for employment
- hours of work
- minimum wages
- overtime, holiday, and vacation pay
- paid public holidays
- parental leave
- individual and group terminations of employment
- the recovery of unpaid wages

In addition to employment standards, each province has human rights legislation. Human rights codes make it illegal to harass or discriminate against an employee or potential employee on the grounds of gender, race, religion, sexual preference, physical disability, age, and so on. These characteristics are called **protected grounds**. Denying a qualified individual an interview, a job, or a promotion because of religion, gender, or physical disability is job **discrimination. Harassment** occurs when specific people or groups are made to feel threatened or uncomfortable because of who they are. Harassment can include making rude jokes, offensive comments, and inappropriate sexual suggestions. Employees who experience discrimination or harassment can complain to the appropriate human rights body.

The Rights of the Employer

Employers have the right to hire, dismiss, and promote employees, and to establish conditions of employment that best serve their business goals. In doing so, they must not discriminate on the grounds protected by human rights legislation. Specifically, employers have the right to

- decide what their employment needs are
- require that employees have job-related qualifications and/or experience

- hire, promote, and assign the most qualified person for a position
- establish standards for evaluating job performance
- require that employees adhere to clearly defined job descriptions and performance criteria
- discipline, demote, or dismiss incompetent, negligent, or insubordinate employees
- set employment terms and conditions
- establish salary and wage scales either independently or through negotiations

Review Questions

11. List five rights of the employee.
12. List five rights of the employer.

Ethical, Moral & Legal Considerations

Employment Laws

Several different laws in Canada protect the rights of the employee. Human resources managers and employers should be familiar with all of them. A brief summary of each one follows:

The Ontario *Human Rights Code*

Inspired by the 1948 Universal Declaration of Human Rights, the Ontario *Human Rights Code* protects employees from discrimination and harassment in the following areas: race, ancestry, place of origin, colour, ethnic origin, citizenship, creed (religion), sex (includes pregnancy), sexual orientation, disability, perceived disability, age, marital status, same-sex partnership status, family status, and record of offences.

The *Canadian Human Rights Act*

The *Canadian Human Rights Act* covers workplaces that are under the jurisdiction of any federal department or agency and protects these federal employees from discrimination and harassment at work in the same areas that the Ontario *Human Rights Code* does. If an Ontario organization is federal or federally regulated, the *Canadian Human Rights Act* applies, and not the Ontario *Human Rights Code*: these two laws are mutually exclusive.

Employment Standards Act

The *Employment Standards Act* is an Ontario law that outlines an employee's minimum rights in the workplace. The rights include minimum wages, overtime, notice of termination, severance pay, pregnancy and parental leave, vacation time, public holidays, and hours of work.

The Ontario *Labour Relations Act*

The Ontario *Labour Relations Act* covers unionized workplaces. Its purpose is to ensure that employees have the right to organize, encourage collective bargaining, promote harmonious labour relations, and provide for effective and fair dispute resolution.

The *Occupational Health and Safety Act*

This legislation outlines businesses' legal requirements with regard to on-the-job safety issues, and their responsibilities to maintain a safe workplace and a healthy work environment.

The *Workplace Safety and Insurance Act*

Injuries in employment-related accidents are covered by the *Workplace Safety and Insurance Act* (formerly the *Workers' Compensation Act*). This act provides an insurance plan that protects injured workers from salary loss while unable to work. It also limits employer liability through a funding system based on payroll assessment.

Ontarians with Disabilities Act, 2001

The purpose of the *Ontarians with Disabilities Act* (ODA) is to improve opportunities for people with disabilities and to provide for their involvement in the identification, removal, and prevention of barriers to their full participation in the life of the province. The ODA establishes annual accessibility planning requirements for the following organizations: Ontario government ministries, municipalities, public transportation organizations, hospitals, school boards, and colleges and universities.

The *Ontario Building Code*

The *Ontario Building Code* (OBC) governs the construction of new buildings and the renovation and maintenance of existing buildings. The OBC includes accessibility requirements for the construction and renovation of all buildings in Ontario, ensuring that the facilities can be approached, entered, and used by persons with physical or sensory disabilities. These provisions present standards relating to the installation and construction of doors, elevators, paths of travel, washrooms, and so on, that provide barrier-free wheelchair access. Assistive listening devices are also required for public auditoriums, meeting rooms, and theatres.

The *Freedom of Information and Protection of Privacy Act*

The *Freedom of Information and Protection of Privacy Act* sets out privacy laws that are limited to the public sector, namely to Ontario government ministries, agencies, cities, and towns. Government organizations are, with limited exceptions, prohibited from disclosing personal information in their control to third parties. Private-sector employers cannot obtain personal information, such as medical history, from a government agency without the employee's consent.

The *Canadian Charter of Rights and Freedoms*

The *Canadian Charter of Rights and Freedoms* is a constitutional document that is the "supreme law" in Canada. It can be used in the courts to challenge or strike down unconstitutional laws or government practices. The Charter applies only to the acts and conduct of government and does not apply to acts of, and conduct between, individuals.

International Human Rights

Canada is a signatory to numerous international human rights conventions, documents, and treaties. Examples of such documents are the following:

- the Universal Declaration of Human Rights
- the International Covenant on Civil and Political Rights
- the International Covenant on Social and Economic Rights
- the International Convention on the Elimination of All Forms of Racial Discrimination
- the International Convention on the Elimination of All Forms of Discrimination against Women

In Canada, international documents are not laws. However, the values reflected in international human rights law may aid in interpreting human rights laws in Canada, as well as the Charter.

CHAPTER REVIEW

Knowledge

1. Provide an example or a brief explanation of the following terms:
   a) productivity
   b) headhunter
   c) skilled labour
   d) professional labour
   e) stock option

2. What two things do provincial human rights codes prohibit on the job?

Thinking

3. Is high employee turnover good or bad? Explain.

4. What do you think is the most important employability skill? Give several reasons for your selection.

5. What do you think is the best form of compensation? Explain why.

6. Research the training program at any major corporation in which you are interested.

Communication

7. Find an ad for a job on the Internet or in the newspaper that you think you could get. Write a one-page covering letter asking for an interview.

8. Select one of the business careers listed in this chapter. Research that career, providing a detailed job description, average compensation, specific companies that provide that career path, and details of at least two programs available at Canadian educational facilities that would prepare you for an entry-level position.

Application

9. Prepare a one-page report on your school with regard to health and safety.

10. What is the minimum wage in your community?

11. Have a "Dress for Success" day in your business class. Wear to school what you would wear to a job interview, and have someone you trust provide an evaluation of your choices.

Team Activity

Team Goal: Writing a resumé

Team Assignment: The Perfect Resumé

- Select one person from your team.

- Your team will develop the perfect resumé for that team member.

- The team that creates the best resumé wins this competition.

Portfolio

Complete the Skills Credentialing Tool for Individuals and include it in your portfolio. Your instructor will tell you how to access the site, or simply visit the Conference Board of Canada's website and search for the tool.

Reflect on Your Learning

Now that you have read Chapter 6, compare your new list of employability skills with the skills you listed initially. What changes did you make? Why did you make them?

Disney

Walt Disney once said, "You can dream, create, design and build the most wonderful place in the world but it requires people to make the dream a reality." Disney's success is not because of magic pixie dust or a twirl of Tinkerbell's wand—it is thanks to a well-trained, enthusiastic, and motivated work force. However, getting consistent and superior service from a staff of approximately 54 000 is no easy task.

When Walt Disney opened Disneyland in 1955, he realized that employees, or "cast members," needed a structured environment where they could learn the unique skills necessary to excel at Disney. The company's reputation is built on its service quality. Seventy percent of visitors are repeat visitors and a bad Disney experience could be detrimental.

A child enjoys the company of Minnie Mouse during his trip to Disneyland Park.

To ensure exceptional service, Disney University was born.

Disney's world-renowned selection and training program starts with "casting the show" at the first "audition." Before the interview process even begins, a video is played outlining the high expectations and the downside of working at Disney. At this point, 10 percent of the applicants usually leave. Disney selects for attitude and fit with the culture, not skills. Upon being cast, all employees go through "Traditions," an introduction to Disney and their first experience at Disney University.

Disney University provides a wide variety of training and education programs to its employees throughout their careers. In addition to its new hires and college programs, Disney offers executive development, management and leadership skills, ethics programs, and computer skills. Disney also offers non-work-related courses on topics such as television and radio production, animation, gardening and the great outdoors, culinary arts, performing arts, design arts, lifestyles, story arts, sports and fitness, and more. Disney is currently working to create e-learning programs for its cast members. And the benefits of these programs are visible both in the level of service at Disney and also in their full-time turnover rates. Full-time employee turnover is about 20 percent, which is half of the industry average.

The business world took notice of Disney's exceptional training programs after they were featured in the 1985 book *In Search of Excellence*, by Tom Peters. Since the book's publication, one of the most prominent attractions at Walt Disney World has no rides, parades, or movie characters. The Disney Institute—or the public arm of Disney University—teaches the business behind the magic. It has trained more than one million corporate executives since 1986 in courses such as The Disney Approach to People Management and The Disney Approach to Creative Leadership. Courses are taught by Disney cast members at Walt Disney World and are hugely popular among major corporations. This is no Mickey Mouse business.

QUESTIONS

1. Do you think that corporate executives might be skeptical of taking business advice from Disney? If so, why? If you had to convince a corporate executive to take part in Disney's training program, what would you say to convince them?

2. Many of the programs that Disney offers to its cast members have no relevance to Disney's business (such as courses in gardening). Why do you think Disney offers them?

SPECIFIC EXPECTATIONS

After completing this chapter, you will be able to

- describe how different management styles can influence employee productivity
- explain the importance of ethical behaviour with respect to employees, the environment, and communities

- demonstrate business teamwork skills needed to carry out projects and solve problems
- explain how information and communication technology affects the functions of a business and how it affects employability at various skill levels

GoodLife Fitness Clubs

GoodLife Fitness Clubs—Canada's largest fitness chain—was founded in 1979 in London, Ontario. Since then, the company has achieved a consistent revenue growth of 25 percent, brings in an annual revenue of C$100 million, employs more than 3300 staff, and has earned numerous Canadian awards, including the 2002 Consumer Choice Award for Greater Toronto Area for Health & Fitness Club. This all sounds typical of yet another successful business, right? Well, there is something just slightly out of the ordinary when it comes to GoodLife's founder and CEO, five-time Canadian rowing champion David Patchell-Evans.

A young woman goes to work out at a GoodLife club.

To begin, David does not conform to formal titles—he asks his colleagues to call him "Patch." Nor does he care much for the traditional business dress code; he is notorious for sporting the athletic shorts and T-shirt look. Indeed, David believes in doing things differently when it comes to managing GoodLife. He explains, "In my business, people don't want a typical CEO. What they want is a leader." And he seems to be right. In 2004, he was inducted as the youngest member of the Business Hall of Fame of London, Ontario, and was selected as Most Innovative Executive by *Canadian Business* after an open call for nominations.

But David's innovative approach to management extends beyond his informal attitude toward titles and style of dress. In 2004, he acquired exclusive Canadian rights to Visual Fitness Planner, a software tool that provides clients of GoodLife with the ability to visualize themselves both before and after meeting their personal fitness goals. It's also able to provide clients with customized exercise and diet recommendations depending on lifestyle and genetic traits. David explains that "You can take your 'after,' put it on the fridge and say, 'That's what I'm going to be.'" But, he adds, "You have to come to me to get it." David recognizes that to be successful in his business, he must be able to both attract and retain customers. That is why GoodLife also offers its clients free DVD rentals, babysitting, and tanning services.

Also, David manages his business in cost-effective ways that his clients don't see. For example, GoodLife is partnered with the Ontario-based company RenewABILITY Energy, which has a system for recycling hot water that would normally go down the drain into usable energy. Thus far, David has fitted seven of his locations with the technology and estimates that GoodLife saves between $6000 and $20 000 per year at each site.

QUESTIONS

1. What makes David Patchell-Evans different from a typical CEO?

2. Explain the innovations that David has implemented.

How Management Functions

Managers are people who get things done by directing individuals and teams. They develop employees and are responsible for the efforts of the workers who report to them. Management tries to achieve a company's goals by deciding how best to use the business's human, financial, and material resources. Management performs four major functions for any business: planning, organizing, leading, and controlling.

Planning

Planning is the process of setting realistic goals for a business— both short-term and long-term—and deciding how best to achieve them. Goals are occasionally social and always economic. (See Chapter 3 for information on corporate social responsibility.) The long-term economic goal of any business is to maximize profits. Short-term goals are often expressed as a sales or income target. For example, a business may plan to increase sales by 10 percent in the next quarter or to increase profit by 5 percent in the next year.

Managers must understand these goals and develop strategies to achieve them. If a beverage company plans to increase sales by 10 percent, all of its managers have to work to meet this goal. The marketing manager creates a promotional plan. The sales manager arranges new contracts with companies that will distribute the beverages. The human resources department hires the necessary employees. And the production manager arranges the necessary resources to produce an increased amount of the product.

Frank and Ernest

©1998 Thaves. Reprinted with permission. Newspaper dist. by NEA, Inc.

Organizing

Organizing is arranging people and tasks to carry out the business's plans. Each department within a company has its own manager, who is responsible for organizing the department. That manager determines tasks and duties for the department and establishes relationships with other departments to help achieve the company's goals. The manager hires the employees and also writes job descriptions for each member of the department so each employee is aware of his or her role.

Many companies are organized into three levels of management.

To see how levels of management are connected, imagine a company that is looking for ways to expand.

- The upper management determines that setting up a factory in China will allow the company to increase sales by taking advantage of China's growing population.

- The middle management is responsible for building and running the factory.

- The lower management hires operating workers and is responsible for the day-to-day running of the factory.

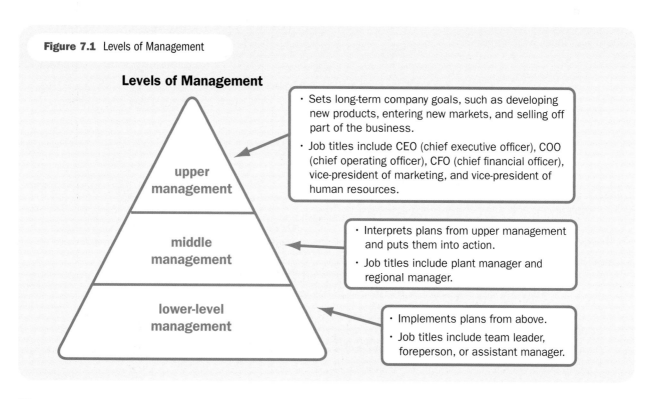

Figure 7.1 Levels of Management

Levels of Management

upper management
- Sets long-term company goals, such as developing new products, entering new markets, and selling off part of the business.
- Job titles include CEO (chief executive officer), COO (chief operating officer), CFO (chief financial officer), vice-president of marketing, and vice-president of human resources.

middle management
- Interprets plans from upper management and puts them into action.
- Job titles include plant manager and regional manager.

lower-level management
- Implements plans from above.
- Job titles include team leader, foreperson, or assistant manager.

The World of Business DVD

"The Hostile Skies"
from *The World of Business DVD*

Leading

Managers are leading when they focus employees on achieving objectives and motivate their staff to accomplish these objectives. Leadership involves activities such as leading teams, and managing conflict and stress. Managers spend substantial amounts of time motivating people to excellence, communicating effectively, and encouraging staff.

Motivating

Some people work hard at their jobs, some do not. What is the difference? It is their level of motivation. Managers must motivate workers to do their best work at all times. There are many ways to increase motivation. Compensation can be a strong motivating factor. Some employees work harder to receive a pay increase, promotion, or a well-situated office. Others work hard because their managers appreciate them, provide challenging work, and trust them to do a good job. In other words, motivation means different things to different people. A skillful manager discovers how to best motivate each employee, and uses these motivating factors to increase employee productivity.

Stretch Your Thinking

What disadvantages might there be to participative planning? Share your ideas with a partner.

Communicating

Leading others means letting them know what needs to be done. A good leader communicates directions, urgency, corporate values, plans, and goals clearly and effectively. Failure to do so may mean that tasks are poorly done or not done at all. A task completed improperly wastes labour. Employees will have to redo the task, and the company's reputation may be damaged.

In the News

The Pike Place Fish Market in Seattle has become world famous. The employees decided some years ago that retail work, which is often boring and repetitive, could be rewarding and enjoyable. They developed four principles to motivate themselves. These rules were

1. Be there—pay attention to customers and work in the moment.

2. Play—have fun at work. At Pike Place, staff achieve this by throwing fish.

3. Make their day—focus on the customers; make them feel important.

4. Choose your attitude— decide to have a positive attitude every day.

The market thrived with the new philosophy. Customers flocked to the store to see the workers entertaining the shoppers and enjoying their jobs. The mood was contagious. Sales quickly grew, and so did the market's reputation. A series of management training videos have been made and books published about the success of this business.

These principles can be used in any workplace. How can you use these principles at your job? at school?

The playful and popular Pike Place Fish Co.

Encouraging Participation

Many progressive businesses allow employees to direct the training, promotion, and dismissal of other employees in their department. This type of employee participation is called participative planning, because the people affected by the decision (stakeholders) get to make the decision. For example, in a beverage company that practises participative management, telephone receptionists may contribute to decision making about promoting sales representatives because they talk to customers every day and know which sales representatives the customers prefer. Not only can employee participation result in better decisions, it can also improve staff motivation. Many employees enjoy the sense of purpose that comes from being involved in making decisions.

Controlling

Controlling is the method managers use to increase, maintain, or decrease the resources they are allocated. Activities involved in controlling include employee discipline, performance appraisals, and budgeting. The number of employees in a department, the amount of money the department receives, and the extent of its physical supplies are all based on the budget it is given.

If the department fails to reach its goals, its budget may be cut and resources reduced. If the department exceeds its goals, more resources are required and usually supplied. If the department simply reaches its target, little changes. The budgeting process, in other words, is a very important means of control.

Managing Resources

A manager's ability to plan, organize, lead, and control is one of the most important skills he or she can possess. But businesses have resources other than people that must also be managed. For this reason, many businesses have different managers for each resource area.

Purchasing

The purchasing manager negotiates deals for the supply and delivery of **raw materials** (which the manufacturer transforms into another product), equipment, supplies, and goods for resale. If a beverage company's purchasing manager negotiates a small reduction in the price of sugar (e.g., 5¢ per kilogram), it may not seem like a big savings. But if the company uses 2 000 000 kilograms of sugar a year, the reduction in cost is considerable. The company will save $100 000 a year! A good purchasing manager also arranges for inventory to arrive when it is needed. **Just-in-time** delivery reduces shipping costs and warehouse needs to save the costs of space and warehouse staff. The company simply orders supplies exactly when it needs them and then demands quick delivery services.

Production

Production managers ensure that their business makes the things it is supposed to make. They balance many activities, from arranging for raw materials to be processed into a finished product to packaging and storing that final product. Production managers often have to arrange and coordinate plant maintenance, shift scheduling, machinery repair, and technological improvements.

Keep in Mind

1. purchasing
2. production
3. marketing and distribution
4. research and development
5. finance

This purchasing manager is helping to inventory a new shipment.

Business Fact

A Japanese electronic company, Maspro Denkoh Corp. needed to decide between Sotheby's and Christie's art sellers to sell its US$11.8 million Cézanne painting. How did it make the decision? It used the rock, paper, scissors method. Christie's scissors beat Sotheby's paper.

Marketing and Distribution

Marketing and distribution managers try to ensure that what the company produces gets sold. The marketing manager develops sales strategies, which include advertising, promotional activities, and publicity. The distribution manager (who is often the marketing manager as well) focuses on sales, often attempting to improve product distribution through direct sales efforts (sales representatives) or indirect ones (vending machines, catalogues, and Internet sales). Marketing and distribution will be covered in greater detail in Chapter 8.

Research and Development

Research and development (R&D) departments create new products or services, or come up with new and better ways to produce the same product or service. An R&D department's work is sometimes based on feedback from the marketplace. A company will conduct studies to find out what consumers like or dislike about their product or what new products they would like to see. Then, R&D managers analyze and interpret the market data and give direction to their department. They also prepare reports that help the purchasing, production, and marketing managers make decisions for their departments.

Finance

The **comptroller,** or manager of the financial department, is often an accountant. His or her major responsibilities are keeping records of the company's financial transactions and controlling the company's money, which includes setting the budget of each department along with the department manager.

A scientist researches the development of a new drug.

Stretch Your Thinking

Explain what research and development could be done to improve a fast-food restaurant.

Review Questions

1. Define the four functions of management.
2. Why is it important that managers plan?
3. Explain four ways that managers can motivate employees.
4. What are the advantages of participative planning?
5. List the resources that a manager must manage.

Leadership Styles

All leaders have different styles. The style depends on the manager's personality and on the situation. For example, an emergency calls for quick, decisive action, which requires certain leadership skills. However, an experienced employee who needs little direction will require very different leadership. And a long-term plan needing input from many sources will require yet a different set of leadership skills.

Autocratic Leadership

The **autocratic leader** takes control of the situation. He or she does not allow employees to participate in decision making. This type of leadership works when decisions need to be made quickly, when additional input from others would not change the decision, and when unpopular decisions such as laying off employees need to be made. However, too much autocratic leadership leads to discontentment. Employees feel undervalued and rebel against decisions made without their input.

Laissez-faire Leadership

The **laissez-faire leader** leaves employees alone to do their job. This is appropriate when employees are mature and have years of experience. However, all employees need direction, guidance, and motivation from time to time, and all need to believe their input is valued. Without feedback, they become uncertain about their work. Employees led by laissez-faire leaders can become unmotivated and directionless and often do not work well as a team. In addition, this is a very poor leadership style for employees who are new to their jobs.

Napoleon is an example of a famous autocratic leader.

Ethical, Moral & Legal Considerations

Managers now have the technical means to monitor employees. Managers can listen to their staff's telephone calls, read their e-mail, and search their Internet activity. Many managers believe they should monitor employees because they need to measure productivity, gather information for performance reviews, and prevent legal problems for the company. They also feel justified in keeping track of their employees' actions because the technology is owned by the company. The majority of employers using electronic-monitoring technology notify the employees that they will be monitored. What do you think of this management practice? Is it ethical, moral, and legal?

Democratic Leadership

The **democratic leader** provides opportunities for employees to contribute to the decision-making process. Employees provide input, information, and creativity to the department's goals. This leadership style encourages staff, recognizes achievement, and increases team spirit and morale. Employees feel appreciated and work harder because they know their contributions are valued. Productivity in the department increases. This is the most effective of the three leadership styles in most situations, although there are certainly appropriate times to use the other styles. An excellent leader knows when to apply each of the different styles and can seamlessly change among the three, as the situation requires.

Review Questions

6. Define the three styles of leadership.

7. Explain when each of the three styles of leadership is appropriate.

8. Which form of leadership do you think would be the most effective most of the time? Why?

Ethical Behaviour and Management

In Chapter 3, you learned that social responsibility and ethics are critical elements to a business's success. The people in the business that make decisions about ethical behaviour are the managers. As Henry David Thoreau once said, "It is truly enough said that a corporation has no conscience; but a corporation of conscientious men is a corporation with a conscience."

Management and Employees

Ethics are important at all levels of a corporation. Managers need to lead by example—to be ethical role models. One of the ways they can do this is to treat their employees ethically. Managers need to provide fair pay, reasonable hours, vacations, and interesting work. They need to treat their employees with

A company's environmentally friendly practices result in these large bales of plastic drinking bottles on their way to be recycled.

🌐 **E-ACTIVITY** ☐⊡☒

Visit www.nelson.com/WOB and follow the links to learn more about becoming an environmentally friendly business.

Stretch Your Thinking

Create a list of appropriate team behaviours. Example—arrive at meetings prepared.

respect and dignity. Many companies have an ethical code of conduct. Included in this document are the company's policies on discrimination, sexual harassment, bribery, kickbacks, and theft of company property. The code also includes whistle-blower protection. This means that an employee who reports corporate wrongdoing cannot lose his or her job because of the disclosure.

An example of a company that treats its employees ethically is Starbucks. It pays benefits to its employees, even to part-time workers. Howard Schultz, the CEO, believes this is important because when he was young his father suffered a serious injury and could not work. This caused great hardship in his family. When he started his own business, he took steps to ensure that none of his employees would suffer the way his family had. In addition to paying benefits, Starbucks' guiding principles emphasize treating employees with respect and dignity and embracing diversity.

Management and the Environment

In their homes, most people participate in environmentally friendly practices, such as recycling. But these practices also need to be used in businesses. Companies need to consider the impact of their decisions on the environment and minimize environmental damage. This can happen in many ways. Companies should construct factories and offices that use green building materials, have guidelines for energy conservation, and avoid polluting. For a list of how businesses can improve their environmental practices, see Table 7.1.

An example of a company that is serious in its support of the environment is Ben and Jerry's. This American-based ice cream company uses unbleached paper products in its packaging, napkins, sundae bowls, and paper bags. It also has a plan to reduce greenhouse gases, total energy consumption, and carbon dioxide emissions.

Using environmentally friendly practices is good for a company. It improves its public relations. Consumers are more inclined to buy from a company that cares about the environment. It also has an impact on the bottom line. Environmentally friendly practices can increase sales and decrease costs, therefore increasing profits in the long run.

Management and the Community

In Chapter 3, you learned the impact a business has on the local community. Management makes daily ethical decisions that impact the local community. One such decision is to contribute to charitable organizations. An example is the United Way. The purpose of the United Way is to improve lives and communities by collecting money for local charities and not-for-profit service organizations. In addition to organizing fundraising drives, many companies also support the United Way by sending company staff to work for the organization while being paid by the company. These employees help raise money for the United Way by talking to other companies and convincing them and their employees to make contributions. Another example of a corporation that supports local communities is The Body Shop. Over the last 10 years, The Body Shop has raised more than one million dollars for programs to stop violence in the home.

"Miss Dugan, will you send someone in here who can distinguish right from wrong?"

Table 7.1

10 Ways to Be an Environmentally Friendly Business

1. Turn off equipment.
2. Encourage communications by e-mail.
3. Reduce fax-related paper waste.
4. Produce double-sided documents.
5. Do not leave taps dripping.
6. Install displacement toilet dams in toilet reservoirs.
7. Find a supply of paper with maximum available recycled content.
8. Choose suppliers who take back packaging for reuse.
9. Instigate an ongoing search for "greener" products and services in the local community.
10. Before buying new office furniture, see if your existing office furniture can be refurbished.

Review Questions

9. Explain how managers can act ethically.
10. Why should managers be ethical role models?
11. What is an ethical code of conduct? What is included in it?
12. How is Ben and Jerry's environmentally friendly?
13. How can businesses give back to the community?

Table 7.2

Advantages and Disadvantages of Teamwork	
Advantages	**Disadvantages**
<ul><li>improved creativity</li><li>more ideas</li><li>more information</li><li>improved decision making, especially when no expert is available</li><li>greater commitment to the decision</li><li>higher motivation</li><li>improved employee discipline</li><li>improved morale</li><li>shared risk</li></ul>	<ul><li>one group member may do less (or no) work and coast on the efforts of others</li><li>takes more time</li><li>costs more</li><li>a group may produce a great idea, but with no one taking responsibility for implementing it, it may never get done</li><li>personality conflicts may occur among group members</li><li>it can be difficult to get everyone ready to work together at the same time</li><li>some group members may arrive unprepared</li></ul>

Figure 7.2 Types of Teams

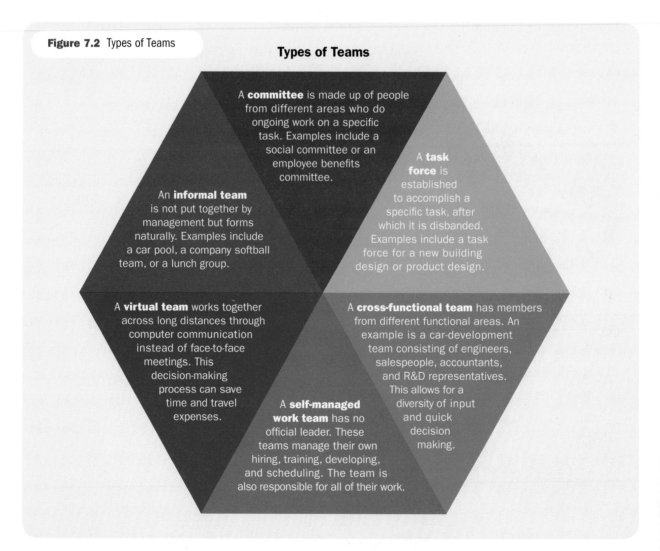

Types of Teams

A **committee** is made up of people from different areas who do ongoing work on a specific task. Examples include a social committee or an employee benefits committee.

A **task force** is established to accomplish a specific task, after which it is disbanded. Examples include a task force for a new building design or product design.

An **informal team** is not put together by management but forms naturally. Examples include a car pool, a company softball team, or a lunch group.

A **virtual team** works together across long distances through computer communication instead of face-to-face meetings. This decision-making process can save time and travel expenses.

A **cross-functional team** has members from different functional areas. An example is a car-development team consisting of engineers, salespeople, accountants, and R&D representatives. This allows for a diversity of input and quick decision making.

A **self-managed work team** has no official leader. These teams manage their own hiring, training, developing, and scheduling. The team is also responsible for all of their work.

Teamwork in Companies

A team is a group of people with different skills. Teamwork is the ability of people to work together for a common goal. Teams are common in corporations because they lead to better decisions and let people have input into their working environment.

Types of Teams

Many types of teams are used in businesses. The type of team depends on the purpose and the duration of the group.

Companies establish teams because of their advantages, but there are disadvantages as well. Being aware of these disadvantages can help each team member avoid bad team habits and can help the team achieve the best possible results.

Review Questions

14. Define team and teamwork.
15. Describe the six types of teams.
16. What are the advantages of teamwork?
17. What are the disadvantages of teamwork?

From the boardroom to the operating room, good teamwork is essential.

CHAPTER REVIEW

Knowledge

1. What is the purpose of management?

2. What goals are set by managers in the functions of a business such as production, human resources, marketing, and accounting?

3. You are the manager of an ice cream stand. State one short-term and one long-term goal for the company.

4. Explain why companies would pay to have an employee work for the United Way.

5. Why do companies organize their workers into teams?

Thinking

6. State an example of a time when you were motivated to work hard. What factors motivated you?

7. How do you manage yourself? What planning, organizing, leading, and controlling will you need to do in the next year? In the next five years?

8. Using the information from this chapter, explain ways that your school can become more environmentally friendly.

9. Make a list of companies that have a good reputation. Explain why each has a good reputation.

10. Some would say that businesses contributing to local charities are giving away shareholders' money. What do you think of this statement?

11. Think of a time when you enjoyed working on a team. What made it a successful experience? Think of a time when you disliked working on a team. What made it an unpleasant experience?

Communication

12. Interview a manager of a local business. Ask him or her for specific examples of each management function that he or she performs in a typical day.

13. Prepare an illustrated report that profiles a local business. Be sure to show each of the departments, their responsibilities, and the management levels.

14. Research and create a poster of a current business leader.

Application

15. You have an employee who is constantly late for work and who seems unmotivated when she is at work. How will you deal with this situation? What leadership style will you use?

16. Your company has decided to contribute $10 000 to a local charity. With a partner, research and find a charity in your community that you believe deserves the contribution. Present your findings and justification to the class.

Team Activity

Team Goal: Using the four functions of management to run a lunchtime barbecue

Team Assignment: Managing a Meal

- Each team will set up and run a specific section of a lunchtime school barbecue (sections could include: hot dog, hamburger, chicken, drink, ice cream, potato chips, and so on).

- Each team must be part of and help coordinate the overall barbecue.

- The team that generates the greatest profit wins this competition.

Portfolio

Visit two corporate websites of businesses within your industry. Who are the leaders (president, CEO, VPs, and so on)? What is the corporate structure? (List the departments or divisions, and the people that run them.)

Contact at least one of these companies and request an organizational chart for your portfolio.

Reflect on Your Learning

In your opinion, what are the characteristics of an excellent manager? Think about when you will have a full-time job. How important is it to you that the company has a good ethical reputation?

Whole Foods

Whole Foods is not an ordinary grocery store. When you walk in, you will see beautifully displayed products including mounds of organic fruit, terra cotta pots full of vegetables, wooden signs, and lots of natural light. You can pick up a prime rib dinner, select from more than 10 varieties of hot, homemade soup, or take home one of the many pastries.

Founded in Austin, Texas, in 1980, Whole Foods is now the largest natural and organic food store in the world. It has 183 store locations throughout North America and the United Kingdom, including one in Vancouver and two in the Toronto area. There are eight distribution centres, seven regional offices, and four subsidiaries, including a seafood

Fresh organic produce abounds at Whole Foods.

processing plant and a coffee manufacturer. The company has 39 000 employees.

John Mackey has been the chairman of the board and CEO of the company since it was founded. He dropped out of university six times while studying philosophy and religion. He is a vegetarian and a strong environmentalist—his office is made out of mostly recycled products. Mackey believes that businesses can combine capitalism with social responsibility. This is a combination that obviously works. In 2005, Whole Foods had revenues of $4.7 billion and a net income of $1.3 million.

Whole Foods harnesses the collective energy and enthusiasm of its employees by organizing everyone into self-managed work teams. The teams have the power to hire and train employees and select product lines. Teams meet on a regular basis to discuss issues, creatively problem-solve, and acknowledge each others' contributions. Whole Foods believes in combining work and fun by fostering friendly competition to improve stores. Knowledge is shared at all levels of the company. The financial books are open to all employees. This means that a team member can find out the compensation of any other team member at any level. The company provides good wages and a profit incentive program. There is also a salary cap for senior executives that limits their salary to 14 times that of the average full-time employee. For 10 years in a row, Whole Foods has been listed on *Fortune Magazine*'s Top 100 Employers to Work For.

Whole Foods believes in the importance of acting ethically. It purchases products grown from organic farms that practise sustainable agriculture. Waste is reduced, recycled, and reused where possible. Whole Foods donates a minimum of 5 percent of its profits to charities and local communities. It also pays its team members while they work at non-profit community organizations. This company lives up to its motto of "Whole Foods, Whole People, Whole Planet."

QUESTIONS

1. Describe how the motto "Whole Foods, Whole People, Whole Planet" applies to Whole Foods.

2. State the good management practices used by Whole Foods.

CHAPTER 8 Marketing

SPECIFIC EXPECTATIONS

After completing this chapter, you will be able to

- explain the role and the impact of marketing
- identify the four Ps (product, price, place, and promotion) and the two Cs (competition and consumer) of marketing and apply the concepts by developing a strategy to market a good, service, or event

- compare the advantages and disadvantages of the major types of advertising
- design an advertisement appropriate for a specific good, service, or event
- identify and describe different types of marketing research tools
- design and implement, using appropriate tools, a marketing research plan for a good, service, or event, and produce a report on the results

Research In Motion Limited

What is that strange, flat, handheld device that everyone seems to be using? It's a BlackBerry—the first successful handheld electronic device that integrates e-mail, phone, SMS, and organizer features. Research In Motion Limited (RIM) is among the leading designers and manufacturers of wireless technologies currently serving the market of mobile communications. Located in Waterloo, Ontario, RIM was founded in 1984 by Mike Lazaridis in partnership with Douglas Fregin.

The pair viewed the business as an opportunity to invest in a technology that was still very poorly understood. Mike felt that the potential for wireless technology presented the company with such an unparalleled business opportunity that RIM would continue to invest in it for 10 years before their vision of success would begin to be realized. Since then, the company has erupted in size. It now employs 3500 people and

BlackBerry is the first successful handheld electronic device that integrates e-mail, phone, SMS, and organizer.

has offices located in Canada, the United States, Europe, Hong Kong, Australia, and Singapore. The monetary success of RIM is apparent from its 2005 fiscal earnings of more than $200 million.

Mike Lazaridis and James L. Balsillie are the current co-CEOs of RIM. Mike is also the company's president. Mike began RIM while still an undergraduate, and now holds an honorary Doctor of Engineering degree from the University of Waterloo. He has earned more than 30 patents and numerous awards for his innovative wireless technology and software, including being named Canada's Nation Builder of the Year for 2002 by readers of the *Globe and Mail*.

BlackBerry was launched in North America in January 1999 and gets its name from a chance remark that its keyboard resembled the seeds of a berry. Not only did RIM supply the exterior product, they were also responsible for every other component—from writing the operating software to providing the servers required for e-mail. Indeed, RIM even leased airtime from phone carriers, truly making themselves the sole producers of the impressive device.

RIM markets BlackBerry to a range of customers, including the individual, small- to medium-sized businesses, as well as enterprises and government, with the corporate sector constituting the bulk of RIM's clients. In order to appeal to a diverse market, RIM offers its customers a variety of products from which to choose.

Despite the BlackBerry's tremendous success, it is not without competition. In 1996, Palm Computing launched the first handheld computer, the PalmPilot. Although PalmPilot set the innovative precedent as the first wireless computer to hit the market, many customers have opted for RIM's more recent BlackBerry. Where the PalmPilot requires a pen-based mode of data entry, the BlackBerry utilizes a built-in keyboard; a feature that has largely contributed to its success.

QUESTIONS

1. How is RIM's manufacturing and marketing of the BlackBerry product different from any other company's efforts?

2. Why did RIM expand to countries outside of Canada?

3. What are some of the interesting accomplishments of Mr. Lazaridis? What is an honorary degree?

The Role and Impact of Marketing

Have you ever tasted Diet Rite Cola? It was the first diet cola ever sold. It was made by the RC Cola Company and was introduced to consumers in 1958. That was 24 years before the Coca-Cola Company introduced Diet Coke. Diet Rite Cola is still sold as a Cadbury Schweppes Americas Beverage. So why aren't you drinking Diet Rite Cola? Probably because Coca-Cola launched Diet Coke in July 1982 with a US$100-million advertising campaign and has kept on marketing the brand very aggressively ever since (Coca-Cola Limited's marketing budget was US$400 million in 2005). Marketing made Diet Coke a success; lack of marketing keeps Diet Rite Cola a minor brand.

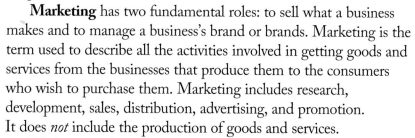

Marketing has two fundamental roles: to sell what a business makes and to manage a business's brand or brands. Marketing is the term used to describe all the activities involved in getting goods and services from the businesses that produce them to the consumers who wish to purchase them. Marketing includes research, development, sales, distribution, advertising, and promotion. It does *not* include the production of goods and services.

Without marketing, not much would get sold. Consumers wouldn't know what goods and services were available. They wouldn't know about new trends or fashions, or how products have been improved. Manufacturers wouldn't have research to know what to make. Importers, wholesalers, and retailers wouldn't have channels of distribution to get their products into the hands of consumers all over the world.

Keep in Mind

1. branding
2. the product life cycle
3. non-traditional product life cycles

Before You Begin

Describe your favourite advertisement. Explain why you like it. What is your favourite store? Why do you prefer that store to other stores? What soft drink do you consume most often? Why that product instead of any others?

Figure 8.1 Roles of Marketing

Can you imagine choosing to buy a black-and-white television instead of a colour television?

example, might develop a campaign to target an old product to a new consumer group (Walkman for senior citizens, for example). If the campaign succeeds, the brand becomes more popular. A lower price may also boost the brand's popularity. If these marketing strategies work, the brand regains its original sales figures and brand equity. If the decline continues in spite of efforts to stop it, the manufacturer discontinues the product and removes it from the market.

Often, new technology makes old products obsolete. DVDs have replaced videotape, MP3 players have replaced portable cassette players, and flat-screen television sets have all but replaced the picture tube type. No amount of marketing will restore life to these products.

Non-traditional Product Life Cycles

Many products do not go through the stages of the traditional product life cycle. There are at least three non-traditional product life cycles: fad, niche, and seasonal.

Women are a new customer-market for Vespa motor scooters.

The Role and Impact of Marketing

Have you ever tasted Diet Rite Cola? It was the first diet cola ever sold. It was made by the RC Cola Company and was introduced to consumers in 1958. That was 24 years before the Coca-Cola Company introduced Diet Coke. Diet Rite Cola is still sold as a Cadbury Schweppes Americas Beverage. So why aren't you drinking Diet Rite Cola? Probably because Coca-Cola launched Diet Coke in July 1982 with a US$100-million advertising campaign and has kept on marketing the brand very aggressively ever since (Coca-Cola Limited's marketing budget was US$400 million in 2005). Marketing made Diet Coke a success; lack of marketing keeps Diet Rite Cola a minor brand.

Marketing has two fundamental roles: to sell what a business makes and to manage a business's brand or brands. Marketing is the term used to describe all the activities involved in getting goods and services from the businesses that produce them to the consumers who wish to purchase them. Marketing includes research, development, sales, distribution, advertising, and promotion. It does *not* include the production of goods and services.

Without marketing, not much would get sold. Consumers wouldn't know what goods and services were available. They wouldn't know about new trends or fashions, or how products have been improved. Manufacturers wouldn't have research to know what to make. Importers, wholesalers, and retailers wouldn't have channels of distribution to get their products into the hands of consumers all over the world.

Keep in Mind

1. branding
2. the product life cycle
3. non-traditional product life cycles

Before You Begin

Describe your favourite advertisement. Explain why you like it. What is your favourite store? Why do you prefer that store to other stores? What soft drink do you consume most often? Why that product instead of any others?

Figure 8.1 Roles of Marketing

Roles of Marketing
1. sell what a business makes
2. manage a business's brands

research
development
sales
distribution
advertising
promotion

Marketing is important to all businesses. Producers use it to sell products to stores. Stores use it to sell products to consumers. Service businesses use it to let people know where they are and what they offer. Non-profit organizations use it to promote their services. Politicians use it to spread their ideas. If you have something you want others to buy or believe in, you will use marketing, too.

Branding

Some businesses spend hundreds of thousands of dollars to create an image. Others spend very little. In either case, three things can be part of the image: a brand name, a logo or trademark, and a slogan.

Brand Name

A **brand name** is a word or group of words that a business uses to distinguish its products from competitors' products. The brand name is the most important part of a product or company's image because it is how the company is identified. If you buy a Roots cap for the first time and feel stylish in it, the company will want you to remember the name for a number of reasons. It may want you to purchase other Roots items. If you can't recall the name, you could easily buy a competitor's product instead. If you're talking to friends about style preferences and mention Roots to them, you're giving the company free publicity. Brand names should be distinctive and stand out from the competition. They should also be easy to remember.

Some very popular fast-food brand names

Logo or Trademark

Many products combine their name with a special symbol that is associated with the product. This symbol is called a **logo** or **trademark**. The logo or trademark helps the product compete for consumer awareness. Peter Pan peanut butter, for example, has a cartoon of Peter Pan on the label. Its logo indicates that the product is aimed at young people.

Logos take one of three possible forms. The first is a *monogram*, which is a stylized rendering of the company's initials or a combination of initials and numbers. IBM (International Business Machines), KFC (Kentucky Fried Chicken), and 3M (Minnesota Mining and Manufacturing Company) are all examples of monogrammatic trademarks. Some companies use monograms to update an image that has become outdated or undesirable. KFC wanted to de-emphasize the word "fried" in its original name; IBM wanted consumers to associate its name with computers rather than adding machines; and 3M had moved far from its roots as a sandpaper manufacturer.

Other companies use *visual symbols* as logos. These are usually line drawings of people, animals, or things, such as Apple Computer's apple, the United Way's hand and rainbow, and Kellogg's Frosted Flakes' Tony the Tiger. The logo is seen everywhere and becomes directly associated with the brand name. Almost any child who sees Ronald McDonald thinks about McDonald's restaurants, for example.

Many companies select an *abstract symbol* as a logo. Abstract symbols are shapes that carry a visual message but are not representative of actual things. Some symbols seek to communicate a company's initials but are obscure enough to be considered abstract. Often these types of logos are difficult to remember. Many are not distinctive enough to stand out from other symbols. However, the Nike "swoosh" is an abstract symbol and is one of the world's most famous logos.

Slogan

The third method of brand identification is the **slogan**—a short, catchy phrase that is usually attached to the company's name and logo. MasterCard's "Priceless," Canadian Blood Services' "It's in You to Give," and Sprite's "Obey Your Thirst" are examples of effective slogans. Each one is also a tagline for both print and broadcast advertisements. Just hearing the slogan will often remind you of the entire ad. A good brand name is helpful. An effective logo is worthwhile. Put them both with an effective slogan: Priceless.

The creation of an identifiable image through logos or trademarks, monograms, and visual symbols are popular ways in which companies brand and market their products.

Frank and Ernest

© 2001 Thaves. Reprinted with permission. Newspaper dist. by NEA, Inc.

Brand Identification

Once a company develops a name, slogan, or logo for a product, everything associated with that product should carry the identification. If the name is written in a distinctive style, such as Coca-Cola or Pepsi, the name should always be written that way. If there are specific colours associated with the brand, these colours should appear on everything associated with the product. Some brands develop a distinctive design for the package. That, too, becomes part of the brand's identification. No consumer should ever have to guess whether this is the product they want. Competition is so fierce that no company wants its product to get lost on a store shelf, especially after spending a great deal of money promoting the brand.

The Product Life Cycle

The impact of marketing can be measured in two ways. The most obvious way is with a sales analysis. Have sales increased? Have we sold more than our competitors have sold? The other way is to measure a consumer's reaction to the brand—a reaction based on marketing efforts. Effective marketing increases **brand equity**: the value of the brand in the marketplace. Good marketing develops brand awareness: customers can name your brand as part of a specific category, whether it is a product, service, non-profit organization, or event. Better marketing develops brand loyalty: customers prefer your brand and support it. The best marketing is marketing that develops brand insistence: the customer will accept no substitutes. Some people will drink only Coca-Cola as a soft drink, for example, or insist

Oops!

Here are some foreign brands that might not be successful in Canada unless they found another name:
Looza Orange Juice (France)
Skum Candy (Sweden)
Rasch Dish Detergent (Chile)
Pocari Sweat Energy Drink (Japan)
Puke Playing Card (Turkey)

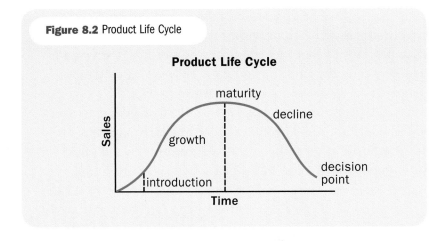

Figure 8.2 Product Life Cycle

Product Life Cycle

(Graph: Sales on vertical axis, Time on horizontal axis. Curve shows stages labelled introduction, growth, maturity, decline, and decision point.)

The Coca Cola brand name is recognizable in any language.

on a BlackBerry as their personal handheld computer, or buy only a PlayStation, even if they have to wait an extra six months to get it. Products that have reached the brand insistence level have enormous brand equity.

A brand's equity develops in a predictable way. The progress of the brand can be charted on the **product life cycle**. The traditional product life cycle consists of five parts: product introduction, growth, maturity, decline, and decision point. A graph of the product life cycle, which can also be called the **style curve**, illustrates product sales over time. Marketers use the product life cycle to determine what type of marketing efforts they should use on the brand.

Product Introduction

The product enters the marketplace through a product introduction, often called a **launch**. Sometimes, businesses introduce a product nationally or even internationally. At other times, they introduce their products by city, region, or province. At the introduction stage of the product life cycle, consumers don't even know the product exists. The business needs to inform them about the product's features, availability, package design, and brand identification. Usually, curious or adventurous consumers (or consumers who like to be the first to own new products) buy the product first.

Marketers often call these first consumers **early adopters** and focus their selling efforts on them. Other consumers look to early adopters, or trendsetters, for style information. Trendsetters can be celebrities, sports heroes, politicians, or even students in your school. Professional athletes often help businesses introduce new products. When a television star wears a new hairstyle, for example, fans of that star often copy him or her. Other early adopters copy the clothing and dress styles worn by famous people at celebrity events such as award shows.

Many products, however, are introduced to the mass market with hopes that some people will become early adopters. In its introductory stage, the advertising campaigns and sales promotions for the new individual serving size of Crystal Light—an instant drink mix now packaged in tubes so it can be added to bottled water—aimed the product at women. (Advertising campaigns and sales promotions will be discussed later in this chapter.)

Growth

Once early adopters find and use a new product, others soon try it and sales increase rapidly. Samples of Crystal Light's individual-serving-size packages were sent to millions of householders. Within days, women in fitness clubs, offices, and factory lunchrooms were using the new product (which turned ordinary bottled water into Crystal Light). Other women saw these early adopters using their sample and tried out their own free product. Soon, sales started to rise.

During the growth stage, marketers manage their products very carefully. As a product's popularity increases, competitors enter the market. These competitors modify the original product either by adding features and improving quality or by making a similar product more cheaply and offering it at a lower price. Nestea and Kool-Aid have both introduced individual serving sizes for their products. Who will be next: Gatorade, Snapple, Lipton?

Competition fuels growth. Consumers see the battle for market dominance and become interested in knowing what all the fuss is about. The new product lines are featured in commercials, billboards, print ads, even on talk show interviews and news broadcasts. The line becomes very visible and highly promoted. A buzz surrounds the line, and everybody has to try it. New competitors enter the market and dilute profitability. Others, unsuccessful at making any money or attracting enough customers away from the originators, drop out of the race. Finally, at the top of the growth cycle, only a few winners survive.

Although these products are very similar, each product is designed to stand out from and out-compete the other leading brands.

Maturity

At the maturity stage, growth is flat—it does not increase or decrease. New consumers replace those who leave to purchase a competing product. Brand equity is at its highest at this point. Companies manage mature products through continued advertising. This advertising keeps the brand in the public eye and reminds consumers of the advantages this product has over the competition. Kellogg's Corn Flakes, Coca-Cola, and Tide detergent are all products at the maturity stage.

By the time a product reaches maturity, the manufacturer has long since paid for all the major costs of production and product development. Because a mature product has established an effective distribution method, the costs of sales and distribution are low. As a result, products at the maturity stage usually make large profits. Businesses can use income generated by their mature products, often called **cash cows**, to develop and fund new products.

Decline

At some point, most products fail to attract new customers to replace those who leave to buy other brands. As sales decrease, the product enters the decline stage. Seasonal changes or new competition may cause a temporary decline. But if the decline continues, businesses research their markets to determine whether consumers are actually rejecting the brand. A small change in price or a new advertising campaign can reverse a temporary decline. If, on the other hand, brand equity drops, then the business has a serious problem.

The Decision Point

At the final stage of the product life cycle, the decision point, marketers make very important brand-management decisions. Often, they use what equity they have left in the brand and try to reposition it—that is, they try to make it popular again with a new consumer market. Vespa is making motor scooters in new colours specifically designed for women, for example. Businesses also reformulate, repackage, and re-introduce a "new and improved" product. For example, an old brand of liquid detergent could re-enter the market with a convenient new pour spout.

Most often, however, decision-point management involves new promotion and repricing. An advertising agency, for

Tide detergent is an example of a product that has reached the maturity stage.

Stretch Your Thinking

Think of a product that has declined in popularity. How could you increase sales?

The World of Business DVD

"Rethinking the Advertising Game"
from *The World of Business* DVD

Can you imagine choosing to buy a black-and-white television instead of a colour television?

example, might develop a campaign to target an old product to a new consumer group (Walkman for senior citizens, for example). If the campaign succeeds, the brand becomes more popular. A lower price may also boost the brand's popularity. If these marketing strategies work, the brand regains its original sales figures and brand equity. If the decline continues in spite of efforts to stop it, the manufacturer discontinues the product and removes it from the market.

Often, new technology makes old products obsolete. DVDs have replaced videotape, MP3 players have replaced portable cassette players, and flat-screen television sets have all but replaced the picture tube type. No amount of marketing will restore life to these products.

Non-traditional Product Life Cycles

Many products do not go through the stages of the traditional product life cycle. There are at least three non-traditional product life cycles: fad, niche, and seasonal.

Women are a new customer-market for Vespa motor scooters.

Fads

A **fad** is a product that is extremely popular for a very short period of time. Many people misuse the term and call trends fads. A trend lasts a lot longer than a fad and influences numerous other areas. Low-carb diets were a trend that crippled businesses such as Krispy Kreme and hurt numerous other carb-friendly producers. Fads, on the other hand, appear in a very select target market (usually the under-14 set) and last less than a year. Some popular fads over the years have been hula hoops, yo-yos, Pogs, and Tamagotchis. You can still find these items but they are no longer as popular.

Companies can make or lose a great deal of money on fads. If a business can sell most of its stock and get out of the market just as the fad reaches its peak, the business will make an excellent profit. Many fad marketers—especially imitators who create a cheaper version of the fad, called a **knock-off**—enter the market at the wrong time or stay too long. When a fad dies, it dies very quickly, and many businesses get caught with a large inventory that no one wants to buy.

Niches

Some products have a very short growth stage that leads to a solid, but not financially spectacular, maturity stage. These products have a **niche**—a section of the market in which they dominate and into which very few competitors enter. Niche marketers usually invent their products and hold exclusive patents or formulas. By the time other businesses can invent a competing product, the original manufacturer has already distributed its brand to most of the businesses or stores that wish to purchase it. Competitors, then, have no one to sell their product to. Often, niche marketers manufacture specialty parts. Recently, niche marketers have shown rapid growth in the high-tech industry, manufacturing specialized computer parts for large computer firms.

Many factors prevent competitors from being profitable in a given market. These factors, called **barriers to entry**, include the small market size, the cost of research and development, advertising expenses, factory and equipment costs, design costs, lack of distribution channels, and the cost of raw materials. High barriers to entry usually mean that competitors don't enter a market, leaving a niche marketer alone.

Stretch Your Thinking

What are some fads you remember as you were growing up? Are there any current fads of which you are aware?

Oops!

Excerpt from *The Simpsons*, episode 2F14: "Homer versus Patty and Selma"
Lenny: Hey, Homer! How come you've got money to burn? Or singe, anyway?
Carl: Yeah, Homer, what's your secret investment?
Homer: Take a guess.
Barney: Uh, pumpkins?
Homer: [*pause*] Yeah, that's right, Barney. This year, I invested in pumpkins. They've been going up the whole month of October and I got a feeling they're going to peak right around January. Then, bang! That's when I'll cash in.

For a farmer, this pumpkin field represents significant income at the beginning of October but, come November, this same field would mean a huge financial loss!

Seasonal

Try to sell a Christmas tree the day after Christmas, or a snowblower on the hottest day in August. Ice cream parlours have lineups from July to the end of August, but are often closed in January and February. These examples demonstrate that many products are popular only during a specific time or season. The product becomes popular again only when that season returns. The new season, however, brings with it new styles. Even Christmas ornaments change in style from year to year. Retailers, wholesalers, importers, and manufacturers of seasonal products need to make the most of their selling season. These businesses must keep adequate stock. However, if they have too much inventory left over at the end of the season, many of the products will be out of style when the season starts again the next year. This balancing of product quantity with sales is called **inventory management**.

Review Questions

1. What are two major roles of marketing?
2. What is the most important way to measure the impact of marketing?
3. List and describe briefly the three parts of effective brand identification.
4. List a product *not* mentioned in the text for each of the stages in the product life cycle.

Keep in Mind

1. the four Ps of marketing
2. the two Cs of marketing

Marketing Concepts

Did you know that Sony Corporation had portable digital audio technology two years before Apple did? What Sony did not have, however, was a way to connect this technology to a product and connect the product to a consumer. Apple figured that out and put together a marketing mix that saw the iPod become one of the most successful products in the past decade. Sony missed out by not having the right marketing concepts.

You can divide marketing into two major concepts: the product concept and the market concept. Product concept marketers can answer questions about a firm's internal operations: What should our company make and sell? What price will stimulate sales and generate a profit? Where and how do we sell the product? What advertising and promotion should we create for the product to boost sales? These make up the four Ps of marketing: product, price, place, and promotion.

Market concept marketers work with the external environment by examining both the competitive market and the consumer market. The competitive market consists of all the products or services that might take sales away from a firm. The consumer market consists of all the people who are or might at some point be interested in buying the product or services. These make up the two Cs of marketing: competitive market and consumer market.

The Four Ps of Marketing

A good marketing campaign considers the **four Ps of marketing**: product, price, place, and promotion. All four elements must be combined properly to have an effective campaign. When all four parts are assembled, it is called the marketing mix.

Products and Services

Businesses develop products and services for two reasons: because they can and because they see a need. Good product and service development takes into account quality, design, features, and benefits.

Quality

Ralph Waldo Emerson wrote, "If a man can…make a better mousetrap than his neighbour, though he build his house in the woods, the world will make a beaten path to his door." Simply put, if you improve the quality of your product, you will attract more customers. Vacuum cleaners that pick up more dirt, dry cleaners who sew on buttons, skateboards with better wheels, movie theatres with stadium seating and great sound, and jeans with higher-grade denim are all examples of products that are of better quality than other similar products. Many established brand names take pride in their quality, and consumers come to depend on it.

Low quality is a part of product development as well. Most consumers know that you pay for quality. If some products can meet a consumer's needs and be less expensive because they don't provide high quality, that product or service has a good chance for success as well. For example, Food Basics and no-name products remove the frills but lower the price.

The World of Business DVD

"Igniting the Buzz: I-Buzz"
from *The World of Business* DVD

Figure 8.3 The Marketing Mix

The Marketing Mix

The Four Ps of Marketing

Product (or service)
- quality
- design
- features
- benefits
- service and support

Price
- how our product compares with the competition
- customer's perception of our product's value
- impact on sales and profit

Promotion
- how our company encourages consumers to buy a product (coupons, contests, premiums, samples, special events)

Place
- how our product gets to the consumer (channels of distribution)

Business Fact

Product designers also create product features that you cannot see, such as the flavour of a soft drink or the scent of a perfume.

Not only is the Coca-Cola Classic brand name distinct, but so is the shape of the bottle.

Design

Most often, we think of style and design in relation to clothing. Jeans, for example, come in many different styles—slim fit or wide leg, button fly or zipper, straight leg or flare. Every detail is part of the design, from the colour of thread used in the stitching to the colour of the denim itself. However, every product has a design component. We often buy one product instead of another because we like the way it looks. For example, all cars will transport us from one place to another, but many of us would prefer to get there in a Porsche.

Even if the product itself is not interesting to look at (e.g., liquid detergent), the package design can capture the customer's attention. When designing a package, product developers consider the package's functions. Packages protect the product from light, dirt, germs, air, water, tampering, and damage. A good package also makes it easy for the consumer to use the product—for example, cartons with spouts, bottles with handgrips, or resealable cereal bags. Consumers may also identify a particular product by the shape or colour of the package design. The traditional Coca-Cola bottle is one of the most identifiable packages in the world.

Package labels also help consumers identify the product and can make the product stand out from the competition.

An attractive label can help sell a product. For example, Arizona Iced Tea shrink-wraps colourful plastic labels around the entire bottle. This labelling method, which results in a bottle that attracts consumers' attention, has helped sales. Labels also provide information about a product's size, weight, ingredients, and nutritional content.

Services have a design feature as well. Even if the business is web-based, the web page design is important. A computer repair shop can look sterile and high-tech or down-and-dirty and hands-on. A hairstylist's shop can be a luxury spa or a busy salon. Each design feature of the business attracts a specific type of customer.

Arizona Iced Tea's packaging is designed to catch consumers' attention.

Features

Product developers consider the features of products, such as the material used in construction, the scent, the size, or the taste. Pillows are foam or feathers. Perfumes all smell differently. Cocoa Krispies cereal does not taste the same as Raisin Bran. Detergents come in liquid or powder, large boxes or small, scented or unscented.

Service providers outline what they do. As a car rental company, is pickup part of the service? As a house-cleaning firm, do you do windows? If you were a DVD rental place, how long would you allow customers to keep new releases? Service features are in the details.

Benefits

People buy most products and services for a particular purpose—towels for drying, furnace repair for warmth, microwaves to cook food quickly. But some towels are more absorbent than others, some furnace repairers more efficient, and some microwaves cook food faster. Each product or service has benefits that attract different consumers. The consumer must perceive these benefits in order to be interested enough to buy.

The Product/Service Mix

Retail stores provide services that add value to the products they sell. These include delivery, installation, extended warranties, alterations, advice, carry-outs, gift-wrapping, and free parking. Many stores provide coffee or relaxation areas. Some have a cafeteria or restaurant. Every service that a store offers gives consumers another reason to select that store instead of another.

On the other hand, many service businesses also sell products. Movie theatres sell popcorn, video stores sell candy, veterinarians sell pet food, universities sell sweatshirts, and salons sell hair care products. The right product/service mix can increase sales to existing customers. It can also attract new customers by helping the store be competitive.

Price

Pricing decisions can make the difference between a successful product and a failure. You could have a well-designed, top-quality product with great features, but if the consumer thinks the price is too high, you will not sell it. Consumers are very price aware these days, especially with the ability to check out competing prices on the Internet. To compare prices, all they need to do is spend a few minutes at their computer.

If you lower the price to sell more product, you might increase your profit, but you could also end up with less. For example, let's assume the total cost of producing your gadget is $25.

- If you can sell 100 gadgets at $100 each, you will make a profit of $75 for each gadget sold (because it costs $25 to make). Your total profit will be 100 × $75 = $7500.

- If you lower the price to $50 per unit and sell 1000 gadgets, you will only earn $25 profit for each gadget you sell, but your total profit will increase to $25 000 because 1000 × $25 = $25 000.

- However, if you lower the price to $50 and sell only 200 gadgets, you will still earn $25 profit for each gadget but your total profit will only be 200 × $25 = $5000.

Clearly, marketers need to know how **price sensitive** their product is: how much sales will go up or down when the price goes up or down.

Price must always be similar to the price of competitive products. If the product appears to be similar, but carries a much higher price, the marketing mix should increase the promotional component and make sure consumers know they are paying more for more.

Place (Channels of Distribution)

Channels of distribution are the paths of ownership that goods follow as they pass from the producer to the consumer. They are the methods that a business uses to sell and distribute its products. A product does not change as it moves through

Figure 8.4 Channels of Distribution

Channels of Distribution

Direct
- the business that makes the product sells it directly to the consumer (e.g., at a farmers' market, bakery, or factory outlet store)
- allows for direct communication between producers and consumers

Indirect
- the business sells to an intermediary who then sells the product to the consumer
- the intermediary could be a retailer, or it could be an importer or wholesaler who will then sell to a retailer
- intermediaries add to the cost of a product

Specialty
- the consumer buys from a place other than a retail store (e.g., vending machine, catalogue, website)

channels of distribution (also known as a distribution chain). If a product does change in any way, it has reached the end of that particular channel. For example, a farmer sells wheat to a business that stores grain. Because it does *not* change the product, the storage company is part of the wheat's distribution chain. The storage company then sells the wheat to a flour mill, and the mill processes the wheat into flour. Because the mill *does* change the wheat into another product, the channel of distribution for the wheat ends, and a new channel of distribution for the flour begins.

A marketer can use three types of channels of distribution: direct, indirect, and specialty channels.

Direct Channels

Selling directly to the consumer is the simplest form of distribution. It has a number of advantages. Other channels of distribution use **intermediaries** or businesses that take possession of the goods before consumers do. Intermediaries add costs to a product so that they make a profit. Eliminating intermediaries cuts out these costs.

Direct channels of distribution connect buyers to the businesses providing the goods or services. This connection is known as a **maker–user relationship**. Through this relationship, consumers can inform businesses about their needs. Consumers may also feel more confident because they know the actual source of the products they are buying.

This farmer is selling his produce to customers through a direct channel of distribution.

Indirect Channels

Indirect channels of distribution have one or more intermediaries. These intermediaries might be importers, wholesalers, or retailers.

Importers

Many foreign businesses want to sell their products in Canada. An **importer** searches for these businesses, negotiates distribution deals with foreign manufacturers, buys the manufactured merchandise, stores it in Canada, if necessary, and then sells it. This arrangement makes it easier for foreign businesses to ship their goods to Canadian customers. Sometimes, importers arrange only delivery of foreign products to Canadian businesses. In this way, they assume no risk in buying the goods.

Normally, importers hire a sales force to sell the products across Canada. When an importer actually buys the foreign merchandise and distributes it nationally, the foreign business usually gives the importer exclusive rights to the product. Having exclusive rights means that no other business can buy or sell these products in Canada. An exclusive distribution deal is usually for a year or more. (Review Chapter 4 on International Business.)

Stretch Your Thinking

Why would an importer want to have exclusive rights to a product? Why would a manufacturer want to give exclusive rights to an importer?

Wal-Mart is known for its low prices. The company tries to do everything it can to shave a few cents off the selling price of its products. The company pays low wages and discourages labour unions. Numerous charges have been levelled against Wal-Mart for age discrimination (laying off workers when they get old in order to make room for younger, less costly employees), failure to pay overtime, and widespread sex discrimination to keep women at lower wages. In the United States, where Wal-Mart is based, almost 70 percent of Wal-Mart workers can't afford to participate in the company's health insurance plan, which costs about 20 percent of a worker's paycheque. Some people view Wal-Mart's employee practices differently. They argue that everyone who works for Wal-Mart makes the choice to work there and knows the wages being offered when they take the job.

Most consumers are grateful to Wal-Mart for keeping prices low. It is considered a better retailer than most other companies because it carries the merchandise consumers want at a lower price than competitors, and merchandise is always in stock, when the customer wants it.

Would you be willing to pay more for the items you buy at Wal-Mart if the extra money Wal-Mart received went to benefit its employees?

Wholesalers

Wholesalers buy goods from producers or importers and resell the goods to retailers. Retailers use wholesalers, rather than buying directly from suppliers, for a number of reasons. Manufacturers often require retailers to purchase a minimum quantity of goods. Smaller stores may not have the space or money to buy in such large quantities. Wholesalers can afford to buy in volume and will sell to retailers in much smaller quantities. As well, wholesalers are usually located close to retailers, which means wholesalers can provide storage space and reduce transportation costs. Retailers who use wholesalers, however, often pay more for a product than those who buy directly from the manufacturer.

Canadian Tire is just one familiar retail centre that is constantly stocked with large quantities of merchandise.

Retailers

In the distribution chain, retailers link directly to consumers. Retailers buy merchandise that consumers want, have it in stock when consumers want it, and display the merchandise so consumers can examine it in an easy-to-reach location.

Specialty Channels

A **specialty channel of distribution** is any indirect channel of distribution that does not involve a retail store. There are many different specialty channels, including vending machines, telemarketing, catalogue sales, e-commerce, and door-to-door sales.

Lee Valley Tools catalogue

Figure 8.5 Specialty Channels of Distribution

Vending Machines

Vending machines sell everything from soft drinks to blue jeans. Marketers can place their products in vending machines where consumers work, study, shop, rest, eat, or travel. If the manufacturer owns the machine, it dispenses only their products—there is no competition unless a rival producer's machine is nearby.

Telemarketing

Many businesses use the telephone to sell products and services. Businesses may hire a telemarketing company to create a **sales pitch**—a scripted presentation that anticipates consumer responses. Telemarketing companies may set up call centres, or they may hire an **independent call centre**. Call centres use **automatic call distributors (ACDs)**—computers that automatically dial phone numbers. Telemarketers may call at random, or they may get lists of targeted recipients from coupons, contest-entry forms, or surveys that consumers complete. The main problem with telemarketing is that it often annoys consumers, which may lead to negative reactions to the product or service.

Catalogue Sales

Catalogues from retailers, such as Sears, provide information about merchandise that consumers can purchase by mail, by phone, or at the store. However, there are also catalogue distributors who sell mainly by mail. Lee Valley Tools, for example, makes a high quality line of woodworking tools. It offers these to consumers primarily through its catalogues (it also has retail stores across the country). Catalogues are expensive to produce when they are printed in colour and include photos taken by professional photographers. But catalogue businesses can be very successful, and many companies have added online catalogues to their distribution chain.

E-commerce

By far the most important specialty channel is e-commerce: selling online. Almost all major retailers provide customers with an online catalogue and electronic shopping cart. Online shopping offers consumers convenience and competitive prices. For manufacturers and retailers, distribution costs are much lower. For importers and wholesalers, it is possible to sell directly to consumers, cutting out intermediaries entirely. Online shopping allows even small entrepreneurs to compete globally. You can buy almost anything online today, have it shipped within 24 hours, probably save money, and never have to leave your home.

Promotion

Most people associate advertising with promotion. That part of promotion will be covered later on in this chapter, under a separate section. Promotion, though, means more than advertising. Promotion is any attempt to sell a product. **Sales promotion** encourages consumers to buy a product by using coupons, contests, premiums, samples, and special events.

The eBay logo

Coupons

Coupons offer consumers money off the price of a product. When a consumer presents a coupon at a checkout counter, the cashier treats it as cash. On average, Canadian consumers are exposed to more than 1200 coupons a year. Most coupons end up in the trash. Advertisers measure the effectiveness of a coupon promotion by the **redemption rate**, or the percentage of coupons that consumers actually use. An average redemption rate is 5 percent. In general, the larger the value of the coupon, the higher the redemption rate will be.

Contests

Contests are an exciting way to increase brand recognition and sales. By law, businesses must organize contests so that anyone can enter—the business cannot require consumers to buy a product in order to enter. As a result, you often see "no purchase required" included in contest rules. Businesses, however, can make it easier for consumers who buy the product or service to enter contests. Purchasers of the product may receive an entry form at the cash register, for example, or receive a game card to scratch or collect.

What could be better than to "roll up the rim" and win?

There are laws that forbid the use of gambling in contests. Contests must require people either to demonstrate a skill—for example, drawing a logo, thinking up a name, responding to a quiz—or to answer a skill-testing question (usually a simple math problem). Consider the Tim Hortons "Roll Up the Rim to Win" contest. People could enter their name in the contest by writing to the Tim Hortons head office, but most consumers bought coffee in specially marked cups and "rolled up the rim" themselves to see if they had won a prize. Contestants did not have to exhibit a skill to enter, but winners did have to answer a skill-testing question.

Premiums

Premiums are giveaways—something a consumer gets free with the purchase of a product. Premiums can be unrelated to the product—for example, a free CD with the purchase of a certain amount of coffee, or a free T-shirt with the purchase of a case of pop. To establish brand recognition, these free products usually carry the company's logo.

Many businesses encourage brand loyalty by giving free products to regular customers. Coffee and sandwich shops, florists, video-rental businesses, and CD retailers issue **customer loyalty cards**. These cards are stamped each time the customer buys the business's product. When the card is completed, the consumer is entitled to a free product. Because the consumer must buy the product to get the premium, this method of promotion ensures sales.

When customers buy this box of Kellogg's Raisin Bran, they will get two scoops of raisins and a free gift.

Samples

Samples encourage brand trial. Usually, samples are small "trial" sizes of the product being promoted. Often, the company distributes these samples door to door. Sometimes, marketers hire product-sampling businesses to set up booths in supermarkets, big box stores, and shopping centres. They give out samples of the product to shoppers passing by. They also provide information about the product, its price, and where it can be found in the store. Sampling is a very effective method of sales promotion, and it usually results in increased sales. Costs are very high, however.

Special Events

Marketers organize special events to attract customers and increase product sales. Authors visit bookstores to autograph their newly published books. Sports heroes, television stars, actors, and music celebrities take part in special events that promote their athletic shoe, new perfume, latest movie, or current CD. Sometimes, special events also include other types of sales promotions, such as contests, premiums, and samples. The main purpose of a special event is to excite consumers, encourage their participation, and, ultimately, get them to buy the product. Consumers are more likely to buy if they are having fun.

The Two Cs of Marketing

In order to properly put together a marketing mix, the marketing department must consider two major external factors: the competition and the consumer. These are called the **two Cs of marketing**.

The Competitive Market

The **competitive market** consists of all the sellers of a specific product, and is expressed most often in terms of the total dollars spent annually on this product. Table 8.1 defines the size of that market in dollars. For example, the American soft drink industry is worth $68 billion, which means all the manufacturers, bottlers, importers, and distributors share that $68 billion among themselves. The percentage of the market that a company or brand has is called its **market share**.

Assume that in 2007, the soft drink market is worth $70 billion, and the leading soft drink brands and their market shares are as illustrated in Table 8.1.

The total market share for these top seven brands is 62.9 percent—almost two-thirds of the market. That leaves only 37.1 percent of the market for the other 200 brands available in the United States. However even one-tenth of a 1 percent share of this market is worth $68 million!

Although Coca-Cola Classic has the largest *market share* of the soft drink industry, Coca-Cola still has to share the *competitive market* with other soft drink companies, such as Pepsi.

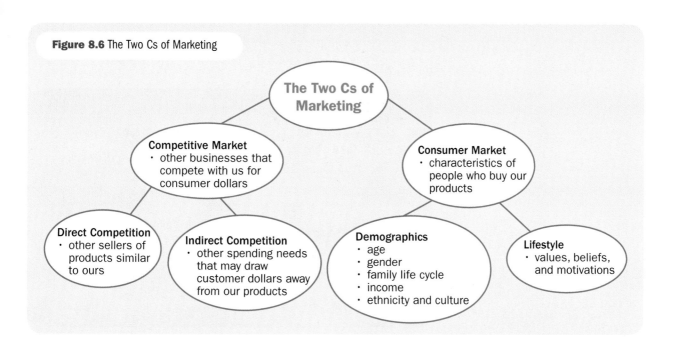

Figure 8.6 The Two Cs of Marketing

- **The Two Cs of Marketing**
  - **Competitive Market**
    - other businesses that compete with us for consumer dollars
    - **Direct Competition**
      - other sellers of products similar to ours
    - **Indirect Competition**
      - other spending needs that may draw customer dollars away from our products
  - **Consumer Market**
    - characteristics of people who buy our products
    - **Demographics**
      - age
      - gender
      - family life cycle
      - income
      - ethnicity and culture
    - **Lifestyle**
      - values, beliefs, and motivations

Table 8.1

Estimated U.S. Market Share for Major Soft Drink Brands*	
Brand	**% Market Share**
Coca-Cola Classic	16.5
Pepsi	12.3
Diet Coke	10.2
Mountain Dew	6.5
Diet Pepsi	5.9
Sprite	5.8
Dr. Pepper	5.7
Total	**62.9**

*2007

Coca-Cola has a major portion of the cola segment of the soft drink market. A **market segment** is a part of the overall market that has similar characteristics. The soft drink market would have flavoured segments, such as root beer (Barq's has the largest piece of that pie), a diet segment (Diet Coke is the leader here), and an energy drink segment (Red Bull owns this market segment).

A company can increase market share in two ways. The first is by increasing the size of the overall market. When energy drinks became popular, a whole new segment of the overall beverage market was created. New soft drink users were added

The energy drink Red Bull played a major role in expanding the beverage market.

to the market, and the size of the market increased, meaning many competitors could see an increase in sales.

The second way to increase market share is by taking sales away from competitors. If you look at the market shares of U.S. beverage brands next year (or next month, perhaps), you will see different market shares, as Sprite attracts more customers than Mountain Dew, or Diet Pepsi takes customers away from Diet Coke. Market shares are like pieces of a pie. If five people are sharing the pie and one person gets half, all the others get much smaller pieces. For the last 100 years or so, Coca-Cola has always had the biggest piece.

Competition among Products

The most obvious type of competition is competition among similar products. All products compete for the consumer's money in some way. If you have $25 and decide to spend it taking a friend to a movie, each theatre and each movie competes for your money. Once you spend $25 on the movie, that $25 is gone—you can't spend it on anything else. So it's not just movies and theatres that compete for your $25; CDs, pizzas, clothes, and any other products you might buy also compete for your money. This type of competition is called **indirect competition** because the products or services are not directly related to each other. Every business is in competition with every other business for your **discretionary income**. Discretionary income is the income you have that is not committed to paying for basic necessities, such as food, clothing, and shelter. **Disposable income**, on the other hand, is used to pay for basic necessities. It is the amount of income left after taxes have been paid.

Products in direct competition

Products that are very similar are in **direct competition**. The consumer chooses among them because of minor differences. There really is not a large difference between two brands of sunscreen—they both have the same sun protection factor, both are waterproof, and both are non-greasy. These products compete mainly on image. Other products compete directly in more obvious ways, through all of the quality, price, design, features, and benefits that compose the product (see the four Ps of marketing, earlier in this chapter).

The Consumer Market

Companies also compete by studying the **consumer market**, or the types of consumers who buy their products. These consumers can be identified in at least two ways: by demographics and by lifestyle.

Demographics

Demographics is the study of obvious characteristics that categorize human beings. Businesses use demographics to target specific consumers. Examples of demographic variables are age, gender, family life cycle, income level, and ethnicity and culture.

Age

Children want toys, teens want computer games, adults are interested in cars, and seniors may want more products related to health or retirement activities. Age defines our tastes, as well as our needs and wants. Some age groups are consumers, but not often customers. For example, an adult—most often a parent—usually directs his or her child's purchases. Businesses consider this adult a **gatekeeper**, or a person who makes buying decisions for others. Cereal makers compete by selling their products to the gatekeepers, advertising that their cereal is low in sugar or has added vitamins for good health. However, cereal makers also know that children have some influence over the decisions that their gatekeepers make, so these companies also target young people in their advertisements.

Gender

Many products, like jeans and athletic shoes, are worn by both genders. However, businesses that sell jeans and shoes still distinguish between their men's and women's product lines. The businesses market their men's athletic shoes to the male market and their women's athletic shoes to the female market.

In the area of shopping, gender roles have changed a great deal. At one time, women did the family grocery shopping and men purchased the family car. Today, the act of shopping has become a task for males and females alike, and purchase decisions are more likely to be shared. A number of successful businesses have recognized this change. Many products that were formerly targeted at females (detergents, disposable diapers, food products) or males (cars, power tools, sporting equipment) are now being advertised and sold successfully to both genders.

Family Life Cycle

Newly married couples need furniture. Parents with a new baby need a crib, carriage, and car seat. A couple with three teenagers wants to save for their children's college or university educations. Retired seniors want to travel. Your stage in the family life cycle often determines your wants and needs. Businesses are aware of this demographic. They compete for consumer dollars in

What products would this family buy...

...that this family wouldn't need?

different ways for various groups. For example, a cruise could be a honeymoon for a newly married couple, a break for a couple with a baby, a family holiday for a couple with teenagers, or a retirement escape for a senior. The advertising, destination, onboard activities, and meals will all depend on the type of customers the cruise is trying to attract.

Income Level

Consumers are often grouped by how much money they have or earn. This grouping affects what products or services a business tries to sell them. Products such as Kellogg's Corn Flakes are targeted at consumers in every income bracket, but a Mercedes automobile could be purchased only by wealthy customers. Businesses have many ways of determining the income of specific groups of consumers. One way is to look at the postal codes of affluent, or upper-income, neighbourhoods. If a consumer has an address in this postal code, it is likely that he or she has a high income. Similarly, a business can look at programs for ballets, book readings, and other special events in the community to find out who sponsors these events. If a business wants to target a particular high-income group, it might place an advertisement in a certain type of publication, such as a luxury travel magazine.

Businesses that make or sell luxury goods and services are interested in the wealthy customer, but most manufacturers and retailers make and sell products to consumers with average incomes. These businesses are mainly interested in competing for the discretionary income that almost all consumers possess. They sell their products and services to everyone.

Ethnicity and Culture

Canada has a diverse population with a wonderful mix of customs and traditions. Many cities have ethnic communities with stores and businesses that target the various wants and needs of a particular ethnic group. These businesses compete for a cultural market by importing goods from the consumer's country of origin or producing goods reflective of that country. The food-service sector has a multitude of restaurants that reflect different cultural tastes in food. Newspapers and magazines in Canada are available in more than 100 languages. Of course, many of the products and services that first attracted the business of a specific ethnic group now compete for the business of all Canadians. Italian restaurants, for example, certainly have many non-Italian customers.

Lifestyle

Lifestyle is less obvious than demographics but equally important to businesses competing for specific groups of consumers. **Lifestyle** is the way people live, which includes their values, beliefs, and motivations. The study of lifestyles is called **psychographics**.

A person's beliefs influence what he or she purchases. An environmentally conscious person would not buy an SUV, for example. A sedentary person would not be interested in running shoes or skis. These lifestyles cross all demographic boundaries. Unless companies consider lifestyle marketing, the potential consumers in these groups will miss their message.

Review Questions

5. What are the four Ps of marketing?

6. Provide an example for each of the following:
   a) slogan
   b) family life cycle
   c) premium
   d) specialty channel of distribution
   e) product/service mix

7. What are the two Cs of marketing?

8. Define and give an example of market share.

9. Explain two possible ways in which a business could increase its market share.

Advertising

Keep in Mind

1. creating good advertising
2. types of advertising
3. comparing types of advertising

Has an advertisement ever made you cry? Or laugh out loud? Some television commercials are better than some movies; they do in 60 seconds or less what some movies can't do in two hours. There is an art to good advertising, and more than a few major artists have started their careers in the industry. Spike Jonze, for example, directed videos for the Beastie Boys, Beck, REM, and Fatboy Slim, as well as films such as *Being John Malkovich*. Today, he is considered one of the best advertising minds in the business (look for his Levi's ad on the Internet).

Creating Good Advertising

There is no magic formula for genius. Really great advertising has genius in it, and that cannot be taught. But most advertisers are simply looking for good ads—ads that consumers will see and remember. Advertisers want consumers to remember the brand name of the product in particular. Even ads that are artistic or funny or incredibly creative might not be good ads if you can't remember the name of the product being sold. Good ads sell products. The Apple Computer advertisement called "1984" that introduced the Macintosh onto the market during the 1984 Super Bowl had thousands of customers looking for Macs the day after it was aired.

There are four standard rules for creating good advertising: attract attention, gain interest, build desire, and get action.

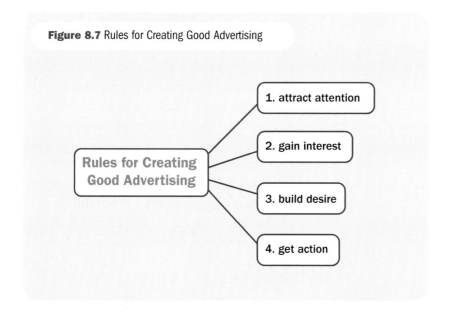

Figure 8.7 Rules for Creating Good Advertising

Rules for Creating Good Advertising

1. attract attention
2. gain interest
3. build desire
4. get action

Attract Attention

For print advertisements, a good headline works. It should be a headline that mentions the brand: "Sprite: Obey Your Thirst," for example. Even if the consumer only sees that much of the ad, he or she will associate Sprite with thirst. A good print headline is rarely more than seven words (easier to remember) and always leads the reader into the rest of the ad. The Sprite ad, for example, should talk about thirst.

Broadcast ads attract attention in various ways: sound, unusual visuals, an attractive person, a famous celebrity, or a hilarious moment (a singing cow attracted attention for HP sauce several years ago). For broadcast advertising, the task is to hold the attention for up to 60 seconds when the fridge or bathroom beckons.

Gain Interest

Print ads should be simple and easy to read. Avoid complex or mixed typefaces. Keep the message clear and to the point. Broadcast ads, too, should get to the main message right away. New advertisers should *not* try to do humour. It is very hard to make something funny, and very embarrassing when no one laughs. Provide a direct, interesting sales message and a great illustration. The old proverb that one picture is worth a thousand words is absolutely true in advertising. Of course, television ads must have strong visuals and radio ads can't have any (except those that the imagination creates). Make people want to read (or watch or listen to) your ad.

Build Desire

Connect the sales message to your visual message. Help the customer want your product. Set up a problem that your product solves or put the product in a situation with which the customer identifies. The Sprite ad creates a scene in which someone is very thirsty. A cold bottle of Sprite solves the problem. The consumer, if thirsty, desires Sprite. Print ads build desire with words, adding benefits with each line. Broadcast ads describe the benefits thoroughly and repeat the brand name often to make sure the desire is associated with the brand. It is counterproductive to remind the audience of their thirst if they don't remember that Sprite is the best product to quench it.

Literacy Link

Persuasive writing

Persuasive writing is used to convince others to think like you do. There are many ways to suggest that others see something your way. You can use

- a brochure (written details to highlight your position)

- an advertisement (written words and visual pictures to persuade)

- a speech (spoken emotional words to convince)

Get Action

Always ask for the sale. Summarize the reasons to buy. Be sure to have your logo, slogan, brand name, and contact information at the bottom right-hand corner of the print ad (the North American reader looks at a printed page from top to bottom, left to right, and always ends in the bottom right-hand corner). Both print and broadcast ads should repeat a phone number or simple website address to encourage consumers to find out more or even order online. Retail advertisers should include the store address and hours. A map is helpful. Limited-time offers are effective ways of providing a reason to "buy now." All advertising should be about buying now.

Types of Advertising

Advertising is the paid-for promotion of a business's goods and services over a variety of mass media to a target market of consumers. Businesses pay a great deal of money to advertise, and they carefully control what their ads say. In other words, an advertisement gives only the advertiser's point of view. **Publicity** is media information about a business that the business doesn't pay for. Publicity can be either positive or negative. As a result, it is more believable than advertising. Many companies try to control their publicity by hiring public relations firms. Public relations firms try to influence the media to use only positive stories about their clients. In fact, public relations firms often write and distribute positive stories about the businesses they represent, hoping that the media will use them.

We see, hear, and read hundreds of advertisements every day. Ads are played during movie previews at the cinema and during our favourite television programs each night. We hear advertising messages on the radio when we wake up. We read ads on buses and in subway stations; in magazines, newspapers, and flyers; and on the Internet. Most often, advertising is classified by the type of medium that is used to carry the message: direct-to-home, out-of-home, radio and television (broadcast media), newspapers, magazines, and the Internet.

Oops!

In 1996, Clearly Canadian Beverage Corporation introduced a soft drink called Orbitz. Orbitz contained edible balls of a somewhat chewy substance. The balls gave Orbitz a unique look, but made many consumers reject the product. The balls had the consistency of tiny oysters, and lots of people didn't like drinking solid things, instead of just a liquid.

Although Orbitz looked cool, it was not the number one beverage that customers turned to in order to quench their thirst!

Direct-to-home

Any advertising message that comes to your home, such as a flyer or catalogue, is a **direct-to-home advertisement**. Advertisements on the Internet, which are quite new, are also considered direct-to-home advertisements. Businesses are still testing the effectiveness of Internet advertisements, which are usually interactive graphic banners across web pages. Consumers do not ask or pay for direct-to-home advertisements, and residents often ignore them or throw them out.

Out-of-home

Out-of-home advertising is any advertising message that the consumer is supposed to receive while not at home. These messages are sometimes carried on billboards, which can reach 100 percent of a city's mobile population if the advertiser rents the right number of billboards. Out-of-home ads are also shown in buses, subways, and transit shelters. Some advertisers have their ads painted on the outside of buses, making each ad a billboard in transit. These ads attract consumers' attention during the commute to and from work, school, shopping, or entertainment. Clever advertisements also provide an interesting diversion for bored or weary travellers.

Advertisements are placed in all kinds of places, including on buses and train cars.

Radio

Because the radio is often playing in the background, many people call it the "go anywhere" medium. Clock radios wake us up; car radios entertain us on the way to school or work; desk radios keep us amused while we work; radios at the cottage or beach help us relax. Effective radio advertisements skillfully use words and sound effects to draw us in. Although we may never have seen a flying crocodile, we can certainly imagine one when it's described. In fact, you're probably imagining one right now. (What kind of sound effect would you use?)

Television

Because television combines words, sounds, and images, it is an extremely effective advertising medium. It is also very expensive. Nonetheless, television has the size of audience that many businesses want. Millions of people watch popular television shows and sporting events. Some programs appeal to a particular group of consumers. Others reach a large, general audience. If a television advertisement is creative and well made, a large percentage of the target audience will remember the product's name, and many will purchase the product. If an advertisement is especially creative, it may become popular itself.

> ### Business Fact
>
> A 30-second commercial spot during the televised broadcast of the 2006 Super Bowl football game cost an average of US$2.6 million. By way of comparison, 30-second ads on prime time typically run about $400 000.

Newspapers

Businesses advertise in both local and national newspapers. Small companies usually advertise in just local papers, while large companies might advertise both locally and nationally. It can be expensive to place a large ad in a newspaper, but inexpensive to place a small ad in the classified section.

Magazines

Magazines offer advertisers many advantages over newspapers. Magazines print colour advertisements, which attract consumers to the product. Many advertisers use specialty magazines to target specific groups of consumers. They advertise products that appeal to skiers, for example, in *Ski Magazine*. *Flare* has advertisements for fashions for young women. Advertisements for stores that sell bridal gowns appear in *Brides* magazine. Other magazines target specific demographics. There are magazines for men, women, business executives, new parents, young people, and senior citizens. General interest magazines, such as *People* or *Maclean's*, have enormous readerships and appeal to a large cross-section of people.

The Internet

There are three types of Internet advertising: company websites, banner advertising on other websites, and e-mail advertising. Company website advertising attracts consumers who are interested in the company in the first place (enough to look it up). This is a good action medium, as it can easily convert interest into sales. Banner ads can target consumers on one website and direct them to another (if you are looking up a website on skateboarding, for example, a skateboard shoe company like Vans could have an effective banner ad on the site). E-mail advertising is a bit of a mixed bag. If consumers have subscribed to a specific site and are expecting updates, offers, and advertising, then e-mail advertising can be very effective. But it can be very annoying to get messages from companies you don't know. This type of non-permission-based e-mail is called spamming.

Comparing Types of Advertising

Advertisers use eight categories to compare media and select the right one for their advertising. The categories are as follows:

- Reach: The number of people who are exposed to a message. Magazines express reach as circulation. Television describes it as ratings. Super Bowl ads reached 140 million people, for example.

- Frequency: The number of times an audience will see or hear the advertisement over a given period of time. To get frequency on some media (such as radio) requires payment for each placement. Some media have frequency built in. A billboard will be seen 20 times a month by commuters who take the same route to work each day, and a bus advertisement might be seen 40 times a month by the same audience.

- Selectivity: The ability of the medium to focus on a target audience. Internet advertising can be very selective (skateboard ads on skateboard websites), while television ads are only slightly selective (female products advertised on shows that attract more women than men).

- Durability: How long the advertisement lasts in the house. Television ads survive 30 seconds. Newspaper

Table 8.2

Media Rating Chart								
	TV	Radio	Magazines	Newspapers	Out-of-home	Direct-to-home	Internet	Specialty
Reach	8	7	7	7	10	10	7	3
Frequency	1	1	8	3	9	1	10	8
Selectivity	6	7	10	3	1	9	10	5
Durability	1	1	10	7	9	3	10	10
Lead-time	2	9	1	8	2	4	10	4
Mechanical Requirements	3	9	2	7	1	4	8	10
Clutter	3	2	3	4	7	2	2	9
Costs	3	6	6	6	3	7	9	5

This chart rates the advantages and disadvantages of each of the major advertising media on a scale of 1 to 10, where 1 is poor, 10 is excellent, and 5 is variable.

ads last a day. Magazines might hang around for a month. Certain specialty advertisements, like the Milk Calendar, last a whole year.

- Lead-time: How fast the ad can be ready to run. Television ads require months, radio and newspapers only a few days. E-mail advertising is instantaneous.

- Mechanical requirements: How complex it is to prepare the ads for the medium. Television and magazines have very complicated mechanical requirements. Radio ads are simple.

- Clutter: The competition for the audience's attention. Most advertising exists alongside other advertising and competes with other ads for the audience's attention. Ads on the second page of a newspaper, for example, compete with ads on page 3. One television commercial in the middle of eight others feels very cluttered.

- Costs: The accumulated costs of running the advertisement. This includes the costs of preparation as well as the costs of the space or time in the medium used to run it.

Review Questions

10. What are the two most selective media? Explain why.

11. List five types of advertising.

12. What are the four standard rules for good advertising?

13. Why does out-of-home advertising have a reach score of 10 in Table 8.2?

14. Describe an advertisement you think is good. Why do you think that?

Keep in Mind

1. types of marketing research
2. marketing research tools

Marketing Research

What was your favourite movie this month? What television shows do you watch the most? What is your favourite ice cream? You have just been involved in marketing research. If all the students who are reading this book called in their answers to a special number, and the person answering the phone wrote the answers down and sorted through the responses, then movie producers, television networks, and ice cream makers would know a little more about the preferences of young men and women in high school for their products.

Types of Marketing Research

Marketing research is the collection and analysis of information that is relevant to the marketing strategy. There are several different types of marketing research, including consumer, market, motivation, pricing, competitive, product, and advertising research. Marketers do not use every type of research in every situation. Instead, they select which type to use based on what information they require, how they want to collect the information, and what they are going to do with the information after it has been analyzed.

- **Consumer research** discovers what type of product consumers want and predicts the overall sales potential for that product. Researchers use primary-data collection methods, such as phone surveys and personal interviews, to get consumer opinions.

Market surveys can be conducted face to face, on the telephone, or online.

- **Market research** identifies specific groups of consumers who would use a particular product or service. Marketers then create profiles of these groups using demographic and psychographic studies.

- **Motivation research** examines both the emotional (the way we feel) and the rational (the way we think) motives that influence our buying decisions. It tries to find out why we buy.

- **Pricing research** helps the marketer determine if the company can sell the product for a competitive price and still make a profit. Pricing research also looks at how different prices affect demand and, consequently, sales.

- **Competitive research** looks for opportunities in areas where competition is weak or absent and determines what competitors are doing.

- **Product research** examines each detail of a product or service and analyzes the impact these details might have on the market.

- **Advertising research** provides information on the most effective ways to get a message about a product to potential consumers.

Marketing Research Tools

Marketing research relies on two types of data: secondary data and primary data. It uses different tools to collect each type.

Secondary Data

Secondary data is information that others have collected. Researchers re-interpret this information for their own or their clients' purposes. Secondary data can be collected from websites, databases, books, periodicals, indexes, and professionally prepared marketing research reports. Much secondary data is free and provides a background for the company's research strategy. Access to many databases or marketing research reports, however, can be costly. One report on the beverage industry, for example, costs almost $10 000. The questions that secondary data can't answer become the basis for the marketing research plan. This research plan involves primary data.

Primary Data

Primary data is current information that researchers collect and analyze for a specific purpose. Researchers collect this data in a number of ways: test marketing, internal information sources, surveys, observation, and focus groups.

Test Marketing

Companies will sometimes produce a limited quantity of a new product and introduce it into one or two specific areas. Researchers select a test market area based on its demographics and how well it reflects a typical Canadian city. In Ontario, London, Peterborough, and Kingston are often selected. Consumers in the test markets may be unaware that they are testing a new product, and the test markets are often kept secret so competitors cannot influence results. Test marketing is very expensive and must be done very carefully if the results are to be used for major decisions.

Internal Information Sources

A business can analyze its own sales records, inventory data, advertising and promotional results, and production statistics to gather primary data on product histories and/or customer behaviour. This is called **data mining**. Client cards that require customers to provide personal data (age, income, marital status, family size, and so on) help companies gather important information about who purchases what, when. Businesses use data mining to determine relationships between the personal information and purchasing habits. Some stores, through data mining, can tell you what you will buy on your next visit to the store before you even know. The store tracks your purchases and can tell when you are about to run out of bread, for example. If that data is shared with a bread company, they can target you with special coupons at the moment you are ready to purchase.

Surveys

A **survey** is a set of carefully planned questions that are used to gather data. Most surveys use **closed-ended questions** that ask respondents to select one answer from two or more choices. Closed-ended questions usually fit one of the following types: Yes/No; Agree/Disagree; 'Select a, b, c, or d'; or 'Rate on a scale of 1 to 10.' Each of these types of questions is easy to answer and easy to score.

Open-ended questions are more complicated and require respondents to develop their own answers. They are difficult to answer and difficult to analyze, so researchers use them only when they need some very specific data. An example of an open-ended question is, "What words do you associate with this brand of soft drink?"

Observation

Researchers often watch the behaviour of people without those people knowing it. Even if they know they are being observed (two-way glass, cameras, observer in the room, and so on), the researcher and subjects do not interact. The purpose of observation is to note how people really react in situations.

Focus Groups

One of the most popular forms of consumer research is the focus group. A **focus group** is a company-arranged meeting of potential consumers. Marketers observe the focus group during an organized discussion. The meeting usually lasts a few hours, and there is often an incentive for consumers to participate. For example, the company might offer participants a meal, product samples, or money. Before Nike introduced a line of soccer shoes in North America, it had to determine whether there was a large enough market for the product. Nike organized several focus groups of soccer players. Interviewers asked people of various ages and skill levels questions in a group discussion. With the participants' permission, Nike marketers observed and taped the discussion. The answers must have been positive, because Nike is now making soccer shoes.

Companies often test new products or services by conducting a focus group.

CHAPTER REVIEW

Knowledge

1. What is the difference between advertising and publicity?

2. What are the four parts of most print ads? Describe them briefly.

3. What are the three possible forms that logos can take?

Thinking

4. Which part of the marketing mix do you think is the most important? Give reasons for your answer.

5. Find several different methods for the distribution of chocolate. Describe them with examples.

6. Select a print ad that you dislike and give your reasons.

7. Name a product or service that is in the decline stage of the product life cycle. Make recommendations for the product at this stage and give reasons for your answer.

Communication

8. Design a good print ad for the new iPod or BlackBerry.

9. Write a critical appraisal of a commercial you liked or disliked. Be sure to mention its effectiveness as a marketing vehicle.

Application

10. Find two examples of each of the promotional methods described in this chapter.

11. Evaluate the branding on two products in direct competition.

12. Describe in detail the target market for a Vespa.

13. Discuss the marketing mix for any cereal on the market.

Team Activity

Team Goal: To increase attendance at a school function

Team Assignment: Marketing a School Event

- Your team will select one of the many events at your school, such as a play, parents' night, fashion show, or school dance. It will be the team's task to market the event and make it more successful than the last time it was held.

- Use the attendance records from the last time the event was held as a baseline for comparison.

- Members of your team should prepare all of the advertising and publicity for the event, and consider both the four Ps and the two Cs of marketing in your planning.

- The team with the highest percentage increase over the last time the event was held wins.

Portfolio

Design and implement a marketing research plan. Use one or more of the research tools to collect primary data from your school and/or community that you can use to describe trends, evaluate advertising, outline consumer preferences, or make other judgments that would be useful to the marketing managers of companies within your selected industry. Produce a report on the results.

Describe the marketing mix of at least two products in direct competition within your selected industry.

Collect examples of good and bad advertising for products or services within your selected industry.

Reflect on Your Learning

How has your knowledge of marketing affected your opinion regarding your favourite advertisement, your favourite store, and your favourite soft drink? Have you altered how you feel about any of these things, based on what you have learned? If so, how and why?

Apple Computer

The story of Apple began in 1972 when Steven Jobs and Stephan Wozniak (both Hewlett-Packard employees) joined a group of computer enthusiasts. During the next few years, the two Steves would work together to create a personal computer called Apple 1. On April Fools' Day, 1976—in partnership with Ronald Wayne (who designed the first Apple logo)—Apple was founded.

Apple soon became successful. In 1978, Xerox invested one million dollars in Apple stocks; in 1980, the company went public, and within one year, the value of Apple stock increased by 1700 percent. By 1983, Apple had become the fastest growing company in history.

Marketing has always been a vital part of Apple's success. In December 1983, Apple Computers ran its now famous "1984" Macintosh television commercial—they ran it once in 1983 so it would be eligible for awards during 1984. The commercial cost US$1.5 million

Imaginative marketing has played a huge role in Apple's extreme success.

and was so popular it made TV history. The next month, Apple ran the same ad once more during the NFL Super Bowl, and millions of viewers saw their first glimpse of the Macintosh computer. The commercial was directed by Ridley Scott (*Hannibal*, *Gladiator*) and showed the IBM world being destroyed by a new machine, the Macintosh. The launch of Macintosh was one of the great marketing stories of the twentieth century.

Apple has also pulled off one of the great marketing stories of the twenty-first century. In October 2001, Steve Jobs announced the release of Apple's portable music player, the iPod. Despite its initial hefty price (US$400), the iPod quickly became the most used portable music player on the market. Why? Because it looks great and is simple to use. In fact, iPods have generated so much customer interest that, according to the *New York Times,* the iPod has become "the number one motivational electronics product" used by marketing incentive programs. In other words, companies have begun offering a free iPod to those who sign up for a service or product.

Just nine months prior to the release of the iPod, Apple announced its first version of the free music-download software, iTunes. Even though the market was already crowded with competing software, it did not take long for the popularity of iTunes to overtake its rivals.

Following the success of the first iPod, Apple released several versions that provided a range of storage capacity and price. Then, the company launched a wide range of accessories for the iPod. Other companies piggybacked by producing clothing with iPod pockets and "wired" jackets and backpacks.

In October 2005, Apple introduced the next generation of the "world's most popular music jukebox and online music store," iTunes 6.0. The new software not only allows customers to download more than 2000 music videos and six short films for just US$1.99 each, but also provides the ability to download certain television shows. These shows can then be viewed on a Mac, PC, or even a new iPod. Clearly, Apple has revolutionized the market for digital music and video.

QUESTIONS

1. Provide an example of how Apple has marketed itself (hint: consider both advertisement and the products themselves).

2. What is a possible iTunes and/or iPod feature that Apple could provide for its customers in the future?

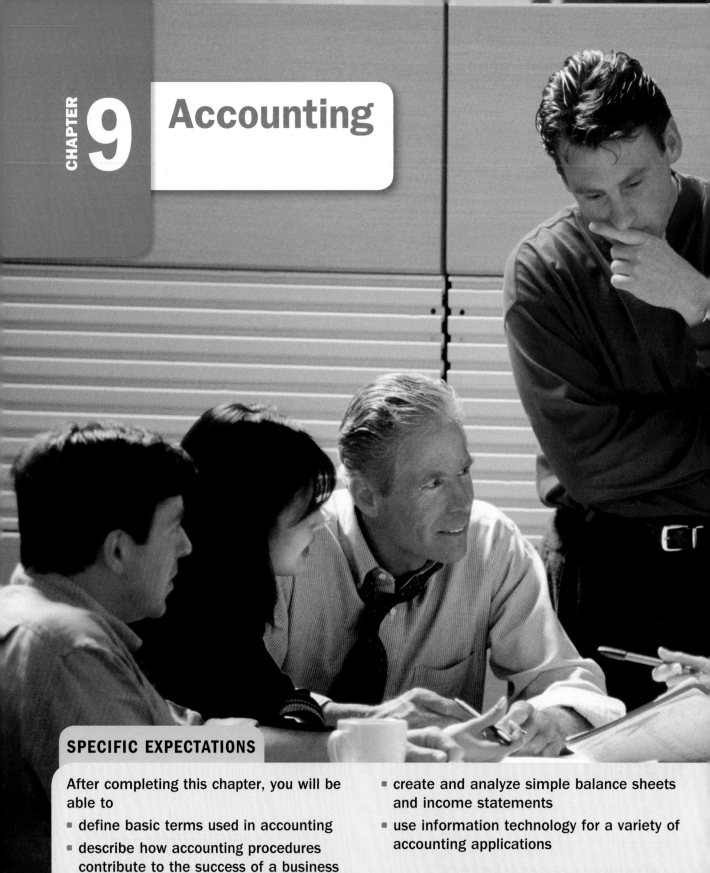

CHAPTER 9

Accounting

SPECIFIC EXPECTATIONS

After completing this chapter, you will be able to

- define basic terms used in accounting
- describe how accounting procedures contribute to the success of a business
- create and analyze simple balance sheets and income statements
- use information technology for a variety of accounting applications

Liquidation World

As a retailer or manufacturer, what do you do when you order too much merchandise, are going out of business, or a customer cancels a large order? One option would be to write it off as a loss, possibly leading to more financial hardship. Another option would be to drastically cut prices in order to sell off the merchandise as quickly as possible. But a more attractive option is to call Liquidation World. Established in 1986, Liquidation World is Canada's largest liquidator, with more than 100 outlets in North America.

Liquidation World provides solutions to inventory problems by buying and marketing merchandise from businesses that are in distress situations. If a business were in trouble, difficulty, or danger, that business would be considered to be in distress. Distress situations include fire, insurance or freight claims, bankruptcies, receiverships, buybacks, overproduction, and cancelled orders.

Dale Gillespie, founder of Liquidation World, realized that the relationship between manufacturers and retailers

The entrance of a Liquidation World

often needs a third party to maintain balance. Liquidation World specializes in liquidating overstocked products, goods damaged by natural disaster, and inventory from bankrupt or financially weak companies. When companies have products that they cannot sell, Liquidation World can take over. A business may not make a profit by selling off their inventory to Liquidation World, but such an option can be better than not getting anything for the sale of that inventory. Liquidation World, with annual sales of more than $185 million, generates a profit by selling this acquired merchandise for more money than they paid to buy it.

Liquidation World provides its services to insurance companies, banks, manufacturers, distributors, and retailers. As well as buying and selling distressed inventory, the company provides auction and appraisal services for its customers. The company also has advanced logistic solutions to get the products off a business's hands within 24 hours, and will gladly ship items out of the province or country.

Liquidation World does not advertise the brand names that they sell (unless specifically asked to), thus ensuring discretion to its customers. In disposing of inventory through its stores, Liquidation World recognizes the importance of brand and label control. If Liquidation World buys brand-name merchandise because of a cancelled order, it tries to be sensitive to prices charged by other retailers operating in the same community. For example, if the company had acquired 30 new brand-name stoves because of a cancelled order, it would sell them at prices that would be competitive with other retailers.

Liquidation World is a bargain hunter's dream. The inventory is constantly changing and no one really knows what brand names they will find when they arrive at the store. More than 750 000 bargain hunters flock to the stores each month. Yet the bargain hunter's dream is usually the result of a retailer's or manufacturer's biggest nightmare. Saving money is usually the result of Liquidation World making the best of a bad situation.

QUESTIONS

1. When a company approaches Liquidation World to do business, the company is often in a dire situation. What help does Liquidation World provide for these businesses?

2. Why is it important for Liquidation World to recognize and honour the importance of brand and label control?

Basic Accounting Concepts

Most of the activities that a business engages in are about financial worth.

- How much money did a business make in a year?

- How much can a business afford to spend on a new store addition?

- How can a business reduce its expenses?

- Is it wise for a business to merge with another company so that it can sell its services in international markets?

- How much will any or all of this cost?

What Accountants Do

Accountants are those individuals who are responsible for finding answers to these questions concerning the financial side of business. Making sure that the records of a business are kept up to date and accurate helps ensure that the accountant can make business decisions that are meaningful and effective. The purpose of accounting is to provide the necessary financial information so that accurate and timely decisions can be made.

Keep in Mind

1. what accountants do
2. accounting and individuals
3. accounting and businesses

Before You Begin

An individual's equity is often called their "net worth" because it expresses what a person is worth financially. Net worth represents the difference between what you own and what you owe. What do you think that your net worth would total? Predict a dollar figure that you would place on your net worth so you can review it after studying this chapter.

⊕ E-ACTIVITY

Visit www.nelson.com/WOB and follow the links to learn more about the accounting profession.

If a business does well financially, the company may expand, leading to the construction of additional space.

For example, if a business is successful and makes a profit, decisions about the use of that money will have to be made. On the other hand, if a business loses money, other decisions will have to be made.

Accounting is the process of recording, analyzing, and interpreting the economic activities of a business. In accounting, any business activity involving money is recorded as a **transaction**. A transaction occurs when something that has value is exchanged for something else that has value. A business pays an employee $80 in exchange for eight hours of work; a customer buys a computer printer in exchange for $150; a clothing manufacturer sells 100 sweaters to a retail outlet in exchange for $5000. The monetary part of these exchanges can be paid in cash, by cheque, or on credit.

A large business can conduct hundreds—even thousands—of transactions daily. For example, a supermarket might serve several thousand customers on a busy Saturday. In addition to customer transactions, businesses conduct many other types of monetary exchanges on a regular basis. These include paying staff; paying bills, such as heat and electricity; and buying and storing inventory. Because each transaction affects a business's finances, companies keep records of these transactions. **Bookkeeping** is the recording of all of these business transactions. Since the introduction of computers and computer software, the majority of businesses use accounting software packages to record and track financial information. Two popular software packages are QuickBooks and Simply Accounting.

Double-Entry Bookkeeping

Most businesses use a double-entry bookkeeping system. **Double-entry bookkeeping** is based on the principle that each transaction involves two changes. The transaction could result in one increase offset by one decrease, two increases, or two decreases. For example, if a business pays $80 for labour, it decreases its cash balance while increasing its expenses. If a business borrows money from a bank, it increases both its cash balance and the amount owing to the bank. And if a business uses some of its cash to make a payment on a mortgage, both the cash and the amount owing on the mortgage will decrease. All of these transactions and the changes they bring about are part of the recording procedure for accounting.

This individual is using an accounting software package to record and organize his business's monetary transactions.

Accounting and Individuals

Individuals, as well as businesses, have to keep accurate financial records. Many people keep personal records of transactions with a chequebook or a computer program. Each time they write a cheque, they record it in a chequebook or in an online file. In either case, the cheque written decreases the current chequebook balance. Other deductions to the chequebook balance could result from the use of a debit card or a preauthorized payment. A **preauthorized payment** occurs when you have given prior permission for someone else to automatically take money from your bank account, normally on a regular basis. For example, a utility bill could be preauthorized and therefore be deducted each month from a chequing account.

Increasing the chequebook balance could result from a deposit made, such as a pay amount. The account goes up in value as a paycheque is directly and electronically deposited to the account. The transaction is recorded in the chequebook or in an online file. Over the course of a month, you could have a dozen or so entries in your chequebook. Keeping accurate records is a method of making sure you don't write cheques on an account that does not have enough money to cover the cheque, also known as having insufficient funds. See Chapter 13 for more details on banking procedures for individuals and businesses.

Currency, stocks, and indexes are all part of the language of business.

Personal accounting isn't always about keeping track of transactions. Individuals can also use accounting to determine their net worth—the value of everything they own after all their debts are paid. To do this, they need to determine the value of their assets (what they own) and their liabilities (what they owe). Terms like "asset," "liability," and "net worth" are part of the language accountants use to communicate about money—the language of business.

Assets

In accounting, an **asset** is something that has value and is owned by a person. A more formal definition of an asset is a resource controlled by an individual as the result of past events and from which future economic benefits are expected to flow.

If you own a bicycle, it is considered to be one of your assets. It does not matter whether you purchased this item or received it as a gift. When you take ownership it becomes yours and you can consider it one of your assets. Even if you owe money on that purchased item, it is still considered to be your asset. How many assets do you possess? What is their value?

Liabilities

Having lots of possessions—or assets—is nice, but sometimes you have to borrow money to acquire these assets. You may not currently have any debts, but as you acquire more assets of higher value, such as a car, you may have to rely on credit to help pay for them. Most individuals owe some money because of a credit purchase or a loan of some kind and therefore have a debt. **Liabilities** are debts or amounts that are owed to others. For example, if you purchased a music player for $150 and put $50 toward a down payment, you have a debt, or liability, of $100. Remember that the music player is still considered to be one of your assets, worth $150, even though you have not completely paid for it. As the music player gets old, it will lose some of its value, but that doesn't mean it is of no use to you.

Personal Equity or Net Worth

If you can put a dollar figure on the assets you own, and if you know how much money you owe to others, you can calculate your personal equity. Sometimes this is also referred to as your net worth. **Personal equity**, or **net worth**, is what you would have left if you paid off all your debts. You can express a person's net worth with this equation:

Stretch Your Thinking

What do you think will happen to your music-player asset if you fail to pay off your $100 debt? Will it change your asset total?

Assets – Liabilities = Net Worth

For example, let's assume that Sonia has calculated her asset total as $1400. If Sonia has debts totalling $300, then her personal equity, or net worth, would amount to $1400 − $300 = $1100. Sonia's net worth is $1100.

Accounting and Businesses

Like individuals, businesses have assets and liabilities. Accountants can use this information to calculate the net worth of the business—the owner's equity.

Owner's Equity

As you learned in Chapter 2, there are many different forms of business ownership. Some businesses have one owner (sole proprietorships) while other businesses have a few or even thousands of owners (such as in partnerships, co-operatives, and corporations). **Owner's equity**, the net worth for a business, is calculated in the same manner as that for an individual, that is *Assets − Liabilities = Owner's Equity*. Because shareholders own corporations, the owner's equity for a corporation is normally called shareholder's equity.

Balance Sheet Equation

Accountants using these terms form what is known as the **balance sheet equation**. This equation can be expressed in two ways, depending on which part of the equation is unknown.

To determine the owner's equity, use
Assets – Liabilities = Owner's Equity

To determine the total assets, use
Assets = Liabilities + Owner's Equity

> **Business Fact**
>
> In the spring of 2006, Toyota Motor Corporation had assets of US$245 billion and liabilities of US$155 billion, resulting in a net worth of US$90 billion.

The second equation is set up in the same way as a balance sheet, with assets on one side and liabilities + owner's equity on the other. A **balance sheet** is one of the financial statements used in a business and prepared by accountants to show the financial position of that business on a particular date. If the information in the balance sheet is correct, the left side and right side will balance, that is, will be equal in value. (See page 281 for more information about balance sheets.)

Cost Principle and Depreciation

A particular asset, such as a building or piece of machinery, can increase or decrease in value over time, but balance sheets are not set up to accommodate these changes. For reasons of consistency, assets are always recorded at the actual amount they cost the business. This is called the **cost principle**. An owner may think that the business's assets have increased in value over time, but the asset values on the books are never increased. An asset may be sold at some future point for more than it cost to buy it, but that does not mean its cost value on the books should be increased. Similarly, if an asset loses value over time, a process called **depreciation**, the original cost figure of that asset remains on the books. For example, if a truck were purchased by a business for $25 000, that purchase price (or cost amount) would remain as an asset on the books even though the truck will lose value over time as it depreciates.

Mark's Repair Shop

Let's use an example to examine some of the assets and liabilities that could exist for a small business. Mark Bianchet of Mark's Repair Shop has been in business for several years and specializes in fixing small appliances such as toasters, shavers, fans, microwave ovens, coffee makers, and vacuum cleaners.

All the items within this bicycle repair shop, including the store out of which the business is run, are considered to be part or all of the company's assets.

The business has a bank account, a few supplies, and several customers who buy on credit. Mark keeps a limited parts inventory for repairs, and he has many tools and equipment that he uses in his business. He also has a computer to keep track of his inventory and to help handle the invoicing for his customers. Mark owns the land and the building where his business is located. He has a mortgage on the building and a bank loan for his truck.

The assets Mark has available include

- cash that he has in the business and in the business bank account ($6500)

- money owed to him by customers—this asset is called **accounts receivable** ($8100)

- supplies needed for invoicing ($500)

- parts inventory ($4000)

- equipment, including a truck, that is necessary to run the business ($25 500)

- building and land ($175 000)

Total Assets = $219 600

Mark has some debts that haven't been paid off. These include

- debts he owes to another business—this liability is called **accounts payable** ($7350)

- bank loan for the truck ($11 050)

- mortgage on building—this liability is called **mortgage payable** ($110 000)

Total Liabilities = $128 400

Mark can now use this information to calculate the equity he has in the business. Using the asset and liability information, the balance sheet equation for his business would be: *Assets – Liabilities = Owner's Equity*, or $219 600 – $128 400 = $91 200.

This amount—$91 200—represents the equity or net worth of the business. It is the claim that Mark could make on the assets of the business. In other words, if Mark were to sell all of his assets and pay off all of his liabilities, he would be left with $91 200.

Review Questions

1. What is the purpose of accounting?

2. Define double-entry bookkeeping.

3. What is the difference between an asset and a liability?

4. Using Sonia's example (see page 277), calculate her net worth if she had the same asset total, but no debts.

5. How can you calculate the owner's equity in a business?

6. What is the cost principle?

Keep in Mind

1. preparing a balance sheet
2. preparing an income statement
3. preparing a statement of cash flow
4. interpreting financial statements

Preparing Financial Statements

Financial statements present financial information in a way that helps business owners and managers keep track of the financial health of the business. These statements are also used to communicate information about a business to outsiders with an interest in a business, such as lenders, government employees, and other businesspeople. In the next part of this chapter, you'll learn how to prepare three different types of financial statements used in business—the balance sheet, the income statement, and the statement of cash flow.

Figure 9.1 Types of Financial Statements

Types of Financial Statements

Balance Sheet
- summarizes information about assets, liabilities, and owner's equity
- a snapshot that shows how a business is doing on a given day
- the sheet is balanced because *Assets = Liabilities + Owner's Equity*

Income Statement
- summarizes information about revenues and expenses
- indicates profit or loss over given periods
- like a movie that shows how much money a business made or lost over a period of time (net income or net loss)

Statement of Cash Flow
- reports on the flow of cash into and out of the business over a period of time
- helps business operators estimate the amount of cash that will flow in and out during a given period of time

Preparing a Balance Sheet

A balance sheet is the device used to record and summarize financial information about assets, liabilities, and owner's equity. As mentioned earlier, a balance sheet shows the financial position on a particular date. For example, if a balance sheet was prepared on September 30, and another balance sheet was prepared the very next day, it is highly unlikely that the two would look the same. Assuming that Mark's business was open on both days, changes to any asset or liability would have an impact on the balance sheet equation. That is why a balance sheet is like a photo; it is a snapshot of the financial history of a business at a particular moment in time.

Balance Sheet Equation Method

You've already learned that the balance sheet equation *Assets = Liabilities + Owner's Equity* is used in the preparation of the balance sheet. A balance sheet gets its name because the left side of the equation (*assets*) must always equal the sum of the right side of the equation (*liabilities* plus *owner's equity*). The equation must always be in balance.

All of the assets of a business are owned by one of two groups: (1) the owner or owners of the business (owner's equity); or (2) the individuals, or businesses, to whom the business owes money (liabilities). If a business did not have any debts, the balance sheet equation would be *Assets = Owner's Equity*. In business, it is possible to be debt free but it is highly unlikely.

Just like a company's balance sheet equation, these scales are also in balance.

The following sequence of steps is used to prepare a balance sheet for Mark's Repair Shop at the end of September.

Step 1: Fill in the Statement Heading

A three-line heading is used for all balance sheets and is designed to answer three simple questions: Who? What? and When? The heading should be centred at the top of the page.

Who?   Mark's Repair Shop
What?   Balance Sheet
When?   September 30, 20—

Step 2: List the Assets

On a balance sheet, assets are listed in order according to how easily they can be converted into cash. For example, cash requires no conversion and therefore is the first asset to be listed. Accounts receivable, which is money owed to a business by customers, is normally received within thirty days. A building is more difficult to convert into cash than supplies or inventory and therefore is listed after those two assets. **Liquidity** is the term used to describe the ease of converting an asset into cash. In Mark's Repair Shop, cash is the most liquid asset, and the building and land the least liquid assets.

Mark's assets will appear on the balance sheet as follows:

Assets		
Cash	$	6 500
Accounts Receivable		8 100
Supplies		500
Parts Inventory		4 000
Equipment		25 500
Building and Land		175 000
Total Assets		$ 219 600

Step 3: List the Liabilities

Like assets, liabilities on a balance sheet are listed in a particular order. Liabilities are listed in order by **maturity date**, that is, the date by which they must be repaid. For example, accounts payable will likely be paid before loans or mortgages will be paid off and therefore will appear higher in the list of liabilities. The individuals and businesses that appear under the heading of liabilities are commonly called the **creditors** of a business.

Mark's liabilities will appear on his balance sheet as follows:

Liabilities		
Accounts Payable	$	7 350
Bank Loan		11 050
Mortgage Payable		110 000
Total Liabilities		$ 128 400

Step 4: Calculate Owner's Equity

Use the balance sheet equation *Assets – Liabilities = Owner's Equity* to calculate the owner's equity for Mark's Repair Shop. It's already been determined that the shop has $219 600 in assets and $128 400 in liabilities. The owner's equity must be $219 600 – $128 400 or $91 200.

Owner's Equity	
Mark Bianchet, Equity	$91 200

Step 5: Put It All Together

Using the information from Steps 1 through 4, the balance sheet for Mark's Repair Shop would appear as follows:

Mark's Repair Shop
Balance Sheet
September 30, 20—

Assets			Liabilities		
Cash	$	6 500	Accounts Payable		7 350
Accounts Receivable		8 100	Bank Loan		11 050
Supplies		500	Mortgage Payable		110 000
Parts Inventory		4 000	Total Liabilities		$ 128 400
Equipment		25 500			
Building and Land		175 000	**Owner's Equity**		
			Mark Bianchet, Equity	$	91 200
Total Assets		$ 219 600	Total Liabilities and Owner's Equity		$ 219 600

Balance-sheet Conventions

The balance sheet is one of the financial statements used in business and it is considered to be a formal document. Since balance sheets are used for decision making and are shared with owners both inside and outside of the business, they should always be prepared with care. To ensure that everyone can readily understand a balance sheet, certain conventions of style are expected:

- Never use abbreviations in a balance sheet.

- Never have corrections or changes appear on the final version.

- Always take care to line up figures and dollar signs. (Use the Mark's Repair Shop balance sheet as an example.)

- Underline when totalling a column, and double underline a final total.

Balance Sheet Report Form Method

Another way of presenting information on a balance sheet is to use an up-and-down column format rather than a side-by-side format. The report form approach is easier to use, and most computer software programs prefer this method for recording data. However, it is important to remember that the end result is still the same. The balance sheet equation must remain in balance.

Mark's Repair Shop Balance Sheet September 30, 20—	
Assets	
Cash	$ 6 500
Accounts Receivable	8 100
Supplies	500
Parts Inventory	4 000
Equipment	25 500
Building and Land	175 000
Total Assets	$ 219 600
Liabilities	
Accounts Payable	$ 7 350
Bank Loan	11 050
Mortgage Payable	110 000
Total Liabilities	$ 128 400
Owner's Equity	
Mark Bianchet, Equity	91 200
Total Liabilities and Owner's Equity	$ 219 600

Balance sheets provide financial data for a variety of different purposes. Here is a summary of four groups that might be interested in the financial dealings of a business.

Figure 9.2 Who Might Need to Review a Balance Sheet?

Creditors
By examining a business's balance sheet, a creditor can see how much of a claim other creditors have on the business and how solvent that business is at a particular point in time. That lets them know if they should lend money or extend credit to the business.

Investors
Potential investors are concerned about solvency so they will not lose their investment.

Owners
A balance sheet lets the owners know exactly what their claim is on the assets as compared to creditors. Examining several balance sheets over time will let the owners know how their financial position is changing, and how solvent the business is at certain times. Being solvent for a business means having the capability to pay its bills, in other words, to meet its financial obligations.

Government
The Canada Revenue Agency is interested in the business's ability to pay its taxes. Other government departments, such as Statistics Canada, may be interested in statistical data for reporting purposes.

Preparing an Income Statement

So far, we have examined business transactions that have an impact on balance sheet accounts. How would you handle other transactions? For example, a service business owner must pay a sum of cash to business employees working part time. The easy part is dealing with the change to the cash account. The asset account—cash—decreases and the total assets decrease as well. However, we do not have a way of recording the salary paid to employees. At least, not yet. To take care of this transaction, and thousands like it, income statement accounts are used. An **income statement** is a second financial statement used to help a business calculate and report its profit or loss on business operations. While a balance sheet is like a snapshot of one day in the life of the business, an income statement is more like a movie that shows what happened over a period of time. An income statement can show a business how much money it made or lost over the past week, month, quarter, or year.

Stretch Your Thinking

Do you think that it is possible for a business to be solvent but not profitable? Why or why not?

In Chapter 1, we defined a business as an organization that produces or sells goods or services to satisfy the needs, wants, and demands of consumers for the purposes of making a profit. It follows then that we need a way of recording the sale of goods or services. Also, since businesses generate costs and expenses that relate to the sales of goods or services, there must be a method of recording these changes. The money, or the promise of money, received from the sale of goods or services is called **revenue**. On the other hand, **expenses** are things like salaries, advertising, maintenance, and utilities, and are used to help generate the revenue in a business.

If a business sells a cellphone for $150, and that business had to spend $85 in expenses to produce the cellphone and complete the sale, the profit on the sale of that item is $65 because $150 − $85 = $65. Because the total revenue exceeds total expenses, there is a profit, which is referred to as net income. However, if the business sold that same item for half the price ($150 ÷ 2 = $75) because of discounting, and if the expenses to sell that item were twice as much ($85 × 2 = $170), there would be a loss of $95 on the sale of that item. When total

Ethical, Moral & Legal Considerations

How does one go from being a teenage millionaire to appearing on the *Oprah Winfrey Show* to being featured in *People* magazine to lecturing in business schools to owning a Ferrari—and then ending up in jail? Barry Minkow went to prison after he was convicted for attempting to pull off one of the largest stock market frauds in history. His white-collar crime netted him seven and a half years in prison.

In the beginning, Barry Minkow started small with an investment of $1600 in a carpet cleaning business, ZZZZ Best. Within four years, the company was employing 1400 people and

was worth more than $280 million. Minkow's company was a pyramid scheme: it used new investors' money to pay off early investors. To generate even more money for the scheme, ZZZZ Best went public and sold shares to more new investors, again using the new money to pay off old debts. Minkow fooled even the accountants by producing thousands of fake documents with hundreds of transactions describing business procedures that never took place. Along the way, in an effort to raise even more money for the business, Minkow factored the accounts receivable of ZZZZ Best. Factoring

accounts receivable is a process whereby a business sells its customers' accounts for cash and pays a fee to the buying company for this service. According to Barry Minkow's confession of this deceptive practice, he was convinced that he could make all the money back and repay everyone. But the hole just kept getting deeper!

These days, Minkow is out of prison. He has been paying back some of his institutional investors and pays up to $2000 a month into restitution funds. You may not be surprised to find out that he has a book for sale called *Cleaning Up*!

expenses exceed total revenue, a net loss occurs. When a net loss is reported on an income statement, the total amount is put in parentheses rather than shown with a minus sign. For example, a loss of $95 is recorded as ($95) rather than −$95.

Income Statements for Service Businesses

The following sequence of steps has been used to prepare an income statement for Mark's Repair Shop for the month of September.

Step 1: Fill in the Statement Heading

The three-line heading for an income statement is similar to the one prepared for a balance sheet. It answers the questions Who? What? and When? and is centred at the top of the page. Notice the change in the third line, however.

Who?	Mark's Repair Shop
What?	Income Statement
When?	For the month ending September 30, 20—

Step 2: Organize the Revenue Section

All sources of revenue should be listed in the revenue section. Let's assume that Mark has one source of revenue from his business.

Revenue		
Repairs Revenue	$ 9 900	
Total Revenue		**$ 9 900**

Step 3: Organize the Expenses Section

The following expenses applied to Mark's business in September. There is no particular order for listing expenses, but larger ones tend to get listed first.

Expenses		
Salaries	$ 2 600	
Rent	2 000	
Advertising	850	
Supplies	185	
Utilities	235	
Insurance	150	
Delivery Expense	770	
Total Expenses		**$ 6 790**

Step 4: Calculate Net Income or Net Loss

Use the information from Steps 2 and 3 and the equation for calculating profit (*Total Revenue – Total Expenses*) to calculate the net income for Mark's Repair Shop for the month of September:

$$\$9\ 900 - \$6\ 790 = \$3\ 110$$

The complete income statement will look like this.

Mark's Repair Shop
Income Statement
For the month ending September 30, 20—

Revenue		
Repairs Revenue	$ 9 900	
Total Revenue		**$ 9 900**
Expenses		
Salaries	$ 2 600	
Rent	2 000	
Advertising	850	
Supplies	185	
Utilities	235	
Insurance	150	
Delivery Expense	770	
Total Expenses		**$ 6 790**
Net Income		**$ 3 110**

When expenses are shown on the income statement, those expenses should be shown on the same monthly statement as the revenue they helped generate. For example, a business spends money on deliveries, which count as an expense, in order to help repairs revenue. Let's take a look at what would happen if items weren't matched correctly. Assume that Mark's Repair Shop had a $600 delivery expense in September when Mark paid the delivery driver for deliveries made in August. Customers paid Mark when their appliances were delivered in August, so the delivery cost was recorded against August's revenue, not September's. If the delivery cost were added to September's expenses, the result would give a false picture of the health of the business.

For this reason, delivery and other expenses should be matched with the revenue they generate. This process of matching is referred to as the **matching principle**. For Mark's Repair Shop, total expenses during September came to $6790, and that expenditure helped generate the repairs revenue of $9900. If this matching principle is not followed, accounting figures could be distorted.

Table 9.1

Matching Principle Example				
	Incorrect* (*counts a $600 August expense in September)		Correct	
	Aug	Sept	Aug	Sept
Revenue	$ 8 000	$ 9 900	$ 8 000	$ 9 900
Expenses	$ 5 000	$ 7 390	$ 5 600	$ 6 790
Net Income	$ 3 000	$ 2 510	$ 2 400	$ 3 110

The incorrect figures overstate the net income for August ($3000 when it should have been $2400) and understate the net income for September ($2510 when it should have been $3110). Why would that matter? Any accounting information that is not accurate will influence the decisions accountants and owners make. For example, if profits were overstated, a decision might be made to use some of that profit to reduce a business's debt. However, since that money is not really available, allocating money to reduce debt could lead to a shortfall in October or November.

Income Statements for Retail Businesses

Balance sheets for retail merchandising businesses are quite similar to those for service businesses, except in the case of a few types of accounts. (Note: We will refer to a retail merchandising business simply as a retail business.) However, the income statements for the two types of businesses are somewhat different because retail businesses need to take into account the cost of **inventory**—the goods they have on hand to be sold.

Income Statement Equations

In a service type of business, the costs of the goods or services used by the company are simply recorded as expenses on the income statement.

> Income statement equation for a service business:
> **Revenue – Expenses = Net Income**

In a retail business, the costs of goods and services used are treated differently, because this kind of business buys and sells finished products to consumers.

> Income statement equations for a retail business:
> **Revenue – Cost of Goods Sold = Gross Profit**
> **Gross Profit – Expenses = Net Income**

Gross profit is the money left over after deducting the cost of goods sold from the revenue, but before deducting the business expenses that helped generate the revenue. Gross profit is sometimes referred to as gross margin.

A retail business starts with an inventory on hand, purchases more goods, sells the goods, and has inventory left at the end of the year. In order to keep track of the costs of changes in inventory, a "cost of goods sold" component is added to the income statement. **Cost of goods sold** is calculated by starting with the opening inventory figure (goods and services purchased in previous months but not yet used), adding the new purchases made during the period, and subtracting the inventory remaining at the end of the time period. The cost of goods sold section can appear on an income statement, or it can be prepared as a separate schedule, with just the final total being transferred to the income statement.

Income Statements and Inventory

The vastness of a grocery store's warehouse inventory

Using accounting to keep track of inventory is critical to a retail business because good inventory control saves the company money and increases customer satisfaction. Businesses check that the quantity of goods shipped matches the quantity of goods recorded on the shipper's invoice. As inventory sells, businesses deduct it from the quantity they have on hand to provide an accurate, up-to-date total. At least once a year, companies physically count the inventory to check that records are accurate.

Every retailer starts the fiscal year with inventory on hand. A **fiscal year**, or business year, is any 12-month operating period. Often, but not always, the fiscal year corresponds to the calendar year. For example, one business might have a fiscal year that begins on January 1 and ends on December 31, but another business could have their fiscal year begin on April 1 and end on March 31 of the following year.

Imagine that you own a shoe store. At the start of your fiscal year, you have $50 000 worth of inventory. In other words, your current inventory cost the company $50 000 over previous months. Throughout the following year, your store updates styles, replaces sold stock, and prepares for seasonal changes by purchasing $75 000 worth of additional inventory. Therefore, over the course of the whole year, the store has a total of $125 000 worth of inventory to sell.

Twelve months later, a physical, or actual, count of the inventory shows that your shoe store has $40 000 in unsold inventory to start the next fiscal year. If this amount is subtracted from the cost of goods available for the year ($125 000), the store must have sold goods that cost $85 000. Keep in mind that this is the cost the business paid for these goods, not the price their customers paid. In retail accounting, this amount is expressed as the cost of goods sold.

Beginning Inventory, Jan. 1, 20__	$ 50 000
Inventory Purchased	+ 75 000
Cost of All Goods Available for Sale	125 000
Ending Inventory, Dec. 31, 20__	– 40 000
Cost of Goods Sold	$ 85 000

Let's assume the store collects $150 000 in sales revenue during the year. This sales revenue is generated entirely by the goods sold. Because $85 000 worth of goods was sold to bring in $150 000 in sales, the store makes a gross profit of $65 000. (Recall that gross profit is the money left over after deducting the cost of goods sold from the revenue, but before deducting the business expenses that helped generate the revenue.)

Sales Revenue	$ 150 000
Cost of Goods Sold	– 85 000
Gross Profit	$ 65 000

The store must now use a portion of the gross profit to pay expenses such as rent, salaries and wages, supplies, and advertising. Once these expenses are deducted from the gross profit, the amount of money left over is the **net income**, or **net profit**. If the expenses, sometimes referred to as operating expenses, are $25 000, then the net profit would be $40 000.

Oops!

Based on Nike's worldwide success, one might assume that anything the company touches turns to gold. Not so. When Nike wanted to expand into the outdoor gear and clothing market, the company had to make a decision: develop a new product line or purchase a company with an established foothold in that market? In 2000, Nike had an opportunity to buy The North Face, Inc.—a move that might have doubled its outdoor business. Instead, Nike dragged its feet, and the opportunity passed. In hindsight, Nike might have done better to follow its own advice: "Just do it!"

Gross Profit	$ 65 000
Expenses	– 25 000
Net Profit	$ 40 000

Net profit is the amount of money the storeowner can declare as income for income tax purposes. As you learned in Chapter 2, if the company is a corporation, net profit is divided among shareholders in the form of dividends or retained by the corporation for investment in the business.

Donahue's Shoe Store
Income Statement
For the year ending December 31, 20__

Revenue			
Sales		$ 150 000	
Cost of Goods Sold			
Beginning Inventory, Jan. 1, 20__	$ 50 000		
Inventory Purchased	75 000		
Cost of All Goods Available for Sale	125 000		
Ending Inventory, Dec 31, 20__	40 000		
Cost of Goods Sold		85 000	
Gross Profit			65 000
Expenses			25 000
Net Income			$ 40 000

Retail is not the only type of business that uses this accounting method. Wholesalers and importers use it as well. These businesses do not manufacture goods; instead, they buy inventory from manufacturers and resell it to other companies or stores. Wholesalers and importers calculate the cost of goods sold just as retail stores do.

Owner's Equity Account

What happens to the profit made by a business? In the retail business example, the net profit of $40 000 goes to the owner. That is why an income statement is prepared *before* a balance sheet. The net profit has to be calculated and then transferred to the balance sheet as part of the owner's equity. After the financial statements are complete, the owner knows how much to claim as profit for the year. To help identify the owner's account, the word "Capital" becomes part of the account name.

Owner's Equity	
C. Donahue, Capital, January 1, 20__	$ 75 000
Add: Net Income	40 000
C. Donahue, Capital, December 31, 20__	$ 115 000

Remember that two groups have claims upon the assets of the business: the creditors and the owners. In the above example, because the business made a profit, C. Donahue increased her claim upon the assets of the business. She can now lay claim to $115 000 of the business asset total.

Preparing a Statement of Cash Flow

Cash flow is the movement of cash in and out of a business. Some businesses generate a **statement of cash flow**, which reports on a business's cash flow over a stated period of time. For example, a business might prepare a projected statement of cash flow to estimate the amount of cash it will likely receive in a given period of time and the amount of regular and extra expenses it will have to pay during that time. Sources of cash moving into a business include sales, interest received from investments, accounts receivable that will be collected, the sale of capital equipment, new loans, and investments. On the other hand, expenditures of cash moving out of a business include rent, payroll, accounts payable, interest payable, and insurance. Extra commitments to be paid, such as the purchase of capital assets and payment of loan principal, are harder to predict but must also be carefully considered.

Projected Cash Flow Statement Mark's Repair Shop October 31, 20__		
Transaction	**In (+)**	**Out (−)**
Investment Income	+$ 500.00	
Accounts Receivables	+750.00	
Equipment to be Sold	+1,250.00	
Payroll Not Yet Paid		−$ 460.00
Loan Repayment		−930.00
Insurance Due		−200.00
Projected Cash Flow		**$ 910.00**

Macy's is among the business holdings of Federated Department Store Inc.

Ways to Increase Cash Flow

By examining the cash-in and cash-out sections of a statement of cash flow, a business can predict whether it will have enough cash to meet obligations. If it will not, the business must take steps to correct the problem. These steps could include seeking extra investment (e.g., extra money from the owner, a short-term loan from a bank, or finding a partner or investor), reducing inventory purchases (to keep accounts payable down), and increasing activity to collect accounts receivable. At the end of the stated period, the business updates the budgeted cash flow to include the actual numbers. In this way, the business can validate or change predictions as needed. See Figure 9.3 for more tips on how to boost cash flow.

Figure 9.3 Eight Ways to Boost Your Cash Flow

8 Ways to Boost Your Cash Flow

1. Increase the price of goods: Consider increasing prices, especially on those goods that have a small mark up.

2. Minimize costs: Is the business paying too much to its suppliers? Shop around for better deals.

3. Spread out expenses: Consider leasing instead of buying. Leasing reduces the amount of money paid up front or in advance.

4. Reduce inventory: A lot of money can be tied up in inventory that may not be selling. If possible, keep fewer items on hand.

5. Use the right kind of debt: Use long-term debt to finance long-term assets rather than using a line of credit (short-term). Long-term debt leaves more money available for other transactions.

6. Collect what is owed to the business: Make sure that you collect money when it is due. If necessary, use a collection agency to collect debts.

7. Shorten the deadline for accounts receivable: Don't let customers take forever to pay for purchases. If necessary, offer a small discount to encourage early payment.

8. Stretch the deadline for accounts payable: Don't pay bills early unless there is a worthwhile discount. Take as long as possible to pay the debts.

It is not uncommon for a businessperson to confuse cash flow with profit. Cash flow is the difference between money coming into a business and money leaving a business over a given period of time. If there is more money coming into a business, that money can be used to pay debts or expenses. It is not considered profit. Here are some suggestions for ways to maximize a business's cash flow.

Cash-flow Implications of Credit and Debit Cards

Most big-box stores ask customers to pay in cash or use a credit or debit card. Using these methods of payment means that the stores do not have to wait for their money (accounts receivable). Instead, the stores get their money (sales revenue) up front.

The exchange of money—between a customer and the owner of a fruit stand—for produce is an example of cash flow.

Misappropriation of funds is a type of accounting fraud. Here is an example that occurred in a not-for-profit organization. The duties of an accounting clerk in this organization included submitting money to the government for payroll deductions, such as Canada Pension Plan (CPP), Employment Insurance (EI), and income tax on behalf of the company's employees. The accounting clerk's duty was to submit these numbers accurately. However, each time the clerk submitted a cheque to the government, he increased the amount on the cheque by even thousand-dollar amounts. For example, the clerk would remit $45 000 instead of $40 000. What happened to that extra $5000? The accounting clerk kept track of it and added the amount to his own T4 slip at the end of the year. This made it appear as if he had contributed much more to CPP, EI, and income tax, and therefore would qualify for a larger tax refund. The clerk was caught when accountants at the Canada Revenue Agency noticed that there was an unusually high tax refund—approximately $17 000 on gross earnings of only $35 000! What might a not-for-profit organization do to its accounting procedures to prevent such a fraud in the future?

On the opposite side of the cash flow, big-box stores often take as long as possible to pay their own bills (accounts payable). In the interim, they may invest their customers' cash to make money on money. In many cases, these stores actually make as much or more on their money-on-money investments as they do from selling the goods in the stores. A business with a positive cash flow has more money on hand than it needs to meet all of its short-term commitments. A positive cash flow is an objective that almost every business strives to achieve.

Interpreting Financial Statements

How will you measure your financial success? Is the successful person one with lots of assets, very few debts, lots of money in the bank, or a high net worth? Using financial data such as that found on balance sheets and income statements can help summarize the information you need to answer those questions. Businesses use a similar approach and answer similar questions when measuring financial success. One role of an accountant is to interpret the financial information found in the financial statements of a business and then to make recommendations to the owners about future decisions.

To gather information, accountants compare financial data over a set period of time, usually two or more years. For example, if an accountant has balance sheets for the past two

Table 9.2

Thomson's Used Car Dealership Comparative Balance Sheet December 31, 2007 and 2006			
	2007	**2006**	**Increase (+) Decrease (−)**
Assets			
Cash	$ 23 000	$ 33 000	− $ 10 000
Accounts Receivable	77 000	42 000	+ 35 000
Supplies	3 700	4 100	− 400
Car Inventory	65 000	84 500	− 19 500
Truck Inventory	27 000	10 000	+ 17 000
Office Equipment	13 000	14 000	− 1 000
Building	150 000	150 000	no change
Total Assets	$ 358 700	$ 337 600	+ 21 100
Liabilities			
Accounts Payable	56 000	17 000	+ 39 000
Bank Loan	24 000	4 000	+ 20 000
Mortgage	120 000	140 000	− 20 000
Total Liabilities	200 000	161 000	+ 39 000
Owner's Equity			
G. Thomson, Capital	158 700	176 600	− 17 900
Total Liabilities & Owner's Equity	$ 358 700	$ 337 600	+ 21 100

fiscal years, the information contained in those balance sheets can be compared. This comparison provides a clear picture of where the company was and where it currently finds itself. The accountant lists the key data for both years and determines increases and decreases. He or she will first look for account

Costco is just one example of a big-box store.

balances that seem to be out of order and then analyze and interpret why these account balances are not in order. Let's compare the balance sheets for Thomson's Used Car Dealership on page 297.

An analysis of these balance sheets reveals the following interesting points:

1. The total assets from 2006 to 2007 have not changed much. As well, the cash position has decreased somewhat. But more importantly, the accounts receivable have almost doubled. This suggests that the cash may be lower than it should be—perhaps the business is not collecting money that is owed to it from its customers. This should be a concern to the owner.

2. Both the car and truck inventories have changed. Are there enough cars on hand to satisfy customers? Are there too many trucks left in inventory? The owner should examine this change further.

3. The total debts of the business have increased, mostly because the accounts payable have more than tripled and also because the bank loan increased dramatically. As long as the business does not have to pay for charges on overdue accounts, this may not be a major problem. However, these are debts that have to be paid. If more money was available from accounts receivable, it might help solve the situation.

4. The net worth of the owner has decreased because of an increase in liabilities. This should cause some concern to the owner.

A Final Measure of Success

An owner's equity in a business is an investment. By spending the time and effort to run the business, risking capital, and worrying daily about its success or failure, the owner hopes to see a return on his or her investment. What kind of return can an owner reasonably expect? For a business to be successful, the return from the business should be equal to or greater than the return from a savings account, bond, or mutual fund.

Stretch Your Thinking

In November 2006, Microsoft Corp. introduced the Zune portable player and music service to compete with Apple Computer Inc.'s iPod and iTunes. This is an example of how to use equity as an investment. Has it worked?

 **E-ACTIVITY**

Visit www.nelson.com/WOB and follow the links to learn more about annual reports.

Review Questions

7. What is the purpose of a balance sheet?

8. Who owns, or can lay claim to, the assets of a business?

9. Why is it highly unlikely that a business's balance sheet would appear as follows: *Assets = Owner's Equity*?

10. What four groups are interested in the financial dealings of a business?

11. Define the following terms: net income, net loss, revenue, and expense.

12. How is the heading of an income statement different from that of a balance sheet?

13. Why is the matching principle important in accounting?

14. Does a fiscal year always coincide with a calendar year? Explain.

15. Why is it important to have accurate inventory figures when preparing an income statement?

16. How is gross profit calculated?

17. Why is it important for a business to calculate and predict its cash flow position?

18. Identify three important comparisons an accountant could focus on when analyzing a comparative balance sheet.

Knowledge

1. Use the following personal data for P. Karkoulis to calculate his net worth on June 3, 20__.

Bank Account Balance	$ 185
Electronic Equipment	1 800
DVD Collection	225
Motor Bike	1 200
Money Owed to Him	100
Money Owed by Him	650
Clothes	1 000
Computer	740

2. Fill in the missing amounts for each of the following balance sheet equations. Record your answers in your notebook.

   Assets   = Liabilities + Net Worth

   a) $24 000 = $14 000 + $ _____

   b) $ _____ = $56 000 + $110 000

   c) $87 000 = $ _____ + $40 000

3. Why are assets listed in order of liquidity and liabilities in order of maturity on a balance sheet?

4. Write each of the following terms in your notebook and classify each one as asset, liability, or owner's equity.

   Cash
   Mortgage
   Accounts Payable
   Partner #1's share in the business
   Truck
   Accounts Receivable
   Supplies
   Land
   Bank Loan
   Partner #2's share in the business

5. Use the following account information to prepare an income statement for ABC Company for the month ending November 30, 20__.

Sales	$ 7 000
Rent Expense	770
Salaries	2 350
Advertising	550
Utilities Expense	240

6. Use the following information to prepare an income statement for Presotto Realty for the three-month period ending March 31, 20__:

   Rental Revenue $13 300
   Employee Salaries $8750
   Promotion Expense $1000
   Maintenance Expense $2000
   Heat and Utilities $2100
   Supplies Expense $740
   Insurance Expense $1200
   Cleaning Expense $450

7. Use the following data to prepare a cost of goods sold section for an income statement:

   Inventory, April 30 $20 000
   Inventory, April 1 $35 000
   Purchases during the month of April $12 000

8. Complete the following equations by supplying the missing dollar amounts. Record your answers in your notebook.

   Revenues – Expenses = Net Income
                                (Loss)

   a) $13 500 – $12 000 = $ _____

   b) $76 000 – $ _____ = $57 300

   c) $ _____ – $1350   = $13 000

   d) $112 000 – $122 500 = $ _____

   e) $ _____ – $4550   = ($3450)

9. Sergei has $23 000 in assets and $13 200 in liabilities. If Sergei used $3000 of his cash to pay off his bank loan, how would that impact his owner's equity? Use the balance sheet equation to illustrate your answer.

10. If a business lost $20 000, how would the capital account of the owner be adjusted? Where does this adjustment take place?

Thinking

11. Increasing sales can increase profits in a business. Suggest how a business might increase sales. When would increasing sales not increase profits?

12. Use the following data to prepare a cost of goods sold section for an income statement.

Inventory, June 30 $65 000
Inventory, June 1 $
Purchases during the month of June $43 000
Cost of Goods Available for Sale $92 000

13. What does the word "solvent" mean in reference to a business? Can a business be profitable but not solvent? Explain.

14. Make the necessary corrections to the following financial statements for My Enterprises. When preparing the balance sheet, use the report form. Remember to double-underline the key totals.

Balance Sheet
My Enterprises
For the month ending May 31, 20___

Assets		Liabilities	
Building	$ 25 500	Cash	500
Accounts Payable	1 400	Accounts Receivable	780
Furniture and Fixtures	1 100	Mortgage Payable	18 000
Supplies	120	Total Liabilities	19 280
Rent Expense	750		
Inventory	4 200		
Bank Loan	2 000	**Owner's Equity**	
		I'm Confused, Capital	$ 10 800
Total Assets	$	Total Liabilities and Owner's Equity	$

My Enterprises
Income Statement
May 31, 20___

Revenues		
Advertising Expense	$	2 200
Sales Revenue		35 900
Utilities		1 800
Expenses		
Rent Revenue	$	12 000
Salaries Expense		21 700
Insurance Expense		1 750
Miscellaneous Expense		2 300
Net Income		$

Communication

15. The four groups that would be interested in the financial health of a business are owner(s), creditors, investors, and government. Using Mark's Repair Shop as an example, describe what interest each of these groups would have in an income statement. Discuss with a partner and write a one-page summary.

16. A friend has sent you a scrap piece of paper listing financial information. Your friend knows you have been studying accounting and has requested your financial advice. After analyzing the data provided, write an e-mail to identify any concerns you may have and make any appropriate recommendations. Explain the concept of personal or net worth to your friend as part of your response.

Cash on hand and in bank	$ 125
Savings bond (gift from grandparent)	350
Everything else I own	540
Money owed to my brother	440
Money owed to my father	750
Money owed to friends	120
Money owed to my mother	440

17. Using Figure 9.3 (Eight Ways to Boost Your Cash Flow) as a checklist for research, interview a businessperson to find out how practical this list of suggestions is in the real world. Have they used any of those suggestions, and if so, to what effect? Would they add anything to the list? Write a one-page summary of your findings.

18. Not many businesses are profitable in their first year of operation, so financial planning is necessary. How might an owner obtain enough money to operate the business until it becomes profitable?

Application

19. Use the following information to prepare two balance sheets, one using the balance sheet equation approach and the second using the report form approach.

    Building $160 000
    Cash $56 000
    Accounts Payable $12 000
    Supplies $2700
    Merchandise Inventory $34 500
    Bank Loan $43 000
    Accounts Receivable $44 000
    Taxes Payable $13 400
    Equipment $78 900
    Salaries Payable $16 500
    Mortgage Payable $111 000
    N. Droulis, Capital $

20. The following income statement information was taken from Roma Pastry & Bakery:

    Revenue
    January $20 000
    February $25 000
    Expenses
    January $12 000
    February $10 000

    Use the concept of the matching principle to correct a $ 1000 mistake. That amount was *incorrectly* charged in February when it should have been charged in January.

	Incorrect		Correct	
	Jan	Feb	Jan	Feb
Revenue	$ 20 000	$ 25 000	$ 20 000	$ 25 000
Expenses	12 000	10 000	$	$
Net Income	$ 8 000	$ 15 000	$	$

21. Use a personal contact and/or the Internet to research one of the following accounting designations: the chartered accountant (CA), the certified management accountant (CMA), or the certified general accountant (CGA). Make a list of duties performed by the one that you choose.

22. Comparative financial statement analysis tells an accountant a lot about what took place in a business over a period of time. Use the following comparative income statements for Aisenthal's Used Car Dealership to do a comparative analysis. Use the analysis provided in the text (See Table 9.2) as a guide when answering.

Aisenthal's Used Car Dealership
Comparative Income Statements
December 31, 2007 and 2006

	2007	2006	Increase (+) Decrease (−)
Revenue			
Sales of cars	$ 92 000	$ 42 000	+ $ 50 000
Sales of trucks	8 000	29 000	− 21 000
Total Revenue	100 000	71 000	+ 29 000
Cost of Goods Sold			
Inventory, January 1	94 500	89 000	+ 5 500
Net Purchases	40 000	30 000	+ 10 000
Cost of Goods for Sale	134 500	119 000	+ 15 500
Inventory, Dec. 31	92 000	94 500	− 2 500
Cost of Goods Sold	42 500	24 500	+ 18 000
Gross Profit	57 500	46 500	+ 11 000
Operating Expenses			
Advertising	2 000	1 800	+ 200
Salaries	35 000	52 000	− 17 000
Utilities	1 500	1 300	+ 200
Interest and Bank Charges	2 200	2 600	− 400
Total Expenses	40 700	57 700	− 17 000
Net Income (Loss)	16 800	(11 200)	+ 28 000

Team Activity

Team Goal: To identify business profitability

Team Assignment: Who Made the Most Last Year?

- Your team should find the most profitable five businesses for the last fiscal year.
- List each business and its profits (document your sources).
- Add the profits for the five businesses that your team selected.
- The team with the highest profit total will win this competition.

Portfolio

Obtain and examine the annual reports of two businesses within your selected industry. You can use these annual reports (and more, if you can get them) as artifacts for your portfolio. Annual reports are available from a company's website, in libraries, or from a variety of online annual report providers. Your teacher will have some websites for you, or you can search Google for "annual report [name of company]."

For each company, determine:

- total assets
- total liabilities
- total equity (in annual reports, the owner's equity is listed as shareholders' equity)
- total income
- total expenses
- net profit
- Select two terms you do not understand from each of the balance sheets. Look the terms up and record their definitions.
- If you had money to invest, which of the two companies you have examined would be the better investment? Explain why you think so.

Reflect on Your Learning

On page 273, you were asked to make a prediction about your personal net worth. Use what you've learned in this chapter to re-estimate your net worth. How did your prediction hold up?

KPMG

The world of accounting has been rapidly changing and undergoing much scrutiny since the corporate scandals in early 2000. Prior to the collapse of Enron Corp., there were the "Big Five" accounting firms worldwide. Post-Enron, a "Big Five" firm that was intimately involved in the Enron scandal, Arthur Andersen, folded into Deloitte & Touche, leaving the "Big Four" accounting firms to ensure the credibility of corporate financial statements worldwide. The "Big Four" firms are Ernst and Young, Deloitte & Touche, PricewaterhouseCoopers (PWC), and KPMG.

KPMG stands for Klynveld Peat Marwick Goerdeler. However, the KPMG name was only standardized in 1996. That's because each name making up the KPMG initialism originates from a smaller firm, many dating back to the eighteenth century and coming from the United States, the United Kingdom, Amsterdam, and Germany. Through a series of mergers and acquisitions KPMG grew to its current size. KPMG currently operates in more than 144 countries around the world, including Canada, with more than 104,000 employees.

Why is it so important to have an accounting firm, such as KPMG, generate credible financial statements? By examining and validating financial statements produced by public companies, firms like KPMG help establish

KPMG is a member of the "Big Four."

confidence in investors. This examination and validating process is commonly referred to as auditing financial statements. Accurate and timely financial statements also allow lenders and management, as well as investors, to make important business decisions. Using financial statement data, lenders can assess whether they will be repaid for the money they loan, management can evaluate the profit picture, and investors can judge the net worth of the company.

As well as providing auditing services, KPMG also provides tax and advisory services. One of the advisory services offered is in the area of forensic accounting. KPMG Forensic offers a wide range of fraud-investigation and related services to assist clients in effectively managing their exposure to corporate crime and other irregularities, resolving disputes and conflicts, improving their recoveries from losses, safeguarding their assets, and limiting damage to a company's reputation. For example, a forensic audit is an examination of a company's records and reports by auditors who look for suspicious spending practices, such as excess amounts charged to miscellaneous accounts, or credit card charges that are not company related.

Yet for all the work that KPMG has done to ensure that the public companies it audits operate legally, KPMG itself has run into some recent legal trouble. The United States member firm of KPMG LLP admitted to criminal wrongdoing in 2005. KPMG created fraudulent tax shelters to help wealthy clients avoid paying $2.5 billion in taxes. In order to avoid criminal prosecution, KPMG agreed to pay $456 million in penalties. This fraud represents the world's largest criminal tax fraud case.

KPMG continues to audit some of the world's largest companies, including PepsiCo, Burger King, Apple Computer, General Electric, and Visa International. Transparency and ethical conduct have been made major priorities at KPMG, as seen in their Transparency Reports and whistle-blowing hotlines in some countries. Yet, all it took were 19 partners at KPMG to cause the tax scandal, which tarnished the entire company.

QUESTIONS

1. What does it mean when one refers to auditing financial statements? Why is this process important in the business community?

2. Why would some of the world's largest companies continue to deal with an accounting firm after it had been involved in a fraud case?

UNIT 3

Entrepreneurship

"The critical ingredient [in entrepreneurship] is getting off your butt and doing something. It's as simple as that. A lot of people have ideas, but there are few who decide to do something about them now. Not tomorrow. Not next week. But today. The true entrepreneur is a doer, not a dreamer."

Nolan Bushnell, founder of Atari and Chuck E. Cheese's

OVERALL EXPECTATIONS

- describe the characteristics and skills associated with successful entrepreneurs
- demonstrate an understanding of the contributions to Canadian business of selected entrepreneurs
- analyze the importance of invention and innovation in entrepreneurship

10 Characteristics and Skills of an Entrepreneur

SPECIFIC EXPECTATIONS

After completing this chapter, you will be able to

- describe the characteristics and skills often associated with successful entrepreneurs at the local, national, and international level

- describe the lives and accomplishments of a variety of Canadian entrepreneurs

- analyze your own entrepreneurial strengths and interests

- describe and evaluate either your own or an existing idea for an entrepreneurial endeavour in your school or community

Rumba Games Inc.

Jean-Paul Teskey, the founder of Rumba Games, is the new king of board games. But don't challenge him to a game of Survivor or Urban Myth—he doesn't like to play. Board games just aren't fun for Teskey anymore. He'd much rather take on a competitor or a new idea. That's what gets Teskey excited.

Teskey has always had the heart of an entrepreneur. At the age of 17, he saw an opportunity in the tie-dyed T-shirt market. The market, which was dominated by artists and manufacturers, was in need of a distributor. Teskey developed a distribution system that involved buying the best designs in bulk from the artists and then reselling them to customers. Teskey was the crucial middleman who got the tie-dye shirts from the artists to the customers in an efficient and profitable way.

After graduating from the University of Toronto with a degree in political science, he was headed straight for law school, but had a change of plans. His part-time job at Loblaws became full time and he became a Loblaws buyer. This gave him valuable business experience and a secure job. Yet Teskey wanted more.

As a favour, he used his marketing and merchandising background to help a friend launch a board game. While doing so, he saw the "cocooning" trend emerging. That is, people were choosing to spend time at home and required more at-home entertainment. Board games, he thought, fit perfectly into that trend. Teskey decided to leave the security of his position at Loblaws and enter into the uncertain and risky board-game market.

In 1998, Teskey founded Rumba Games. Rumba has developed its own games, such as Urban Myth, Real Vegas, and Trivia on the Road. Rumba was also selected by CBS as the licensee of the Survivor Game. Rumba's games are fun, imaginative, easy to play, and often educational—and all have a creative twist.

The world has taken notice of Rumba. *Profit* magazine named Rumba Games as one of the fastest growing companies in Canada in both 2003 (No. 5)

Jean-Paul Teskey, the founder of Rumba Games

and 2004 (No. 3). This is exceptional as the major toy and entertainment market was extremely unstable at that time. Rumba excelled while major players, such as FAO Schwartz and KB Toys, filed for bankruptcy protection. Rumba has succeeded due to its persistence and imagination—both of which are key qualities of its founder.

As an entrepreneur, Teskey has the freedom to set his own hours, be his own boss, and make his own choices. He also gets to travel and meet famous people. And he has a constant sense of amazement about what he's accomplished. But life as an entrepreneur has not been easy. Teskey has had to be persistent, hardworking, a risk taker, and flexible. His work never stops and his business is always on his mind. Beyond the obvious hard work involved, what does Teskey consider to be crucial to his success? Insatiable curiosity, and constantly dreaming and asking, "What if...?"

QUESTIONS

1. What risks has Teskey taken to pursue his entrepreneurial dreams?

2. Why is imagination important in being a successful entrepreneur?

3. What other ideas could cater to the cocooning trend in society?

Entrepreneurial Characteristics

Did you hear the one about the kid who dropped out of high school to start a new business and is a multimillionaire today? It has happened a few times (John W. Sleeman, founder of Sleeman Breweries, was a high-school dropout, for example). But by far the most common way to achieve financial success is by developing your entrepreneurial characteristics and skills through education, hard work, and planning.

There is a route to entrepreneurial success, but it is not an easy one, and not everyone wants to take it. Not everyone is entrepreneurial. Many people are comfortable working for others, and they look for stability and security. Other people are driven to make changes. It is these people who become entrepreneurs. All entrepreneurs possess similar characteristics. They are risk takers, and they are perceptive, curious, and imaginative. They are persistent goal setters who are hardworking. They are self-confident, flexible, and like to be independent. You must possess at least some of these characteristics to succeed.

Risk Taker

If you had $50 000, you could do several things with it. You could buy a new car with the money. You could give it to charity. You could invest in Canada Savings Bonds or other safe investments, or you could invest in areas that are less safe. Risky investments often promise better financial rewards than safer investments. With risky investments, however, you could lose all your money.

Entrepreneurs often take on a high degree of risk. Because there are no "sure things" in business, every business faces risk. A failed business can mean bankruptcy for its owners, leaving them with few or no business and personal assets. Not everyone can cope with this stress.

Successful entrepreneurs minimize and manage risk. Business owners research opportunities to be sure they have covered all the potential problems. Some risks are simply unacceptable. For example, it would not be acceptable to bet all your business capital on a horse race or at a casino. In these examples, financial success depends only on luck. On the other hand, if you have a plan to produce and distribute a product you know people will buy, starting a factory to manufacture this product

What risks does this entrepreneur face?

is an acceptable risk. If you've done the research and acquired the knowledge and skills to make the factory efficient, there's a good chance you'll be able to earn a profit on the money you've invested.

Perceptive

Entrepreneurs do not avoid problems. Instead, when faced with problems, they welcome them as opportunities or challenges. During the mid-1980s, Canadian soft-drink manufacturer Cott Corporation had a problem. How could it hope to compete with Coca-Cola and Pepsi, the two giants in the soft-drink industry? Gerald Pencer, Cott's entrepreneurial CEO, was very perceptive. Research indicated that soft drinks were one of the biggest selling items in supermarkets. Pencer decided to develop Cott as a **private-label** bottler. Cott contracted with supermarkets and other retail stores to provide a variety of soft drinks that could be packaged under the retailer's brand, such as President's Choice at Loblaws or Master Choice at A&P. Cott's product challenged Coca-Cola and Pepsi by developing a whole new method of distribution— one that allowed retailers to make more profits by offering consumers a much cheaper soft drink. Today, Cott is the world's largest retailer brand/private label soft-drink provider.

Curious

Entrepreneurs like to know how things work. Before American Ray Kroc, founder of the McDonald's fast-food franchise, got into the restaurant business in the 1950s, he worked as a salesperson. One of the products he offered was a multimixer, a blender that could make five milkshakes at a time. Two of Kroc's customers, the McDonald brothers, ordered many of these machines. Kroc wondered why. Instead of simply sending out the order, Kroc decided he needed to see what kind of restaurant used so many mixers. When he saw the restaurant in operation, Kroc immediately perceived that the McDonald brothers had a formula for producing good, inexpensive food. They had created a kind of food assembly line that could deliver meals to customers in a matter of minutes. Kroc suggested that he could open additional restaurants for the McDonald brothers and translate their "fast food" concept into a business

Ray Kroc smiles for the camera while proudly displaying a McDonald's hamburger.

venture. In 1961, he bought out the McDonald brothers. Ray Kroc's curiosity made him a very successful businessperson—his McDonald's restaurant chain spread throughout the United States and, eventually, the world. He was a leader in the development of the modern franchise system.

Imaginative

Entrepreneurs are creative. They imagine solutions to problems and create new products or generate new ideas. Entrepreneurs have a vision. As a young boy, T.P. Phelan sold newspapers to train and steamship travellers in 1883. He saw that the travellers who bought his papers were always looking for someplace to eat. He opened a small newsstand and lunch counter on one of the steamships, which was very successful. He continued to expand the service to other ships and eventually formed the Canadian Railway News Company. That rather unwieldy name was shortened much later to Cara Operations Ltd.—owner of Harvey's, Swiss Chalet, Kelsey's, Second Cup, and numerous other restaurants and catering businesses.

Persistent

Rarely is a new venture successful right away. Often, dealing with bureaucracy, making mistakes in the market, confronting criticism, and having money, family, or stress problems are part of the entrepreneurial experience. Many people would say "Enough!" and give up. True entrepreneurs stick with their ideas until they're sure they've tried everything to make the venture work. The famous children's story *The Little Engine That Could* serves an example of the quality of persistence.

Goal-setting

For many entrepreneurs, one success may not be enough. In fact, entrepreneurs are often motivated primarily by the excitement of starting a new venture. They set a goal, then develop a venture to achieve that goal. Once the goal is achieved, a new goal needs to take its place. Most often, setting a new goal means starting a new venture. Manoucher Etminan, the founder of Manoucher's Bread, an upscale bakery in Toronto, was an amazing success in the Toronto area. Not satisfied with having achieved his initial goal, he decided to open new markets—in Europe!

Canada's Second Cup is owned by Cara Foods.

To be successful, entrepreneurs need to exhibit persistence and perseverance; qualities exemplified by *The Little Engine That Could*.

The tailfin of a Virgin plane

Hardworking

Entrepreneurs see the task in front of them, but do not let hard work deter them. During the Christmas season, for example, a retailer may work 16 hours straight for days in a row. If a new plant is opening or a special order needs to be filled, a factory owner may not get home for days. To succeed, entrepreneurs need a great deal of energy. J.M. Schneider, the founder of Schneider Foods, worked in a button factory all day and made his famous sausages long into the evening after he got home from work, to satisfy the growing list of customers for his delicious products.

Self-confident

Entrepreneurs believe in themselves. In order to take risks and work so hard, entrepreneurs must be certain their ideas are worth the effort. Doubts may exist, but the self-confidence of entrepreneurs takes care of these doubts. Can you imagine how much self-confidence it took for Sir Richard Branson, the founder of Virgin Records, to start Virgin Airlines?

Flexible

There are no sure things in business. The only thing an entrepreneur can count on is that things will change, sometimes for the better, sometimes for the worse. A true entrepreneur looks at change as an opportunity. He or she must be flexible in order to adapt to changing trends, markets, technologies, rules, and economic environments. As the popularity of videotape declined and the demand for DVDs increased, flexible video rental businesses were able to change over to the DVD format and capitalize on the new trend.

Independent

The most common entrepreneurial characteristic is the desire for independence. Entrepreneurs do not like to be told what to do. They need to control their own lives and make their own decisions. People with an entrepreneurial personality find it hard to work in a controlled environment. As a result, they would not likely enjoy working on an assembly line or in the military.

Entrepreneurs' need for independence helps them achieve their goals. No one possesses exactly the same characteristics.

It is the particular mix of characteristics in each entrepreneur that defines each new project. Entrepreneurs, then, must find their own opportunities, make their own plans, and create their own solutions. Each venture is a reflection of the independent entrepreneur who started it.

Review Questions

1. List and describe in a sentence or two the 10 characteristics of an entrepreneur.

2. Name three of the characteristics you think you have. How would you illustrate that you have those characteristics?

3. Name one of the characteristics you feel you lack. How might you develop that characteristic in yourself?

Stretch Your Thinking

Consider a task you would willingly stay up all night to finish. Now think about what kind of business you could start that would use your interest in this area.

Entrepreneurial Skills

Keep in Mind

1. research skills
2. management skills
3. relationship skills

Do you ski? Can you hook up a sound system? Do you know how to knit? These are skills you may or may not possess. Having a **skill** means that you have the ability to do something specific. Carpenters have woodworking skills, chefs have cooking skills, and doctors have diagnostic skills. It is easier to learn a skill than it is to develop a characteristic. Skills enable you to translate knowledge into action. To be successful, entrepreneurs need a variety of skills, including research, management, and relationship skills.

Research Skills

To run a successful venture, an entrepreneur needs to perform marketing and accounting tasks, as well as many of the other business activities described in this textbook. Entrepreneurs must identify what they need to know, and then use research techniques to obtain this information.

It is not necessary for entrepreneurs to know everything about their chosen venture before they begin. What they do need, however, is the ability to learn or acquire knowledge. The first step in knowledge acquisition is asking a good question. In fact, knowing what questions to ask is one of the most important research skills an entrepreneur can possess.

Entrepreneurs often ask questions about problems or information that most people pass over or take for granted. Entrepreneurs may wonder about something they read in a newspaper or see on a television program. Perhaps a question is sparked by a chance remark overheard in a supermarket or on the street. In any case, the entrepreneur asks questions such as "Why is that?" or "How does that work?" These initial questions often lead nowhere in particular; sometimes, however, the question is the first step in a process that leads to a venture plan.

Most people who struggle to find their house key in their cluster of keys day after day never wonder about the problem. An entrepreneur, however, might ask, "How could I make it easier to find the right key?" Such a question is the beginning of research and may lead to a new venture.

Once you formulate your initial research question, the first step is to gather information that will help you answer it. During this process, you may discover things that lead you to ask new questions or to reformulate old ones. As your investigation moves further along, your questions become more specific and focused, and may even lead to the creation of a new business.

Gathering Information

Once entrepreneurs form their questions, they need to know how to find answers. Often, their search begins at a library or on the Internet. Complex questions such as "How will I advertise my product?" or "What channels of distribution would be best for this item?" may require the entrepreneur to research a variety of sources.

Books

In a library or bookstore, you can find books on all aspects of business. Hundreds of books have been written about advertising, for example. Some of these books offer very specialized advice, such as how to create advertisements for a specific product.

Periodicals

Magazines, newspapers, and newsletters are good sources of business information. Some periodicals, known as trade journals, focus on a particular industry. *Convenience Store News*, for example, is written for people who are interested in the convenience store business. *Automatic Merchandiser* is a monthly magazine published for people in the vending machine industry.

<aside>
Literacy Link

Identifying main idea and supporting details
As you read or do research, use a graphic organizer such as an idea web to summarize the text. Jot down the main idea in the centre of your notebook and connect supporting details to it.
</aside>

In 2005, according to *Profit* magazine, the fastest-growing company in Canada was Rutter Inc. Founded in 1998 by Byron Dawe, Rutter makes voyage data recorders (VDR) for large ships. The VDR is like the "black box" on airplanes, but instead of flight data it records sailing data. On old sailing ships, a rutter was the diary or log in which the ship's navigator kept a detailed record of every voyage.

Dawe needed capital to fund expansions and development. Another entrepreneur, Donald Clarke, came to the rescue with the necessary capital. Clarke and his partners had become established as concrete suppliers and formed the ConPro Group as they expanded into providing construction, engineering, and technology services to the offshore oil and gas industry in Newfoundland. Clarke, whose grandfather founded Montreal-based Clarke Steamship Company, had a love of ships and the sea, and saw Dawe's VDR as a golden opportunity.

To fund Rutter's expansion, ConPro took the company public in 2002. Since then it has grown quickly. In 2000, Rutter's income was $223 800. In 2005, it was $70 939 704. This represents a five-year growth of 31 598 percent, more than enough to qualify as the fastest-growing company in Canada.

This icebreaker records its sailing data using a VDR made by Rutter.

Indexes and Databases

Indexes and databases are excellent research tools. A **periodical index** lists articles that have been published about a specific topic over a particular period of time. Most indexes provide the article's title, a brief description, and the name and date of the periodical in which the article appears. **Databases** are lists of information organized by category. These categories can be very specific—for example, kite manufacturers—or very broad—for example, Canadian businesses that export to the United States. The CanCorp Financials website posts a database of detailed information on more than 8000 Canadian companies. Using the Thomas Register of American Manufacturers, entrepreneurs can access information on 156 000 North American manufacturers and more than 450 000 products. The federal government's

The federal government of Canada's Strategis website.

Industry Canada website Strategis maintains a comprehensive database of Canadian companies. Frasers website provides access to detailed information about 30 000 Canadian industrial suppliers. Some databases charge a fee, but others are free. Your public library may also provide free Internet access to some databases.

The Internet

The Internet can offer many advantages to entrepreneurs, but there are potential disadvantages as well. See Table 10.1.

Consultants

Experts, or consultants, can help entrepreneurs gather needed information. Consultants are often entrepreneurs themselves and charge for their services. However, certain university business departments, some government departments, and most financial institutions offer free business consulting. Local chambers of commerce and business development offices are often the best sources of free and valuable information when opening a venture in a particular city or region. They have a wealth of knowledge about topics such as business trends, available locations, and local tax rates and rental costs.

Professionals

Many different kinds of professionals can assist entrepreneurs with their research. Advertising agencies can help figure out what types of ads to create and where to place them. Accountants can give advice on maintaining financial records. Sales agents can provide information on distributing a product. Lawyers can offer advice about patents and copyrights. Professional help is expensive, however, and should be factored into your start-up costs.

School

Most universities and community colleges offer extension courses in business subjects. Usually, the courses are offered at night. Many schools and community colleges also offer general-interest courses, which may provide other sorts of information. If the entrepreneur has more complex information needs, he or she may need to enroll in a full-time program and obtain the necessary skills and knowledge over several years.

Table 10.1

Using the Internet	
Advantages	**Disadvantages**
• Government and association sites can be especially valuable to entrepreneurs with particular interests. • Internet search engines such as Google can help the entrepreneur find relevant information. • Groups of people interested in sharing information on specific topics can join Internet chat groups or **listservs** (e-mail lists that distribute queries and information to people who subscribe to them). For example, entrepreneurs interested in starting a wool-production business could acquire information from sheep ranchers, weavers, or sweater designers.	• So much information is available that it can be difficult to find exactly what you need. • Some information is inaccurate, unedited, or outdated. • Some people use the Internet for illegal or unethical activities, so it is very important to never give out personal or financial information to an unknown source.

Using Information

Not all information is usable. Once entrepreneurs gather information from a variety of sources, they need to extract data that will answer their initial question. As mentioned previously, while gathering information, entrepreneurs may ask other questions and start on new quests. They may discover alternative solutions or new opportunities. For example, Nelia was interested in textile making. Through her research, she found lots of information on this topic, but she also found information on textile dyeing and colouring. Nelia then wondered what plants were used to produce dyes. By doing research on this connection, she saw an opportunity to produce and sell potted plants that each produce a different colour of dye. She thought she could sell these plants to craftspeople who dye and weave their own cloth.

The initial venture creates more questions. As the business develops, the questions and answers become more specific and focused on particular aspects of the venture. Entrepreneurs acquire new knowledge as they look for ways to solve problems:

How do I adapt new equipment? find new markets? develop new products? Nelia, for example, needs a tray that can hold the plants for shipping and also display them in the customer's home. This problem is specific to the new venture. Research should be aimed at finding a practical solution. Once Nelia solves the problem, the new tray design becomes part of the venture.

Management Skills

In Chapter 7, you learned that the role of management in business is to achieve the goals of an organization by directing the allocation and use of the organization's human, financial, and material resources. Management performs four major functions for any business: planning, organizing, directing, and controlling.

The definition of management can be rephrased for entrepreneurs in this way: Entrepreneurs achieve their individual goals by applying their management skills to their personal, financial, and material resources. For entrepreneurs, management skills still involve planning, organizing, directing, and controlling.

Planning

Entrepreneurs do a great deal of planning. They develop financial, production, and marketing plans. Ultimately, they incorporate all these individual plans into an overall business plan. Entrepreneurs must be careful, however, to avoid overplanning. If they focus on every tiny detail, they may panic and give up.

A colourful representation of various plant dyes

Organizing

The main thing entrepreneurs need to organize is their time. Detailed schedules, "to do" lists, reminder files, and personal planners help entrepreneurs keep appointments and remember all the things that need to get done, such as meeting with suppliers, purchasing or repairing equipment, and interviewing potential staff. Organizing the venture is very important. Entrepreneurs need to develop job descriptions and know who is responsible for each job. Communication must be organized as well, so that each person involved in the venture knows its structure and the lines of communication.

Ethical, Moral & Legal Considerations

Peninsula Farms was a small business in Lunenburg, Nova Scotia, that began with one cow. The Joneses owned the cow and kept her around to maintain their lawn. The cow produced milk, of course, but the Joneses didn't know how to milk her. So they learned proper milking techniques. The cow was producing more milk than they could use, and the surplus was going to waste. The Joneses researched the local market to find out what kind of milk product would sell. They discovered that whole-milk yogurt was in demand. They then found out how to make yogurt in large batches. They also studied the health and safety regulations to make sure they were meeting government standards. The Joneses were so successful that they exceeded the government criteria. The Joneses then bought more cows—enough to make Peninsula Farms a profitable business.

Government inspectors had always given Peninsula Farms a high rating on their regular inspections. It was a surprise to the Joneses, then, when six federal inspectors from the Canadian Food Inspection Agency (CFIA) visited the farm and, with just a cursory examination of the plant and its procedures, impounded more than $50 000 worth of yogurt. This halted the production and left Peninsula Farms' customers without the product they wanted to buy. The Joneses faced a total loss of more than $100 000, as they were now behind $50 000 worth of new production in addition to the yogurt that had been impounded. (Their cooler was full of the impounded yogurt and there was nowhere to put any new yogurt.) They were losing sales and customers as well. The space that Peninsula Farms' product took on grocery shelves was soon filled with competing brands. Faced with such a loss, Peninsula Farms was forced out of business. It was discovered after the fact that their plant was above standard and their yogurt tested totally clean, with no trace of offending bacteria.

No one wants to be poisoned by the foods we eat. The Canadian Food Inspection Agency does a wonderful job of protecting us from dirty factories, unsafe packaging, and dangerous storage practices. As a result, we eat foods that do not, as a rule, make us sick. Canadians are grateful that the CFIA is diligent in their efforts on our behalf. 1) Was the Canadian Food Inspection Agency too diligent in this case? 2) Should there be special rules for small ventures that cannot afford such an interruption to their businesses? 3) If you were the Joneses, would you start over? Explain your decision briefly.

Directing

Directing isn't simply telling people what to do. Good entrepreneurs learn to empower their staff, which means giving their employees the feeling that their work and contribution to the business are important. This task is most often accomplished by sharing the goals of the company with the employees and illustrating how their particular jobs fit into the overall picture. An entrepreneur who takes this approach can encourage more initiative and self-direction in his or her staff. In other words, a good boss doesn't really "boss." Instead, he or she shares the operation of the business with the people who make it work.

Controlling

Because entrepreneurs have limited resources, they need budgets to help them control expenses, inventory, and other material resources. An accurate bookkeeping and accounting system helps an owner keep control of the finances. In fact, the inability to control spending is the primary cause of most venture failures. An entrepreneur should have accounting knowledge and skills or hire someone who does.

Relationship Skills

When starting and running a venture, an entrepreneur establishes many different relationships. The relationship skills that

---

In the News

Doug Zell, the founder and director of Intelligentsia Coffee in Chicago, Illinois, does not believe in the old business saying, "Buy low, sell high." Instead, his philosophy is "Buy high, sell high." Buying high gets Intelligentsia the very best coffee in the world.

To ensure that his coffee is indeed top of the line, Zell hired Geoff Watts to "buy high." To do this, Watts says, "I find a coffee I love, build a direct relationship with the grower, and pay at least 25 percent above the fair-trade price." Customers love Intelligentsia's coffee, and Doug Zell doesn't mind paying the extra $200 000 a year it costs to support Watts's relationship building.

The grower connections also include financial incentives for improving growing methods and producing superior coffee beans. Geoff Watts gets to know each of the growers he buys from and helps them remain a supplier by maintaining the quality of their coffee. The business model is obviously working: Intelligentsia had sales of almost $10 million in 2005 and a 21 percent growth rate in 2006. And Chicago coffee lovers had great coffee.

entrepreneurs need vary, depending on the kind of association the entrepreneur has with each person. Each business contact can be categorized as a staff, supplier, or customer relationship.

Staff Relationships

To maintain good relationships with their staff, entrepreneurs need the ability to motivate. Employees must feel that they are being treated fairly; they need to feel that they are being rewarded for their efforts and that their needs are being met. Each employee is unique and has different needs and different ideas about fair and equal treatment. And, as you read in Chapter 6, each employee is motivated by different rewards—money, job satisfaction, self-worth, profit sharing, holidays, employee-of-the-month awards, and so on.

Motivation skills rely on matching rewards to an employee's needs and personality. Entrepreneurs should try to get to know and empathize with their employees. **Empathy** is the ability to understand what other people think and feel. It can help entrepreneurs realize what motivates each employee to work hard and stay with their business. For example, Tawanda is single and lives alone. She likes the social aspect of her work because it allows her to meet people and develop relationships. Staff parties, casual Fridays, and organized staff events such as bowling and movie nights are all reasons why Tawanda likes coming to work. Matthew, on the other hand, is married with a young son. He likes time with his family. Friday afternoons off and additional holidays are two rewards that would motivate Matthew to make an extra effort. He would also jump at the chance to work from home more often.

Supplier Relationships

Communication is the most important relationship skill required to deal with suppliers. Regardless of who your suppliers are—the government, service providers, merchandise suppliers, or material and equipment sellers—they are all sources of information about new products, processes, and materials. They also want feedback from you if there are problems so that they can improve their service.

Paying bills when they're due is one way to maintain good relationships with suppliers. If cash flow makes prompt payment seem temporarily impossible, send a partial payment with an explanation and a request for an extension. Be sure to state the

Oops!

Florida-based Goosebumps Products made gel-filled shoe inserts. However, purchasers found that the inserts produced "flatulence-like noises," like a novelty "whoopee cushion," when worn. It turned out that the gel had bubbles in it, which caused the shoes to make these noises when people walked in them. Goosebumps sued the supplier, Bell Chem Corp., claiming that the company had sent the wrong compound, which had caused the bubbles to form. Goosebumps had to dispose of 35 000 pairs of inserts.

length of the extension (30 days is common) and to pay the balance before the time is up. If the problem is more serious and requires some financial restructuring, inform your suppliers and ask how you can work together to solve the problem. It's important to remember that suppliers want your business to succeed. If it doesn't, they may never receive payment. They also lose the distribution channel or source of income your business provides. Most suppliers are willing to help out their customers to some extent, as long as they feel that honest communication is taking place.

Customer Relationships

Entrepreneurs are motivated to be independent, but they do have a boss: the customer. An entrepreneur should be able to make each customer feel important. This skill sets the standard for every member of the organization. If an entrepreneur maintains positive customer relationships, the "customer is boss" attitude is adopted by the entire staff. The restaurant owner who greets customers at the door and visits each table personally not only makes the customers feel special, but also sets an example that motivates staff to make service even better. The software manufacturer who requires employees to visit customers to see how the product is actually being used shows both staff and customers how important customers are. The first question an entrepreneur should ask every morning is, "How will I make my customers feel good today?"

Some Canadian Entrepreneurs

How rich do you want to be? In a good career, you could eventually earn a salary of $60 000 or more. As a professional, you could earn $400 000 or higher. CEOs of major corporations earn several million dollars per year or more. But no one earns more than entrepreneurs. Of the 23 Canadian billionaires, every one is an entrepreneur or inherited their money from entrepreneurial parents or grandparents. Unless you inherit, the only way you can ever become that rich is by starting your own venture. Let's look at some examples of Canadians who made it.

Jimmy Pattison

Jimmy Pattison, 74, is a true entrepreneur. His dad was a used car salesman in Vancouver, and Pattison certainly inherited his selling spirit. When he was 12, Pattison sold garden seeds door to door. He moved up to magazine subscriptions soon after, and then took on a paper route.

When he attended the University of British Columbia, he earned his tuition by washing cars at a used car lot. Seeing more opportunity in selling cars, he began buying the $150 bargains that came onto the lot, fixing them up, and making a profit selling them to his fellow students for $250. Many afternoons Pattison would drive one of his bargains to a buyer's house, collect his money, and then take the bus home. He was so successful in car sales that he was asked to manage a car dealership before he had finished his UBC degree (he was nine credits short).

Over the next four decades, Pattison continued to build his business empire. Today, he owns supermarkets, car dealerships,

One of Canada's wealthiest individuals, Jimmy Pattison

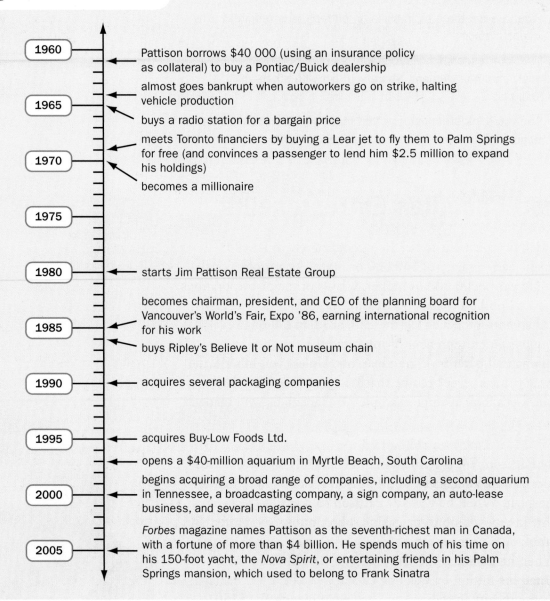

Figure 10.1 Pattison's Timeline

1960 — Pattison borrows $40 000 (using an insurance policy as collateral) to buy a Pontiac/Buick dealership

almost goes bankrupt when autoworkers go on strike, halting vehicle production

1965 — buys a radio station for a bargain price

meets Toronto financiers by buying a Lear jet to fly them to Palm Springs for free (and convinces a passenger to lend him $2.5 million to expand his holdings)

1970 — becomes a millionaire

1975

1980 — starts Jim Pattison Real Estate Group

becomes chairman, president, and CEO of the planning board for Vancouver's World's Fair, Expo '86, earning international recognition for his work

1985 — buys Ripley's Believe It or Not museum chain

1990 — acquires several packaging companies

1995 — acquires Buy-Low Foods Ltd.

opens a $40-million aquarium in Myrtle Beach, South Carolina

begins acquiring a broad range of companies, including a second aquarium in Tennessee, a broadcasting company, a sign company, an auto-lease business, and several magazines

2000

Forbes magazine names Pattison as the seventh-richest man in Canada, with a fortune of more than $4 billion. He spends much of his time on his 150-foot yacht, the *Nova Spirit*, or entertaining friends in his Palm Springs mansion, which used to belong to Frank Sinatra

2005

print media distribution firms, an outdoor advertising company, numerous radio stations, a few television stations, and, of course, the world-famous Ripley's Believe It or Not museum chain. This timeline shows some of the steps that helped Pattison become a billionaire.

Vickie Kerr

When Vickie Kerr began making her own potato chips in her kitchen in 1986 she thought about two things: how she could make use of some of the potatoes she and her husband grew on their 165-acre potato farm, and how to make something the kids would like, but was a healthy snack as well. The potato farm was a good, solid business, but the family was not rich, so an inexpensive homemade family treat was worth researching.

Kerr was persistent and experimented with different recipes for more than a year, finally finding one she liked. She left the skin on each potato slice, to preserve all of its healthy vitamins and nutrients. She cooked the chips in small batches, in hot peanut oil, which is low in cholesterol. She even hand-stirred the slices so that each chip browned evenly and didn't stick. The finishing touch was a dash of sea salt on the cooling chips. The result was a delicious potato chip, extra crispy and free of cholesterol and any added preservatives. The chips also contained the vitamins that commercially produced chips lost, especially when they were peeled.

A sample of Miss Vickie's tempting flavours of potato chips

Everyone loved her chips and Kerr felt sure she had a product she could sell. She certainly hoped the profit resulting from her idea might supplement the income from the potato farm. The potato-farming industry was becoming very competitive, and it was increasingly difficult to make a living from just potatoes. Calling her product Miss Vickie's, she managed to place bags of potato chips in several retail stores around her community of New Lowell, Ontario.

Her product was successful locally, so in 1989, she and her husband bought a potato-chip manufacturing plant with money they borrowed from the bank, using their farm as security. They were risking everything they owned on Vickie's idea. They bought the necessary equipment, created a marketing plan that focused on health-food stores, and started making potato chips in large quantities. Kerr insisted, however, that everything be done according to her original recipe.

Miss Vickie's was a premium potato chip, which, at the time, was a novelty. They sold for twice as much as other potato chips on the market. Customers loved the crunch and the taste, however, and Miss Vickie's chips were immediately popular. Kerr expanded her operation from one kettle to six, and within a year, she was selling chips in Toronto, the best retail market in Canada. The increased demand called for expansion, and the business converted a potato-storage building into a processing plant. Sales in the first year exceeded a million dollars. Her second-year sales grew 200 percent!

By now Miss Vickie's was a big business, adding several new flavours to the line, and opening manufacturing plants in Quebec and British Columbia. It became so big, in fact, it caught the eye of North America's biggest potato chip manufacturer, Hostess Frito-Lay. The company made a generous offer to buy, and Vickie and her husband accepted. In 1993, they moved to Phoenix, Arizona, to enjoy the success they had worked so hard to achieve. Today, Miss Vickie's is still a strong brand for the American-owned Hostess Frito-Lay Company, and still sticks to Vickie Kerr's original recipe.

David Tuccaro

David Tuccaro is a Fort McMurray businessman from the Mikisew Cree Band. Tuccaro is using his businesses (Neegan Development Corp. and Tuc's Contracting) and his cultural knowledge to become a local ally for Syncrude Canada. Syncrude is a major participant in the multibillion-dollar development of Northern Alberta's Athabasca oil sands. Energy, forestry, and mining companies affect Aboriginal communities every day, and Tuccaro's expertise can make the contacts between the two groups easier.

Neegan Development at work.

A true entrepreneur, Tuccaro bought Neegan Development Corporation Ltd., the earthmoving and mining services firm, in 1991, after working for a year as the company's president. He turned the struggling $2-million concern into a robust $10-million company by 2003. Tuccaro also owns and operates Tuc's Contracting, which provides water and vacuum trucks to clear industrial and human waste from work sites. Tuc's has grown in seven years to become a $4-million business. Tuccaro owns environmental consulting, furniture-making, and other companies as well.

Tuccaro is committed to the Aboriginal community and has the respect and trust of community leaders. In addition, he is an advocate of using local labour and is proud of the fact that Neegan is 70 percent staffed by Aboriginal workers; Tuc's has 60 percent Aboriginal staff.

Tuccaro operates his companies with world-class standards, a policy that's allowing him to expand globally. He has started a new project in New Zealand, where Aboriginal Maori communities have sought his help to create commercial properties. They would prefer to be involved in these undertakings rather than have huge multinational corporations come in and operate major projects. Tuccaro's Aboriginal roots make him sensitive to the needs of Aboriginal communities. He proposes to assist in developing a long-term management approach for his Maori clients, who he believes have similar goals to those of First Nations communities in Alberta.

"The majority of the [Aboriginal] people I've encountered want to have a chance to play a part in the economies of Canada and the world," he observes. "There has to be a huge commitment to education by the Aboriginal leadership at First Nation locations. Economies come and go, up and down, booms and bust, but if our kids are educated, there's always something they can do."

🌐 E-ACTIVITY ☐▣☒

Visit www.nelson.com/WOB and follow the links to learn more about successful Canadian entrepreneurs.

Review Questions

7. Select one of the entrepreneurs profiled above. List five entrepreneurial characteristics that he or she possesses. Provide proof for each one.

8. How does being Cree help David Tuccaro's businesses?

Venture Evaluation Criteria

Keep in Mind

1. feasibility
2. marketability
3. profitability

Do you have an idea for a business? Before you risk all your cash and your self-esteem, examine the criteria below, and make sure that your business plan meets each one.

Feasibility

Can you really do this? Use this feasibility chart to make sure.

Financing	List the amount required in the form of a budget.	Include the source of the capital with details (bank, terms, etc.).
Location	Explain your choice of location.	Outline details regarding location (address, rent, taxes, utilities, etc.).
Licences and Permits	List the licences and permits you require.	State where, when, and how you will obtain them.

continued on next page

Suppliers	Make a list of everything you need.	Next to each of the items on your inventory needs list, name the supplier, price, and terms.
Staff	Describe your staffing needs.	What is your detailed plan for obtaining the necessary employees?

Marketability

Ask yourself the following questions about your product, service, or charity:

- Does your target market want this product? Prove it.

- What is your competition? How much of the market do they own already? How will you take it away from them?

- Are you competitively priced?

- Is this a short-term venture? How long will it last?

- What does your product, service, or charity offer that no other product, service, or charity offers? Why would a customer pay money for whatever you provide?

Profitability

If you are expecting a profit from this venture, you should be sure that your revenue exceeds your costs—all of your costs. Be sure to prepare an income statement that lists projected revenue and every expense you can foresee. When you deduct the expenses from the revenue, that's what's left for you. Is it enough? (See Chapter 9 for more information on income statements.)

With the international success of the iPod, manufacturers of iPod accessories were more easily able to predict the feasibility, marketability, and profitability of products, such as the ezTattoo.

Review Questions

9. What are the three criteria you could use to evaluate an idea for a venture?

10. What licences and permits might businesses require?

CHAPTER REVIEW

Knowledge

1. List and describe briefly the four functions of management.

2. What entrepreneurial characteristics do the following people illustrate?
   a) Ray Kroc   b) Manoucher Etminan
   c) T.P. Phelan   d) Gerald Pencer

3. What three research questions did the Joneses need to ask before they could start Peninsula Farms?

Thinking

4. Are you an entrepreneur? Take at least two online entrepreneur quizzes and report on your findings about yourself. Were the results of the quizzes what you expected? If not, how were they different from your expectations? (To find these online tests, go to the Nelson website at www.nelson.com/WOB.)

5. What rather difficult situation has been a common event in the lives of many of the entrepreneurs featured in this chapter?

6. Do you think there are differences between a profit-driven enterprise and a charitable enterprise? Explain your reasoning.

7. Select a business in your area that failed over the past few years. Why do you think it failed? Which new venture in your community do you think might not last long? Why do you say that?

Communications

8. Interview a female entrepreneur in your area. Describe her business, and ask her to comment on the characteristics of an entrepreneur that she feels she possesses. Ask her for her opinion on whether female entrepreneurs have more difficulties than male entrepreneurs.

Application

9. Describe and evaluate either your own or an existing idea for an entrepreneurial endeavour in your school or community. Use the criteria outlined in this chapter to assist you.

10. Miss Vickie's Potato Chips is now owned by the U.S. firm Hostess Frito-Lay. Many other popular Canadian companies have also been purchased by American firms. If you were a successful Canadian entrepreneur, would you sell to an American firm? Explain why or why not.

Team Activity

Team Goal: Raise money for a worthy cause

Team Assignment: A Fundraising Plan

- As a team, formulate a plan to make money for a worthy cause. Once your instructor has approved your plan, put it into effect.

- The team that makes the most money in one week for their cause will be declared this week's winner.

Portfolio

Prepare detailed biographies of some of the entrepreneurs who have started businesses within your industry. Collect photos and entrepreneurial stories about them. Show how they illustrate the characteristics and skills of most entrepreneurs.

Reflect on Your Learning

Do you want to be an entrepreneur? Why or why not?

Sir Richard Branson

Sir Richard Branson will literally take you out of this world. His latest business venture, Virgin Galactic, is currently taking reservations. For approximately US$200 000 you too can fly into orbit on the VSS *Enterprise* rocket with the likes of William Shatner and Paris Hilton. Sound outrageous?

Branson is the wildly successful British entrepreneur behind the Virgin empire. With an estimated worth of more than £3 billion, he is the ninth-richest person in the United Kingdom. He was knighted by the Queen in 1999 for his "services in entrepreneurship." Yet Branson is not your traditional businessperson. When he is not running his business empire, he is attempting to circle the world in a hot-air balloon or breaking the world record for crossing the

Sir Richard Branson just hanging out in front of one of his product advertisements

Atlantic Ocean in his boat. His major competitor, Sir Stelios Haji-Ioannou, summed it up, "Let's be honest—Branson is some hippy from the 1960s whereas I'm a university graduate who went through formal training to become a businessman." Yet that is exactly what makes Branson successful and iconic.

Branson was an entrepreneur from birth. By the age of 15, he had two failed business ventures—Christmas-tree growing and pigeon farming. However, he was never a good student. He suffered from dyslexia and an overly curious spirit. At the age of 16, he dropped out of school and moved to London. There he started his first successful venture, *Student Magazine*, and then, at age 17, a Student Advisory Centre (a charitable organization). In 1970, he began a mail-order record business, and in 1972, he started the Virgin Records label, opening a recording studio with a partner, Nik Powell.

The Virgin Records label welcomed controversy. It signed bands that other record labels did not dare to release, such as the Sex Pistols. This risk won praise and business success for exposing the public to fresh music. Virgin Records was the primary business in the ever-expanding Virgin brand, but it was sold off in 1992 to keep one of Virgin's newer ventures—its airline business—afloat. It is rumoured that Branson wept while finalizing the sale, as the record label was the genius of the Virgin empire. Virgin re-entered the music market with the V2 label once financial stability was attained.

Today, the Virgin brand is best known for its airline and music divisions, yet the brand encompasses business ventures ranging from space travel to fine wines to cell phones to bridal needs. Virgin's eclectic business ventures are based on what Branson thinks he himself would consume. Yet not everything he touches turns into a success. He has had many business failures, including Virgin Cola and Virgin Vodka.

How does Branson cope when things do not go as planned? "Whenever I experience any kind of setback, I always pick myself up and try again…. The amount of time that people waste on failures, rather than putting that energy into another project, always amazes me…. So a setback is never a bad experience, just a learning curve."

QUESTIONS

1. Describe Sir Richard Branson and what you think makes him a successful businessperson.

2. Why do you think people say failure is an important ingredient in becoming a better entrepreneur?

11

Invention and Innovation

SPECIFIC EXPECTATIONS

After completing this chapter, you will be able to

- describe how entrepreneurs discover opportunities in people's needs, wants, and problems

- describe a variety of Canadian inventions and innovation, including Aboriginal inventions and innovations

- explain how innovation has affected a variety of goods and services over time

Ballard

Ballard Power Systems Inc., originally known as Ballard Research Inc., was founded in 1979 by Geoffrey Ballard, Keith Prater, and Paul Howard in Vancouver, British Columbia. Together, they formed an alliance with the intention of developing a rechargeable, lightweight lithium battery. Within the first few years, it became clear to the founders that in order

to see their pursuit realized, they would have to deviate from their initial plans. So, in 1983, the company changed gears and began working to produce a solid polymer fuel cell, which later became known as the proton-exchange membrane (PEM) fuel cell. Since then, Ballard Power Systems Inc. has become the world leader in the development, manufacture, and marketing of PEM fuel cells, which the company then commercializes for a variety of transportation, stationary, and portable applications.

What exactly are PEM

A bus powered by a Ballard fuel cell engine

fuel cells and why are they important? A fuel cell combines hydrogen fuel with oxygen from the air to produce an efficient form of electrical energy, with the only by-products being water and heat. The result: little (if any) noise, vibration, air pollution, or greenhouse gases.

By 1986, Ballard's PEM fuel cells were producing four times the amount of power that any comparable company had been able to achieve. What this meant was that fuel cells were beginning to emerge as potential sources of alternative energy that could be used for automobiles. Seven years later, in 1993, Ballard developed the first prototype fuel-powered bus. Since then, more than 125 Ballard fuel cell–powered vehicles have been produced—the greatest number of fuel cell vehicles ever demonstrated. Furthermore, in 2003, Ballard provided fuel-cell engines for the manufacture of 33 Mercedes-Benz Citaro buses, which were designed to carry passengers for daily service as part of a two-year field trial in nine major European cities.

There are few companies in history that have relied upon innovation to tackle hurdles and achieve success in the same way that Ballard has. In 2004, Ballard Power Systems received two Frost & Sullivan awards at the Annual Excellence in Industrial Technology Awards Banquet. A hydrogen-fueled stationary fuel cell generator, the Nexa RM Series, was named the 2004 Energy Product of the Year and Alternative Technology of the Year. Additionally, Geoffrey Ballard himself has received numerous awards, including *Material Handling Management Magazine*'s Innovation Award in 2004; the first Lifetime Achievement Award in the Energy Sector, where he was credited at the World Energy Technologies Summit in 2004; and recognition by *The Economist* in 2003 with Leadership in Energy and the Environment. There is no doubt that Ballard Power Systems' non-stop innovation has made it a clear winner when it comes to technological development.

QUESTIONS

1. How has Ballard Power Systems proven itself as an innovative leader in the technology sector?

2. What does Ballard hope to achieve by developing the company's products?

Entrepreneurial Opportunities

Choosing a Venture

If you've determined that you have the characteristics and skills necessary to be an entrepreneur, and you feel that you may enjoy starting a venture, only two questions remain: What kind of venture will you start? How will you do it? Entrepreneurs can seek a venture opportunity in one of two ways—as an idea-driven opportunity or as a market-driven opportunity.

Idea-driven Enterprises

An **idea-driven enterprise** is one that you create as a result of an invention or innovation. Imagine that one day, while looking at a kitchen-drawer organizer, you come up with a great idea for a similar device that will help people organize their ties. Your innovation—a tie organizer—is a wooden device designed to fit in a wide variety of bureau drawers. The retail price might range from $10 to $50, depending on the type of wood that is used.

Now that you have an idea for a venture, you have to find a location for your business, invest in equipment to produce the tie organizer, gather the necessary raw materials, and hire staff. Then, you can begin production. Once the tie organizers are made, you have to start selling them. At this point, idea-driven entrepreneurial ventures sometimes run into trouble. What if no one wants to buy a tie organizer? No customers have expressed

Keep in Mind

1. choosing a venture
2. bringing ideas and marketing skills together
3. finding entrepreneurial opportunities
4. setting your venture apart

Before You Begin

What do you consider the most important invention in the history of the world? Why?

The DVD player in this van is an example of an idea-driven venture.

a demand for the product, so you can't tell for sure if there's a market. Perhaps the current trend is toward *not* wearing ties. Perhaps people already have other ways to organize their ties. You hope that your idea is good enough to bring the customers you need to your business.

Market-driven Enterprises

A **market-driven enterprise** develops in a different way: market-driven entrepreneurs look for a customer base and then develop a product those customers indicate that they need and want. This time, imagine that you are interested in fashion. Your research indicates a real growth trend across the country in ties. Men are using ties to dress up casual clothing, wearing them with jeans or khakis and a shirt. To see whether there is a need for another tie manufacturer, you design a survey to determine how many ties most men own. The results surprise you. Most men don't know how many ties they have. They keep their ties on racks, hangers, and hooks, but the ties tend to fall off and become disorganized. The more ties men get, the more disorganized the ties become, making tie selection difficult.

You realize that what men need isn't more ties; what they need is a way to organize the ties they have. Again, you wonder: What types of tie organizers are on the market today?

Frank and Ernest

© 2002 Thaves. Reprinted with permission. Newspaper dist. by NEA, Inc.

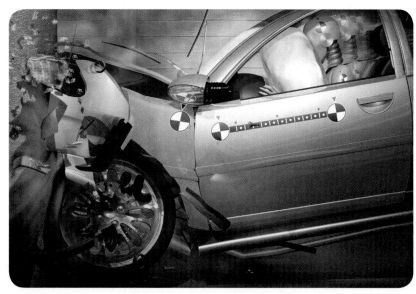
The airbag in this car is an example of a market-driven enterprise.

What types used to be available and why are they no longer sold? How do men organize their ties? How much are men willing to pay for a tie organizer?

Your new research points to a real need for a tie organizer. There is certainly a venture opportunity for anyone who can design such a system. This is the point at which market-driven entrepreneurial ventures often run into trouble. What if you can't design the product yourself? Maybe you don't know anything about woodworking, or you just aren't an inventor. You have a great market, but no idea how to tap into it.

Bringing Ideas and Marketing Skills Together

No successful venture can be purely idea-driven or purely market-driven. The idea person needs help with marketing, while the marketing expert needs help with ideas.

People can learn marketing skills from various sources, including courses, texts, websites, and magazines. If you don't want to learn these skills yourself, you can hire a marketing consultant. Advertising firms, research companies, and consulting firms all provide services to help people assess the market potential of their ideas.

People can also learn technical skills. Many high schools and community colleges hold woodworking and design classes. How-to books are available on a wide variety of technical subjects.

In a metalworking class, you can learn skills such as welding and sheet metal bending.

The Internet and magazines can help as well. If you don't want to do the technical work yourself, you can always hire someone else to do it. Drafting firms, industrial design companies, and technical consultants will, for a fee, take an idea for a product and construct a model. They will design plans and help with technical specifications. They can also advise you about which materials and manufacturing processes you will need to make the product.

When an idea person forms a partnership with a marketing person, each partner brings different strengths to a project. A partner can also increase the venture's capital and share the risks involved. You can find partners at venture capital trade fairs, which are held in major cities, or by placing an advertisement in a national newspaper or magazine. The Internet is also being widely used to bring together entrepreneurs with different types of knowledge.

Ultimately, the entrepreneur wants the answer to one question: Is my venture feasible? A **feasible venture** is one that has the potential to succeed—the entrepreneur has set reasonable goals, and there is both an idea and a market for the product.

Finding Entrepreneurial Opportunities

Every new venture fits into one of the following categories: manufacturing, importing or wholesaling, retail sales, or service (other than retail). When you're looking for venture opportunities, start with the area you like most.

A venture is feasible only when it solves a problem or satisfies a need or want. To identify problems, needs, and wants in the area you chose, you have to find out what is and what is not already available in the market. Products and services that already exist have achieved a certain level of success and acceptance. You may be able to innovate or improve on these products or services with your new venture. It's equally important to find out what's *not* available; doing so may help you identify customer needs and wants that are not currently being filled.

To investigate the market for a new business, an entrepreneur should do two things: segment the current market and create a product or service map.

Segmenting

Chapter 8 has already defined a **market segment** as any part of an overall market that has common characteristics. Market segments can be large or small. For example, the carbonated soft-drink segment represents a large part of the overall

Figure 11.1 What Area Do You Most Like?

If you enjoy building things, manufacturing may be for you.

If you enjoy travel and have a good eye for merchandise that will sell, consider importing or wholesaling.

If you have a great deal of knowledge or passion about a particular type of product, such as sporting goods, books, or clothes, you might enjoy selling this type of product through your own retail venture.

If you like helping others or have a special talent, such as gardening or designing web pages, you might find your place in the service sector.

beverage market, while the caffeine-free diet cola segment is much smaller. The smaller the segmentation, the easier it is to determine what is available in a particular market. It's very difficult to list all the beverages sold in North America, but it's much easier to identify just the available caffeine-free diet colas. Before you launch a new venture, it's important to analyze the segment of the market in which your business will fit.

Product or Service Mapping

Product mapping allows an entrepreneur to visualize all the products or services that are available in a particular segment and to group them by a specific feature—root beer available in long-necked bottles, premium root beers, foamy root beers, and so on. This stage also involves analyzing sales statistics, taste-test data, product histories, consumer motivation data, and any other information that has been found about individual brands. The aspiring root beer maker or importer looks for connections between sales figures and specific attributes, such as packaging, product history, and taste.

After thorough research, the entrepreneur creates a product map. This map illustrates all the characteristics that make each type of root beer popular. When the map is complete, the new entrepreneur can decide which type of root beer to make or import in order to fill a need or want in the market. For example, an entrepreneur's product map might reveal a need for a premium, strong-flavoured root beer that is packaged in a long-necked brown bottle and yields five centimetres of frothy foam when poured into a glass. These characteristics remind consumers of old-fashioned types of root beer, with which they have positive associations. Consumers will pay more for this type of treat than they would for a beverage purchased only to quench their thirst.

Setting Your Venture Apart

As you conduct segmenting and product or service mapping, it's important to keep the following question in mind: How will your venture be different from the ones that are already in the market? If you're interested in manufacturing, importing, or wholesaling, you would ask, "What product can I introduce that's different from what's already there?" For example, if you want to manufacture root beer, you might ask yourself, "Which Canadian root beer brands are not already available in my market area? Which brands could be imported from the United States

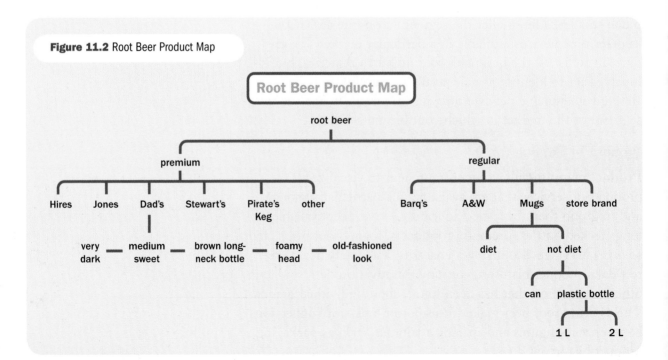

Figure 11.2 Root Beer Product Map

or another country? Which brands would meet the need for a premium root beer with lots of foam?"

Retailers and other service providers can ask themselves, "What services could we add to set our ventures apart from ones that already exist?" For example, Kamloops, British Columbia, with a population of only 80 000 people, has about 20 video stores. A new video store would have to provide something special in order to succeed in this market. What could the store offer to draw customers away from the competition? Perhaps drive-through service, home delivery, 24-hour video vending machines, an attached laundromat, or specialty products like old movies or cult favourites? In fact, there are many possible answers that could lead to a successful venture opportunity.

Review Questions

1. What is an idea-driven enterprise?
2. At what point does an idea-driven enterprise run into problems?
3. What is a market-driven enterprise?
4. At what point does a market-driven enterprise run into problems?
5. What two things can an entrepreneur do to investigate the market for a new venture? Describe them briefly.

The Automatic Lubricating Cup is the real McCoy!

Some Canadian Inventions

Did you know that the BlackBerry was a Canadian invention? So were basketball and insulin. Canadians have made a major contribution to the world with their inventions. The following section outlines some of those contributions.

What Is an Invention?

Paul Nipkow, Philo Farnsworth, Vladimir Zworykin, and John Logie Baird have something in common. They were all inventors who experimented independently with ways to transmit pictures and moving images from one place to another. Each one is given credit for discoveries that led to the development of modern television broadcasting.

An **invention** is a product or process that does something that has never been done before. When this product or process fills a market need, it sets the stage for entrepreneurship. Entrepreneurs look for ways to use the invention in a product or service that can be sold to a consumer. Some inventors are also entrepreneurs— they build a business to produce, distribute, and market their invention. Other inventors are not entrepreneurs. They prefer to focus on experimentation and discovery. Sometimes they do not even realize, or care, that their work has commercial potential.

Canadian Inventors and Inventions

Canadians are responsible for inventing thousands of products, many of which have had (or still have) a global impact. Table 11.1 is a list of the inventors that called Canada home, and their famous inventions.

⊕ E-ACTIVITY

Visit www.nelson.com/WOB and follow the links to learn more about Canadian inventors and inventions.

Review Questions

6. What would be your vote for the most important Canadian invention? Why did you pick this invention?

7. What entrepreneurial ventures are associated with the invention you selected?

Imax is an example of a Canadian invention that can be seen worldwide.

Table 11.1

Canadian Inventions and Inventors		
Invention	**Description**	**Canadian Inventor(s)**
Balderdash 1994	a game in which players win points by defining obscure words	Laura Robinson and Paul Toyne
basketball 1892	a game in which two teams try to place a ball into each other's hoop	James Naismith
Canadarm 1981	a robotic arm used for construction and repair during space exploration	SPAR Aerospace Limited
canoe	a watercraft; the original was made out of birchbark	Canada's Aboriginal peoples
cardiac pacemaker 1950	a device that is surgically implanted to regulate heart rhythm	Dr. John A. Hopps
electron microscope 1937	a device that allows scientists to "see" particles as small as electrons	Eli Franklin Burton, Cecil Hall, James Hillier, and Albert Prebus
goalie mask 1960	a device used to protect hockey goalkeepers from facial injury due to pucks, sticks, and skates	Jacques Plante, Montreal Canadiens goalie
IMAX movie projection 1968	a process used to project giant movie images on large screens for super-realism	Graeme Ferguson, Roman Kroitor, and Robert Kerr
insulin 1921	a life-saving drug for diabetics	Dr. Frederick Banting and Dr. Charles Best
Java 1994	computer programming language	James Gosling
lacrosse	a game played with sticks and a ball	Canada's Aboriginal peoples
newsprint 1838	an inexpensive paper made from wood fibres ground into pulp	Charles Fenerty
poutine 1957	a popular snack or side-dish made with French fries, gravy, and cheese curds	Fernand LaChance
snowmobile 1922	a vehicle used for travelling across snow and ice	Joseph-Armand Bombardier
Standard Time 1878	the division of the world into 24 time zones, in order that all the clocks in each zone show the same time, and the time in one zone can be determined by counting on or back from the time in another	Sandford Fleming
zipper 1913	a closing device for clothing	Gideon Sundback

Keep in Mind

1. patents and copyrights
2. licensing agreements
3. franchising agreements
4. producing the invention
5. selling the rights

Taking the Next Step

Inventions usually get their start when somebody asks, "What if?" Once the invention is finished, it's time to ask, "What now?" Inventing something new is not enough to make someone an entrepreneur. Even creating an innovation is not necessarily an entrepreneurial activity. Entrepreneurship begins when the new invention or innovation becomes the inspiration for a venture.

There are different ways for aspiring entrepreneurs to answer the question, "What now?" The first step is usually to protect the invention or innovation by obtaining a patent or copyright. Then, the creator may decide to license the idea, franchise it, produce it, or sell the production rights to someone else.

Patents and Copyrights

A **patent** gives the holder the sole right to make, use, or sell an invention for a set period of time, preventing others from using it without permission. A **copyright** gives someone the exclusive right to publish, produce, sell, or distribute works of literature, music, art, and software.

An inventor asks her lawyer for advice about obtaining a patent.

Ethical, Moral & Legal Considerations

More than 3 million BlackBerry owners held their breath in February 2006, waiting for Judge James Spencer, of the U.S. Federal Circuit Court, to decide on the patent infringement case of *NTP v. Research In Motion* (RIM). Research In Motion is the Canadian company that invented and manufactures BlackBerry, a hand-held information device that acts as a phone, text message centre, Internet link, and computer. NTP is a small patent-holding company co-founded by Tom Campana that exists solely to protect Campana's wireless technology concepts (as a sad footnote to this case, Tom Campana, a tireless inventor, died on June 8, 2004, before the case was settled).

Fortunately, the two companies settled out of court. RIM agreed to pay NTP US$612.5 million for the rights to all five patents NTP claimed that BlackBerry used without permission. Had there been no settlement, it was entirely possible that the courts would have forced BlackBerry to shut down its U.S. operations. The millions of subscribers who depend on their BlackBerries breathed a sigh of relief when the settlement was announced.

The high-profile case directed a great deal of attention to American laws governing the protection of ideas and to the rights of the so-called patent trolls. These are companies or individuals that buy patents, not for the purpose of developing the idea but to profit when someone else uses it. The patent trolls then sue, claiming infringement. There are other legal issues as well. Should juries decide these complicated patent litigation cases? They would rarely have the expertise to decide cases dealing with complex technical problems. Patent injunctions, which halt the manufacturing and sales of a product found to be in infringement of someone else's patent, could harm millions of innocent product owners. Perhaps the law could create another way of settling patent infringement lawsuits, such as mandatory product royalties.

The process of obtaining a patent is complicated and expensive. The inventor may need a lawyer's help to fill out the application form (including technical drawings with exact specifications) and to perform a patent search. This search uncovers any previous patents for a similar invention that may already have been filed. If one person's invention or creative work is too similar to someone else's, the patent or copyright will not be granted. During the patenting process, the invention is considered to be legally protected as long as products are marked "patent pending" to show that an application for the patent has been filed.

Many patent services are available to new entrepreneurs. Most are reputable, but a thorough background check on the company in question should be undertaken before any inventions or ideas are shared to prevent the theft of your idea.

Licensing Agreements

One of the easiest ways for an inventor to capitalize on his or her invention or innovation is to license it. **Licensing** an invention means that the inventor allows another business to use his or her invention for a fee. The fee, or **royalty**, can be either a fixed amount or a percentage of the total sales revenue that the user pays the patent or copyright owner. The inventor is not responsible for manufacturing or distributing the product; he or she simply sells these rights to someone else.

Many computer software programs are licensed to computer manufacturers and software developers. When Sun Microsystems created JavaScript, it sought out companies that would benefit from its invention, such as Microsoft and IBM, and arranged licensing agreements with them.

Licensing agreements don't necessarily involve a specific invention. An entrepreneur might start a new venture by licensing an idea, an image, or a name from the owner and then use it to create an innovative product. For example, various companies hold licensing rights to Franklin, a turtle who is the main character in a popular series of children's books created by Paulette Bourgeois and Brenda Clark. These companies produce Franklin television programs, computer software, plush animals, backpacks, and many other products. Sports teams and stars, famous musicians, and fashion designers also license the use of their name, pictures, and logos on products.

Franchising Agreements

Franchising agreements are similar to licensing agreements. A **franchise agreement** is an arrangement for one business, such as MotoPhoto, to license the rights to its name and procedures to another business or person. The entrepreneurs in this situation are both the franchisor and the franchisee. If the inventor has already launched a business, the franchisor could give the franchisee the right to sell or distribute the product in a certain area, or even to set up a similar business in another location. Chapter 1 contains more information on franchises.

Producing the Invention

The riskiest thing for an inventor to do is to manufacture the product that results from his or her invention. This process

---

Business Fact

An inventor can make money by selling the patent or copyright to his or her invention. Although this sale results in a profit, it doesn't make the inventor an entrepreneur unless the inventor makes a business out of the regular sale of patents or copyrights.

---

usually requires a large amount of capital and expertise that many inventors do not possess. Entrepreneurial inventors who wish to minimize their personal risk can form a partnership with an established business or a financial investor. The inventor gets start-up funds and business help from the venture partner, and the venture partner gets an opportunity to invest in a new invention that could become very successful. Just as trade shows bring manufacturers and distributors together in central locations, **venture capital markets** bring inventors together with financial investors who are interested in developing new ideas. This type of partnership arrangement is similar to a licensing agreement, except that the inventor has some personal control through an ownership stake in the business.

Inventors and innovators have started many famous companies. Roots, Bombardier, Clearly Canadian, and Tim Hortons are just a few examples. Although the risks are great, the rewards for the inventive or innovative entrepreneur can be great as well.

Selling the Rights

If an inventor is prepared to completely give up control of his or her invention or a related business, then he or she may decide to sell the patent or copyright to someone else. Inventors may sell their inventions if they prefer to receive a fairly large sum of money for the sale of their invention, rather than wait for profits from licensing or franchising to come in slowly over time. However, conflicts sometimes arise when the purchaser takes an invention in a direction other than what the seller expects. There is also the risk that, over the long term, profits from licensing, franchising, or developing the business will be greater than the amount the inventor earns from a one-time sale. On the other hand, the buyer assumes the risk of financing, producing, and marketing the product.

Oops!

Body-supported hoop game and device
US Patent # 4,871,178
Issued October 3, 1989
The invention comprises a body-supported hoop device and a team game utilizing the hoop device. The hoop device comprises a hoop, a net connected to the hoop and means for attaching the hoop to the legs of a goalie. In the game of the invention, the body-supported hoop devices are worn by each of two goalies. The object of the game is for team members of the goalie to place a projectile, such as a soccer ball, through the hoop of the goalie on their team and to prevent members of the opposing team from placing the projectile through the hoop of the goalie of the opposing team.

Will this Invention Create a New Craze? Any volunteers?

Review Questions

8. What is the difference between a patent and a copyright?

9. What is the riskiest thing for an inventor to do?

The Impact of Innovation

What's an icebox? a coal scuttle? a 45? These are inventions that have been changed so much that they are no longer recognizable to this generation. An icebox was a refrigerator that kept things cool with a block of ice (that an ice-man delivered to your home regularly). A coal-scuttle was a special container for coal that helped you carry it from the coal pile and put it on the fire. A 45 was a vinyl disk, with a large hole in the centre, that played music when turned at a speed of 45 revolutions per minute (rpm).

A pile of vinyl 45s

What Is an Innovation?

Would Reginald Fessenden, a Canadian-born inventor who did pioneering work in the field of communication, recognize today's flat-screen plasma television, with digital sound and on-screen menus? No one really *invented* colour television—newer technology was simply used to improve an existing product. The colour television was an innovation. **Innovation** means using new technology, materials, or processes to improve existing products, or how they are produced and distributed.

To see how invention and innovation work together, consider the history of soap. No one knows who invented soap. Perhaps prehistoric people found foam around the ashes of their fires after a rainfall and discovered that this foam was useful for cleaning their tools. We do know that by 2800 BCE, the Babylonians were using soap to clean fibres that they made into cloth. The soap-making process didn't change much over the next 4500 years. By the late seventeenth century, early North American settlers were still making soap by creating a solution from wood ashes and then boiling this solution with animal fat. In the early nineteenth century, sodium hydroxide became widely available. Manufacturers began to use this compound to make firmer soaps with far less effort, changing the production process.

Over the years, people have experimented with making soap in slightly different ways, adding an endless variety of colours and scents. Soap manufacturers today create their own innovations by combining other products, such as skin lotion or lemon scent, to improve their product. Soap manufacturers have also made innovations to their distribution processes. Today, consumers can buy soap at the supermarket, at the drug store, from a catalogue, over the Internet, and even from vending machines! The person who created the soap-manufacturing process was an inventor. The people who improved the production process, as well as those who made different types of soap and first sold soap on the Internet, were innovators.

Both inventors and innovators were required to produce this array of soaps.

Innovators as Entrepreneurs

It is usually easier for innovators to be entrepreneurs than for inventors to be entrepreneurs. Inventors need to start from scratch as they plan ways to manufacture, distribute, and market their inventions. Innovators can build on what inventors have already done.

Most innovations are spurred by a business looking for ways to gain a competitive advantage over another business. There are many ways for entrepreneurs to use innovation to gain a business advantage. For example, they can change the way a product is used, packaged, marketed, distributed, designed, or manufactured.

Changing How a Product Is Used

When was the last time you used Scotch tape? What did you use it for? When 3M introduced Scotch tape in 1948, an advertisement suggested that the tape could be used to

- cover clothespins to prevent clothing snags
- prevent plaster cracks when hanging pictures
- cover bandages
- attach coins to cards sent in the mail
- attach new window shades to old rollers
- smooth the ends of curtain rods
- fix tears in plastic aprons
- repair frayed shoelace ends
- wrap household garbage

If 3M had depended on the clothespin market for Scotch tape sales, the company would be in financial difficulty today—most people don't use clothespins any more, and the clothespins we do use don't snag clothes. Fortunately for 3M, someone decided to promote Scotch tape for other purposes, such as wrapping gifts. The company developed a whole new market by finding an innovative use for a familiar product.

E-ACTIVITY

Visit www.nelson.com/WOB and follow the links to learn more about the impact of innovation.

Business Fact

Thomas Edison initially tried to market his phonograph as a dictating machine for offices. When others recognized its potential for playing music, the recording industry was born.

In 1985, 12-year-old Rachel Zimmerman created an innovation based on Blissymbolics. Blissymbolics is a system of symbols that non-speaking people use to communicate. It was invented by Austrian engineer Charles Bliss in 1942. With Charles Bliss's invention, people pointed to symbols on a board or page to communicate with someone in the same room. With Rachel Zimmerman's innovation, the "speaker" touches the symbols on a touch-sensitive board and the symbols and corresponding words appear on a computer screen. The message can then be read on the screen, sent by e-mail, or printed out. Rachel's innovation allows for faster communication, and enables non-speaking people to communicate with others who are not in the same room.

Changing the Package

Changing the way a product is packaged can create a whole new industry. In 1944, two Swedish inventors, Ruben Rausing and Erik Wallenberg, created a milk package that provided maximum protection for milk using a minimum of material. Their invention was a tetrahedron-shaped paper package with a waterproof coating. Together, Rausing and Wallenberg founded a company, AB Tetra Pak, in Lund, Sweden. Since then, the company has continued to create innovations in the packaging industry, adding new package sizes and shapes, including the familiar brick-shaped drinking boxes that many people put in their lunches every day.

Package innovations occur for a variety of reasons. For example, many packages, including drink containers, are now reusable or recyclable. This kind of environmentally friendly innovation can help a product's reputation and its sales. Other packaging innovations help a company market a product to a new audience. For example, one company sells yogurt in squeeze tubes, which have become very popular among children. These squeeze tubes contain a product that is itself an innovation—yogurt that doesn't have to be refrigerated.

Changing the Marketing Strategy

Marketing strategies determine the target market for a product and give companies direction on how they can use advertising and promotion to encourage people in this target market to buy. For example, many breakfast cereals appeal mainly to children. Marketers try to enhance this appeal with promotions,

The World of Business DVD

"The Next Level"
from *The World of Business DVD*

In the News

A research lab at Trent University in Peterborough, Ontario, is using forensics to find new ways to preserve wildlife and plants. Researchers examine deer and other game carcasses to collect DNA evidence to catch poachers. Game wardens can match the animals' DNA to samples in an existing database that tells them where the animal is from. Since the database was created in 1985, more than 1000 poaching cases have involved DNA as evidence. But the Wildlife Forensic DNA Laboratory database, which extracts DNA from animal tissue and blood samples, isn't just an enforcement tool. It uses genetics to understand wildlife population structure, disease management, and the conservation of endangered species. "It allows us to interpret if some populations are becoming isolated, or if there are more animals there than we originally thought," says Bradley White, the Director of the Natural Resources DNA Profiling and Forensic Centre (NRDPFC) at Trent University.

Having a thorough genetic database also allows researchers to track the appearance of animal diseases that are potentially lethal to humans. Currently the centre is helping to track the spread of rabies in raccoons. Over the last four years, more than 150 rabid raccoons have been found between Kingston and Cornwall, Ontario. This type of study is very important considering that Toronto has one of the highest densities of raccoons in North America.

The NRDPFC is creating DNA profiles to save endangered and threatened species such as wolves, moose, deer, black bears, caribou, and elk. These profiles provide valuable information on the impact of roads and highways on each species' habitat, and the effects of this encroachment on the animal population.

The future of DNA profiling for animals is cutting edge and revolutionary, and should continue to help protect the public and the animal population.

such as contests or mascots, and with advertisements that are shown during children's television programs. In the late 1990s, Kellogg's designed a series of innovative Corn Pops commercials aimed at teens as well as children. With these commercials, the company hoped to expand the market for Corn Pops and, as a result, increase the product's sales.

Advertising is certainly not limited to broadcast media. For example, Montreal's Zoom Media rents washroom wall space from universities and other places where 18- to 34-year-olds will see its ads. Companies who want to target this demographic group pay Zoom to display the ads. Over the past decade, this innovative approach has helped Zoom expand internationally.

Companies are always looking for new ways to promote their businesses, and many innovative entrepreneurs have developed innovative promotional ideas into personal ventures. Dianne Pepper, also known as Pepper the Clown, makes kids *and* adults laugh at promotional events, such as store openings, in the Toronto area. She attracts large crowds of parents and children to malls and retail stores, and has lots of fun in the process.

Changing the Distribution Process

The target market for a product is closely linked to the way the product is distributed. If the distribution process improves, then more customers, or different kinds of customers, will be able to buy the product.

Another way for a business to reach more customers is to display products at a trade show. A **trade show** is an exhibition where a large number of manufacturers and distributors of a particular type of product show their goods. Some trade shows are open only to people involved in the particular industry, while others invite the general public to attend. Trade shows not only allow entrepreneurs to reach potential customers, they also help entrepreneurs make contact with retailers or distributors who may want to carry their products.

Sometimes, a business decides to expand its market by distributing its products internationally. Until the mid-1980s, most Canadians had never heard of the kiwi fruit. The popularity of this fruit in other countries encouraged overseas producers to try marketing their product in Canada. Canadians loved the taste. By the early 1990s, the taste of kiwi fruit was in products as diverse as salads, drinks, and ice cream.

Changing the Design

There are many reasons for changing the design of a product, including improving its function and appealing to a new market segment. For example, an innovator named Alexandra Finley created The Green Box, based on the traditional composter. This air-tight plastic container was designed to make composting kitchen scraps easy—especially for apartment dwellers who have nowhere to compost. The Green Box is small enough to fit under a kitchen sink, is odour-free, and has compartments that separate solid and liquid waste.

Sometimes, simply revising the size, colour, or shape of a product can help spark or sustain customer interest. For example,

Rows of booths crowd a convention centre, where a trade show is taking place.

some companies that sell canned pasta have changed the shapes of their pasta to look like alphabet letters, zoo animals, and cartoon characters. This innovation has increased the product's appeal to children, and has resulted in improved sales.

Changing the Manufacturing Process

You've already learned that when sodium hydroxide became more widely available, soap manufacturers changed the process they used to make soap. As technology changes and new materials become available, manufacturers constantly review their production processes to look for innovations that make their products better or less expensive to produce.

New processes and new machinery improve efficiency and lower production costs; faster machinery makes more products in the same amount of time; and quality-control processes ensure more reliable products. A Swiss machine that processed metal to one-thousandth of a millimetre allowed Marcel Bich to make innovations to ballpoint pens. These innovations led to the development of the BIC pen.

What kind of innovation is this?

Sometimes, a slight change to the manufacturing process can result in a wider range of products. For example, a company that makes regular potato chips can add equipment to its production facility that allows it to make chips with other flavours, such as ketchup or dill pickle. These flavours may encourage people who do not like regular potato chips to try the new products. Sales for the company could increase, resulting in increased profits.

New raw materials also have an impact on the production process. Like many other companies, Columbia Sportswear relies on the latest technology to stay in business. Columbia has developed and trademarked a number of fabrics, such as Omni-Tech, that make its outdoor clothing waterproof, windproof, and breathable. Columbia's innovative approach increases sales for the company, but it provides other benefits as well. By raising the standard for quality, Columbia encourages its competitors to develop better products and improve service to their customers.

The automobile is yet another example of a product that has undergone significant changes in its design.

In the News

Domino's Pizza has more than 8000 stores around the world. To appeal to international tastes, the company has created some new pizza toppings for its stores outside of North America.

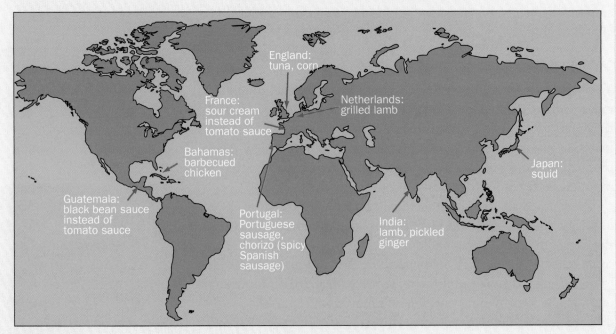

England: tuna, corn

France: sour cream instead of tomato sauce

Netherlands: grilled lamb

Bahamas: barbecued chicken

Japan: squid

Guatemala: black bean sauce instead of tomato sauce

Portugal: Portuguese sausage, chorizo (spicy Spanish sausage)

India: lamb, pickled ginger

CHAPTER REVIEW

Knowledge

1. Compare a licensing agreement with a franchising agreement. What do they both have in common? How are they different?

2. What potential risks are there for an inventor who wants to move into entrepreneurship? How can an inventor reduce these risks?

Thinking

3. "Necessity is *not* the mother of invention." Explain why you agree or disagree with this statement.

4. Use the news media and the Internet to identify inventions from the past 12 months. Describe one invention, and tell who invented it. How could an entrepreneur use this invention to create a venture?

5. Are all ventures innovative? Why or why not?

6. Give examples that show how innovation and invention have led to the development and application of new technologies.

Communication

7. Many inventors, such as Alexander Graham Bell and Thomas Edison, create more than one invention. Choose an inventor in this chapter and find out what else he or she created. Present your findings in a collage.

8. Pick one product that has gone through a number of innovations over time (e.g., rotary phone, touch-tone phone, cellphone). Illustrate these innovations with pictures, a timeline, and reasons for why the product changed.

Application

9. Prepare a chart that analyzes a Canadian invention. Choose one of the following: the Avro Arrow, Pablum, Trivial Pursuit, caulking gun, and space suit. Use the following chart headings to record your information: Invention, Inventor, Brief History, How It Works, Ventures Based on the Invention, and Innovations Based on the Invention.

10. Select a product that you buy on a regular basis and discuss the impact of invention and innovation on that product.

Team Activity

Team Goal: Create an innovation for a common product

Team Assignment: New Products from Old

- Your teacher will assign each team the same product, such as a can of soup or a bottle of water.

- Over the course of a few days, your team must create an innovation for the product.

- The team with the most marketable innovation wins the round.

Portfolio

What were the most significant inventions and innovations in your industry? Collect pictures of them, especially illustrations that show how some products have changed over time.

Who were the inventors of some of these products? Write a short profile of two of them. Be sure to include a Canadian inventor if possible.

Reflect on Your Learning

Using the invention you named as the world's most important at the beginning of this chapter, describe several innovations that have occurred to this invention over the years. What businesses depend upon it today?

Sony

Few companies have come close to paralleling Sony Corporation's innovation, invention, or imagination. Founded in 1946 in Tokyo, Japan, Sony was created by an engineer, Masaru Ibuka, and a physicist, Akio Morita. Initially, the company's focus was repairing electrical equipment and experimenting with building novel products. The company's name is based on a combination of the word "sonus" (the Latin root word for "sound" and "sonic") with the popular Japanese expression "sonny boy" (which refers to a young person with a free and pioneering spirit).

From the start, Akio Morita knew that in order for Sony to be a success, its products would have to be marketed worldwide. So, two companies were formed, Sony Corporation of America (1960) and Sony United Kingdom Limited (1968).

Originally, Sony Corporation had just 20 employees in Japan, but by 2006 the company employed more than 158 500 people around the world. If Sony's worldwide presence isn't enough to signal the degree to which the company has been a success, just consider Sony's 2006 net income, reported at

Imagination and innovation have turned the Sony Walkman into more than just a listening device.

the end of March, which totalled US$1057 million.

In 1954, Sony acquired the rights to manufacture transistors in Japan. The transistor was a small electrical circuit, larger than a computer chip, but much, much smaller than a vacuum tube. Vacuum tubes were used in radios, and Sony was the first to replace them with the tiny transistors, making radios much smaller, cheaper, and totally portable (about the size of a modern portable compact disc player).

Today, it's hard to believe that the transistor radio was one of the most important innovations of the twentieth century and was, in part, responsible for the growth of a huge new industry—rock and roll! Sony was just getting started. The list of Sony's subsequent innovative and inventive landmarks is impressive and includes: the first "Trinitron" colour television in 1968; the colour video cassette in 1971; the Betamax VCR in 1975; the Walkman in 1979; the electronic camera in 1981; the first CD player in 1982; and the first consumer camcorder in 1983. And who can forget PlayStation, which was launched during the mid-1990s throughout Japan, North America, and Europe, and which has been updated several times since then.

Sony's inventive flair has been recognized with numerous awards, including an unprecedented five awards from the European Imaging and Sound Association (EISA) in August 2006. Furthermore, three of Sony's products were listed by *PC World* as among "The 25 Most Innovative Products of the Year" in 2006. What will they think of next?

QUESTIONS

1. Describe what makes Sony an innovative and inventive company.

2. Based on what you know of the items that Sony has launched in the past, make a prediction regarding the types of products the company could come out with in the future.

UNIT 4 Finance

"Annual income twenty pounds, annual expenditure nineteen nineteen six, result happiness. Annual income twenty pounds, annual expenditure twenty pounds ought and six, result misery."

Charles Dickens, from the novel *David Copperfield*

OVERALL EXPECTATIONS

- show how income and spending issues affect individuals and businesses
- explain how banks and other financial institutions operate
- demonstrate an understanding of effective investment practices
- analyze the role and importance of credit in personal and business finance

12 Income Management

SPECIFIC EXPECTATIONS

After completing this chapter, you will be able to

- distinguish between types of personal income and types of business income

- identify the factors that need to be assessed in order to make effective purchasing decisions

- demonstrate financial-planning skills and produce a business or personal financial plan, using appropriate software

The War for Your Home-Improvement Dollars

In Canada, the market for home improvement is no small business. Where there are individuals willing to spend record amounts on renovating their homes and gardens, there are companies ready to capitalize and supply customers with the products they want. In 2006, Canadians were

expected to spend more than $43.6 billion dollars renovating their homes, a 7.1 percent jump from 2005. Vying for the customer's attention, and dollars, are the two big-box stores, Home Depot and RONA, as well as thousands of smaller, independent hardware stores found in towns and cities across Canada.

Prior to 2001, big-box store competitors also included Revy, Revelstoke, Lansing and Reno-Depot stores. However, during an aggressive growth program, the Quebec-based RONA Inc. acquired Revy, Revelstoke, and Lansing, with 51 locations in Western Canada and Ontario. RONA also purchased 20 Reno-Depot stores located across

Quebec and Ontario. Even with this acquisition for RONA, the Atlanta-based Home Depot is currently Canada's largest big-box store operator, with 138 stores operating in Canada in 2005 and collective annual sales hitting $5.5 billion. Furthermore, the company announced the opening of 18 additional stores in Canada by the end of 2006.

Customers looking around the garden section of Home Depot during the summer months

But Home Depot Canada is far from secure in its position of dominance in the home-improvement market. Competition is still on the horizon, with RONA planning to build 40 more stores across Canada in 2006 and 2007, and Lowe's, the second largest home-improvement business in the United States, making its Canadian debut in 2007. And then there are the small- and medium-sized independent home-improvement stores, which total about 5000 in Canada and serve close to 50 percent of the market.

Among the major non-big-box store competitors is Home Hardware, based in St. Jacobs, Ontario, which consists of 1019 independent dealer-owned co-operatives throughout Canada. The company pulled in over $4.3 billion in sales in 2005 and, during the first few months of 2006, increased its sales over the same period of the previous year by 11 percent.

A key difference between the small independent and the big-box stores is the demographic that each target. For example, in addition to catering to renovating firms and new-home builders—a niche that has typically been men—RONA has adjusted the big-box layout to include lighting and flooring boutique sections. By creating a more department-store aesthetic and focusing on décor-oriented themes, the big-box stores have attracted a much greater mixed-gender clientele, with women representing over half of RONA's customers. The smaller home-improvement stores such as Home Hardware attract consumers interested in customer service and the convenience of a smaller store.

The appearance of numerous television programs focused on interior design and home renovating has also influenced the market and, in 2004, prompted RONA to join the Global Television network in launching a 10-week series called RONA Dream Home. The reality show narrated the renovation and decorating done by two families in two similar houses, and a jury decided which home they liked best. The winning family was then awarded the renovated home and its contents.

At this time, the winner of the war for home-improvement dollars is still anybody's guess. Although independents such as Home Hardware may be flourishing now, some feel that the sustainability of their success is questionable. As RONA spokesperson Sylvain Morissette put it, "If the strip mall is open until 9 p.m., the independent hardware store can't close at 7 p.m. and expect to get customers." It appears as though, unlike the jury for the RONA Dream Home, in this contest the jury is still out.

QUESTIONS

1. How are stores like Home Depot and RONA different from stores such as Home Hardware?

2. What are the demographics of the customers who are more likely to shop at the big-box stores and the independent stores, respectively?

What Is Money?

"Money makes the world go 'round." At least, that's what the song from the play and the movie *Cabaret* says. Without money, businesses could not operate, and consumers could not buy the goods and services they need and desire. But what exactly is money and how does it function in a modern economy?

Forms of Legal Tender

Under federal law, **legal tender** must be accepted as payment for goods and services. The two main forms of legal tender are coins and Bank of Canada notes (or "bills") at face value. Cheques and credit cards, although widely used and accepted as payment, are not legal tender. No law states that they must be accepted as payment, but they are seldom refused.

Coins are **minted**, or manufactured, at the Royal Canadian Mint headquarters in Ottawa or at the Mint's Winnipeg branch. The Government of Canada decides when, and if, to issue new coins. For example, the government replaced the $1 and $2 paper notes with coins because coins are much more durable and, therefore, more cost effective.

The Bank of Canada issues paper money, also known as **bank notes**. The Bank issued its first notes in separate French and English versions in 1935. In 1937, it released a redesigned, bilingual series. Interestingly, the Bank of Canada does not run its own facilities to print bank notes. Instead, it uses two privately owned, high-security printing companies.

Keep in Mind

1. new Canadian bank notes
2. special features of bank notes

Before You Begin

People get money from a variety of sources. Where do you get your money? What do you spend it on? Where do your parents get their money? What do they spend it on? Where do your grandparents get their money? What do they spend it on?

The Royal Canadian Mint headquarters located in Ottawa

New Canadian Bank Notes

In 2001, the Bank of Canada began issuing a new series of Canadian bank notes. The new $10 bill was introduced in 2001, the $5 bill in 2002, and the $20, $50, and $100 bills in 2004. The $10 bill and $5 bill in this series were updated again in 2005 and 2006 to improve their security features. The new series, called the Canadian Journey series, features Queen Elizabeth II and Canada's prime ministers on the front. New designs on the back of the notes reflect Canada's culture, history, and achievements.

Special Features of Bank Notes

Canada's new bank notes have state-of-the-art security features to discourage high-tech counterfeiting. **Counterfeiting** is the production of fake money. Figure 12.1 shows some of the protective features that make Canadian bank notes very difficult to forge. These features are always being reviewed and changed.

The new notes also have features that enable people who are blind or have a visual impairment to distinguish between the different denominations. Each denomination has a unique texture so that people can recognize it by touch alone. Canada is one of the first countries in the world to incorporate these tactile features in its paper bills.

Counterfeiting is not limited to bank notes. Credit cards, travellers' cheques, passports, and other identification documents can all be counterfeited as well.

Figure 12.1 Security Features on This $5 Bill

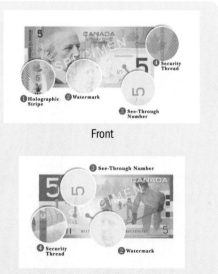

Note the various security features that are found on this $5 bill.

1. **Holographic stripe.** When you tilt the note, brightly coloured number 5s and maple leaves move within the shiny stripe on the side of the bill.

2. **Watermark portrait.** Hold the bill to the light. On the front and back, ghost-like images of the portrait appear.

3. **See-through numbers.** Irregular marks form a number 5 when the bill is held to the light.

4. **Security thread.** When you hold the note to the light, a solid line appears.

Front

Back

Money's Changing Purchasing Power

Money's true value is its purchasing power. The paper used to print our currency is virtually worthless, as are the metals used to make coins. Our "silver" coins (nickels, dimes, and quarters) no longer contain silver. Just a few cents' worth of metal is used to make a toonie. In other words, our currency has almost no value in itself. It is worth something only because we accept that it has a specific value—two nickels equal 10¢, four quarters equal $1, ten $10 bills equal $100, and so on.

Although money serves as a standard of value, its purchasing power changes as prices for goods and services change. In general, prices tend to rise (inflation), so the dollar buys less from one year to the next. Today, $10 buys much less than it did 30 years ago. You have probably noticed that the prices of clothing, magazines, and movie tickets have increased over the past few years.

Purchasing power is measured by the **Consumer Price Index (CPI)**, which is calculated monthly by Statistics Canada. It measures 600 products typically bought by Canadian households. This basket of goods includes food, shelter, transportation, clothing, and recreation.

Review Questions

1. What is legal tender?

2. What features on the $5 bill help to stop it from being counterfeited?

3. What is the Consumer Price Index? What does it measure?

4. Explain why the dollar's purchasing power changes.

Frank and Ernest

© 2004 Thaves. Reprinted with permission. Newspaper dist. by NEA, Inc.

In the News

Who says you need money to purchase a house? Kyle MacDonald, a Montreal resident, offered one red paper clip in the barter section of the Craigslist website in hopes that he would end up with a house. A year later, he was successful. He traded the paper clip for a fish pen; then traded successively for a ceramic knob; a Coleman camping stove; a generator; a beer keg and a Budweiser sign; a snowmobile; a vacation in the Canadian Rockies; a cube truck; a recording contract; a year's rent in Phoenix, Arizona; an afternoon with Alice Cooper (the rock star); a KISS snow globe; and a part in a new movie with Corbin Bernsen (the actor from *L.A. Law* and *Major League*). Finally, the town of Kipling, Saskatchewan, offered MacDonald a house. The town is going to set up a talent search for the part in the movie.

Kyle began with one red paper clip and, fourteen trades later, ended up with a house!

What Is Income?

Income is money that an individual or business receives from various sources, such as wages, sales, interest, or dividends. For some people, most of the money they earn is used to pay for necessities such as food, rent, and clothing. People who have higher incomes can afford to spend more money on non-essential items such as vacations and flat-screen televisions. Regardless of your income level, it is a good idea to have a financial plan so you can get the most out of the money you earn. (Money management will be discussed later in the chapter.)

Types of Personal Income

Personal income comes in many forms. The major way people earn money is through a full-time job. Forms of employment income include salary, wages, commission, piecework and profit sharing. Employees also receive benefits, including medical insurance, paid holidays, paid sick days, drug plan and dental benefits. There are other sources of income as well. These include dividends from investments and interest from savings accounts. Teenagers often receive income from a part-time job, or as allowance or gifts.

Gross Income

The total amount of income received by a person is known as his or her **gross income**. For example, Nadira Sahota is a 35-year-old working as a sales manager. She has three children and is a single parent. This pie chart shows the amounts that make up Nadira's gross income.

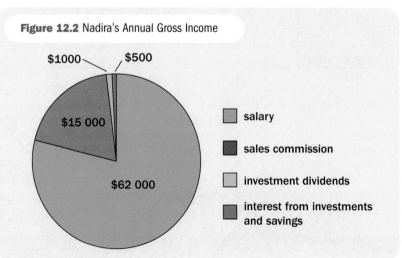

Figure 12.2 Nadira's Annual Gross Income

$1000
$500
$15 000
$62 000

- salary
- sales commission
- investment dividends
- interest from investments and savings

Nadira earns a total of $78 500 per year from her salary, her commission, her investments, and interest payments. That's $6542 per month. This is her gross income.

Disposable Income

Nadira does not get to keep the total amount of her gross income. Before she receives her paycheque, her employer deducts income tax, Canada Pension Plan (CPP) and Employment Insurance (EI). What is left is known as take-home-pay or **disposable income**. Nadira pays income tax, a CPP (Canada Pension Plan) contribution, and an EI (Employment Insurance) contribution. This leaves her with about $47 500 in disposable income, or $3959 per month.

It is important that people be aware of their disposable income because that is the amount available for them to spend. The amount of income tax each Canadian is required to pay depends upon a variety of factors. Union dues, charitable contributions, and pension payments are deductions that will decrease the amount of tax payable. Taxes are paid to the Canada Revenue Agency and to the province in which the person lives.

<aside>
Oops!

The Fraser Institute estimates that in 2006, Canadians worked until June 18 to pay off their taxes. This means that out of 365 days of work each year, approximately 169 days of work go toward paying taxes. These taxes include income, property, sales, fuel, corporate, import duties, and many more. This is one week less than in 2005.
</aside>

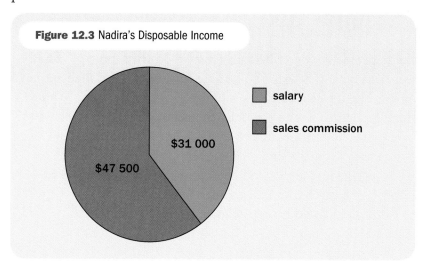

Figure 12.3 Nadira's Disposable Income

- salary
- sales commission

$31 000

$47 500

Discretionary Income

Nadira does not get to spend all of her disposable income on whatever she wants. She has to spend money on mortgage payments, food, car payments, insurance, electricity, and other necessities. The income that is left after necessities have been paid for is called **discretionary income**. Discretionary income is used to purchase luxury items such as vacations and eating out.

Nadira has committed $3770 per month in necessities payments out of a total disposable income of $3959. Her discretionary income is what's left—$189 per month.

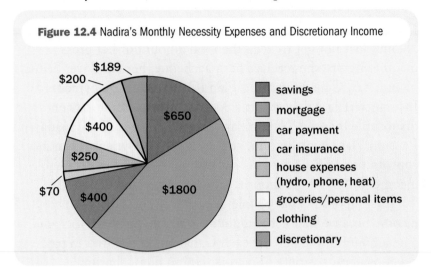

Figure 12.4 Nadira's Monthly Necessity Expenses and Discretionary Income

Legend:
- savings
- mortgage
- car payment
- car insurance
- house expenses (hydro, phone, heat)
- groceries/personal items
- clothing
- discretionary

Pie chart values: $189, $200, $650, $400, $250, $400, $70, $1800

Managing Money for Personal Use

Some people are described as being "good with money." They were not born that way. To be able to earn and use their money effectively, they developed a money management plan. **Money management** refers to the daily financial activities connected to using your limited income to satisfy all your needs and wants. It means getting the most for your money through careful planning, saving, and spending. Money management is a very important part of your education. You may already have begun to form ideas about money management by observing how adults close to you earn and spend money.

Whether you earn $2000 a year or $200 000, it is very important to know how much money you have to spend and where you spend it. It is equally important to know what you want to achieve. Understanding why we make purchase decisions, knowing how to spend money wisely, learning when to buy, and practising budgeting are all important elements of money management.

Why We Buy

Consumer decision making is the process of choosing among all the alternatives available in the marketplace. Sometimes, however, trade-offs are necessary—the expensive vacation has to be cancelled in order to save money for college or university, or the new car purchase has to be delayed to pay for repairs to a leaky roof.

We all buy products for different reasons, but there are five key factors that influence consumer buying decisions: income and price, status, current trends, customs and habits, and promotion.

An employee accepts a paycheque from his supervisor.

Income and Price

The amount of money consumers have to spend has a big influence on what they buy. A low-income family has to spend a larger portion of its income on basic necessities (food, clothing, and shelter) than a high-income family does. People who are responsible for children or aging parents often make different consumer and financial decisions than do people without these obligations. Families with more available income can invest, travel, and spend more on entertainment and recreation.

Price is still the most important consideration for consumers. It greatly influences the types and quantities of products and services that consumers buy. Some consumers believe that the higher the price, the better the quality or design of the product, but this is not always true.

Today, consumers expect good value for the money they spend. Most will not pay more than what they believe an item is worth.

Status

You may know people who brag about how much they paid for a product. They always want to have the biggest and the best, the latest and the greatest of everything. They feel that owning these items improves their status, making others admire or at least notice them. This desire to flaunt purchases to impress others is called **conspicuous consumption**. Unfortunately, some consumers purchase these expensive items even when they can't afford them and seldom use them.

Peer pressure can sometimes influence people to buy things they don't necessarily like.

Current Trends

Although jeans and T-shirts remain fashion basics, it is the "in" look that lures both teenage and adult consumers into retail stores. For many people, clothing helps create an image. For teens, clothing is often seen as an indicator of status, popularity, or group identity. As a result, clothing is a key area of youth spending. You might even be strongly influenced by your friends to buy something you don't really want. This type of influence is called **peer pressure**. Teenage peer pressure comes into play most often at school and in social settings. Buying to belong is a common motive in the buying patterns of young people and a popular strategy in product advertising targeted at teens.

Staying in style can be costly. The latest fashions quickly become outdated and are replaced by something new. You can easily spend hundreds of dollars putting together a single outfit that soon you will no longer wear because it has gone out of fashion. Keeping up with the latest trends often leads to unwise purchases.

Customs and Habits

Family, religion, community, and customs often affect consumer choices. For example, weddings, birthdays, and baby showers are customary gift-giving times. In fact, special occasions and certain holidays result in dramatically increased consumer spending. Without proper planning, holiday spending can also lead to disastrous consumer debt.

Habit also plays a part in what you buy. You may buy a particular magazine each week or month, rent a DVD every Friday, go out to a movie every week, or eat at the same fast-food outlet every day. These behaviours are habits—they are formed over time and done repetitively, often with very little thought.

Promotion

Business advertising and promotion are designed to influence consumer spending and create a desire for products and services. Through advertising, consumers learn about the many products and services available to them.

It is no coincidence that this GAP jeans advertisement is featuring women who are attractive, young and having fun!

Sometimes, advertising methods are deceptive. For example, advertising can lead consumers to believe that one product or service is far superior to another, when in fact little or no difference exists. False or misleading advertising comes in many different forms. One form, known as **lifestyle advertising**, shows attractive, healthy, successful, and appealing people using the product or service. The ads suggest that if you use the product or service, you will be just like these ideal people and your lifestyle will improve. Advertisements for soft drinks, snack foods, jeans, and athletic shoes often use this technique. To be a smart consumer, you must pay careful attention to the intention of advertisements and not be taken in by the unrealistic expectations they promote.

Spending Money

Today's society is often described as (and sometimes criticized for) being consumer-driven. We are all consumers, and the economy offers us a never-ending supply of exciting and innovative goods and services. These goods and services, as wonderful as they may be, mean that most families must be more careful about what they buy—and how much they pay for it. Unwise choices can have costly consequences.

Comparison Shopping

Before buying anything, smart consumers compare. You can find almost every available product at more than one store. For this reason, it is important to shop around before you buy and compare the price, quality, and special features of a product offered in one store with those of the same (or a similar) product in several other stores. By comparison shopping, you'll get better value for your money when you make a purchase.

Comparing Price and Quality

Comparison shopping does not always mean paying the lowest price. It means selecting the least expensive product or service that best suits your needs and wants. At times, quality may be more important than price. If you want the product to last for many years, you may spend less money in the long run if you pay more for a high-quality product now. High-quality sports equipment, electronic components, and automobiles generally last much longer than lower-quality goods.

Figure 12.5 The Wise Shopper

The Wise Shopper
- compares what's available from different stores and online
- looks for higher-quality products that will last
- makes sure a product has the right features before buying it
- asks the vendor about delivery policies and warranties
- does research before buying
- watches for sales
- considers buying things second-hand
- avoids impulse buying

Features

Sometimes, the features of goods and services are the most important consideration. Imagine that you need a new bike to get to school. You live in a hilly area, so you need a bike with at least 21 gears. A bike with fewer gears costs less, but you'll likely arrive at school tired and sweaty from working so hard to make it over the hills. In this case, you should shop at several stores to compare features, quality, and price—you want to find the best deal on a bike with 21 gears. You may be able to find a good-quality bike with the features you want in your price range, or you may have to make a trade-off—perhaps buying a bike with more features, but paying more than you expected.

Services

It is important to check what services different retail stores offer. For example, if you're making a large purchase, will the store deliver it to your home? If delivery service is available, is it free or is there a charge? What type of guarantee, or warranty, does the product have? A **warranty** is the manufacturer's or dealer's promise, usually in writing, that a product is of a certain quality. It may apply to the entire product or to parts only. It usually promises that the product or defective parts will be replaced free of charge for a certain period of time—for example, the first 90 days or the first year after the purchase date.

If prices are almost identical in all stores, you may want to choose the store nearest you or the store that has the best services or reputation. If the product costs less at a store far from your home, you may still decide to buy the product at a local

Oops!

The Hudson's Bay Company (HBC) is Canada's oldest business. It was founded in 1670 by a group of British merchants who wanted to take advantage of Canada's resources. Originally, it controlled the fur trade in Canada. Today, the Hudson's Bay Company is one of the largest retailers in Canada. Its divisions—The Bay, Zellers, Home Outfitters, Designer Depot, and a chain called Fields in Western Canada—have stores all across Canada. For over 300 years, the company was owned and operated by Canadians. However, in early 2006, the Hudson's Bay Company was sold to U.S. industrialist Jerry Zucker. Should Canadians be worried about Canadian companies being sold to foreign purchasers?

Customers catch the streetcar after a day of shopping at the Hudson's Bay Company.

store. The cost of transportation for follow-up services, such as tune-ups for a car, could easily cancel out any money saved on the purchase price.

Planning and Comparing

Besides visiting stores, you can usually compare the prices and features of a particular product and find out about delivery terms and follow-up services by looking at catalogues and newspaper advertisements, phoning stores that sell the product, or doing research on the Internet. Sometimes, it is helpful to ask the opinion of people who have already used the product or service. In addition, product reports in consumer magazines, such as *Consumer Reports* and *MoneySense*, can provide vital information. *The Globe and Mail* and other large daily newspapers often run consumer-information features as well. You can access these sources at your local library or on the Internet.

A page from Future Shop's online catalogue

Table 12.1

	Where to Buy	
Type of Store	**Types of Goods and Services**	**Examples**
department stores	• wide variety of goods and services • emphasis on customer service • conveniences such as delivery, telephone-ordering, gift-wrapping, return and replacement of defective merchandise • prices often higher	The Bay Sears
discount stores	• low prices on well-known brands and products • stores buy in large quantities • high-volume sales • fewer conveniences and services	Zellers Wal-Mart Giant Tiger
factory outlets	• goods come directly from producer • lower prices • goods may have minor flaws	McGregor Socks Factory Outlet Store
specialty stores	• carry a specific line of products • small in size • known for quality, customer service, and higher prices	Sport Chek La Senza Roots
supermarkets	• carry food and household products • wide variety of items	Loblaws Sobeys
convenience stores	• small neighbourhood stores • carry food, essential household products, magazines, newspapers • open long hours • prices higher than supermarkets	Mac's Hasty Market 7-Eleven
warehouse clubs	• membership fee • goods sold in bulk quantities • lower prices • usually large, plain, and functional	Costco Sam's Club
big-box stores	• large stores • wide variety of products • low prices • also known as "category killers" because they cause the smaller competitors to go out of business	Chapters Home Depot Future Shop
online shopping	• e-commerce is quickly growing • easy to comparison shop • access to greater number of products	eBay.com Staples.ca FutureShop.ca

Keep in Mind

1. clearance sales
2. promotional sales
3. second-hand shopping
4. avoiding impulse buying

When to Buy

Do you need to buy your item immediately? Can you wait for a sale? When goods are on sale, their price should be lower than the regular selling price. If you have any doubts about whether or not a price is a sale price, do some comparison shopping to see what other stores are charging for the same product. Most stores use two basic types of sales to attract consumers: clearance sales and promotional sales.

Clearance Sales

At the end of a season, stores usually reduce prices on seasonal stock they have left over. Stores hold **clearance sales** (or end-of-season sales) to make room for new merchandise. For example, clothing stores usually have sales in January and in June (or July). Many people buy next year's Christmas cards and wrapping paper at Boxing Day sales when prices are often reduced to 50 percent of the regular price. Car dealerships usually lower prices in August and September, just before new models arrive in October. However, you may not find exactly what you want at a clearance sale. Because the store is clearing out its leftovers, selection is limited. You have to decide which is more important to you: a lower price or getting exactly what you want.

Promotional Sales

Stores hold **promotional sales** for a number of reasons. A retailer may want to publicize the opening of a new store or a new location. The retailer hopes you will become a regular customer at that store. A retailer also uses sales to draw you into a well-established store, hoping that you will also buy products that are not on sale. Manufacturers might put their goods on sale when they want to introduce a new product. If you like the new product, the manufacturer hopes you will buy it again—at the regular price.

Second-hand Shopping

Second-hand shopping lets you save money while supporting the three Rs of waste management—reduce, reuse, and recycle. You might consider making your purchases at "nearly new" stores in your community, through the classifieds in your local newspaper, at garage sales or online. The obvious advantage of second-hand purchases is that they cost much less than new items. You can find second-hand bargains that will provide you with years of service and pleasure. On the other hand, the disadvantage of second-hand purchases is that they come with no guarantees or return policies. Also, you might not find the item in exactly the colour or style that you want.

Avoiding Impulse Buying

The time you spend planning purchases usually pays off in savings. Taking your time means slowing down, visiting more stores (real or online), and giving yourself a chance to look for the best values. A smart shopper refuses to be hurried into buying anything. With careful planning, you can avoid buying things that you really don't want or need.

Most people indulge in **impulse buying** at some time. For example, have you ever been in a music store and bought a CD because you heard it being played in the store and liked it at the time? Most of us have also impulsively bought chocolate bars, gum, or magazines from displays at supermarket and drugstore checkout counters. In fact, these stores deliberately place these types of items at the checkout counter, hoping that you will buy them on impulse.

Some consumers always buy impulsively and put little or no thought into their purchases. Impulse buying can be a mistake

This teen went to buy just one CD but, while he was at the store, saw several other CDs that he thought looked interesting, so bought them on impulse.

for many reasons. If you're on a tight budget, you might not have enough disposable income left for essential items after you've given in to an impulse. Most impulse purchases cost you more than purchases made after you've taken the time to comparison shop. People who buy on impulse also end up with many items that they don't really need or want. The biggest disadvantage of impulse buying is that you waste money.

Review Questions

10. Describe the factors to be considered when comparison shopping.

11. What are some advantages of comparison shopping? What are some disadvantages?

12. List the nine different types of stores where consumers can buy goods and services. What are the features of each type of store?

13. Describe the differences between a promotional sale and a clearance sale.

Keep in Mind

1. setting personal goals
2. preparing a personal budget

Budgeting

A **budget** is a plan for wise spending and saving based on income and expenses. With a budget, you can organize and control your financial resources, set and realize goals, and decide in advance how your money will work for you. A personal budget allows a family to determine how their disposable income will be spent. A business uses budgeting to allocate resources to different projects. It is an important part of the planning process (see Chapter 7).

Personal Budgeting

A personal budget can be as simple or as complicated as you want to make it. You can make a daily, weekly, or monthly plan. If you receive a paycheque every other week, you might develop a two-week budget to make sure that your money will last until your next payday.

Deciding what to do with your allowance is one example of budgeting. Think of your allowance as a whole that can be

 E-ACTIVITY

Visit www.nelson.com/WOB and follow the links to learn more about personal budgeting.

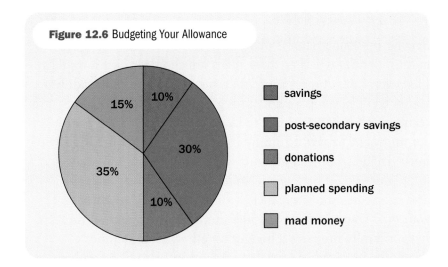

Figure 12.6 Budgeting Your Allowance

- 10%
- 15%
- 30%
- 35%
- 10%

■ savings

■ post-secondary savings

■ donations

■ planned spending

■ mad money

Stretch Your Thinking

Would you consider building a house without blueprints? Would you plan a driving trip to Florida or California without using maps and planning a route? How is the way you earn, spend, save, and invest your money related to these situations?

broken into parts. (See Figure 12.6.) It makes sense to consider a "savings" component. For example, why not save 10 percent each time you get your allowance? As well, you need to save for specific goals. For example, if you are hoping to attend college or university, you need to start saving now. If donating is important to you, put aside another set percentage (a "donating" component) for a charitable or religious contribution. The remaining portion of your allowance could be divided into two parts. Your "mad money" is the portion that you can spend on whatever you want. Your "planned spending" is for items that you know you will need, for example, school supplies and lunches.

Because many people feel that budgeting involves going without, "pinching pennies," or not having any fun, they avoid the subject completely. What they don't understand is that creating and following a budget can actually help them find the money for the things they really want. Think of budgeting as financial planning for your dreams and wants. Budgeting gets money to work for you, rather than you working for the budget. Thinking in this way may provide you with the motivation you need to get started. The time to begin managing your money is now, regardless of how much or how little you have. Planning means setting goals and establishing the financial targets that enable you to reach those goals. To be able to plan, you first need to know your gross income and expenses. Then, figure out how much you need to put aside regularly to keep your targets in sight. Budgeting is all about planning. Fortunately, with practice, most people can learn how to create and stick to a budget.

Setting Personal Goals

Setting up your financial plan requires you to establish goals and to identify whether those goals are short term or long term. However, budgeting is more than just setting goals. In addition, you need to develop a regular savings plan so that your budget is realistic. To achieve a long-term goal, you must make a strong commitment to save a minimum amount *every* month, and you must decide what that amount will be.

Goals should be realistic and achievable. They should also be specific and have a clear time frame. For example, your goal could be to save $50 a month for the next 24 months. If your family prepares a budget together, each member should be involved in setting goals and in identifying which are most important. These are the goals that you will work toward first.

Preparing a Personal Budget

Some budgets are very simple records of how much money you have, how much you plan to save, and how much you plan to spend. Other budgets use computer software programs to alter input data and predict future financial results. A useful budget should not take much time to prepare, but it should still be specific enough to let you know what is happening with your money.

The first step of budgeting is to calculate the amount of income you expect to earn. In a personal budget, this is the *gross* income.

The second step is to calculate expenses. There are two types of expenses. **Fixed expenses** occur regularly and cannot be adjusted. In a personal budget, fixed expenses would be mortgage or rent, insurance payments, and car payments. **Variable expenses** differ from one month to another. These expenses include food, clothing, utilities, personal care, and entertainment. Savings are also included here. Remember it is important to put 10 percent of your income into savings. This will be discussed more in Chapter 14.

The third step is calculating the amount left. In a personal budget, you can add this extra money to your discretionary spending or to your savings account. The goal of a personal budget is to have all of your income allocated and not have any left over. An example of a personal budget can be found in Figure 12.7.

Figure 12.7 Nadira's Personal Budget for May

```
                    Monthly Budget
Gross Income                        6542
Income Tax, CPP, and EI            (2583)
Disposable Income                   3959
Necessities
    Savings                                      650
    Mortgage                                    1800
    Car Payment                                  400
    Car Insurance                                 70
    House Expenses (hydro, phone, heat)          250
    Groceries/Personal Items                     400
    Clothing                                     200
Total Necessities                   3770
Discretionary Income                 189
Entertainment and Gifts                          120
Additional Clothing                               69
Leftover Income                                    0
```

The final step in the budgeting process is to review your budget. This allows you to compare your actual spending with your expected spending. You may be surprised just how much it costs to buy the things you want, or you may find that you're doing too much impulse buying. You need to know where your money goes. If you are spending more than you earn, you need to decrease your expenses or increase your income.

Use your expenses for the past few months as a basis for creating your budget. As you develop your budget, continue to record expenses for several months. By regularly reviewing your expenses, you'll see areas where you can reduce spending without altering your lifestyle too much. You may also be able to increase your savings. Understanding your spending habits and changing them whenever necessary are the keys to successful budgeting.

If you've trimmed and cut expenses but still can't meet your savings goals, re-evaluate the goals. You may want to change the time frame or adjust the goal itself. You may have to take a shorter ski trip this winter, or postpone it until next year. You may have to buy a less expensive bike or use public transportation instead. Try to think ahead to the day when you can finally take that ski trip or get that new bike. With smart budgeting, these goals are within your reach.

Nadira now needs to start planning her budget for June. She knows that the budget for May worked because she was careful

Literacy Link

As you read about personal budgeting, consider making connections between Nadira's budgeting decisions and the ones made in your world. This might help you better understand the process.

Figure 12.8 Nadira's Personal Budget for June

Monthly Budget

Gross Income		6542
Income Tax, CPP, and EI		(2583)
Disposable Income		3959
Necessities		
Savings		570
Mortgage		1800
Car Payment		400
Car Insurance		70
House Expenses (hydro, phone, heat)		230
Groceries/Personal Items		320
Clothing		200
Total Necessities	3590	
Discretionary Income	369	
Entertainment and Gifts		300
Additional Clothing		69
Leftover Income		0

and made spending choices that followed her budget. However, she also knows that June is an expensive month and she will have to make some adjustments. Her son in Grade 8 is going on a class field trip to Ottawa. This will cost $300. Her daughter in Grade 10 needs new soccer shoes for $90. Nadira's daughter in Grade 12 is attending the prom. She has borrowed shoes and a purse from a friend, but bought a dress for $300. Nadira has said she will pay for half of the dress but her daughter must pay the other half. The $240 for the new soccer shoes and the dress can come out of the clothing and additional clothing budget. However, this means that Nadira cannot buy a new bathing suit for her son for his trip to Ottawa, nor can she buy a sweater for herself she saw in a store window. The money for the trip can come from the entertainment section; however, that covers only $120. Where will Nadira get the additional $180? Nadira initially thinks of taking it from the savings account. After all, that is why she has a savings account. However, after thinking about this, she realizes that the savings account is her pension contribution and an account for the children's university education. She is reluctant to take all of the money from these areas. Nadira decides to cut back $80 in groceries, eliminate long distance calls to save $20, and take the rest from the savings account. Nadira's budget for June is found in Figure 12.8.

Managing Money for Business Use

Just as managing money for personal use is an important skill, managing money for a business is also critical. Remember that in a business you may be managing someone else's money. You are accountable to the owners and the shareholders. Businesses need to understand the amount of income collected by the business, spend that money wisely, and generate as much profit as possible. A budget helps ensure that all these steps are taken.

One of the major differences between budgeting for personal use and for business use is the overall goal. A person allocates all of his or her money in a budget and, therefore, does not have any money left over. However, a business's goal is to have as much left over in profit as possible.

Another main difference between budgeting for a business and budgeting for personal employment income relates to spending. A business owner spends money to make money, whereas a wage earner makes money to spend money. Thus, a business needs to spend money, sometimes a lot of it, in order to launch a product, make a new sales contact, or reach a target audience. Business budgeting and planning are tools for creating profit and growth, not simply for cutting back on expenses. Therefore, spending in a business is good; it helps increase sales, which increases profit.

Types of Business Income

As discussed in Chapter 9, there are three major forms of business income. **Revenue** is the amount of money collected by the business. Revenue is in the form of sales, fees, and investments. **Gross income** is the total amount of money received by the business minus the cost of goods sold. Gross income is calculated for a retail or product-sales business. Finally, **net income** is gross income minus the business's expenses. Net income can be spent in any way the owners wish. They can spend it on personal needs such as a new car or vacations. Smart businesses reinvest the money into the business. They pay off debt, buy new equipment, or expand operations.

Budgeting for a Business

Budgeting is critical in a business. Staying within a budget can mean the difference between success and failure. Each project, department, and division needs a budget. These budgets are interconnected and are often created at the top of the organization. However, good companies allow budget decisions to be made at all levels.

There are two types of budgets in business. The first type is a **start-up budget**. As learned in Chapter 10, entrepreneurs need to plan for the opening of their businesses. A start-up budget shows the money needed to open the business. Entrepreneurs need to have enough start-up capital to last more than a year, until revenue is generated. Start-up expenses must be estimated accurately. Many entrepreneurs underestimate the amount of money needed to start a business.

The second type of budgeting used in a business is the **operating budget**. This budget, done on a monthly, yearly, or project basis, clearly sets out the on-going revenues and expenses of the company.

Setting Business Goals

As discussed in Chapter 7, managers set company goals in the planning stage. These goals may be to launch a new product, expand internationally, increase research and development, or close down a division. These goals need to be measurable and specific. For example, if a personal care company wants to launch a new type of toothpaste in six months, it will have to create a budget that includes production changes, marketing campaigns, additional staff, and projected profits—and it will have to start that budget now.

For example, Dan Sierra's personal goal is to have enough take-home income to support himself. He believes that he can

Figure 12.9 Before Starting a Business

Start-up Budget
- office
- dental chairs
- dental equipment
- furniture
- computers
- billing software

Operating Budget
- dental supplies
- office supplies
- salaries for a receptionist
- hygienist
- nurse
- insurance
- electricity

support his wife and two children on a disposable income of $3500 a month because his wife also has a job. Dan's business goal is to purchase a building for his business to avoid paying rent. He believes this will be a good investment for the business because it is an asset that has value. His goal is to save at least $1000 each month toward a down payment. Meeting that goal each month will allow Dan to buy a building in three or four years.

Preparing a Business Budget

The steps in preparing a business budget are very similar to those of preparing a personal budget. The first step is to calculate the amount of income expected. In a business budget, this is the total revenue.

The second step is calculating expenses. Fixed and variable expenses also occur in a business budget. Examples of fixed expenses for a business include rent, salaries for full-time employees, and property insurance. Variable expenses include wages for part-time workers, cost of goods sold, utilities, advertising, and bank charges.

The third step is calculating the amount left. This step is very different from a personal budget. Remember, in a personal budget, the goal is to not have any income left over. In contrast, business budgets are supposed to have income left over because that is the business's profit. Business budgets are created to restrict expenses to only what is necessary and to make certain that expenses do not sky rocket. The goal of a business budget is to ensure that as much profit as possible is made.

The final step in the budgeting process is to review your budget. This step allows managers to compare actual spending with expected spending. If the business is spending more than it earns, managers need to adjust expenses or increase income through increased sales, higher prices, advertising, or new product lines.

Figure 12.10 is an example of a budget for a small business. Dan Sierra runs a small catering company. A budget is very important to him because he must control costs to make sure he can make enough money to support his family.

Now Dan needs to create a budget for November. This will be a busier month because he has five major holiday parties to

Figure 12.10 Sierra's Catering Company Budget for October

Monthly Budget

Revenue		$ 25 000
Cost of Goods Sold		7 000
Gross Income		18 000
Expenses		
Salaries	6 000	
Wages	2 000	
Rent	1 500	
Telephone	100	
Utilities	500	
Insurance	800	
Delivery Truck	600	
Advertising	700	
Interest and Bank Charges	500	
Supplies	500	
Equipment	300	
Total Expenses		13 500
Net Income		4 500

cater. This will increase his revenue. However, he anticipates having greater expenses such as food, employees, and supplies. His new budget can be found in Figure 12.11.

Figure 12.11 Sierra's Catering Company Budget for November

Monthly Budget

Revenue		$ 40 000
Cost of Goods Sold		14 000
Gross Income		26 000
Expenses		
Salaries	6 000	
Wages	6 000	
Rent	1 500	
Telephone	100	
Utilities	600	
Insurance	800	
Delivery Truck	600	
Advertising	700	
Interest and Bank Charges	500	
Supplies	800	
Equipment	300	
Total Expenses		17 900
Net Income		8 100

Review Questions

18. List and define the three types of business income.

19. Explain how a business that produces bicycles can spend its income.

20. What is the difference between a personal budget and a business budget?

21. State the steps in establishing a business budget.

22. Explain the difference between fixed and variable expenses. Provide some examples of fixed and variable expenses in a business budget.

23. Describe the purpose of start-up and operating budgets.

24. In November, Dan Sierra's Catering Company runs into a major problem. The truck breaks down and needs $4000 in repairs. How can the company deal with this problem?

CHAPTER REVIEW

Knowledge

1. Explain why the dollar's purchasing power changes.

2. How would you adapt Figure 12.6 to suit your needs?

3. What factors might you consider when deciding where to shop?

4. State the advantages to buying goods on sale. State the disadvantages.

5. Explain the actions you can take if you find that your personal monthly expenses are consistently greater than your monthly income.

Thinking

6. Explain why teenagers with jobs may have more discretionary income than their parents.

7. Do you think that a businessperson who sells good quality products or services wants well-informed customers? Explain your answer.

8. What customs or habits influence your purchasing decisions?

9. Many consumer purchases are the result of a desire to be in fashion or to follow a fad. What items have you purchased recently for these reasons? Were these wise choices? Why or why not?

10. Can impulse buying ever be justified? Explain your answer.

11. State two short-term and two long-term savings goals you have.

Communication

12. Interview an elderly relative or neighbour. Ask them how much each of the following cost when they were young.

   a) bread   b) movie

   c) soda pop   d) bicycle

   e) house

   Create a chart of your findings and insert the current prices of these products. Which price has changed the most? Why do you think it has changed so much?

13. Write a memo to a company suggesting ways the company can improve its profits. You can include suggestions about reducing costs, increasing sales, new advertising strategies, and new products or services. Word it carefully and politely.

Application

14. Think of three products that you would like to purchase in the next year. Using the Internet or telephone, comparison shop for the products at three different stores. Find out the price and delivery costs at each store. Put your findings in a chart.

15. Create a personal budget for a person living in your city. His or her salary is $35 000. Using a newspaper or the Internet, find an actual apartment. Include method of transportation, food, utilities, savings, furniture, entertainment and anything else you think is important. Use a spreadsheet if possible.

16. Make a list of all the operating expenses a small ice-cream shop might need. Create a monthly budget for the shop. Use a spreadsheet. Revise your budget to account for a flood that occurs one night when no one is in attendance.

Team Activity

Team Goal: Prepare a start-up budget

Team Assignment: Calculate the Components for an Effective Budget

- Teams could use the team activity from Chapter 7 as part of their research.

- Assume that your audience consists of 150 potential consumers.

- Gather as many accurate costs of products used in production, as you can.

- The team that produces the most realistic budget for the event wins the competition.

Portfolio

Obtain annual reports from at least two of the companies within the industry you are profiling (or use annual reports you have obtained in the past).

- Illustrate with examples how the companies earn their income. Be sure to include the difference between gross income and net income.

- What do the businesses spend money on? Demonstrate the difference between fixed and variable expenses. Discuss what factors a purchasing agent or other buyer might consider when making one or more of these purchasing decisions.

- Use a PowerPoint or other visual presentation to enhance your work.

Reflect on Your Learning

Assess your earning and spending habits based on the information learned in this chapter. What wise income decisions have you made recently? What poor income decisions have you made? What habits should you change?

What characteristics or skills do you possess that would help you plan and follow a budget? Consider your personality, talents, and any skills you have acquired through school, work, volunteering, and so on. What could you do in your everyday life that would help you improve your planning and budgeting skills?

Wal-Mart

The story of Wal-Mart began in the late 1940s when Sam Walton opened a store in Bentonville, Arkansas, named Walton's Five and Dime. Although, in many respects, the management of this particular variety store was similar to others, there was one critical difference in the style of Walton's management that set his store

apart from his competitors. Specifically, though Sam Walton was careful to always strive to achieve the best possible deals from his suppliers—which in itself is not an unusual characteristic in a store manager—the strategy leading to Walton's success was that, instead of pocketing the resulting extra money, he would pass those savings on to his customers. Walton realized that, by foregoing the small savings, he could reap huge profits by increasing the sheer volume of the goods that he sold. Indeed, this aspect of Sam Walton's style of management formed the foundation of a business that would eventually earn Walton the title of wealthiest man in the United States in the 1980s.

The incredible success of Walton's first store (which was a franchise of the Ben Franklin variety store chain) led him to create his own business, which took the form of the first Wal-Mart store that opened in Rogers, Arkansas, in 1962. By 2006, Wal-Mart's employees numbered 1.8 million worldwide, with close to 6500 stores and wholesale clubs stretching across 15 countries. Named the "most admired retailer" by *Fortune* magazine in both 2003 and 2004, Wal-Mart also set a new record in the fiscal year ending January, 2006, by generating over US$312.4 billion in revenue, where the company's net income in fiscal 2005 was US$11.2 billion.

But Wal-Mart has not been successful in every nation. For example, in July, 2006, Wal-Mart announced that it would be retreating from the German market due to significant losses that it had experienced since entering the country in 1998. Indeed, the estimate of the

A mother and child leave Wal-Mart after picking up some goods.

costs incurred by Wal-Mart, during its attempt to gain a foothold in Germany, is in the hundreds of millions of dollars; Wal-Mart is also expected to lose an additional billion during its withdrawal from Germany alone.

Explanations of why Wal-Mart was unable to capture the German market have mainly focused on the criticism that Wal-Mart's American-style management practices are simply incompatible with many German customs. For instance, Wal-Mart initially offered the service of grocery bagging for their customers, before the company realized that Germans did not want their groceries to be handled by strangers. Additionally, when Wal-Mart clerks were ordered to smile at shoppers, many of the male German customers interpreted such behaviour as being sexually suggestive.

Although Wal-Mart may have closed up shop in Germany, the company's ability to conduct business elsewhere has not been adversely affected. Specifically, as the largest grocery retailer in the United States, in the summer of 2006, Wal-Mart started the process of selling more organic foods in an attempt to attract more urban and upscale customers. Such action on the part of Wal-Mart is expected to drastically change the production of organic foods. Some organic food advocates claim that this will contribute positively to increasing both the amount of organically-farmed land and, in turn, the availability of organic food. However, others say that Wal-Mart's participation in the organic food market will ultimately be both a detriment to the organic farmers, and lower the standards for organic food production.

Whether or not Wal-Mart's style of business is unanimously accepted or credited favourably worldwide, the bottom line is that, as a business, Wal-Mart has flourished. And, as the world's largest retailer, Wal-Mart has shown that it is their bottom line that counts.

QUESTIONS

1. Discuss a Wal-Mart business strategy that both sets the company apart from its competitors and contributes to Wal-Mart's success.

2. Pretend that you are a business consultant. In a hypothetical scenario, if Wal-Mart had yet to open any stores in Germany but was planning to do so in the next year, what kind of advice would you offer them?

SPECIFIC EXPECTATIONS

After completing this chapter, you will be able to

- identify the major financial institutions in Canada

- evaluate the products and services offered by major Canadian financial institutions

- identify trends in Canadian banking and financial services

- compare personal banking needs with commercial banking needs

TD Canada Trust

TD Canada Trust is the product of Canada's largest banking merger. Prior to 2000, Canada Trust was Canada's last independent trust company and the sixth largest financial institution while Toronto-Dominion Bank was the third largest bank in Canada. Facing stiff competition from other Canadian banks, such as the Royal Bank and the Bank of Montreal, and seeing the possibility to greatly streamline operations, TD and Canada Trust decided to merge. On February 1, 2000, TD Bank completed its acquisition of Canada Trust for $8 billion. Their merger, however, led to many questions about the banking industry in Canada.

TD Canada Trust is a personal, small business, and commercial banking division of TD Financial Group. It is TD Financial Group's largest division, serving more than 10 million Canadian customers at more than 1000 branches, 2700 automated banking machines (ABMs), on the phone, and on the Internet. TD Canada Trust is now considered Canada's premier retail banking outlet. Canada Trust specialized in servicing retail customers and, after the merger, brought this expertise to the new company.

In the years prior to their merger, there were other bank merger attempts. Many players in the Canadian banking industry argued that in order to compete internationally and to fight off takeover attempts from other international banks, Canadian banks needed to be bigger. But previous attempts to merge by TD and CIBC and by Royal Bank and BMO were vetoed by the Government of Canada's Competition Bureau, fearing the creation of "megabanks" that would dominate 70 percent of Canada's market.

So why were Canada Trust and TD allowed to merge when others were not? The most probable answer is that both represented fairly small players in the banking industry. Post merger, TD Canada Trust was required to sell either its Visa or MasterCard divisions. Although the TD Financial Group is now considered the second largest Canadian bank in terms of assets and the third largest Canadian bank in terms of market capitalization, they do not overpower the other Canadian banking players.

A branch of TD Canada Trust

QUESTIONS

1. Why would it be bad to create megabanks? List the positive and negative aspects of creating one giant bank in Canada.

2. What were some of the benefits of the TD Canada Trust merger?

Before You Begin

People and businesses use banking services on an almost daily basis. Do you have a bank account? Do you have a debit card? What services does a bank offer for you? Why would a business need a bank? What services does a bank offer businesses?

The Need for Financial Institutions

When someone says, "I need to go to the bank to get some money," that person may not mean a bank as you know it. They might be referring to another one of Canada's financial institutions or to an automated banking machine (ABM). The main deposit-taking institutions in Canada are chartered banks, trust companies, *caisses populaires,* and credit unions. All these financial institutions are essential to our economy. They accept deposits, encourage saving, and keep our money safe. They provide loans to individual consumers and to businesses, and each day, they handle millions of cheques relating to business transactions. They also offer a wide variety of other services to their customers.

Each institution differs in the services it provides, the methods it uses, and its hours of operation. However, all invest and lend their customers' savings and charge fees for many of their services. To use these institutions effectively, and to get the best value for your money, you need to understand how they work and what services they offer.

Canadian Banking

Banks are businesses, just as retail stores and manufacturing companies are businesses. Banks sell services and earn profits on these services. They earn most of their revenue by charging interest on money they loan to consumers, businesses, and government. They also invest a portion of the money that individuals and businesses deposit with them. The banks earn interest on these investments, which contributes to their profits.

The *Bank Act*

The Canadian Constitution of 1867 gave the federal government control over money and banking. As a result, the government created a common, unified banking system—all banks in Canada had to operate under similar rules. In 1871, the federal parliament passed Canada's first bank act. The *Bank Act* outlines the rules and regulations that banks have to follow. All banks in Canada receive a charter from the federal government, which means that the government gives the bank the authority to operate. For this reason, Canadian banks are known as

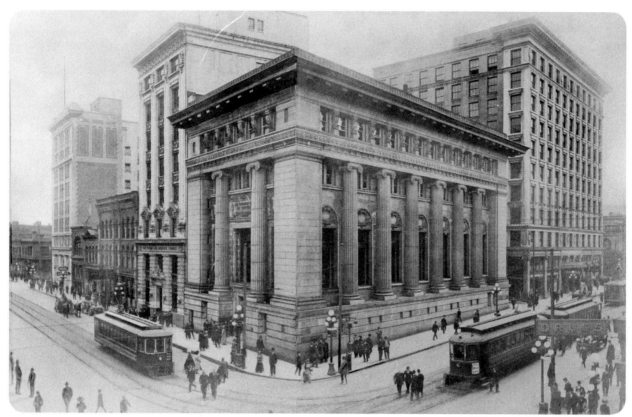
An archival photo of the Bank of Commerce building, c. 1900

chartered banks. Only a chartered institution that operates under the *Bank Act* can call itself a "bank."

The *Bank Act* outlines the procedures for opening new banks and forming mergers and gives other details about what banks can and cannot do. The act also states that banks must make regular reports to the federal minister of finance. Every few years, the federal government reviews and revises the *Bank Act*. The review and revision process ensures that the act continues to meet the needs of society and the business community. For example, the 1980 revisions allowed foreign banks to operate in Canada for the first time. The last revision occurred in February 2001. It introduced a bill designed to provide consumers with improved services and protection and provisions that would enable Canadian financial services providers to compete in a rapidly changing marketplace.

The *Bank Act* established three classes of banks—Schedule I, Schedule II, and Schedule III—to encourage more competition in Canada. The class to which a bank belongs is determined by its ownership.

Table 13.1

The Three Classes of Canadian Banks

Schedule I banks	
	• Schedule I banks are owned by Canadian shareholders.
	• Shares are traded on the major Canadian stock exchanges.
	• Investors buy shares in these banks in order to receive a share of profits.
	• Canada has 19 Schedule I banks, including the "Big Five." (See Table 13.2.)
	• These banks accept deposits and offer investment and financial services.
	• Examples include BMO Bank of Montreal and CIBC (Canadian Imperial Bank of Commerce).
Schedule II banks	• Schedule II banks are mostly foreign-owned banks that are controlled by a small number of shareholders. (These banks generally don't offer shares to the public.)
	• Schedule II banks have the same powers as Schedule I banks; however, the government sets limits on the total number of branches they can have and the total amount of assets they can hold.
	• Examples include the Amex Bank of Canada, the HSBC Bank of Canada (formerly Hongkong Bank of Canada), State Bank of India (Canada), and ING Bank of Canada.
	• Most Schedule II banks concentrate on investment banking and corporate customers.
Schedule III banks	• Schedule III banks are foreign bank branches with permission to operate in Canada.
	• The *Bank Act* sets restrictions on these banks.
	• Most Schedule III banks concentrate on investment banking and corporate customers.
	• Examples include Capital One Bank, Deutsche Bank A.G., and Citibank.

Table 13.2

	Canada's 19 Schedule I Banks
BMO Bank of Montreal	BMO Bank of Montreal*
CIBC	CIBC (Canadian Imperial Bank of Commerce)*
Scotiabank™	Scotiabank (The Bank of Nova Scotia)*
RBC	RBC Royal Bank*
TD	TD Bank Financial Group*
NATIONAL BANK OF CANADA	National Bank of Canada
CANADIAN TIRE	Canadian Tire Bank
citizensbank of canada	Citizens Bank of Canada
	President's Choice Bank
	First Nations Bank of Canada
	General Bank of Canada
	Manulife Bank of Canada
Pacific & Western Bank of Canada	Pacific & Western Bank of Canada
CANADIAN WESTERN BANK	Canadian Western Bank
Alterna Bank	CS Alterna Bank
LAURENTIAN BANK OF CANADA	Laurentian Bank of Canada
	Ubiquity Bank of Canada
	Bank West
DUNDEE BANK OF CANADA	Dundee Wealth Bank

* indicates one of the "Big Five" banks (which combined hold 92% of all bank assets in Canada).

Branch Banking

Each Schedule I bank has a head office in one of Canada's main cities. Each head office determines overall bank policy and is connected to thousands of bank branches across Canada. Canadian banks have also established branches in more than 40 foreign countries. This system of banking is called **branch banking**.

Table 13.3

Branch Banking in Canada	
Advantages of Branch Banking	**How Branch Banking is Changing**
• Branch banking offers residents of both small communities and large cities the same services at the same cost. • Branches link small communities to major financial centres. • Each branch, no matter how small, is fully supported by the expertise and services of the bank's head office. • Customers can go to any branch of their bank anywhere in Canada and, with proper identification, make transactions as easily as at their home branch. • A bank can diversify (spread out) its loans among various segments of the economy to reduce the degree of risk. As a result, poor economic conditions in one area may affect the local branch, but this will be balanced by better conditions in other areas.	• Bank branches are expensive to maintain, and banks are finding that it saves money to close some branches and encourage customers to use automated banking machines (ABMs) and telephone or online banking instead. • In low-income areas, where there is not enough business to support bank branches, retailers such as RBC's Cash and Save and Money Mart are offering cheque-cashing services. (These are retailers, not banks. They do not accept deposits or lend money, and they charge substantial service fees.) • In rural areas, credit unions are replacing banks because of low customer traffic. Credit unions are organized and owned by groups of people who agree to pool and share their resources. (See caisses populaires and credit unions on page 403.)

(See caisses populaires and credit unions on page 403.)

Oops!

Customers in lower-income areas often depend on retailers such as RBC's Cash and Save or Money Mart to cash their cheques. The Cash and Save charges 1.99 percent plus a 99¢ processing fee to cash a cheque. On a $500 cheque, that's a service fee of almost $11! Money Mart charges 2.99 percent and a fee of $2.49. For the same $500 cheque, that amounts to over $17. In addition, these businesses charge the same fees for cashing government cheques—something that banks and other financial institutions will do for free!

Stretch Your Thinking

If you were running a business, how would the rise and fall of interest rates affect your decisions?

The Bank of Canada

In Chapter 12, you learned that the Bank of Canada issues Canada's paper money. The **Bank of Canada** is not a chartered bank—customers cannot open accounts in or borrow money from this bank. (The chartered banks can borrow money from the Bank of Canada, but they seldom do.) Although it offers no direct services to the general public, the Bank of Canada helps keep the Canadian economy as stable as possible.

The most important function of the Bank of Canada is to regulate the **money supply**. The money supply is all the money in circulation. Controlling the money supply is complicated and the Bank of Canada uses a variety of methods. Sometimes, the Bank of Canada raises or lowers the bank rate to control the money supply. The **bank rate**, also called the **prime lending rate**, is the minimum rate of interest that the Bank of Canada charges for loans it makes to chartered banks. Because chartered banks borrow very little and very rarely from the Bank of Canada, raising or lowering the bank rate is actually a symbolic move—it suggests to chartered banks that they should raise or lower their interest rates to borrowers. If interest rates rise, fewer businesses and consumers will take out loans, causing the money supply to contract. On the other hand, if interest rates drop, borrowing money becomes more attractive to businesses and consumers. This causes more money to enter the economy and increases the money supply. The Bank of Canada announces its new bank rate several times a year. The release of this figure is always major economic news.

A CIBC branch located in a small town

Banks in the United States

In the United States, banks operate under a local, or "unit banking," system. The majority of banks are separate institutions that are owned and operated locally. Most American cities and towns have several different banks that do business primarily in that city or town. As a result, there are more than 8000 different banks in the United States. Although American banks offer basically the same services as Canadian chartered banks, most are not part of a unified, national system.

Keep in Mind

1. trust companies
2. credit unions and caisses populaires
3. insurance companies

Other Financial Institutions

The chartered bank is the most common type of financial institution in Canada, but it is not the only one. Trust companies, credit unions, and caisses populaires also play an important role in Canada's economy. With the passage of Bill C-8, insurance companies and money market and mutual fund dealers will also be able to offer many of the same deposit-taking services that banks now provide.

Trust Companies

Trust companies were first established in Canada in the late 1800s to manage and invest the funds entrusted to them by consumers. Today, they also provide many banking services, such as loans and savings and chequing accounts. Because their services are similar to those offered by banks, trust companies are sometimes called "near banks."

In addition to basic banking services, trust companies provide other financial services. They assist customers with the purchase and sale of real estate, administer the estates of deceased people, and maintain trust accounts for charitable organizations and minors.

Either the federal or the provincial government grants a trust company the right to operate. However, the *Bank Act* does not regulate trust companies; instead, each province and the federal government specify the types of investments that these institutions can make with their customers' money. As with chartered banks, the Canada Deposit Insurance Corporation (CDIC) protects depositors' accounts in a trust company.

Business Fact

The main difference between caisses populaires and credit unions is that caisses populaires serve mainly francophone populations while credit unions serve primarily anglophone populations.

Island Savings is an example of a credit union.

Caisses Populaires and Credit Unions

Caisses populaires and **credit unions** are organized and owned by groups of people who agree to pool and share their resources. They are a form of co-operative business ownership studied in Chapter 2. Members share a common bond of association, such as a profession, place of employment, geographic area, cultural or ethnic background, or religion. Both caisses populaires and credit unions belong to the World Council of Credit Unions.

Credit unions and caisses populaires receive deposits, lend money, offer chequing services, and provide investment products, such as RRSPs and GICs, in most of their branches. They offer competitive interest rates on deposits and loans. Credit unions generally concentrate on residential mortgages, consumer credit, and deposits. If you want to borrow money from a caisse populaire or credit union, you must have some savings deposited in that institution. A small committee of members determines how much you will be able to borrow.

Caisses populaires and credit unions have some unique features. They provide services only to members and their families. To become a member, a person must purchase at least one share in the institution. When members make collective decisions, each member has one vote. All members are equal owners regardless of how many shares they hold. Since members are shareholders, credit unions can respond in unique ways to the special needs of their members. For example, during periods of economic difficulty, some credit unions in parts of Canada have developed innovative loan repayment options to accommodate individual members' needs.

Provincial legislation gives caisses populaires and credit unions the right to operate and establishes maximum rates of interest on deposits and loans. Since both caisses populaires and credit unions are not-for-profit organizations, they return any profits they make to their members in the form of dividends or rebates at the end of the year. Provincial governments protect the depositors' accounts through legislation.

Insurance Companies

Insurance companies are financial institutions that insure risks. They generally focus on two areas: life and health insurance, and property and car insurance. Most Canadians have many types of insurance. These may include house, car, life, accident, property, drug, and health insurance, and many more. Many factors influence a person's insurance needs—age, marital status, purchase of a home, car, jewellery, or a rare baseball card. The first time you encounter the importance of insurance will probably be when you start to drive a car.

Businesses also rely on insurance. Fire insurance protects against losing everything in a fire. Property or liability insurance protects against an accident with an employee or customer, and auto insurance allows companies to transport their goods without concern about being sued for an accident. A physician, dentist, or lawyer buys professional insurance against being sued for professional misconduct or malpractice. Product liability insurance protects against a product being faulty and injuring a customer.

Frank and Ernest

©1994 Thaves. Reprinted with permission. Newspaper dist. by NEA, Inc.

How Insurance Works

Insurance is a complicated business. However, simply put, insurance works by using the payments from many policyholders to pay out the claims of a few. This is known as sharing risk. An insurance company has many policyholders that contribute millions of dollars in premiums. These premiums are pooled together so that when a few people make a claim because of a loss, the money comes from this pool. Each year, policyholders have to pay a premium to replenish the pool. A major disaster can quickly drain an insurance company's resources. The ice storm in Eastern Canada in 1998 nearly emptied the pool of resources. Insurance companies make money from premiums; however, most of their profits come from solid financial investments.

The damage caused by the 1998 ice storm in Eastern Canada nearly drained insurance companies' reserves.

Review Questions

6. Define the financial institutions in Canada.

7. Why are trust companies called "near banks"?

8. What services does a trust company provide in addition to its banking services?

9. Provide examples of credit unions or caisses populaires in your community.

10. How do you become a member of a credit union or caisse populaire?

11. What are the different types of insurance?

12. How does insurance work?

About Accounts

All of Canada's deposit-taking institutions accept and hold deposits. The institution holds this money in an account until the depositor needs it. As you will learn in Chapter 14, people open savings accounts because they want to save money and earn interest on it. Interest rates vary from account to account, depending on the minimum balance required and whether or not cheques can be written on the account.

The steps involved in opening an account are basically the same in all financial institutions. Usually, you need to deposit only a small amount of money. A savings account can be in your own name, giving you full control. A **joint account** can be opened in the name of two or more people, such as a married couple or a parent and child. Withdrawals from joint accounts may require one or more signatures, depending on the wishes of the people who open the account.

Opening and Accessing an Account

When you open an account, the financial institution asks you for certain personal information, including your full name and home address, date of birth, telephone number, and occupation. You also need to show two current pieces of identification containing your signature and, if possible, your photograph. Acceptable identification includes a driver's licence, credit card, employer identity card, passport, or student card. You must fill out a **signature card** to provide a sample of the signature you will use when you deposit and withdraw money, write cheques, and engage in other financial transactions. If you wish to change your signature at any time, you have to give the financial institution a copy of your new signature. Finally, you usually receive a card which you can use to conduct transactions in a financial institution or at an automated banking machine. You can also use the card as a debit card.

SURNAME	GIVEN NAMES		TRANSIT
SMITH	Jean		600
SURNAME	GIVEN NAMES		SIGNATURE CODE

ACCOUNT NO.	ACCOUNT TYPE	DATE OPENED	DATE CLOSED
555000	CHEQUING	JAN 01/07	

Specimen Signature(s)

OTHER SERVICES		SIGNATURE CODE
☐ MBB	*Jean Smith*	✓ Single
☐ PLoC		1 Either
		2 Both (ALL)
☐ OTHER		3 Multiple
(See reverse)		4 Non-Writer

See reverse for additional signatures

Your signature card is kept at the branch of the institution where you opened your account. When you conduct a transaction at that branch, tellers may verify your signature by checking your signature card. Usually, however, they check the signature on the back of your ABM card.

Account Statements and Passbooks

The financial institution may give you an **account statement** or a passbook as a record of account transactions. Your account has a unique number, which appears on these documents. Your statement or passbook shows all deposits, withdrawals, transfers of money, service charges, and any interest earned on your account. Account statements are mailed to account holders on a monthly basis or you can select to have them sent every three months or only once a year. The need for monthly statements has decreased because all of this information is quickly available online. Customers can look at their account activity at any time using their bank card number and a special PIN code. Passbooks are still available at some financial institutions, but they are quickly being phased out. The reasons are that online banking is much more convenient, and passbooks are expensive. Passbooks must be updated at the financial institution or at certain automated banking machines.

Making a Deposit

You can deposit money into your account at a financial institution or at an automated banking machine. At a financial institution, you deposit money by having the teller input information—including your account number and the amount of the deposit—electronically or by filling out a deposit slip. (The financial institution keeps the deposit slip for its records.) Then, you give the teller the item(s) being deposited. The teller will give you a receipt for the transaction, which you should keep for your records.

At an automated banking machine, you input the deposit information electronically. **Automated banking machines (ABMs)** are computer terminals that allow customers to deposit

An ABM card cannot be used without a PIN.

This woman has just made a withdrawal from an ABM.

E-ACTIVITY

Visit www.nelson.com/WOB and follow the links to learn how to protect yourself against fraud.

or withdraw funds, pay bills, transfer funds from one account to another, and check their account balances. ABM users need an ABM card, which has a magnetic strip on the back, and a **personal identification number (PIN)**. The PIN is a confidential electronic signature, similar to your signature on your signature card. To use an ABM, insert your card and then enter your PIN. Via an electronic network, the ABM checks the validity of the card and the PIN. After this is done, simply follow the on-screen instructions to carry out your deposit. The ABM prints out a transaction record of your updated account balance. The transaction is generally processed the same day (if you make the deposit before 3:00 p.m.) or the next day (if you make the deposit later). There may be holds on cheques deposited at ABMs or branches, depending on the terms of your account agreement. See page 417.

Security Tips for Using ABMs

1. Your ABM card is a key that opens your account(s) and is for your use only. Keep it in a safe place and never lend it to anyone.
2. Be creative when selecting a PIN. Always avoid the obvious: your name, phone number, date of birth, and so on.
3. Keep your PIN a secret. Never disclose it to anyone, including bank staff, police, clerks, or merchants, and never write it down—memorize it!
4. You cannot use your ABM without the correct PIN. In fact, after a number of incorrect PIN entries, the ABM will keep your card until you claim it later at your financial institution.
5. Conduct ABM transactions only when and where you feel secure. If you are uncomfortable for any reason, do it later or at another location.
6. To ensure privacy when conducting an ABM transaction, use your hand or body to prevent others from watching you enter your PIN.
7. After completing an ABM transaction, remember to take your card and transaction record.
8. When making a withdrawal from an ABM, count the cash you receive and put it away immediately.

Making a Withdrawal

When you want to make a withdrawal, you can go to a financial institution, where a teller will input your request electronically. The teller will give you the money and, as with a deposit, give you a receipt for your transaction. If your account has chequing privileges, you can also withdraw money by writing a cheque on that account.

You can also make a withdrawal at an ABM. Just insert your card, enter your PIN, and follow the on-screen instructions. The machine will give you the money, update your account balance, and print a transaction record.

> ### Review Questions
> 13. What is a joint account?
> 14. What is the purpose of a signature card?
> 15. How is a signature card similar to a PIN?
> 16. What is the purpose of a passbook or account statement?
> 17. List three ways to withdraw money from your account.

Transaction Accounts

Intense competition has led to many changes in the financial-services industry. One sign of these changes is the increased variety of services that financial institutions now offer customers. These services include a greater variety of transaction accounts (formerly chequing accounts).

Reasons for Transaction Accounts

People open savings accounts primarily to earn interest on the money that they save. They open **transaction accounts**, on the other hand, so that they have a place where they can keep money they will use to pay for everyday needs. With a transaction account, they can pay for goods and services with cash, cheques, or debit cards. They can also pay bills using an ABM, telephone banking, and online banking. (You will learn more about debit cards, telephone banking, and online banking later in this chapter.)

When you open a transaction account, the institution gives you a **transaction register**, which is similar to a blank account statement. Each time you deposit or write a cheque, deposit or withdraw cash, use your debit card, or pay a bill electronically, you should record the details in the transaction register. Keeping this record ensures that you always know how much money is in your account.

> ### Keep in Mind
> 1. straight transaction accounts
> 2. transaction-savings (combination) accounts
> 3. current accounts

> ### Oops!
> W.C. Fields was an actor and comedian in the time before ABMs. As he travelled the United States, he hated to be without cash; so he opened bank accounts in almost every city he visited. In keeping with his sense of humour, he did not use his real name on the accounts, but rather made up an amusing, fictitious one. However, he neglected to keep track of the accounts. It is estimated that when he died, there was $1.3 million sitting in unclaimed accounts.

Straight Transaction Accounts

The **straight transaction account** is a simple way to pay personal and household bills. Because this type of account is not meant for savings, most financial institutions pay no interest on account balances.

Transaction–Savings (Combination) Accounts

If you want an account that enables you to save money but still pay expenses, consider opening a **combination account**. This kind of account is part transaction and part savings; you can write cheques, make debit transactions, and also collect a small amount of interest.

With both straight transaction and combination accounts, the financial institution levies a **service charge**, or processing fee, on each cheque unless you have a service plan that includes processing cheques, debits, and other withdrawals. (See page 425 for more information on combination service packages.) The institution may allow some free withdrawals if you keep a minimum balance in your account. The number of free withdrawals and the required minimum balance differ among institutions.

Cancelled Cheques

A **cancelled cheque** is a cheque that has been cashed and paid by the financial institution. Your financial institution stamps each cancelled cheque with the date the money was taken from your account. The institution either returns these cheques with your monthly statement, provides photocopies of the cancelled cheques along with the statement, or stores the cheques for future reference. Cancelled cheques are considered legal proof of payment; you can use them to prove that you paid a bill.

Current Accounts

Current accounts are for businesses. To open a current account, a business must be registered with the provincial or federal government, and the account must be in the business's name. The financial institution that holds the account pays no interest on account balances and charges a service fee for each deposit, withdrawal, and cheque. At the end of the month, cheques are returned to the business, with the statement. Most financial institutions provide a deposit book that contains duplicate deposit slips for clients. The institution keeps one copy of the deposit slip and stamps the other as a receipt for the business.

The World of Business DVD

"Wesley Weber: Counterfeiter"
from *The World of Business DVD*

Frank and Ernest

HAVE YOU NOTICED? WE TRUST THEM WITH OUR MONEY BUT THEY CHAIN THE PEN TO THE COUNTER.

© 2005 Thaves. Reprinted with permission. Newspaper dist. by NEA, Inc.

Reconciling the Statement

The balance on your monthly statement may not agree with the balance recorded in your transaction register on the statement date. Checking your records and bringing the two balances into agreement is called **reconciliation**. It is important to prepare a reconciliation each month so that you know your current account balance. You need to be sure that you have enough money to cover any financial transactions that you've made or will make soon. Businesses, even small ones, also need to reconcile their accounts each month.

Steps in a Reconciliation

Follow these steps to reconcile your account:

1. In your transaction register, check off all the financial transactions that appear on your account statement.

2. List any cheques and withdrawals that are in your register but are not on your statement. These amounts represent withdrawals that have occurred since the statement was prepared and cheques that have not yet cleared through your account. Cheques not yet cashed and deducted from your account statement balance are **outstanding cheques**. Calculate the total of these cheques and withdrawals.

3. List any deposits that are in your transaction register but do not appear on the account statement. These amounts are usually deposits made since the statement was prepared. Add this total to the closing balance of your account statement.

4. Subtract the total in Step 2 from the total in Step 3.

5. Enter into your transaction register any transactions on the statement that are not already in your transaction register, for example, interest, service charges, debit card purchases, and ABM transactions. Then, calculate the register's new balance. The balance at the end of Step 4 should match the balance at the end of Step 5. If the balances do not agree, carefully recheck your work. If you haven't made any errors and the balances still don't agree, contact your financial institution.

Review Questions

18. What is a transaction account?

19. What is the purpose of a transaction register?

20. Define the main types of transaction accounts.

21. Why do financial institutions issue monthly statements?

22. Why is a cancelled cheque a valuable financial record?

23. Why do you reconcile an account statement?

Keep in Mind

1. cheque essentials
2. security features
3. stopping payment
4. cheque clearing
5. holds on cheques

Writing Cheques

A cheque does not have to be written from a chequebook, nor even on paper. You can write a cheque on almost anything and it will still be valid, as long as it contains a few basic elements, described below. Financial institutions have accepted cheques written on some very unusual materials—a roofing shingle, the hide of a cow, an envelope, and even a large piece of white spruce. They will, however, charge an extra fee to process an unusual cheque, since they cannot handle these types of cheques electronically.

Cheque Essentials

All cheques must have the same basic information: the date; the names of the payee, drawee, and drawer; the amount of the cheque in numbers and words; and the account number from which the money is to be drawn.

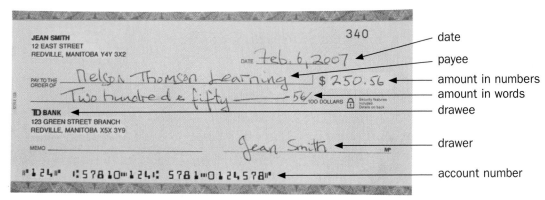

JEAN SMITH
12 EAST STREET
REDVILLE, MANITOBA Y4Y 3X2

340

DATE _Feb. 6, 2007_ → date

PAY TO THE
ORDER OF _Nelson Thomson Learning_ → payee

$ 250.56 → amount in numbers

Two hundred & fifty —— 56/100 DOLLARS → amount in words

TD BANK → drawee
123 GREEN STREET BRANCH
REDVILLE, MANITOBA X5X 3Y9

MEMO _____

Jean Smith → drawer

⑈124⑈ ⑆57810⑆124⑈ 5781⑈0124578⑈ → account number

Essentials of a Cheque

Date

All cheques must show the date, month, and year. Most financial institutions do not accept cheques more than six months after the date shown on them. These cheques are known as **staledated cheques**.

   Postdating a cheque means putting a date on the cheque that is later than the actual date when the cheque is written. If someone presents a postdated cheque before the date written on it, the institution will refuse to cash it. For example, a cheque dated September 15, 2007, is not valid for cashing until September 15, 2007.

Payee

The **payee** is the name of the person or business to whom the cheque is written. Write the payee's name at the extreme left side of the "Pay to the order of" line, followed by a line to fill in any blank space. Filling in this space prevents somebody from changing the name or adding another name. Be sure to spell the payee's name correctly so that the person or business will not have difficulty cashing the cheque.

Drawee

The **drawee** is your financial institution. Its logo, name, and address are usually preprinted on the front of the cheque. In this way, the payee's financial institution knows which institution will honour the cheque.

Drawer

The **drawer**, or the person from whose account the money will be taken, must sign the cheque on the line in the bottom right corner. The signature should be identical to the one on the drawer's signature card.

This woman holds up a large cheque showing the amount of her prize money.

Amount

The amount of the cheque must appear in both numbers and words. Write the numbers close to the dollar sign to prevent someone from adding more numbers in front of the true amount. Write the amount in words as far left as possible, followed by a line to fill in the blank space. Write the number of cents above the /100. To indicate no cents, place small marks (xx) or zeros (00) above the /100.

The amounts in numbers and words must agree. Most financial institutions will not cash a cheque if the amounts are not the same or show a big difference. If they do cash the cheque, they usually cash it for the amount written in words.

Account Number

If you are writing a cheque that is not preprinted, insert your account number where indicated. Your account number indicates from which account the money is to be drawn.

Security Features

Many business cheques are created using software and then sent to the printer. These cheques can be easily altered or forged. Security features can be added to overcome this problem. For example, some cheques have a section using a special ink that changes colour when it is rubbed. Other security features include watermarks and fibres that can be seen only under fluorescent light.

Stopping Payment

If a cheque you have written is lost or stolen, or if you do not want it cashed for some reason, you have the right to stop payment on that cheque. Immediately notify your financial institution that you want a **stop payment** order issued on the cheque. Give them the details on the cheque. Although this action does not officially stop the cheque from being processed, it does delay payment until you can fill out the proper form. This form requires your account number, the date the cheque was written, the cheque number, the payee's name, the exact amount, and your signature. The financial institution charges a fee to stop payment on a cheque.

If payment is stopped because a cheque has been lost, write another cheque to replace it. The replacement should have a new date and cheque number to distinguish it from the original.

Cheque Clearing

Cheque clearing is the processing of cheques and the settling of account balances among financial institutions. Every day, representatives of financial institutions exchange cheques and computer records through their regional data centres. No money, however, actually changes hands. After being sorted, cheques are shipped to the individual financial institutions. The individual institutions process the cheques further and take the money from the drawers' accounts. Branches receive most cheques, regardless of how far they have to travel, no later than two days after they are deposited. (See Figure 13.1 for more information on the cheque-clearing process.) Cashing a cheque involves about 20 different processes. The labour required for these processes represents a significant part of the operating costs of any financial institution.

Cheques move through the clearing process quickly and accurately. Magnetic ink character coding, electronic and digital equipment, and computer terminals linked to increasingly fast central computers have improved the speed and efficiency of this process.

In a single year, Canadian businesses handle more than one billion cheques. The huge cost associated with processing these cheques has led businesses and financial institutions to devise

> **Business Fact**
>
> The six regional cheque-clearing centres in Canada are in Halifax, Montreal, Toronto, Winnipeg, Calgary, and Vancouver.

methods that reduce the number of cheques needed. One way to decrease these costs is to encourage customers to make electronic transactions, including bill payments, withdrawals, and deposits.

Magnetic Ink Character Recognition

Across the bottom of any preprinted cheque is a string of coded numbers, or an encoding line. This line is printed in special ink and is needed for **magnetic ink character recognition (MICR)**. When an institution processes a cheque through an electronic sorting machine, the encoding line is magnetized. The code contains the cheque number, the institution and branch numbers, and the account number. Two more codes are added during clearing: the amount and type of transaction.

Figure 13.1 A Cheque's Journey Through the Canadian Clearing System

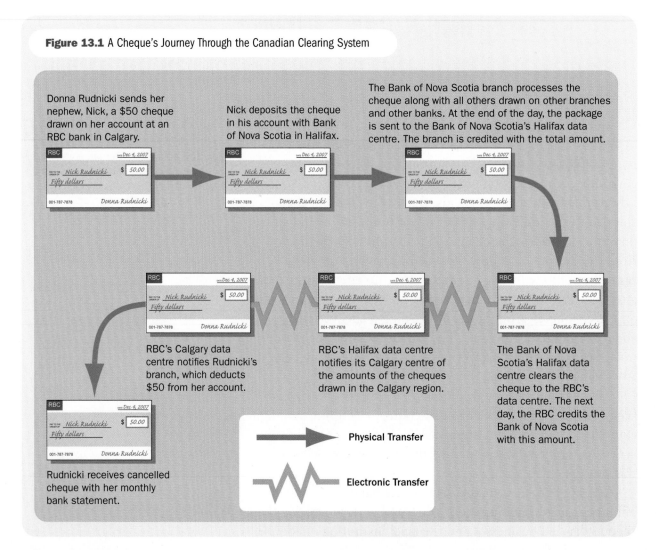

Donna Rudnicki sends her nephew, Nick, a $50 cheque drawn on her account at an RBC bank in Calgary.

Nick deposits the cheque in his account with Bank of Nova Scotia in Halifax.

The Bank of Nova Scotia branch processes the cheque along with all others drawn on other branches and other banks. At the end of the day, the package is sent to the Bank of Nova Scotia's Halifax data centre. The branch is credited with the total amount.

RBC's Calgary data centre notifies Rudnicki's branch, which deducts $50 from her account.

RBC's Halifax data centre notifies its Calgary centre of the amounts of the cheques drawn in the Calgary region.

The Bank of Nova Scotia's Halifax data centre clears the cheque to the RBC's data centre. The next day, the RBC credits the Bank of Nova Scotia with this amount.

Rudnicki receives cancelled cheque with her monthly bank statement.

Physical Transfer

Electronic Transfer

Holds on Cheques

Your financial institution may put a **hold** on a cheque that you deposit. With a hold, there is a delay before you can take the money in cash. The hold gives the institution time to clear the cheque and to make sure that you or the financial institution on which the cheque is written does not present a risk. If your institution knows you well and you have a good record with them, you are less of a risk. Holds are a way for financial institutions to ensure that the person or business who wrote the cheque is willing and able to cover its value.

If you earn interest on money in your account, it is paid even if funds are being held. Holds simply protect you and your financial institution against losses from NSF cheques or cheques written for illegal purposes.

Review Questions

24. List the six essential elements of a valid cheque.

25. Why might someone postdate a cheque?

26. What should you do if you think a cheque that you wrote has been lost or stolen?

27. Describe how a cheque is cleared.

28. Why do businesses want to decrease the number of cheques written? What are the alternatives?

29. What is the purpose of MICR?

Shared ABM Networks

Automated machines provide services more quickly, conveniently, and accurately than the old manual methods. Automation has made services such as ABMs, instant computer updates of passbooks or monthly statements, and the transfer of funds at the push of a button commonplace. The **electronic funds transfer system (EFTS)** is a computerized system of electronic deposits and withdrawals. It provides customers with faster and less costly service, while reducing the need for cash and cheques.

> **Business Fact**
>
> Canadians use EFTS over 18 million times a day. This includes withdrawing cash, using a debit card, preauthorized bill payments, and cheque clearing.

Financial institutions introduced ABMs in Canada in 1970. Today, you can find them in supermarkets, airports, train and bus stations, malls, gas stations, schools, and convenience stores. Many banks, trust companies, credit unions, and caisses populaires are part of a shared ABM network. In addition to providing customers with ready access to their accounts, shared networks save individual institutions the cost of installing their own ABMs at additional locations. Usually, customers must pay a service charge to their own financial institution for each transaction carried out at another institution's ABM. Be careful of these service charges, they can quickly add up. The three main shared ABM networks in Canada are Interac, Cirrus, and Plus. The largest is Interac, a Canadian network that has been in operation since 1986. Many Interac members are linked with Cirrus and Plus, international ABM networks that provide cardholders with access to their accounts while travelling abroad.

Debit Cards and Direct Payment

In 1993, **Interac Direct Payment (IDP)** became available across Canada. With direct payment, consumers can use their ABM cards as **debit cards** to pay retailers on the spot for goods and services, rather than paying cash, writing cheques, or using credit cards. Direct payment is similar to using an ABM. ABM transactions directly transfer money between your accounts, or transfer funds to you in the form of cash. With direct payment, money is transferred directly from your account to the retailer's account. The security tips that apply to using ABMs also apply to using debit cards. For example, always protect your password.

Today, with the increasing use of wireless technology, IDP consumers often use debit cards to pay for purchases or services outside retail stores. For example, in some cities, you can use IDP to pay for taxi rides or pizza delivered to your home. The customer passes, or "swipes," his or her card through a card reader. On a hand-held electronic device, the customer checks the amount of the sale. If the price is correct, the customer presses one key to confirm the amount and another key to indicate the account from which funds are to be taken. The customer then enters his or her PIN (the same as the one used for the ABM). If there is enough money in the account to cover the purchase, the money is immediately debited from the customer's account and credited to the retailer's account. For each direct payment transaction, customers may have to pay a service charge to the institution that issued the card. People

The new Monopoly game: Monopoly Here and Now.

Say goodbye to all that colourful money when you pass Go. Monopoly is updating its game to reflect the way business is done today. Hasbro Inc., the company that produces Monopoly, is introducing a new, cashless version of the game that uses a debit card. Players insert a mock debit card into a plastic device that displays the cash balance of each player. This new version is called Monopoly Here and Now.

The game has been released in the United Kingdom and, as of 2007, in Canada and the United States. The U.K. game has also been updated with new London addresses, higher property taxes, and a cellphone as a playing piece.

Canada is a prime target for this game because Canadians are the highest users of debit cards in the world.

Hasbro Inc. has constantly updated the game to interest new players and make existing players purchase another copy of the game. Different versions of the game include one about Canada, Lord of the Rings, Golf, NHL, The Simpsons, and Star Wars. Don't worry—Hasbro Inc. still sells the traditional version of Monopoly.

to pay a service charge to the institution that issued the card. People who do not like to buy on credit may prefer to use a debit card as a way to make a "cash" purchase without having to carry large amounts of cash or cheques.

Telephone Banking

Technological innovation in banking has led to greater customer convenience. Telephone banking, for example, now lets customers bank at any time and anywhere a telephone is available. To use telephone banking, you need an account, a bank card, and a telephone. Visit your local financial institution or call its toll-free number to get started. Once your account is set up, all you have to do is dial the telephone-banking phone number and follow the voice instructions to use a variety of services. Each institution offers different services. Service charges also vary, depending on how much you use the services and the balance of your account.

Online Banking

Most financial institutions also offer online banking for clients who prefer computer banking. Services are usually available 24 hours a day, seven days a week, from anywhere that customers have Internet access. All services available through telephone banking are also available online. Internet banking, however, has added options such as the ability to buy RRSPs, download files, and print out financial data. Customers can immediately access current information about each of their accounts, including their mortgage, RRSPs, and line of credit. They do not have to wait for their monthly statements to determine their financial status. Financial institutions may or may not charge a monthly service fee for online banking, depending on your account balance and how often you use the service.

Once you are connected to the financial institution online, you enter your PIN, and then follow step-by-step instructions to complete transactions. Generally, banking online is more convenient than traditional banking, and service charges are lower. Online banking is also beneficial for financial institutions because online accounts involve less paperwork and require fewer staff to service them.

Online Banks

Over the past few years, a new form of banking has emerged—**online banks** also known as **virtual banks**. These banks do not have actual, physical branches, but are accessed online. Transactions are completed online, through the telephone, ABM, or independent professionals. Examples of these banks

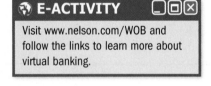

E-ACTIVITY

Visit www.nelson.com/WOB and follow the links to learn more about virtual banking.

Table 13.4

Pros and Cons of Online Banking	
Pros	**Cons**
A wide range of services is available.	Access to a computer and Internet are necessary.
Most services are available 24 hours a day.	Power failures and technical problems can disrupt service.
Transactions are quickly executed and confirmed.	Time is required to become familiar with programs and procedures.
Detailed financial information is available.	Privacy and security may not be guaranteed.
Tools are provided for tracking money and financial planning.	Personal contact between customers and staff at financial institutions is reduced.

are ING DIRECT, President's Choice Bank and Citizens Bank of Canada. These virtual banks provide many of the services offered by traditional banks. They have savings and chequing accounts, mortgages, GICs, RSPs, and loans. Because the costs of running this type of online business are much less, these lower costs are passed on to the customers. Service charges are less, interest on loans is lower, and interest on deposits is higher. However, there are disadvantages to using online banks. Because there is no actual building, online banks have no ABMs. Deposits can be made at other banks' ABMs, but service charges exist. Some online banks will not accept deposits at ABMs. The deposits must be mailed or money transferred from another account. Customer service at an online bank is limited because you have to deal with a 1-800 number. You do not have a chance develop a personal relationship. Another disadvantage is that cheque clearing can be slower at an online bank.

Review Questions

30. Define EFTS. What is its purpose?

31. What are the names of the three main shared ABM networks in Canada?

32. What is a debit card? How does it work?

33. What are the advantages of telephone and online banking?

34. What is an online bank? Provide an example.

Other Financial Services

In addition to different kinds of transaction accounts, financial institutions offer many different services. Some of the more popular services are loans, lines of credit, credit cards, direct deposits, money orders and drafts, night depositories, overdraft protection, preauthorized bill payments, safety deposit boxes, traveller's cheques, and combination service packages. The types and costs of services vary from institution to institution. These services meet both personal and commercial banking needs.

Keep in Mind

1. loans
2. lines of credit
3. credit cards
4. direct deposits
5. money orders and drafts
6. night depositories
7. overdraft protection
8. preauthorized bill payments
9. safety deposit boxes
10. combination service packages

Stretch Your Thinking

Many people entering business partnerships fail to check their new partner's credit rating. Why would this be important?

Loans

Financial institutions lend money to consumers, businesses, and to all three levels of government. Loans range from small personal loans to the multimillion—or multibillion—dollar financing of corporate megaprojects such as the construction of business towers. Loans, in fact, are the most important financial service that financial institutions provide. The interest from loans is a major source of income for financial institutions, and competition among institutions to lend money is very keen.

Institutions lend money only if it seems likely that the loan will be repaid on time. Term loans, student loans, credit cards, lines of credit, and mortgages are the most common forms of loans. A **term loan** involves borrowing money and paying it back at a specified time. The interest rate on the loan can be a fixed rate, which is set for the specific length of the loan, or it can be a variable rate, which rises and falls with general interest rates. (See Chapter 15 for more information about loans.)

Lines of Credit

When it comes to money management, a smart way to make the most of your purchasing power is to establish a line of credit with your financial institution. A **line of credit** is a form of instant access to credit that has been arranged between you and your financial institution. It is a one-time approved loan that allows you to borrow up to a prearranged amount. It is like having cash on hand when you really need it. With a line of credit, you pay interest only on the exact amount you borrow and only for the number of days that you use the money. The interest rates are much lower than basic credit card rates. (See Chapter 15 for more information about credit.) A line of credit is critical for a new business. This business will have inconsistent demands for cash especially in the first few years. For example, bills will need to be paid before the business opens and any revenue is generated, or a company that sells most of its product in the summer months will still have to pay rent in the winter.

Credit Cards

Millions of Canadians regularly use credit cards to buy goods and services. These cards offer a convenient and handy alternative to paying cash or writing personal cheques. Many of Canada's financial institutions offer one of two major credit cards: Visa or MasterCard. Many types of these cards are

Business Fact

Canada's first credit card, Chargex (now Visa), was introduced in 1968. Mastercharge (now MasterCard) was introduced in 1973.

Could consumers afford these without credit?

available, with various features, fees, and interest rates. Visa and MasterCard are known as all-purpose cards because they can be used worldwide to make purchases and to obtain cash from ABMs. (See Chapter 15 for more information on different types of credit cards and their use.)

Direct Deposits

The **direct deposit** service transfers funds from an outside source directly into a specific account that you designate. For example, if you are expecting money from the government, such as an income tax refund or a monthly pension cheque, you can arrange payment by direct deposit. As you read in Chapter 6, many employers also pay employees through direct deposit. Direct deposits give you instant access to your money and eliminate any holds on cheques.

Money Orders and Drafts

A **money order** is a form of payment similar to a cheque. The issuing institution guarantees to pay the amount shown on the order to the payee. The guarantee also protects the payee (and the sender) in case the money order is lost or stolen. If you need to send payment through the mail, a mail order or draft is a safe way to do this. You can purchase a money order up to a certain amount—usually $1000—from a financial institution or from Canada Post. Money orders are also available in foreign currencies. You may have to pay a small service charge for the money order.

A **draft** is similar to a money order except that it is issued only by financial institutions, usually for larger amounts. Some financial institutions no longer differentiate between money orders and drafts—they issue only drafts, regardless of the amount. Unlike cheques, money orders and drafts are not held. As a result, they guarantee the payee instant access to his or her money.

Money orders and drafts are completed in triplicate. The issuer fills in the amount, while the sender fills in the name of the payee, the date, and the sender's name and address. The payee receives the main copy of the money order or draft, the issuing institution keeps one copy for its records, and the sender keeps the third copy as a receipt.

Technology has changed the need for money orders. Many financial institutions e-mail money transfers. These are useful for parents to send money to children at university, deposit into an account in another financial institution, or pay into a common fund for a wedding gift. It is an easy, convenient, secure, and fast way to send money.

Night Depositories

Most branches of financial institutions have a night depository facility, or chute. The **night depository** chute allows customers to make deposits or drop off important financial documents at any time—24 hours a day, seven days a week. This means that businesses do not have to hold large amounts of cash overnight on company premises. As a result, the risk of theft and insurance costs are reduced. Customers place their deposits in locked pouches or bags and then drop them into the chute, which is secure. During business hours, a branch employee accesses these deposits with a special key and processes them. The customer does not need to be present while the deposit is processed.

Overdraft Protection

Even the most careful depositor occasionally runs up an **overdraft**. Having an overdraft means that you write a cheque for more money than you have in your account. For example, if you write a cheque for $300 and your account balance is $250, your account overdraft is $50. In some cases, the financial institution refuses to pay the cheque and returns it marked NSF. With overdraft protection, the institution will lend the depositor the $50 so that the payee can cash the cheque. Institutions charge the depositor for this service.

Night depositories allow businesses to operate in the evening and deposit their day's earnings safely.

Preauthorized Bill Payments

If you have regular monthly bills, such as loans, a mortgage, cable TV, or insurance, you can arrange to make payments automatically through your financial institution. If you give a company written permission to make a **preauthorized debit**, the business can make regular and automatic withdrawals from your account. This type of payment is convenient because you don't need to write cheques as frequently, submit postdated cheques, or pay bills through an ABM, telephone banking, or online banking. Preauthorized payments can also help you prepare your monthly budget.

For regular bills that vary in amount from month to month, the business must provide you with notice of the amount to be debited from your account at least 10 days before payment is due. You should always keep track of what you owe, however, and record the payment in your transaction register to make sure that you have enough money in your account.

Stretch Your Thinking

How can preauthorized payments help you prepare your monthly budget?

Safety Deposit Boxes

Most financial institutions offer safety deposit boxes. Individuals and businesses can use these fireproof, metal boxes to store important documents and valuables, such as birth certificates, stocks and bonds, insurance policies, wills, collector coins, jewellery, and home-ownership papers—though deposit insurance does not cover the contents of safety deposit boxes. Financial institutions are not allowed to know what is in a box. Only the person renting the box, or a person legally named by the renter, can open it. Two keys are required: the renter's key and the institution's key. Rental rates vary according to the size of the box.

Combination Service Packages

Most financial institutions offer their customers package plans that provide a range of services for a flat monthly fee. The most basic plans allow a certain number of cheques and withdrawals each month. The most comprehensive packages usually include unlimited free chequing privileges, personalized cheques, overdraft protection, a MasterCard or Visa card, a credit that covers part of the rental cost for a safety deposit box, free electronic transactions, and a preferred rate on personal loans.

Combination service plans are ideal for people who use most of the services included in the package. To decide if a combination service plan is right for you, determine the separate costs of the services that you use most often. Then, compare the total of these costs with the monthly cost of the service package.

Most financial institutions offer a youth plan, which gives young people a certain number of free in-branch and electronic transactions. Full-time postsecondary students may apply for a special reduced-fee plan, while seniors over 59 or 60 may find a free package plan that offers other benefits as well.

Shopping for a Financial Institution

When you are ready to open an account, visit different financial institutions in your area to compare what each one has to offer. Every financial institution has its own products and services, all of them differently named, priced, and packaged. As a consumer, be as careful in selecting your financial institution as you would be in making any major purchase. Consider reputation, convenience, fees, types of services available, and your level of comfort. Also keep in mind that many people and businesses use more than one financial institution to help them manage their affairs. All financial institutions provide brochures describing their accounts, charges, and other commonly used services. This information is also readily available online.

The Future of Financial Services

Although more and more financial transactions are being done electronically, there will be times when you have to visit a branch of your financial institution, and there will always be some people who prefer the direct contact with employees of the financial institution.

Canada will probably never be a cashless (or cheque-less) society. Many Canadians will continue to write cheques for costly transactions, such as paying rent. And they will continue to use cash—probably coins—to buy low-priced goods or services, such as snack foods, newspapers, bus fares, and so on. Cash is still the only universally accepted form of payment and the simplest way to exchange value. As well, some Canadians are still reluctant to accept the electronic transfer of funds, or do not use credit or debit cards because of personal beliefs and values. Cash is also necessary in case of a blackout or a temporarily out-of-order debit system in a store. For these reasons, financial institutions must continue to offer customers the choice of using cash and cheques.

Over the past years, there has been a lot of discussion about **smart cards**. A smart card looks like an ABM card or a credit card, but has a powerful microchip. It can store different applications, including e-cash, or electronic cash. The microchip provides an additional measure of security because it is exceptionally difficult to duplicate. The Canadian Bankers Association anticipates that the first chip transactions will occur in early 2007. This transfer will be expensive and time consuming because all cards, business terminals and ABMs will have to be replaced.

No matter what a person's personal preferences are, coins and bank notes are no longer the only form of money available. Cheques, debit and credit cards, telephone banking, online banking, and smart cards were all developed to give people increased access to their money and new ways to use it. One thing is certain: electronic and digital technology will continue to transform financial institutions and the way Canadians use and think about money.

Review Questions

35. List services provided by Canada's financial institutions that would be used by a business.

36. List services provided by Canada's financial institutions that would be used by individuals.

37. How are money orders and drafts similar to and different from cheques?

38. Which money options are best for travellers: traveller's cheques, cash, personal cheques, or debit card transactions?

39. What is a combination service package?

40. Describe a smart card.

CHAPTER REVIEW

Knowledge

1. What is the Bank of Canada? How does it differ from a chartered bank? What is the relationship between the Bank of Canada and chartered banks?

2. Describe how to open a bank account.

3. Imagine that you pay your telephone bill by cheque. Six weeks later, you get an overdue notice from the telephone company. What should you do?

4. What are the advantages of using an online bank instead of a bank you can physically visit?

Thinking

5. Why are financial institutions important to you and your community?

6. Why did Canada develop a branch banking system rather than a unit banking system?

7. When the Bank of Canada rate falls, who benefits the most? Why? Who benefits the least? Why?

8. List the ways you can deposit money into your account.

9. Why should you keep your PIN number a secret?

10. Why should you still have to pay a service charge when you use an ABM, a debit card, telephone banking, or online banking?

11. When would you use a joint account? Provide an example from your life.

12. Will Canada ever become a cashless society? Why or why not?

Communication

13. Have a discussion with an adult about the types of insurance they have purchased. Write a description of each.

14. Why do most Canadians open some type of account in a financial institution? Work in groups of three or four and brainstorm as many different reasons as possible. Then, place the reasons in order from the most important to the least important. Select one person from your group to write your ordered list of reasons on the board or on a flip chart. Compare and discuss the various group lists, noting similarities and differences. As a class, develop a final "Top Five Reasons for Opening an Account" list.

15. While high-tech banking provides consumers with convenience and speed, it also collects massive amounts of information on consumers. Should such information be private, or should it be made available to financial institutions and businesses? Prepare three arguments for each side of this issue. Hold a debate with another classmate to discuss this issue.

16. Have a discussion with the person in your family who is responsible for paying the bills. How are these bills paid? Why? What are the advantages and disadvantages of this method?

Application

17. Safoora and Reema are sisters who are roommates at university. They are thinking about opening a savings account, but they aren't certain if they should open a joint account or two separate individual accounts. What advice would you give them? Why?

18. Why are passbooks being phased out of financial institutions?

19. What information is printed on an ABM transaction record? Why is each piece of information important?

20. Explain why the balance in your transaction register and on your account statement may not agree. What can you do to figure out your current account balance?

21. According to your transaction register, the balance in your straight transaction account is $865.84 on October 31. You have just received your monthly account statement and cancelled cheques, and your statement indicates that your balance as of October 31 is $989.24. In comparing these records, you observe the following differences:
    - According to the statement, Cheque 103 for $89.80, Cheque 104 for $187.50, and Cheque 107 for $48.60 have not yet been cashed.
    - A $200 deposit you made on October 30 does not appear on the statement.
    - A deduction of $2.50 for a service charge appears in the statement. This deduction isn't recorded in your register.

    Using this information, determine your current account balance.

22. List the types of banking services that each of the following would most likely use:
    - your school's student council
    - an entrepreneur planning to open a new small business
    - a band in which you play lead guitar
    - your grandparents
    - a large manufacturing plant

    Give reasons for your answers.

23. You are travelling to the United States. What shared ABM network will you look for to withdraw cash?

Team Activity

Team Goal: Research the services of a financial institution

Team Assignment: Gather Data That Relates to a Small Business

- Teams will select or be assigned a different financial institution to contact.
- Visit the financial institution to find out what services are available and the cost of these services for a small business.
- Create a team display and present your findings to the class.
- The team that creates the most comprehensive and useful package for a businessperson will win this competition.

Portfolio

This portfolio activity will require that you investigate both a particular bank in your community as well as a company from your industry.

- Using a company from the industry you are profiling, discuss the role that a *specific* bank might play in the financial operations of the firm (speculate as to the services your company might use, and explain why they might use them). Be sure to include a description of the commercial banking services you select. You could illustrate these services in a variety of ways (brochures, pictures, advertisements, etc.). You might even consider arranging an interview with a bank manager responsible for business banking.

Reflect on Your Learning

Explain why financial institutions are important to individuals, businesses, and the country. What banking services will you need when you enter post-secondary school, leave home, and start a family?

ING DIRECT

Since 1997, ING DIRECT has been helping Canadians save their money. Founded in 1991 as a result of a merger in the Netherlands, ING stands for International Nederlanden Group. However, the companies that make up ING have been in existence for over 150 years. ING Group is a conglomerate of companies specializing in financial services, including banking and insurance. ING DIRECT has over 1 million Canadian clients and over $14 billion in assets.

The front of an ING building

Worldwide, ING DIRECT has eight million customers and banking and insurance assets exceeding C$1 trillion, making ING DIRECT one of the 20 largest financial services companies in the world.

ING DIRECT is not your regular bank—it has no branches. In fact, most customers do all of their banking by Internet, phone, or automatic banking machine (ABM). This is what gives ING DIRECT its competitive advantage—its extremely low rates. Branches add significant overhead costs to any banking operation in the form of real estate and labour expenses. Since it has no branches, ING DIRECT can easily pass those savings along to its customers via higher interest rates on deposits, lower interest rates on loans, and by charging no fees or service charges.

When looking to expand internationally, Canada appeared to be a perfect market for ING DIRECT. Canadian banking customers have been subject to some of the highest banking service fees in the developed world. A no-frill alternative would be seen as giving Canadian banking customers some choice in the market. ING Group also has established successful subsidiaries in Canada, including ING CANADA, BELAIRdirect, ING Insurance Company of Canada, ING Novex, ING Funds, and ING Wealth Management.

Given the ideal circumstances of the Canadian market, ING DIRECT used Canada as a pilot project. If things worked in Canada, it would expand into other countries. In 1997, it opened its first call centre in Toronto and has been expanding ever since. Now ING DIRECT has operations in the Netherlands, Canada, Australia, France, the United States, Italy, and the United Kingdom, and over 115 000 employees in over 65 countries. ING DIRECT has a successful formula for doing business. It fits into the busy lives of its customers and, at the end of the day, provides a higher return to its customers and saves them money.

QUESTIONS

1. ING DIRECT does not have any branches. Is this a good or a bad strategy?

2. Why was Canada an ideal market for ING DIRECT? List reasons why there was a good fit between ING DIRECT's strategy and the Canadian market needs.

14

Savings and Investing

SPECIFIC EXPECTATIONS

After completing this chapter, you will be able to

- compare the benefits of saving with those of investing

- describe various types of investment alternatives available to individuals and to businesses

- assess the factors that will affect the value of investments over time

Who Owns Tim Hortons?

It's hard to drive down a Canadian street and not see a Tim Hortons restaurant. Tim Hortons has been part of the Canadian landscape and people's daily routines since it opened its first store in Hamilton, Ontario, in 1964. The business was founded by Tim Horton, a National Hockey League player. Soon after the company opened, Horton met Ron Joyce, a Hamilton police constable with an incredible entrepreneurial spirit. Joyce and Horton eventually became full partners in the business.

Together they grew their business to 40 stores. However, after Horton died in a car crash in 1974, Joyce took over the business. He bought out the Horton family's share in the business for a mere $1 million. If only the Horton family had known that their donut shop business would develop into a franchise grossing $1.48 billion in sales in 2005 with over 2600 locations in Canada and 260 in northern United States.

Tim Hortons is a Canadian cultural icon. Yet to many people's surprise, it has been American-owned for a decade. In an attempt to break into the American market, Tim Hortons merged with Wendy's International Inc. in 1995. This merger helped Tim Hortons expand into New York, Ohio,

On a cold winter night, Tim Hortons is a popular stop for weary Canadians to refuel with a hot cup of freshly brewed coffee or hot chocolate.

Michigan, West Virginia, Kentucky, and Maine. The merger also led to the creation of numerous Wendy's–Tim Hortons combination stores. This gave Tim Hortons access to a larger market and Canadian travellers a little taste of home.

Yet the "marriage" of Tim Hortons and Wendy's became rocky when the chains became more and more competitive with each other. In late 2005, Wendy's announced that it would sell off its ownership of Tim Hortons by the end of 2006, citing both the competitiveness between the chains and the maturity and profitability of the Tim Hortons brand. In an initial public offering on March 24, 2006, Wendy's began to sell off Tim Hortons at $27 per share. On the first day of trading, Tim Hortons raised over $700 million. Tim Hortons sells under the name THI on the New York Stock Exchange and the Toronto Stock Exchange. Not only can Tim Hortons customers drink their coffee, but now they can also have Tim Hortons stock in their investment portfolio.

The ownership of Tim Hortons has always been a sore point with the Horton family. Numerous unsuccessful legal battles have been fought in an attempt to receive more royalties from Tim Hortons. Unfortunately, for the Horton family, their $1 million buyout was all they were entitled to. Yet, in a strange twist of fate, Ron Joyce's son married Tim Horton's daughter, finally reuniting the partnership and bringing Tim Hortons back to the Horton family.

QUESTIONS

1. There was a long legal battle between the Horton family and Tim Hortons about the amount of money the Horton family was bought out for ($1 million). The Horton family always felt that they were entitled to more money. Argue both why the Horton family is and is not entitled to more money from Tim Hortons.

2. Why do people consider Tim Hortons to be part of the Canadian culture? What is so special about Tim Hortons?

Savings and Investing

Consumers have two choices with money that is left over after consuming. They can put it toward savings or use it for investing.

Saving means safely putting money aside for future use. Savings deposited in a financial institution earn interest and are protected against loss. But this money loses purchasing power over time due to inflation. For example, a savings account that makes 2 percent interest is not a good deal if the current inflation rate is 2.5 percent. You would actually lose purchasing power by selecting this savings option. Examples of options for savings are savings accounts, term deposits, GICs, and RRSPs.

Investing is using your savings to earn extra income. Investing has two major advantages over savings:

1. Investments often yield a higher rate of return.
2. Investments can grow at or exceed the rate of inflation.

However, there are two major disadvantages of investing:

1. The yield is not guaranteed.
2. There is some risk of losing part or all of the money.

While savings are protected, investments can be lost completely. You should consider risky investments only if you are prepared to lose part of your savings. Examples of investments are stocks, mutual funds, bonds, and collectibles.

Smart investors have a combination of savings plans and investments. The amount of each depends on a person's short-term and long-term goals and needs. For example, a family with three teenagers is likely to put the majority of its savings into a house and an education plan to pay for their children's post-secondary education. A couple with no children will spend a greater proportion on investments such as stocks and bonds.

The Need for a Savings Plan

A **savings plan** is a systematic or regular method of putting money aside to reach a financial goal. How much you save, what you save, and where you save are important decisions. Developing a savings plan should be a basic part of your budgeting process and financial future (see Chapter 12).

How much of your earnings you save is your decision. No matter how young you are, saving part of your earnings or unexpected windfalls (such as gifts of money) is a good habit to develop. Many employers help you save by deducting a specified amount of money from your paycheque and depositing it directly in your bank account. Sometimes, the bank will do this for you. If you start saving on a regular basis now, you'll find it easier to save when you're older and earning more money.

Why People Save

People save for many reasons: emergency needs, short- and long-term goals, security, and future needs.

Emergency Needs

What would happen if unexpected events affected the main income earner in your family? There could be sudden expenses and a loss of family income. Insurance offers protection against risks such as an accident, a serious illness, or the loss of a job, but it doesn't always fully cover every cost. Savings can help a family meet expenses during an emergency. The importance of saving to prepare for emergencies or unexpected hardships is what lies behind the familiar expression "saving for a rainy day."

Many financial planners state that you should have three to six months' salary in a savings account. You can use this money in the event you lose a job, or you can use it to allow yourself to resign from a job. For example, if your employer is doing something you think is unethical, such as polluting the environment or selling hazardous products (see Chapter 3), you can afford to quit the company. Three months' savings will be enough to carry you over until you find a new job.

Short- and Long-term Goals

Many people save money to pay for short- and long-term goals. Short-term goals are usually the purchase of inexpensive items

Frank and Ernest

© 2002 Thaves. Reprinted with permission. Newspaper dist. by NEA, Inc.

If you're thinking of buying a new article of clothing, you probably won't have to save for too long before you will be able to afford it. However, to have enough money to buy a sailboat will require many years of saving before making that purchase.

within a short period of time. Examples of short-term goals are the purchase of concert tickets, a bike, or a big-screen television. A long-term goal requires you to save for a year or longer to pay for more expensive items. Examples of long-term goals are the purchase of a car or a house or paying for post-secondary education. If you have a specific goal in mind, it's much easier to save than if you had no goal in mind. Anytime you think of spending the money that you have in your savings, just remember your savings goal and stay away from the ABM.

Security and Future Needs

Knowing that you have money saved for unexpected emergencies, special opportunities, and future needs can give you a sense of security and satisfaction. An important savings goal for many people is to have extra income for their retirement years. People who are free from worries about money are happier people.

David Chilton's bestselling book on financial planning, *The Wealthy Barber*, states that people should pay themselves first. In other words, you should take 10 percent of your earnings from your paycheque as soon as you get paid and put it into a retirement savings or investment plan. This is referred to as paying yourself first because the money never enters your spending account, you never get used to having it. This 10 percent savings builds over time and creates a solid retirement account.

This young man is earning interest on the money that he has in his bank account.

Selecting a Savings Plan

Deciding what to do with the money you save requires effort and thought. You could keep your savings in a jar or hidden under your mattress so that when you need it, the money will be readily available. However, you'll always have the same amount of money as you had before. And over time, inflation reduces the purchasing power of your money (see Chapter 12). So saving without a plan means slowly losing money.

Benefits of Savings Plans

The savings plans of financial institutions offer many benefits. These plans let you earn interest on your money, while keeping your money safe and insured against loss.

Earnings and Yield

When you **deposit** money in a financial institution, you are actually lending the institution your money so that the institution can lend it to other customers who want to borrow it. The financial institution pays you interest on your deposit to pay for the use of your money. **Interest** is money you receive over time for letting others borrow your money. If you were borrowing money, interest would be the price that you pay over time for borrowing money.

When interest is expressed as a percentage of the original investment, it is called **rate of return** or **yield**. Interest rates are usually based on a one-year time period. For example, assume you deposit $1000. If the $1000 earns interest at the rate of 5 percent a year, you would earn $50 interest ($1000 × .05 = $50) by the end of the year. Your total investment is now worth $1050. The $1000 is the original investment. The $50 is the amount of interest. The 5 percent is the rate of return, or yield.

Earnings on savings plans vary depending on how often interest is calculated and paid (for example, daily, weekly, monthly, annually). Usually, the more often interest is paid, the greater the interest earned. Therefore, the return on the money is larger. Earnings on savings plans also depend on how interest is calculated. **Simple interest** is interest calculated only on the **principal**, or the amount you deposited. (See Chapter 15 for the formula for calculating simple interest.) **Compound interest** is interest calculated on the principal *plus* any interest already earned. You earn more interest in each payment period because you are earning interest on interest, as well as interest on principal. And after each interest payment, your total savings increase, so your next interest payment will be even higher.

Stretch Your Thinking

What factors would you consider when comparing interest rates?

Table 14.1

Calculating Compound Interest		
If you deposit $1000 in a savings plan for 5 years at 5% interest compounded annually, interest is calculated as follows:		
Beginning of Year	**During the Year**	**End of Year**
Year 1 $1000.00	+ (5% of $1000.00 = $50.00)	= $1050.00
Year 2 $1050.00	+ (5% of $1050.00 = $52.50)	= $1102.50
Year 3 $1102.50	+ (5% of $1102.50 = $55.13)	= $1157.63
Year 4 $1157.63	+ (5% of $1157.63 = $57.88)	= $1215.51
Year 5 $1215.51	+ (5% of $1215.51 = $60.78)	= $1276.29

Even small amounts of money deposited each month grow when interest is compounded. If you deposited $1 a day in a savings plan at 5 percent interest compounded daily, you would have just over $4700 at the end of 10 years. Compounding makes your savings grow faster than simple interest. Interest can be compounded daily, monthly, quarterly, semi-annually (twice a year), or annually. The more often the compounding occurs, the more your savings grow because interest is being paid on your interest.

A good savings plan should earn a reasonable rate of interest. The yield varies according to the risk involved. Higher yields go hand in hand with greater risks. You should compare interest rates to see where you get the best yield, with a level of risk that you are comfortable with.

Safety

Most savings-plan deposits in banks, trust companies, and loan companies are protected by the Canada Deposit Insurance Corporation (CDIC), an agency of the federal government established in 1967. You do not have to pay for deposit insurance; the financial institutions that hold your accounts pay for it. Each depositor's money is automatically insured to a maximum of $100 000, including principal and interest.

This $100 000 maximum is the total amount insured on deposits in *all* your accounts at *all* branches of the same financial institution. If you have $70 000 in one account and $60 000 in another account with the same institution, $30 000 of your money will not be covered by the insurance.

$$\$70\ 000 + \$60\ 000 = \$130\ 000$$
$$\$130\ 000 - \$100\ 000 = \$30\ 000$$

So, if you have more than $100 000 and you want all of it to be protected, you should make deposits in several different institutions.

Accounts at credit unions are also insured by deposit insurance or deposit guarantee corporations. The extent of protection varies from province to province. For example, the Nova Scotia Credit Union Deposit Insurance Corporation (NSCUDIC) insures deposits up to $250 000, while the Deposit Insurance Corporation of Ontario (DICO) insures deposits to a $100 000 maximum for deposits and an additional $100 000 maximum for each registered savings plan.

Liquidity

An important feature of some savings plans is **liquidity**: in an emergency, you can withdraw money quickly and without notice. In contrast, land, a home, and a valuable painting are examples of assets that are not liquid, since it would be difficult to sell them quickly. Should you need money in an emergency, you might even have to sell these items at less than their fair value. For this reason, it is important for investors to try to keep some liquid investments.

Review Questions

1. What is the difference between savings and investing?

2. What are the advantages and disadvantages of investing?

3. Why do most people save money? List three reasons.

4. Why should you have three to six months' salary saved?

5. Why should you take 10 percent of your income and "pay yourself first"?

6. What are three benefits to having a savings plan?

7. What is the CDIC? What should you do if you have $160 000?

Common Savings Plans

Chartered banks, trust companies, credit unions, and *caisses populaires* offer a variety of savings plans (see Chapter 13). All savings plans operate similarly. They are intended for people who do not plan to withdraw money very often while they are saving toward a goal.

Savings plans are a basic and popular part of most financial planning. They are easy to open, and they pay a fixed rate of interest, while protecting your money against loss. Although the various savings plans may differ from one institution to another, the most common types are savings accounts, term deposits, guaranteed investment certificates (GICs), registered retirement savings plans (RRSPs), and registered education savings plans (RESPs).

Savings Accounts

A savings account is a safe vehicle for savings of any amount. Savings accounts are intended for people who want to save money while earning some interest. Many financial institutions require a monthly minimum balance in some types of savings accounts before paying any interest. These amounts may be as high as $5000. The rate of interest paid and the way the interest is calculated varies among institutions and types of accounts. Interest rates rise and fall with the economic conditions in the country.

Interest may be calculated in different ways:

- daily and paid at the end of each month

- on the average account balance during a specific period

- on the minimum monthly balance, and deposited in your account semi-annually on April 30 and October 31

No matter how it's calculated, the interest paid on savings accounts is the lowest rate of interest paid on all types of investments. It is important to shop around for the best interest rates. Remember, you learned in Chapter 13 that online banks such as ING DIRECT and President's Choice often have the best interest rates on accounts.

Term Deposits and Guaranteed Investment Certificates

Term deposits and **guaranteed investment certificates (GICs)** are both savings plans in which you deposit a fixed sum of money for a specific length of time, or term, at a fixed rate of interest. Terms range from 30 days to five years. Usually, the shorter the term, the greater the deposit required and the lower the interest rate.

Some financial institutions sell both term deposits and GICs. Term deposits offer a lower rate of interest than GICs because they can be redeemed, or cashed in, early. Most GICs are locked in, which means they cannot be cashed in early. However, there are exceptions. Some GICs can be redeemed on the anniversary date of their purchase.

Other financial institutions do not offer term deposits. Instead, they sell GICs that can be redeemed early and GICs that are locked in. GICs that can be redeemed early offer a lower interest rate than GICs that are locked in. When considering term deposits and GICs, it's important to shop around and compare options and interest rates at various institutions.

Registered Retirement Savings Plans

The federal government introduced the **registered retirement savings plan (RRSP)** in 1957 to encourage people to save for retirement. RRSPs help you save money by allowing you to invest a portion of your yearly income without paying income tax on it. For example, if you normally pay 35 percent income tax on your income, and you decide to contribute $5000 to an RRSP, you will receive $1750 back on your tax return for that year. In other words, the government refunds you for all the taxes you paid on that $5000. Inside the RRSP, your contributions grow, along with interest earned, on a tax-free basis until you withdraw the funds after retirement. When you withdraw the money, you must pay income tax on it. Although you are allowed to withdraw funds before your retirement years, it would not be in your best financial interest to do so. Since your income after retirement is usually lower than your pre-retirement income, your tax rate will likely be lower; thus, you will probably pay much lower taxes on that $5000 after retirement than you would now. The government limits how much money you can contribute to your RRSP each year, depending on whether you and your employer also contribute to a pension plan.

Self-employed people and those without a company pension plan can make larger RRSP contributions than employees with company pension plans. RRSPs can be purchased in the form of mutual funds, GICs, stocks, bonds and even small businesses.

The best time to contribute to your RRSP is early in the year so that you can benefit from the interest that will accumulate over the course of the year. Many people make monthly contributions directly from each paycheque.

Who Wants to Become a Millionaire?
The Benefits of Early Savings

You might think you're too young to be concerned about retirement. Well, check it out and you'll be surprised.

Sarah was 19 when she started her RRSP. She contributed $2000 annually for eight consecutive years, earning her a growth of 10 percent per year, compounded. After the eighth year, Sarah decided to attend university and she stopped making contributions.

That year, Sarah's friend Anthony started his RRSP, at the age of 27. Anthony also contributed $2000 annually, earning the same compounded rate of interest each year. Anthony continued contributing until he was 65 years old. Sarah had made only eight contributions, totalling $16 000, while Anthony had made 39 contributions, totalling $78 000. Which person do you think ended up with more money?

The answer is Sarah. Her contributions started compounding interest eight years earlier than Anthony's. As a result, at the age of 65, Sarah's RRSP was worth $1 035 161, while Anthony's was worth $883 185.

Figure 14.1 Who Wants to Become a Millionaire?

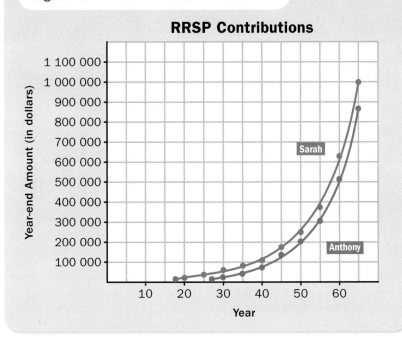

RRSP Contributions

Registered Education Savings Plans

The **registered education savings plan (RESP)** is a tax-sheltered plan designed to help finance post-secondary education. Parents, grandparents, aunts, uncles, or anyone else who wants to help a child save for educational costs can contribute to an RESP. The child is called the beneficiary because he or she is the one who will benefit from the savings plan. The beneficiary must be a resident of Canada.

Unlike an RRSP contributor, the person making contributions to an RESP does not get any tax benefit. However, the income earned from investing in these contributions grows tax-free until the beneficiary is ready to attend a college, university, or other approved post-secondary institution on a full-time basis. Then, he or she withdraws the money. Because students usually have limited incomes, they pay little or no tax when the funds are withdrawn. The government limits the amount that a person can contribute to an RESP each year, and sets a maximum limit for the total RESP contribution.

With the rising costs of post-secondary education, more and more people are turning to RESPs to help finance students' education.

The best part of an RESP is that the government contributes a set amount for every dollar saved in an RESP. The official title for this program is the Canada Education Savings Grant. In 2006, the government contributed 20 percent of the first $2000 of investment in each year up to a maximum of $400 per child.

With rising tuition fees and increasing costs for housing, books, meals, travel, and other expenses, many students may find that post-secondary education is not financially possible. Yet more and more jobs now require a post-secondary education—and this trend will likely continue. It's important to start preparing for your future education now. One way to do so might be through an RESP. Even though you're already in high school, it's not too late for you or a relative to establish an RESP for you. Remember how compound interest adds up!

More about RESPs

If the beneficiary of an RESP doesn't go on to a post-secondary institution, you have the following choices:

- transfer up to $50 000 to your RRSP
- withdraw the original amount of contribution without penalty
- withdraw the entire amount and pay your personal tax rate and a 20 percent penalty
- if the RESP is a family plan (one RESP for all the children in the family), you can transfer the unused amount to another child.

Costs of Post-secondary Education

Tables 14.2 and 14.3 show the estimated costs of post-secondary education and the amount of monthly savings needed for students living at home and away from home. The calculations assume a 5 percent annual increase in education costs (which takes into account inflation) and four years of education. They also assume an 8 percent rate of return on any investment savings. It also assumes that the maximum amount is invested into an RESP, therefore receiving the government grant under the Canada Education Savings Grant program. There are no additional investments once the child starts college or university. The savings are withdrawn once a year for four years. At the end of four years, with inflation and annual investment income taken into consideration, there are no savings left.

Table 14.2

Student Living at Home		
Years until Child Attends a Post-secondary Four-year College or Institution	Estimated Cost of University Program	Monthly Savings Needed
2	$36 000	$1350
4	$40 000	$681
6	$44 000	$449
8	$49 000	$337
10	$54 000	$266
12	$60 000	$221
14	$66 000	$186
16	$73 000	$161
18	$80 000	$144

The estimated cost of post-secondary education is based on $9000 per year in today's dollars, and adjusting for inflation. This includes tuition and books. (All figures are rounded.)

Table 14.3

Student Living Away from Home		
Years until Child Attends a Post-secondary Four-year College or Institution	Estimated Cost of University Program	Monthly Savings Needed
2	$66 000	$2519
4	$73 000	$1270
6	$80 000	$844
8	$88 000	$632
10	$97 000	$505
12	$107 000	$420
14	$118 000	$359
16	$130 000	$311
18	$143 000	$274

The estimated cost of post-secondary education is based on $16 000 per year. This includes tuition, books, and room and board. (All figures are rounded.)

Common Forms of Investments

Even though your money earns interest and is protected against loss in a financial institution, it may still lose purchasing power over time. The same item that costs $100 today might cost $110 in the future because of inflation. If you want a greater and faster yield on your investment, you should consider possibilities other than savings. These include purchasing government or corporate bonds, buying stock in corporations or mutual funds, acquiring real estate, or investing in collectibles. Each investment has a different level of risk and expected return. Some investments tend to be "safer" than others. With safe investments, you have a better chance of keeping your original investment, but the yield may be low. Investments with a high yield are often considered more risky.

As a result, investors usually look for investments that provide security and a reasonable and steady rate of growth. If you have only a small amount of savings, you shouldn't take big risks. Consider risky investments only if you're prepared for the possibility of losing part of your savings. Investors looking for safety in their investments should know that their return will not be as high, but they don't run the risk of losing some or all of their investment.

Good investors **diversify** their investments. This means that they spread their investments across several types. This spreads out the risk of investing. If one investment is performing poorly, it will be balanced by one that is doing well.

Canada Savings Bonds

A **Canada Savings Bond (CSB)** represents a loan made by you to the Government of Canada. The Government of Canada will repay you the value of the bond plus interest earned on or before the maturity date. The **maturity date**, printed on the face of the bond, is the date when the bond becomes due and is paid. Provincial and municipal bonds are also available, but CSBs are more popular.

There are several definite advantages of purchasing CSBs. First, they're guaranteed by the Government of Canada. Also, they're very liquid; they can be cashed at any time. If you cash your bonds within the first three months of purchase, you'll receive only the face value of the bond. The **face value** is the amount that appears on the front of the bond that the government promises to pay you at maturity. If you cash the bond after the first three months, you'll receive the full face value plus all interest earned since you purchased the bond.

Another advantage is that CSBs can be purchased through payroll deduction. This makes it simple and convenient for Canadians to save for their goals from each paycheque. Finally, CSBs can be purchased for as little as $100.

Since 1998, investors have been able to purchase a second type of Canada Savings Bonds—the Canada Premium Bond. This bond has the same security and guarantees as the CSB, but it offers a higher interest rate because it can only be cashed on the anniversary of the issue date or during the 30 days after that date.

Canada Savings Bonds can be purchased at all major financial institutions, including banks and credit unions.

Frank and Ernest

OKAY, LET'S MAKE IT AN EVEN TEN COMMANDMENTS. LEAVE OUT THE, "THOU SHALT DIVERSIFY THY PORTFOLIO."

© 2004 Thaves. Reprinted with permission. Newspaper dist. by NEA, Inc.

Corporate Bonds

Business corporations often need money to increase production, expand their operations, or introduce new products. They raise some of the money by selling **securities**: corporate bonds and shares of stock.

Just as people who buy Canada Savings Bonds lend money to the federal government, people who buy corporate bonds lend money to the corporation. A **bond** is a definite promise to repay borrowed money on a certain future date, along with interest. It is guaranteed by specific assets of the company issuing the bond.

Bondholders receive a fixed interest payment each year, based on the reputation and credit rating of the corporation and on the general interest rates in Canada when the bonds are issued. Bond yields must be high enough to provide serious investors with a reasonable return on their investment.

If bondholders want their money back before the bonds mature, they can sell them to other investors, through investment dealers, at the current value, or **market value**. This amount may be more or less than the bond's face value, depending on what other investors will pay. In this way, corporate bonds are less liquid than savings accounts and CSBs. Although some bonds change in price, such changes are generally slight. People who purchase corporate bonds rather than short-term, high-yield investments generally do so for the regular interest income.

Canada Savings Bonds

Investing in Stocks

As you've just learned, when you invest in bonds you lend money to a government or a large corporation. Investing in stocks is different. When you invest in a stock, you become a part owner, or **shareholder**, of that company. Shareholders share both the risks and rewards of the company. Companies sell shares to raise money to become established or to continue to expand and grow. As you read in Chapter 2, if a business is profitable, part of the profits may be divided and paid to the shareholders in the form of dividends, based on the number of shares they hold.

Unlike bonds, stock shares do not have a maturity date. They can be held as long as the shareholder desires. Stock prices can go up or down from day to day, even from hour to hour. These prices are influenced by supply and demand. If there are more orders to buy a given stock than offers to sell it, prices will rise.

Literacy Link

Before you read this passage, think about what you learned in Chapter 2 about corporations, stocks, and dividends.

Keep in Mind

1. common stock
2. preferred stock
3. stock exchange
4. buying and selling
5. stock quotations

When the demand for and prices of most stocks are high, we say it is a **bull market**. If the offers to sell stocks exceed the orders to buy stocks, then prices will fall. In these circumstances, we say it is a **bear market**. The stock price reflects the investors' overall opinion of the company's prospects. This opinion is influenced by earnings and growth prospects, news of new products or planned services, and the general state of the economy.

Companies issue two different types of stock—common shares and preferred shares. Each type offers distinct advantages to the shareholder.

Common Stock

Most available stock is common stock. **Common stock** gives its owner a voice in the operation of the business. Common shareholders have the right to attend the company's annual meeting and to vote on company matters. Shareholders hoping to influence company policy are likely to purchase as much common stock as they can afford, since each share equals one vote.

If the company makes a profit, common shareholders will share in that profit after bondholders and preferred shareholders have been paid. If any profit remains, common shareholders will see the value of their shares rise or they will be paid dividends. If the company suffers a poor year, or the markets decline (a bear market), share values will fall, and dividends are unlikely.

Preferred Stock

Preferred stock has certain advantages over common stock. The main advantage is that preferred shareholders are paid first if the company makes a profit. The dividends paid to preferred holders are set at a fixed rate, which is usually a higher yield than dividends paid on common shares. There is less risk in owning preferred stock since prices tend to be more stable and dividends are fixed. But there is less chance of big gains in years of high profit. Also, preferred shareholders usually have no voting rights within the corporation.

Both common and preferred shares are liquid because they can be bought or sold on the open market at any time. Companies with long records of regular dividend payments, stable growth patterns, and active trading of their shares are called **blue chip companies**. Large, well-established companies with long records, such as Bell Canada International, Imperial Oil, TransCanada Pipelines, and Weston, are blue chip

Bull statue outside the New York Stock Exchange

companies. They are much less risky than **growth companies**, which reinvest their profits into their operations rather than paying shareholder dividends.

For both common and preferred shareholders, if the company goes out of business, the shareholders are liable, or responsible, only for the amount they invested. Even though they are part owners of the business, they are not liable in the way that a sole proprietor or partner would be liable. As you learned in Chapter 2, this is known as the principle of limited liability.

The Stock Exchange

Investors buy and sell stocks, with the help of stockbrokers or online services, through the stock exchange. The Toronto Stock Exchange (TSX) handles the most trading volume of any Canadian stock market. About $5 billion in shares are traded daily.

The Toronto Stock Exchange was created on October 25, 1861. It listed 18 securities, and membership was $5. In 2003, the TSX listed 1340 stocks, with listing fees between $15 000 and $150 000. The total market capitalization (number of shares times share price) was $1.3 trillion.

Currently there are over 110 members of the TSX and TSX Venture Exchange. These members, who are generally investment bankers and brokerage firms, provide advice to clients, guarantee new issues, and provide corporate finance services. The TSX generates profits in three ways. It collects brokerage fees, collects fees from list companies, and sells stock data. In the United States, the best-known exchanges are the New York Stock Exchange (NYSE) and the NASDAQ (National Association of Securities Dealers Automated Quotations), both based in New York City. Opened in 1971, NASDAQ is the market for high-tech stocks and emerging technologies.

A stock certificate

Stretch Your Thinking

Why do you think health care equipment and supplies is a growing industry? Why do you think tobacco is a poorly performing industry?

In the News

Every year, *Canadian Business* reports its best investment picks for that year. It also publishes the best- and worst-performing industries for the previous year. In the summer of 2006, the following were selected:

Best-performing Industries
1. energy equipment and services
2. health care equipment and supplies
3. consumer finance
4. metals and mining
5. textiles, apparel, and luxury goods

Worst-performing Industries
1. household durables
2. airlines
3. electrical equipment
4. tobacco
5. food and staples retailing

It is the largest electronic stock market in North America. In Europe, EASDAQ is the equivalent of the NASDAQ; and in Japan, a Japanese NASDAQ was created in 2000. Other major stock exchanges include the London Stock Exchange, the Tokyo Stock Exchange, Euronext, the Frankfurt Stock Exchange, and the Hong Kong Stock Exchange.

Because of the diversity of stock exchanges, the future of the TSX is uncertain. Many large Canadian businesses list their companies on the TSX and on the NYSE, NASDAQ, or London Stock Exchange simultaneously. On a world scale, exchanges have been merging with their counterparts. In the fast-paced world of globalization and the Internet, the TSX could quickly become outdated and be forced to merge with another large exchange.

Buying and Selling Stocks

Many stocks are bought and sold through **stockbrokers** and investment dealers. These licensed financial experts advise buyers on which stocks to buy and sell, and when. They charge a fee, or commission, which pays for the broker's salary and for services

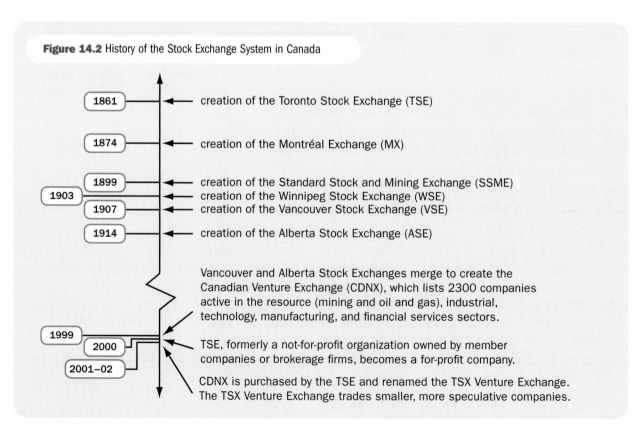

Figure 14.2 History of the Stock Exchange System in Canada

- 1861 — creation of the Toronto Stock Exchange (TSE)
- 1874 — creation of the Montréal Exchange (MX)
- 1899 — creation of the Standard Stock and Mining Exchange (SSME)
- 1903 — creation of the Winnipeg Stock Exchange (WSE)
- 1907 — creation of the Vancouver Stock Exchange (VSE)
- 1914 — creation of the Alberta Stock Exchange (ASE)

Vancouver and Alberta Stock Exchanges merge to create the Canadian Venture Exchange (CDNX), which lists 2300 companies active in the resource (mining and oil and gas), industrial, technology, manufacturing, and financial services sectors.

- 1999
- 2000 — TSE, formerly a not-for-profit organization owned by member companies or brokerage firms, becomes a for-profit company.
- 2001–02 — CDNX is purchased by the TSE and renamed the TSX Venture Exchange. The TSX Venture Exchange trades smaller, more speculative companies.

Table 14.4

Pros and Cons of Online Investing	
Pros	**Cons**
• Online investing costs less than working with a financial planner or stockbroker. • New Internet companies, as well as established investment firms and financial institutions, offer a wide variety of services on the Internet. Some provide tips for the novice investor and even allow customers to maintain investment portfolios right on their website. • Investors can receive stock quotations online and buy and sell stock directly. • Through e-mail, message boards, and newsgroups, investors can exchange information and opinions. • Online investment firms charge a fee per transaction, but fees tend to be modest, often as little as $10 to buy or sell a stock.	• People who act as their own financial planners can't benefit from the advice of a financial expert. • Online investors may buy or sell stocks too quickly, since trading is as quick as the click of a mouse. • Lack of experience can result in serious financial losses. • Data obtained online is not always reliable. There are skilled fraud artists who try to lure investors into investment scams and get-rich-quick swindles. It's very important to do some research before buying a stock.

their firm provides. Commission rates vary between brokers, so it is wise to shop around.

Shareholders interested in selling their shares tell their broker the prices at which they are willing to sell their shares. Interested buyers tell their brokers what they would be willing to pay for these shares. The buyers and sellers adjust their bidding and asking prices until they reach a satisfactory price.

With the rapid growth of the Internet, **online investing** has become more and more popular. Online investing is less expensive and more convenient than using a financial planner or stockbroker, but the wise investor is aware that there are potential disadvantages as well.

If you're interested in buying certain stocks, do some research first. Check out the company's annual reports, financial statements, company news, and background on how the stock has performed recently. You can get valuable information from credible sources, including many on the Internet, and then decide whether to invest online or through a traditional stockbroker.

Stock Quotations

A stock quotation consists of two prices. The **bid price** is the highest price anyone is currently willing to pay for a particular stock. The **ask price** is the lowest selling price that another investor is willing to accept for that stock. The current prices of

the more common and popular stocks are listed in most daily newspapers. These stock quotations usually list the following:

- the highest and lowest price paid for the stock during the current year

- the highest and lowest price paid for the stock the previous day

- the last, or closing, price of the stock that day

- the change in price from the previous day's closing price

- the number of shares traded during the most recent trading session

Mutual Funds

If you want to invest in stocks but don't have the time or patience to follow the stock market carefully on a daily basis, you can buy units in a mutual fund. A **mutual fund** is a pool of money from many investors that is set up and managed by an investment company to buy and sell securities of other corporations.

When you invest in a mutual fund, professional investment managers make day-to-day decisions for you. They research the marketplace and economic conditions around the world before selecting securities to buy and sell. For this service, you pay management fees and additional fees for buying and selling securities. Some funds are no-load funds. This means that no fees of any kind are charged to buy and sell funds or to move investments among different funds. When selecting a fund, make sure that you know what types of fees you'll be paying and how they'll be paid.

Mutual fund managers select investments from many different companies at the same time, which spreads the risk over a large number of securities. If one stock in the fund does poorly, others might do well enough to balance the loss. However, there is no guarantee against loss, and the investment is not protected by the CDIC even if your purchase was made through a financial institution whose savings deposits are insured by CDIC.

Hundreds of mutual funds are available today. These include growth funds, balanced funds, global funds, money market funds, and real estate funds. Most funds now use sophisticated computer programs to move investments among various groups, to adjust to varying economic conditions, and to provide the best rate of return for investors. But even though a professional manager is making decisions for you, you should still follow how your fund is doing to ensure that you're getting a good return on your investment. You can see how your mutual fund is performing by looking at the financial pages of your daily newspaper, the financial reports issued on a regular basis by your fund, and the Internet.

Real Estate

Although savings plans and securities are popular investments, many investors want to see, use, and enjoy their investments. For this reason, they choose to invest in real estate and collectibles.

Real estate is land and anything attached to it. It may involve the purchase of a house, cottage, condominium, or piece of property. For most people, buying a home will be their single most expensive purchase. Nothing requires more careful planning and selection. When you buy a home, you need to consider the cost of maintaining it as well as the amount of the monthly mortgage payment, taxes, and insurance. Another investment opportunity is buying income property, such as an apartment or a commercial building, and renting it to tenants.

Mutual funds, like stock quotations, are listed in the business sections of most daily newspapers.

New highs and lows

stock	symbol	365-day high	low	stock
NEW HIGHS				iShr Cdn Ca
AG Grow	AFN.UN	17.38	11.01	iShr Midcap
Ace Avia	ACE.NT.A	110.00	92.00	Income
Aecon Grp	ARE	8.25	5.05	Laperriere
AlarmForce	AF	5.97	4.00	PanAm Si
Algonq	APF.DB.A	105.00	95.00	PanAm
Allbanc	ABK.A	150.00	104.01	Petrobnk
Anatolia	ANO	5.50	2.50	Primw

Curious about how to read newspaper stock quotations? The stock name refers to the company issuing the stock. The symbol is the abbreviated name and symbol of that company. The year (365-day) high and low represents the highest and lowerst prices paid for a stock in a given year. For example, AlarmForce, known by its symbol as AF, has traded its stock as high as $5.97 and as low as $4.00 during the year.

Collectibles

If you collect baseball or hockey cards, you may have an investment. Any item of personal interest to a collector that can increase in value over time is a **collectible**. A collectible will increase in value only if it is popular and hard to find, or if it is produced in a limited edition so that the demand for it far exceeds the supply. Maybe you or someone you know collects comic books, art, antiques, dolls, stamps, coins, glass bottles, or a variety of other items. Think of almost any item, and there is probably someone somewhere who collects it.

The main advantage of collecting is the personal pleasure you get from the process of buying, storing, arranging, and displaying what you collect. Many collectors form clubs or organizations where they meet to buy, trade, sell, and display their prized collections. For many investors, collectibles combine an interesting and enjoyable hobby with a potential investment.

Remember, though, that collectibles do not provide dividends or interest. You will not realize a return until you sell the item; and to sell, you need to find someone who wants to buy your collectible at a price satisfactory to you. Thus, many experts suggest that you only collect items you really enjoy. Investing in collectibles requires as much serious effort and study as any other investments discussed in this chapter.

Business Investments

Just as individuals invest, corporations also invest their money. There are three main reasons why businesses invest.

Ethical, Moral & Legal Considerations

Would you invest in a stock knowing that the product the company makes can potentially hurt someone? Does this matter to you as long as the stock is performing well? To many investors, it is important that the companies they invest in practise social responsibility. If social responsibility is important to you, there are mutual funds available called "ethical funds." Ethical funds screen out companies that do business in the areas of gambling, animal testing, pornography, weapons, alcohol, tobacco, or use unethical labour practices. Investors in ethical funds are satisfied with a fair return knowing that their investment is also improving the quality of life for employees and society.

Figure 14.3 Why Businesses Invest

Why Businesses Invest

1. to accommodate excess cash until it is needed

Businesses have several options for making the most of their excess cash. They can reinvest it in the company, buy new businesses, expand the current business, or purchase new capital assets. For example, Toyota is investing $800 million on a new assembly plant in Woodstock, Ontario, which will employ 1300 workers and produce RAV4 sport-utility vehicles.

A company can also invest excess cash. Typical investments for this purpose would have a low risk and be highly liquid. Examples include
- putting cash in a higher-rate savings account
- buying **treasury bills** (short-term government bonds issued in large denominations, sometimes as high as $1 million, available for short-term investing, but difficult to cash in before the maturity date)
- purchasing back their own company shares if the shares are perceived as undervalued

2. to generate income

In Chapter 13, you learned that insurance companies profit by investing the pool of claim money in stocks and bonds. Other companies use investments to increase their profits. They often choose preferred shares because of the consistent dividend payments.

3. to advance a corporate strategy

A company that's trying to grow may purchase another company in the same industry. This investment expands the customer base and eliminates a competitor. For example, in 2000 the Toronto-Dominion Bank purchased Canada Trust to form TD Canada Trust.

A company trying to reduce its costs or provide a guaranteed source of high-quality raw materials may purchase a supplier. For example, Starbucks bought a coffee-roasting plant to ensure that the plant would use socially responsible manufacturing principles.

In the News

Ever wonder if your toys or games are worth any money? Margaret Matsui of Mississauga turned her love of Barbie into a $4 million business. As a young girl, she collected Barbie. Years later, she found her childhood dolls and felt a rush of nostalgia. It was at that time she became a collector. In 1994, My Favourite Doll officially became a company. It originally sold collectible dolls through catalogues but switched to Internet sales to increase its potential market and cut mailing costs. There is also a store in Mississauga. The Internet has been a mixed blessing for the business. Although it increased sales dramatically, it also increased competition and made it easier for customers to shop around and compare prices. However, business is extremely successful. My Favourite Doll is Mattel's number one account in collectibles.

Whether she is a new doll or a collectible, Barbie remains popular to this day.

Review Questions

13. What is meant by diversifying investments? Why do good investors diversify?

14. What are four advantages of Canada Savings Bonds as an investment? Which advantage do you think is most important? Why?

15. How is investing in stocks different from investing in bonds?

16. Define the two types of stocks.

17. List the stock exchanges in Canada.

18. What is the advantage of online investing?

19. What is a mutual fund? What are the advantages and disadvantages of mutual funds?

20. What is considered real estate?

21. What are collectibles? List five examples.

22. What are three reasons companies invest?

CHAPTER REVIEW

Knowledge

1. Copy the following chart onto a blank sheet of paper. Complete the chart using the terms "poor," "fair," "good," "very good," and "excellent."

Investment	How Safe?	How Liquid?	Rate of Return?
savings accounts			
term deposits/ cashable GICs			
non-cashable GICs			
registered retirement savings plans			
registered education savings plans			
Canada Savings Bonds			
corporate bonds			
common stocks			
preferred stocks			
mutual funds			
real estate			
collectibles			

2. How does common stock differ from preferred stock, with regard to security, voting, and dividends? Record your ideas in a chart. Which type of stock would you rather purchase? Explain your reasoning.

Thinking

3. Why does a savings account grow when you don't deposit any more money into it?

4. What effect does each of the following have on the value of money over time: simple interest, compound interest, rate of inflation, saving, and investing?

5. Kim deposited $5000 in a savings account. Calculate the interest and principal each year for five years if the interest rate is 4 percent.

6. Why might people want investments such as land or valuable paintings, even though they are not liquid?

7. Why do term deposits and cashable GICs have lower interest rates than non-cashable GICs?

8. Stocks are not as safe an investment as savings plans. Why, then, do many people still buy stocks?

9. Su Mei Cheng wants to invest in stocks that will be highly liquid, very safe, and earn a high yield. Is she likely to find such an investment? Why or why not? What advice would you give Su Mei?

10. Do you own any collectible items? If you do, why did you choose to collect these particular items?

Communication

11. What advice would you give to people who are unable to save money regularly?

12. Explain to a partner why a savings plan earns more with compound interest than with simple interest.

13. You are looking for a financial institution in which to open a savings account. What questions should you ask?

14. At your local financial institution, find out about the interest rates on term deposits and/or GICs. Present your findings in a chart.

15. Ask parents, guardians, or other adults about investing. Have they invested in stocks or bonds? Why or why not? If they have investments, what kind are they? Why did they choose these types of investments?

Application

16. Decide on a goal for which you might save money. Is it a short-term goal or a long-term goal? What might be the best savings plan to meet this goal?

17. What characteristics of savings accounts make them especially good for students?

18. RRSPs are advertised extensively in January and February. Why? (Hint: When are income taxes due?)

19. Find the maturity dates and interest rates on the last two issues of Canada Savings Bonds. Which issue was the better investment? Why?

20. Choose a collectible that interests you. Find out its original cost and its value today. By what percent has the value of your collectible increased or decreased since you purchased it?

21. John Anderson has just inherited $15 000. He is 24 years old, has graduated from a college business program, and works as an assistant manager in a retail store. John shares a two-bedroom apartment with a friend, and regularly saves 5 percent of his monthly paycheque. He wants to invest his inheritance in safe, secure investments because he doesn't want to lose money. But he also wants a good yield on his investment. The only major expense that John plans is a one-week holiday in the Caribbean. From what you learned in this chapter, what advice would you give John about how to invest his $15 000?

22. Using the local newspaper or an Internet site that provides listings of stocks traded on a major stock exchange, select five stocks that interest you. Find answers to the following questions:
    a) What was the high and low price for each stock today?
    b) How many shares of stock were traded today?
    c) What was the high and low price for each stock so far this year?

    For two of your choices, follow the prices for one month. At the end of the month, plot the price changes on a line graph. Can you explain why the price changed as it did during the month? Prepare a report summarizing your findings, indicating which of your stocks you would recommend for an investment, and why. If possible, include newspaper articles or Internet articles that provide additional background on your stocks.

23. The XYZ Company produces jewellery. It has $100 000 in excess cash. State three ways the company can invest the money.

24. What is the moral of the "Who Wants to Become a Millionaire" story? How can you apply this in your life?

Team Activity

Team Goal: Learning about investing

Team Assignment: Preparation of a Stock Portfolio

- Teams have $100 000 to spend and must select at least 10 different stocks.

- On a weekly basis each team keeps track of the 10 stocks and how much they have changed in value.

- Team portfolios will summarize activity over a one-month period and statistics will be recorded on a spreadsheet and graph.

- The winning team will be determined by the largest increase in the value of its portfolio along with a summary of what its would do differently the next time.

Portfolio

Using the annual reports you have collected from at least two of the companies within the industry you are profiling, illustrate how the companies are part of the investment community. Use the questions below as a guide only. Add other observations, illustrations, and explanations if you wish.

- Do your companies have any outstanding corporate bonds? What are they trading for? How have they performed over the past 10 years or so?

- What types of stock have your firms issued? What are they currently trading for? On what stock exchange(s)? Choose one stock and tell how it has performed over the past year or so. Has it paid dividends? How much per share? What is the percentage return on investment from the dividends?

- Have your firms been able to raise money from any other sources? Explain.

- What type of investments do your companies make?

- Compare two of the firms you have selected as potential investment options.

Reflect on Your Learning

Think about the different types of investments discussed in this chapter. Which ones were you familiar with before reading this chapter? What new information did you learn?

Think about the changes you should make in your savings and investing practices. Make a list of actions you want to take because of what you learned in this chapter.

Trump Investments

Donald Trump gesturing and saying "You're fired!" on *The Apprentice*, his wildly successful television show, is etched in the minds of millions of viewers around the world. That phrase sums up what Donald Trump is all about. He's rich, powerful, confident, and cutthroat. His attitude is what has made him such a successful entrepreneur and real estate mogul, never mind that it has also made him a billionaire. That's why it's so hard to imagine that in the early 1990s Donald Trump was broke.

Donald Trump was born in 1946 in Queens, New York. Trump's father, Fred, was in the real estate business, developing housing units for middle-income families. Donald graduated from the Wharton School at the University of Pennsylvania with a degree in economics and finance in 1968. Soon after, he began working at his father's business, Trump Organization.

Initially, Trump stuck with his father's line of business, but eventually moved into high-end real estate. Today Trump owns over 18 million square feet of prime Manhattan real estate and many of the focal points of the New York City skyline, including Trump World Tower. The Trump name is synonymous with some of the most prestigious addresses in New York. Trump also has properties in Chicago, Los Angeles, Florida,

The impressive Trump World Tower in New York City

Las Vegas, Canouan Island, Seoul, Toronto, and Panama. The Trump Organization has major stakes not only in the real estate world, but also in casinos, television and entertainment, bottled water, vodka, corporate education, air travel, golf courses, and even beauty pageants. Trump Organization owns Miss Universe, Miss America, and Miss Teen America.

It was Trump's rapid empire building and investment in Atlantic City casinos that led to his financial troubles in the early 1990s. These factors, combined with the economic recession, led to mounting personal and business debt. Unable to pay his creditors, Trump Organization filed for bankruptcy and Trump himself was on the verge of personal bankruptcy. Banks and bondholders restructured Trump's debt and in doing so, lost hundreds of millions of dollars. In 1994, after selling off some of his assets, such as the Trump shuttle, Trump had paid off $900 million in personal debt and reduced significantly his nearly $3.5 billion in business debt. However, the Trump casinos entered bankruptcy protection again in 2004.

Trump's newest source of fame is his reality television show *The Apprentice*. On the show, contestants vie to earn a job at Trump Organization. Each episode ends in the boardroom meeting, where Trump fires one or more of the contestants based on their performance. Not only is Trump one of the most successful businesspeople in the world, he is also one of the highest-paid television personalities, making over $3 million per episode.

Although Trump is a successful television personality, and has twice considered running for president, Trump's greatest talent is building and developing real estate. And he's the first to admit that he has worked hard for his success. Trump himself has said, "When people see the beautiful marble in Trump Tower, they usually have no idea what I went through personally to achieve the end results. No one cares about the blood, sweat, and tears that art or beauty require. It's the end result that matters." In Trump's world, work hard or "You're fired!"

QUESTIONS

1. Why do you think that Trump has had so much success as a television personality? Do you think that his hard-line approach to business is realistic?

2. What lessons do you think Trump learned from his financial difficulties of the early 1990s?

15 Credit

SPECIFIC EXPECTATIONS

After completing this chapter, you will be able to

- explain the advantages and disadvantages of both consumer and business credit

- describe the process of establishing a credit ranking and applying for and obtaining credit

- calculate the total cost of a variety of loans

Canadian Tire

For generations, Canadians have flocked to Canadian Tire for automotive, sporting, household, and electronic goods. Now add credit to that list. Canadian Tire Financial Services (CTFS) offers a variety of financial services to customers, most notably, the Canadian Tire MasterCard. CTFS is actually one of the Canadian commercial banks. Yet why would an already successful business like Canadian Tire enter into the credit business?

Part of the reason why Canadian Tire is so much a part of Canadian life and culture is due to its Canadian Tire money. Canadian Tire money, first issued in 1958, is Canada's most successful loyalty program. When customers make purchases at Canadian Tire, they receive

Only with Canadian Tire money can you find 10 cents in the form of a bill.

a certain percentage of the purchase price back in the form of Canadian Tire money. That "money" can be used toward their next Canadian Tire purchase. Adding to the charm of the program, Canadian Tire money is printed on the same stock as Canadian currency, making it feel like "real" money.

Yet there is one major problem with Canadian Tire money. There is no way to track how and by whom the paper Canadian Tire money is used. This information is vital in today's business age where tracking the profile and habits of one's customers can greatly increase profitability. Making the Canadian Tire money loyalty program electronic could help collect the information that Canadian Tire needs to better serve its customers.

That's where the Canadian Tire MasterCard comes in. A primary reason for customers to choose the Canadian Tire MasterCard over a regular MasterCard is the benefits they receive. Canadian Tire money is given at a rate of 1.5 percent on all purchases made with the card, regardless of whether or not the purchases were made at a Canadian Tire store. So using the card makes it cheaper to shop at Canadian Tire. It also makes it easier to use Canadian Tire money. Since the Canadian Tire money is electronic, there is no way to lose it!

The Canadian Tire MasterCard is the second largest franchise MasterCard in Canada in terms of the number of accounts serviced. In addition, over 25 percent of Canadian Tire's customer base has a Canadian Tire MasterCard. This idea has caught the attention of other retailers, such as Shoppers Drug Mart, who have developed similar credit card loyalty schemes.

The Canadian Tire credit program seems to provide a win-win situation for both the company and the customer. It provides the company with valuable consumer information and purchase patterns, and it provides the customer with more reason to shop and be loyal to Canadian Tire. Yet for Canadians, a credit card can never fully replace the nostalgia of receiving Canadian Tire money. Luckily Canadian Tire still gives it out on all non-credit purchases.

QUESTIONS

1. The creation of the Canadian Tire credit card appears to be a win-win situation for both Canadian Tire and for the customer. Yet, can you think of any reasons why this may not be a win-win situation?

2. How do you think customers feel about having their spending habits monitored and tracked?

The Wonderful World of Credit

"Buy now, pay later" is a phrase that is frequently used in retail advertising. "Will that be cash or credit?" are often the first words that cashiers say to a customer. Almost without thinking, many customers respond, "Put it on my card." Other customers, however, have a little voice telling them to always pay in cash. In Shakespeare's play *Hamlet*, the character Polonius advises: "Neither a borrower nor a lender be/For loan oft loses both itself and friend." Polonius makes credit sound like a very bad idea. But is it? What exactly is credit? Who uses it and why? What are the advantages and disadvantages of using credit?

What Is Credit?

At some point in their lives, most people need credit. **Credit** is the privilege of using someone else's money for a period of time. It is widely accepted as a substitute for ready cash. Using credit means that a transaction takes place between a creditor and a debtor. A **creditor** is any person or business that grants a loan or sells on credit. A **debtor** is any person or business that buys on credit or receives a loan.

Credit can be good or bad. It can be a very helpful tool in a money management plan, but it can also result in financial disaster. Used wisely, credit lets people maintain a comfortable standard of living without spending all their current income or draining their savings. It helps businesses start up by allowing them to purchase large equipment and factories. But for those who borrow beyond their ability to repay the debt, credit can bring financial difficulties.

Keep in Mind

1. consumer credit
2. government credit
3. business credit

Before You Begin

"Oh, I'll just put that on my credit card" is a statement that is frequently heard. What does this mean? Are there purchases that should be put on credit? Are there purchases that should not? Is it possible to get along in life without using credit?

Frank and Ernest

© 2002 Thaves. Reprinted with permission. Newspaper dist. by NEA, Inc.

Figure 15.1 Advantages and Disadvantages of Using Consumer Credit

Advantages and Disadvantages of Using Consumer Credit

1. Credit allows customers the *instant enjoyment* of buying and using goods and services immediately and paying later. For example, a family could buy a new car on credit, when they need it, rather than save for years to buy it with cash.

2. Credit can replace the need for cash or cheques, which is *convenient* when shopping or travelling. (For convenience spending, it's wise to pay the balance owed in full at the end of each month.)

3. Credit can be a great *help in an emergency*. If your car breaks down on a trip, you might not be able to afford the repairs unless you can use credit.

4. Credit allows consumers to *save money* by taking advantage of sales. However, consumers should make sure that the amount they save is more than the interest charges they will pay for buying on credit.

5. Buying on credit is one way to establish a *credit rating*. A **credit rating** indicates the level of risk that someone would pose if credit were granted to them. People can earn a good credit rating by making payments in full and on time. (Credit ratings will be discussed in more detail later in this chapter.)

6. When you use credit, you receive a *monthly statement* that lists all your purchases. This is a useful record that can help you budget your money and trace your spending.

1. There are *credit costs* involved in buying on credit that are not involved when paying cash. Businesses must keep detailed accounting records of credit sales and credit payments. If customers do not pay on time, the business incurs additional costs and losses, and these are passed on to all customers in the form of higher prices. For this reason, stores that sell on a cash-only basis can offer lower prices than those that offer credit. An additional cost of using credit is that interest charges are added to the purchase price after a period of time. (The interest costs of credit will be further discussed later in this chapter.)

2. With easily available credit, many consumers may not bother to comparison shop or check advertisements carefully. Rather than looking for the best deal, they *buy impulsively*.

3. Credit may lead consumers to *overbuy*, making more purchases, or more expensive purchases, than they need or can afford. For example, a customer using credit may buy a larger, more expensive television than someone who is paying cash.

4. If consumers get carried away with credit and lose track of their monthly spending, they can end up with *financial difficulties* and may not be able to make the required payments. A budget and money management plan can help people make sure that they don't spend more than they can afford.

Consumer Credit

Consumers use credit extensively, as do businesses and governments. Consumers use credit to buy expensive items, such as a home, a car, a home entertainment centre, or a major appliance. They use credit to buy less expensive items, too, such as DVDs, theatre tickets, and restaurant meals, because credit is often more convenient than cash. Consumers also commonly use credit to pay for vacations and, sometimes, to make investments or pay off other debts.

Everyone who uses credit benefits from it in some way, but there are also major disadvantages.

To Use or Not to Use Consumer Credit?

Before buying anything on credit, ask yourself these key questions:

- Do I really need this item, or is it an impulse purchase?
- Is this item a good buy, or should I comparison shop?
- How much could I save if I paid cash?
- If I pay cash, how long will it take me to save enough money?
- How much interest will I pay if I use credit?
- Can I afford the monthly credit payments?
- How will the use of credit affect my budget?
- Is this purchase a wise use of credit?

Your answers to these questions will help you determine if you should use credit and how much credit you can realistically afford. Just pausing long enough to ask yourself the questions means you will probably use credit more wisely.

A credit card monthly statement provides a permanent record of your purchases.

Government Credit

All three levels of government—federal, provincial, and local—borrow money to provide goods and services to citizens. For example, governments borrow money to build schools, hospitals, highways, airports, and buses, and to pay the salaries of government employees. Governments borrow through a variety of sources. In Chapter 14, you learned that Canada Savings Bonds and Government of Canada Treasury Bills are good investments. Essentially, the federal government borrows money from the thousands of people who purchase CSBs and T-bills.

Competitive interest rates provide an incentive to customers interested in making a purchase.

Literacy Link

As you read this section, jot down the main ideas in a graphic organizer similar to the one on page 471. Include a title and split the page in two columns. List the advantages on one side and disadvantages on the other side. Later, use your graphic organizer to help you review the content of the section.

Business Credit

Businesses use long-term credit to purchase land, buildings, and equipment, and entrepreneurs use loans to start new business ventures. Businesses may also borrow money for short-term reasons. For example, a business may need to use credit while it waits for goods in stock to be sold or for credit customers to pay for their purchases. Businesses also use credit to buy goods for sale or to purchase raw materials and supplies.

Why Businesses Grant Credit

Businesses use credit on a regular basis but many also grant credit to their clients and customers. The most obvious companies that grant credit are banks, credit unions, and trust companies. This is how financial businesses make money. They receive deposits for which they pay an interest rate. They then loan out the money for personal and commercial loans at a higher interest rate.

In addition to financial institutions, retail businesses also offer credit. Most retailers allow customers to use credit cards, permit merchandise to be bought with no money down, and establish credit accounts for frequent customers. Businesses that sell to other businesses grant credit to streamline paperwork and to expand their customer base. Credit shows up as accounts receivable in the business's accounting records (see Chapter 9).

Company credit cards allow employees to make purchases in a quick and efficient manner—such as paying for a client's meal after a business lunch.

Figure 15.2 Advantages and Disadvantages of Business Credit

Advantages and Disadvantages of Business Credit

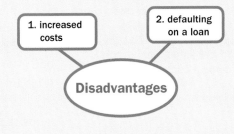

1. Companies borrow money to finance *major purchases* for large projects, such as building new factories or growing product lines. For example, a company wants to build a $1.5 million factory in Ireland. It can borrow the money at an interest rate of 4.5%. If sales in Ireland are expected to return more than the cost of the interest, then borrowing is a good move for the company.

2. Businesses have supplies delivered so often that it makes sense to *consolidate payments*. Instead of paying for each delivery, the business may receive a bill at the end of the month, in effect buying a month's supplies on credit. If a supplier isn't paid within a month, it charges interest.

3. When many people in a business need to make purchases, a company may issue *corporate credit cards*. These cards allow employees to make work-related purchases, travel on company business, and take clients out to dinner without the hassle of cash and reimbursements. Cardholders must keep their bills and submit them at the end of each month so the business can ensure that all charges are legitimate.

4. Many businesses are cyclical; their sales are higher in some months than in others, so they have *cash-flow shortages* in months with low sales. For example, a skateboarding company in Canada likely sells more skateboards in the spring and summer than in the winter. However, expenses such as insurance, rent, and salaries need to be paid every month. A line of credit (discussed in Chapter 13) or a demand loan (discussed later in this chapter) will allow a business to borrow the money in the short term and pay off the loan when its revenues increase.

1. Interest is charged on all loans, resulting in *increased costs*. If the interest is not paid in a timely manner, it adds up quickly. For example, one year's interest on a $100 000 loan at 6% interest is $6000. This added expense does not help a business in the future, since it was not used to buy an asset or employ a worker.

2. If a company *defaults on a loan* (is unable to repay it), the organization that granted the loan may be able to seize company assets, such as products or equipment. This will harm the company's reputation with suppliers and customers. It may also cause the business to become insolvent or declare bankruptcy.

One way that a business grants credit is by accepting universal credit cards, such as Visa and MasterCard.

Businesses can also act as an intermediary between the customer and a financial institution that offers credit. For example, a car dealership may advertise a low interest rate to entice customers. The dealership does not grant the credit but rather puts the car buyer in direct contact with a bank that will issue the loan at that rate. This partnership is advantageous to both the car dealership (which can sell more cars through use of the bank's credit) and the bank (which can lend more money and receive more interest payments through the sale of cars). It also helps the consumer by providing the lowest interest rate available.

Finally, businesses may offer their own form of credit to reliable customers. This type of credit is especially common in business-to-business transactions. Accounts receivables allow a company to process all its payments once a month. If the suppliers do not receive payment on time, they can collect interest. However, they may incur bad debts from companies who can't pay. In such cases, suppliers can pay collection agencies to go after the money or accept that they will never receive payment.

Review Questions

1. What is credit and who uses it?

2. List five advantages of consumer credit.

3. List four disadvantages of consumer credit.

4. Why would a business need credit?

5. What are the advantages of a business using credit?

6. What are the disadvantages of a business using credit?

7. Explain the ways a business can grant credit.

8. What are the advantages and disadvantages of a retailer allowing customers to pay with a credit card?

Types and Sources of Credit

During your lifetime, you will probably borrow money and make many purchases on credit. People with a regular, steady income have several credit options. The type of credit they use depends on their needs, wants, and goals, and on the types of purchases they make. Buying a snowboard, for example, presents different credit needs than buying a car. Buying a house or a condominium requires another type of credit financing.

Like individuals, businesses also need credit for a variety of purposes. They may need to buy supplies, inventory, and land. Each of these requires a different type of credit.

The four most common types of credit are credit cards, installment sales credit, loans, and mortgages. Each type of credit has its own advantages and disadvantages. You should look at each form of credit carefully to decide which type best suits your needs and budget.

Credit Cards

Credit cards are so popular that the average Canadian today carries at least three different cards. In fact, there are more than 600 issuers of credit cards in Canada. There are three basic types of cards: bank-issued credit cards, charge cards issued by retailers, and cards issued by travel and entertainment companies. All three are popular, but bank-issued credit cards, such as Visa and MasterCard, account for the largest percentage of consumer spending.

Except for retail charge cards, credit cards are universal, or multipurpose. This means that they can be used to purchase goods and services at retailers, hotels, airlines, dental offices, and many other places. Many people like to use these cards when they are travelling so that they do not have to carry much cash. Millions of businesses around the world accept major credit cards. By doing so, these businesses attract more customers worldwide and increase their sales.

Using a credit card is like taking out a short-term loan—it is important to be aware of terms and conditions as well as options. Some cards are free, while other cards involve annual or transaction fees to cover expenses. Cards range from basic no-frills cards with low interest rates to "gold" and "platinum" premium cards that offer benefits such as travel and car rental insurance. Many premium cards also offer programs that allow customers to collect points for air or rail travel and other rewards.

Examples of credit cards that offer a customer rewards program

Various types of credit cards, including those two that are the most heavily used: MasterCard and Visa

Bank-issued Credit Cards

Bank-issued credit cards, such as Visa and MasterCard, are the most popular credit cards. Financial institutions issue cards to customers whose credit ratings meet certain standards. Based on the customer's credit rating, the financial institution sets a credit limit for each individual. If the balance owing on the card is paid in full every month, no interest is charged. Otherwise, customers must make a minimum monthly payment on the outstanding balance. With both Visa and MasterCard, interest is calculated immediately on any cash advances. But for purchases, interest is charged only after the payment due date has passed.

Credit cards have several advantages over other forms of credit:

1. Both small companies such as home-based businesses and large companies such as big-box retailers can set themselves up to accept credit card payments.

2. Credit cards are great for web-based businesses. These credit cards are accepted in many countries and make payments across borders easier.

3. Credit cards increase the probability and size of consumer purchases. Most customers don't carry large amounts of cash, especially when travelling. Providing credit allows them to make purchases they may not have cash to pay for.

4. The speed of payment for credit card purchases is faster than many other forms of payment. Businesses do not have to wait for a cheque to clear or an invoice to be paid.

5. Payment is guaranteed. The business does not have to risk a bounced cheque.

There is, however, one big disadvantage to allowing payment through a universal credit card: the business incurs several costs. These include equipment costs, transaction fees, and monthly statement charges. One large cost is charge-back fees for returned items or customer disputes.

The credit extended in a bank-issued card comes from depositors' savings. Since the financial institution must pay depositors interest on their savings, credit cards must make a profit for the issuers. This profit comes from the difference between the interest the financial institutions pay depositors and

Oops!

Businesses allowing customers to use universal credit cards are charged an administration fee for each purchase. These fees are usually between 1 and 3% of the total transaction cost. Therefore, a merchant that processes a $100 transaction will be charged up to $3 for the administration involved in the transaction. A merchant that processes a $1000 transaction will be charged $30—even though the administration would be exactly the same. This is one of the ways that credit card companies make their money. It is also a reason why many businesses don't like accepting universal credit cards.

A purchase using credit is made via a credit card processing machine.

the interest they receive from borrowers. In addition, merchants pay the issuing institution a transaction fee (a percentage of the purchase price) each time a customer uses the card to pay for a good or service.

Consumers like bank-issued credit cards because they are widely accepted. Many also like receiving one monthly bill that lists their purchases.

Ethical, Moral & Legal Considerations

Credit card and identity fraud has become a serious concern in Canada. Credit card fraud comes in several forms, including stolen cards, counterfeit cards, and false credit card applications. To avoid becoming a victim of fraud, police and business organizations recommend that consumers follow these steps:

1. If your credit card is programmed to access an ABM, memorize your PIN and never write it down. Do not select an obvious PIN: for example, your birthday. Some credit card companies will not compensate you for money withdrawn from a stolen card if your PIN is your birthday or any other number that could easily be determined from the contents of your wallet.

2. Never leave credit cards unattended in the workplace—it is the number one place for thefts.

3. Never leave credit cards in your car—the second most likely place for card thefts.

4. Always be sure that your credit card is returned to you after you make a purchase.

5. When travelling, keep your cards with you or place them in a safe location. Only travel with cards you will use.

6. Make a list of all your cards and their numbers. Keep this in a safe place.

7. Sign the back of your new credit card in permanent ink as soon as you get it and destroy all old cards.

8. Report lost or stolen cards immediately. Keep a list of emergency theft report telephone numbers at home, along with your list of card numbers.

9. Always check that the charges on your monthly statements were made by you. If any charges are strange, report them immediately.

10. Only give your credit card number over the phone if you are dealing with a reputable company or if you initiated the call yourself.

11. When you cancel a credit card by telephone, call back a few days later to verify that the cancellation was processed properly. Sometimes errors occur—and your card might not get completely cancelled. This is especially important if you tend to move a lot, since the card company may end up sending a new card to your old address.

Travel and Entertainment Cards

American Express, Diners Club International, and Discover cards are widely used for hotels, airline tickets, and car rentals. Because consumers use these cards to pay for luxury services and products, they are called travel and entertainment cards. Subscribers to these cards usually pay a yearly membership fee that is higher than the fee charged for bank-issued cards. Some travel and entertainment cards require that payment be made in full each month.

Retailer Credit Cards

Stores establish retailer credit card systems to avoid the charges and fees from universal credit card companies. In this way, they can handle the administration of accounts themselves and keep their costs lower. A store credit card provides all the advantages of a universal credit card to the store. An additional advantage is that the store receives the interest payments if the credit balance is not paid on time. The store can also provide credit deals specific to that store to entice consumers to buy with them and not at the competition. For example, a credit card from The Brick offers three months without payments and interest charges.

The disadvantages to administering a store credit card are the paperwork and the cost of the credit never being paid. Trying to collect bad debts is time consuming and often impossible. With a universal credit card, the store always receives payment; and the credit card company has to track down bad debts themselves.

Because customers can use these retail charge cards only at the issuing store, they are known as single-purpose cards. Some stores encourage consumers to get and use the cards by offering special sales that are available only to retail charge card holders. Major oil companies, such as Esso, Shell, and PetroCanada, also issue their own credit cards and offer users special deals and bonuses. For example, many retailers offer reward point systems or air travel points as a bonus for using the card.

Installment Sales Credit

Installment sales credit is a credit plan that requires a purchaser to make a down payment and fixed regular payments, with finance charges added to the purchase price. Consumers making expensive purchases, such as furniture, appliances, or vehicles, often find this kind of credit plan ideal. First, the store draws up a repayment plan in the form of a conditional sales contract between the buyer and the seller. This contract includes the terms of the purchase and payment details, including finance charges. The buyer usually makes a down payment of at least 10 percent of the purchase price. Then over the following months, the buyer makes the remaining payments following the terms of the contract.

Installment credit is more complicated to use than a charge account or credit card, which simply requires the buyer to hand over a card to the salesperson. With installment sales credit, the buyer must fill out a credit application, be approved as a credit risk, and then sign a detailed sales contract each time he or she makes a purchase. The buyer gets *possession* of the goods as soon as the contract is signed, but *ownership* of the goods stays with the seller until the contract has been fully paid.

When companies need to re-equip or expand, they often use bank loans to finance these needs.

Loans

Loans can be used to finance purchases of almost anything other than a house, factory, or commercial property (real estate purchases are usually financed through a mortgage, which will be discussed later). Loans are an alternative to charge accounts, credit cards, and installment sales credit for purchases. Consumers use loans for purchases such as a computer system, family holiday, car, or home renovations. Businesses use loans to buy trucks, raw materials, and new product development. Types of loans include term loans, demand loans, and student loans. Each type of loan provides a number of repayment options. Loans can be obtained from most of Canada's financial institutions.

Term Loans

A **term loan** is a form of installment credit in which the borrower agrees to make fixed monthly payments over a set period of time, or **term**. Usually, the term is one to five years. The biggest advantage of a term loan is that payments can be arranged to fit the borrower's budget. The total amount to be repaid includes the amount borrowed plus finance charges. Because terms and repayment details differ among financial institutions, it is important to consider the kinds of interest rates that the institutions offer. With a fixed-rate loan, the interest rate is set in advance for the full term of the loan. In a variable-rate loan, the interest rate changes because it is linked to the prime lending rate. (See Chapter 13 for more information about the Bank of Canada's prime lending rate.)

This couple discusses the details of requesting a loan with a bank's loans officer.

Many people choose to lease their cars.

Leasing is an alternative to a term loan, used to acquire the use of an asset. A **lease** is an agreement to rent something, such as a car or computer system, for a period of time at an agreed price. Leases are similar to term loans because they require customers to make regular payments over a fixed period of time. Unlike a loan, however, leasing is actually a long-term rental—the borrower doesn't own the asset at the end of the lease. Usually, the customer does have the option to buy the asset at its "residual value," or the worth of the asset at the end of the lease. This value is normally set when the contract to lease is signed.

Demand Loans

A **demand loan** is a special kind of short-term loan with flexible terms of repayment. Demand loans are usually granted to borrowers who have a strong relationship with their financial institution and who have security or collateral to guarantee the loan. **Collateral** is something of value that the lender can take and sell if the loan is not repaid on time. Examples of personal collateral include savings, real estate, or jewellery. Examples of business collateral include factories, machinery, or other valuable assets. With demand loans, borrowers can choose whether or not to make regular payments or to pay the full amount at any time. The lender can also "demand" full payment from the borrower at any time.

This young woman is applying for a student loan.

Student Loans

Student loans are guaranteed by both the federal and provincial governments and are available through most financial institutions. Canada Student Loans are usually interest-free until six months after graduation, when repayment is expected to begin. Canada Student Loan applications are available at most guidance/student services offices in high schools, as well as at most colleges and universities. Almost any full- or part-time student can apply for a student loan, as long as his or her courses and institutions are approved. For students who are still dependants, their family's financial background determines whether or not they qualify for a loan.

Mortgage Loans

Real estate is the largest purchase that most people and business owners ever make, and it usually requires a special kind of loan. A mortgage loan is a long-term credit plan for buying property. The period to repay mortgage loans can vary from 10 to 25 years. The mortgage itself is a legal document in which the purchaser pledges the property as collateral for the loan. Different mortgage options offer flexibility and choice in terms, interest rates, and length of time. Often, the bank and buyer renegotiate the terms of the loan and the interest rate several times during the length of the mortgage because of changing interest rates.

Most home buyers need a mortgage loan.

In the News

The Government of Canada has programs to help small businesses with their financing. The Canadian Small Business Financing program provides small businesses with up to $250 000 for a maximum of 10 years. The owner applies for the loan through a bank or the Internet. The loan payment is guaranteed by the government.

Another source of business credit is the Business Development Bank of Canada. A minimum loan of $5000 is available. The maximum amount depends on the entrepreneur's business plan. This organization does not fund bars or any company that makes over 50% of its profits from alcohol or gambling.

Business owners need to have an excellent grasp of start-up costs and monthly cash-flows when they apply for a loan.

Review Questions

9. List the most common types of credit.

10. What is a universal credit card? What are the advantages of such a card to a consumer and to a business?

11. Define installment credit. When would installment credit be used by a consumer, and when would it be used by a business?

12. How does installment credit differ from a charge account or credit card?

13. List three types of loans. State when a consumer and business would use each one.

The Cost of Credit

Credit is very popular with consumers and businesses, but it does involve a cost. Several factors affect the amount of interest that borrowers pay for credit. The principal, or the amount of money borrowed, is the chief factor in determining the interest cost. Other factors include

- the term for repaying the loan
- current interest rates
- inflation and general economic conditions
- security or collateral
- risk and credit rating

When you borrow, shop around for the best deal, just as you would for a purchase. Remember, financial institutions make their profits on loans, and they compete for customers. You might even ask for a lower interest rate than the one they first offer.

Principal and Term

Obviously, the more money you borrow and the more credit you use, the more you pay in interest charges. Interest is applied to the amount of money that is owed. The term of the loan also determines the interest rate. Short-term loans, usually up to one year, generally have a lower interest rate than long-term loans. Short-term loans have lower rates because the shorter period allows lending institutions to predict interest rates, economic conditions in Canada, and inflation rates with some accuracy. Long-term loans are riskier for lenders because they have greater difficulty accurately predicting long-term economic trends. As a result, lenders charge higher interest rates for long-term loans.

As you can see from Table 15.1, borrowing costs less if you repay a loan over a shorter term. In this example, by making larger payments over a term of three rather than five years, a borrower can save more than $1000 in interest charges. Borrowing also costs less if you make extra payments.

Although credit makes large purchases possible, credit can also place people at risk of financially over-extending themselves.

Table 15.1

Cost of Borrowing $10 000 for a Car					
Total Amount of Loan	Term of Loan	Interest Rate	Monthly Payment	Total Paid	Interest Paid
$10 000	5 years	9.00%	$207.63	$12 457.80	$2457.80
$10 000	3 years	9.00%	$318.08	$11 450.88	$1450.88

How to Calculate Simple Interest

If you are considering arranging a loan, it helps to know and use a few formulas. A formula for quickly calculating simple interest is as follows:

$$I \text{ (interest)} = P \text{ (principal)} \times R \text{ (interest rate)} \times T \text{ (time)}$$

For example, if you borrow $3000 at 7 percent interest for one year, your simple interest payment would be as follows:

$$I = \$3000 \times 0.07 \times 1$$
$$= \$210$$

In other words, if you borrow $3000 over one year at 7% interest, you would repay a total of $3210 ($3000 + $210). If you borrowed the $3000 for three years, your simple interest calculation would be $210 × 3 = $630. You should always know the total cost of your loan, which is P + I.

However, financial institutions do not calculate the interest on a loan using this simple formula. They must take into account any amounts repaid during the term of the loan, and charge interest only on the amount outstanding. Financial institutions must provide borrowers with a payment schedule that includes the total number of payments and the monthly payments for principal and interest.

Security or Collateral

Depending on the principal involved and the borrower's credit rating, collateral may be required as security for a loan. When a borrower offers a home, a car, or stocks and bonds as collateral, the risk of the loan is reduced because the lender can sell this security if the borrower fails to repay the loan. Offering collateral

> **Business Fact**
>
> In 2005, Canadians paid $50 to $60 billion in interest.

usually allows a debtor to borrow a larger amount at a lower interest rate than he or she could without this form of security.

Risk and Credit Rating

The borrower's credit history and credit rating also affect the cost of a loan. A debtor who has a record of borrowing money and repaying it promptly will probably get a competitive interest rate from the lender. An applicant who has no record of borrowing, or a record that indicates the applicant or the business is unreliable, may be denied a loan or charged a higher interest rate. The process of applying for credit and the importance of a credit rating will be discussed in the next section of this chapter.

Review Questions

14. List five factors that affect the interest rate of a loan.

15. "Long-term loans are riskier for lenders because they cannot accurately predict long-term economic trends." What economic trends might this statement refer to? What impact would they have on interest rates?

16. What is collateral?

17. List several examples of things that a business could use as collateral. Which item do you think a loans officer would consider most valuable? Why?

18. What is the formula for calculating simple interest?

19. Explain how length of term and interest rate affect the total amount of money a borrower has to repay.

Frank and Ernest

© 2005 Thaves. Reprinted with permission. Newspaper dist. by NEA, Inc.

Credit Worthiness

Before lenders decide whether or not to grant credit or a loan, they evaluate a potential borrower's **credit worthiness,** or the borrower's ability to assume and pay back credit. In their evaluations, lenders consider the **three Cs of credit**: character, capacity, and capital.

Character

Character refers to a borrower's willingness to repay a loan when it's due, as well as his or her reliability and trustworthiness. Answers to questions such as the following help a lender determine a borrower's character when applying for a personal loan:

- Do you pay your bills on time?
- Have you used credit before?
- How long have you lived at your current address?
- Where do you work, and how long have you held your present job?

Character can also be a factor when a business applies for a loan. The company must have a good reputation and have consistently paid back its loans in the past. Answers to the following questions determine a business's ability to repay credit:

- Does the business pay its bills on time?
- Has the business used credit previously without problems?
- How long has the business existed?
- Are the owners reliable?

The lender looks at the borrower's answers for signs of responsibility and stability. The lender's assessment of character must answer a basic question: "Will the borrower repay the debt?"

Capacity

Capacity refers to a borrower's ability to make payments on time and to pay a debt when it is due. Answers to questions such as the following help a lender determine an individual's capacity:

- Do you have a permanent job or a steady income?
- How much do you earn?
- Do you have any dependants?
- What are your current living expenses?
- How much money do you presently owe?

In the News

The fastest growing fraud in Canada today is identity theft. The increase is caused by home computers and access to the Internet. One method of identity theft known as "phishing" needs the victim's help. Professional-looking e-mails or official sounding phone calls ask people for their social insurance number, credit card number, or passwords. These fake communications are "phishing" for personal financial information that can be used to steal your identity. The Ontario Provincial Police states that consumers should never give personal information to communications such as e-mail or telephone calls unless they themselves have initiated that communication.

Banks also assess businesses on their capacity to repay a loan. A business must answer the following questions to determine its capacity:

- How much income is the business generating?
- What are the business's accounts payable?
- What are the business's current expenses?
- Is the business growing?

If an individual's income or a business's revenue is unsteady or low, the borrower may not be able to handle more—or any—credit. Even with a high income, a borrower may not be able to handle more credit because of other debts. The lender asks this basic question in assessing a borrower's capacity: "Can the borrower repay the debt?"

Capital

Capital is the value of a borrower's assets. Capital can be used to repay a loan if income is unavailable. Answers to questions such as the following help a lender determine an individual's capital:

- How much money do you have in a savings account?
- What assets do you have and what is their value?
- What investments do you have that could be used as collateral?
- Do you own or rent your residence?

Capital is important to assess a business's ability to repay a loan. Answers to the following questions gauge if a business has enough collateral or cash to repay the loan:

- What are the business's liquid assets available in cash, bank accounts, and accounts receivable?
- What assets does the business own?
- What investments does the business own?
- Does the business own real estate?

The value of a borrower's capital gives a lender concrete evidence of whether or not the borrower will be able to meet his or her credit obligations. In assessing a borrower's capital, a lender asks this basic question: "What does the borrower have of value that could be sold if he or she does not repay the debt?"

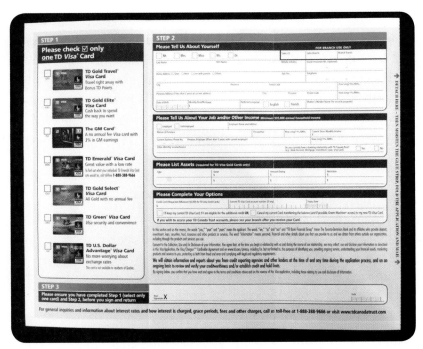

A typical credit card application

Credit Bureaus

Lenders check a borrower's credit worthiness using a credit bureau. A **credit bureau** is a business that gathers credit information on all borrowers in a particular region for the purpose of selling that information to credit grantors, or lenders. Retail stores and financial institutions are the main customers of credit bureaus.

Canada has three major credit bureaus: Equifax Canada, TransUnion of Canada, and Northern Credit Bureaus. The information collected at the bureaus is similar because most national and international creditors are registered with all three bureaus. These credit bureaus maintain a coast-to-coast network of offices and charge annual fees to users as well as a fee for each credit report requested. They collect information on the credit history of both individuals and businesses.

Credit bureaus do not rate or evaluate borrowers. They simply gather information on borrowers, and then keep the information in credit bureau files for seven years. After seven years, they remove the information.

Some people distrust credit reporting because they see it as an invasion of their privacy. Moreover, consumers and businesses who always pay cash have no credit record. But otherwise, the credit reporting system benefits both businesses and consumers. Businesses granting credit know they can use credit reports to make sounder decisions about whether or not to approve credit. Borrowers benefit because lenders are able to make quicker credit decisions, which makes buying on credit fast, easy, and safe for qualified applicants.

Credit Rating

A **credit rating** is an indication of the level of risk that consumers, businesses, or governments will pose if credit is granted to them. In other words, a credit rating is a measure of credit worthiness. Credit ratings exist because businesses that extend credit share the information they gather with other businesses, especially the regional credit bureau. Some lenders, in fact, refer to the credit bureau's report as the credit rating.

A good credit rating results when a borrower

- carries no outstanding balance on credit cards
- pays all bills on time
- keeps debt to a reasonable level, based on income and assets
- has taken out a loan, and met all payment obligations on time

A lower credit rating results when a borrower

- pays bills late
- has too many credit cards
- owes large sums of money as well as a mortgage
- applies for many loans or credit cards in a short time period
- has declared bankruptcy

Getting a Credit History

Students may need a loan for a variety of reasons. Teenagers need to borrow to continue their education, buy a car, or start a summer business. Getting a loan or credit can be very difficult for students. Usually, students have no credit history and therefore no credit file or credit rating. The absence of a credit history makes it difficult for a lender to determine credit worthiness. You can, however, start to build a credit history even while you are a student in high school. As you have learned, lenders consider trustworthiness and reliability to be important character traits. Good marks and regular school attendance help establish these qualities. Lenders often view positive behaviour as an indication that a student is likely to succeed in future education and in the job market. Holding a job and staying with a job for a steady period of time can also help students establish a good credit record.

A simple way to create a credit record is to buy something on credit and pay the bill within 30 days. In this way, you can begin a good credit record and pay nothing in interest charges. If you expect to borrow in the future, consider taking out a small loan before you need larger credit financing—for example, for a car or computer system. Repaying the smaller loan on schedule will help you establish a good credit rating.

As a student, you may be asked to have someone **co-sign** for your loan. This means that a second person, often a relative or a good friend, must also sign the repayment contract. If the borrower cannot repay the loan, then the co-signer is responsible for making the remaining payments. Naturally, the co-signer must also have a good credit rating. A co-signature reduces the risk for the lender. However, be aware that many people, including relatives, don't want to co-sign for loans because they don't want to be responsible for someone else's unpaid debts.

Checking Your Credit File

As a borrower, you are entitled to a copy of all the information that a credit bureau holds about you. In fact, many consumers and businesses check their file regularly. Those who are unsure of their credit rating, have been denied credit, or plan to apply for a large amount of credit might want to check their file. A bad credit rating not only affects credit, but it can also be a deciding factor in job and apartment applications as well.

To get a copy of your credit file, contact Equifax, TransUnion, or Northern Credit Bureaus in person, by mail, by fax, or online. The cost is minimal. Because credit information is confidential, it will not be given over the phone.

> ### Business Fact
>
> The *Personal Information Protection and Electronic Documents Act* came into effect on January 1, 2001. Among other things, this federal legislation ensures that all consumers in Canada have access to the contents of their credit file. Consumers and businesses should check their credit report once a year and three months before a major purchase.

Credit Crisis

How do you know if you are in a credit crisis? Will you be able to identify if you have a credit problem? Many people find that credit can get out of control. Some signs of this problem include

- being consistently unable to pay off your credit cards
- using cash advances for everyday living expenses
- not knowing how much debt you have
- seeming to always be in debt

If you have trouble with credit, you are not alone. However, you need to re-examine your spending habits and get out of debt.

Getting out of Debt

One of the disadvantages of credit is that it can lead to financial difficulties. If credit consumers cannot pay their bills on time, the worst thing they can do is panic and try to avoid creditors. Doing so will only make the crisis worse. Instead, they can take simple steps to help make the situation manageable. They can

- contact creditors immediately and explain their difficulties
- be honest and realistic, and work with creditors to make a plan for paying the debts
- pay a portion of what is owed in overdue payments, if possible
- put credit cards away
- seek help from a credit counsellor if you are unable to make changes yourself

A financial crisis is also a wake-up call to review spending habits, financial goals, and lifestyle. It is important to remember that a budget is the key to financial planning, but it will work only if it is realistic and changes are made when necessary. A borrower with several debts should consider a **consolidation loan**, which combines all debts into one loan. A loan and repayment schedule can usually be developed with the financial institution that will reduce monthly payments to a manageable level, over a longer term. The interest rate charged on a consolidation loan will probably be lower than the interest rate charged on credit card and charge account balances. It is best to consider a consolidation loan when it is combined with credit counselling.

E-ACTIVITY

Visit www.nelson.com/WOB and follow the links to learn more about Credit Counselling Canada.

Credit counselling services are not-for-profit organizations that provide unbiased assistance to individuals and families experiencing money and credit problems. Credit counsellors help clients look at their financial situation, discuss their options, and develop a course of action. Counsellors can offer advice on budget planning and can contact creditors to arrange debt-management plans and reduced payments.

The woman on the right discusses her various debts with a financial counsellor.

Review Questions

20. What two things do lenders want to know before making a decision about granting credit?

21. List and define the three Cs of credit.

22. Why is each of the three Cs of credit important? Which do you think is most important for a consumer loan? Why? Which do you think is most important for a business loan? Why?

23. What is a credit rating? Why is it so important?

24. Why should you check your credit rating regularly? What should you do if you find an error in your credit rating?

CHAPTER REVIEW

Knowledge

1. Describe ways in which consumers, businesses, and governments use credit.

2. Identify a government organization that would use credit. State four purchases it would make using credit.

3. What are some key questions that consumers should ask themselves when deciding whether or not to use credit?

4. Why might a borrower prefer installment sales credit over using a credit card?

5. How do you know if you are in a credit crisis? What should you do?

6. What is the purpose of a credit bureau? Who uses it?

Thinking

7. What do you think Polonius meant when he said "loan oft loses both itself and friend"? Do you agree or disagree?

8. Why might it be a good idea for people who always pay cash to purchase a few things on credit?

9. Canada's credit system is based partly on trust. Who does the trusting: the creditor or the debtor? Explain.

10. Do you think the advantages of credit outweigh the disadvantages? Explain your answer.

11. Many businesses prefer to provide and accept credit cards rather than accept personal cheques. Why do you think this is the case?

12. Would you prefer to have a fixed-rate loan or a variable-interest loan? Explain why?

13. Why do you think the Canadian government funds student loans?

14. Do you agree or disagree with the following statements? Explain why.
    - "If goods were sold only for cash, prices would be lower and everyone would be better off."
    - "If I can't pay cash for something, it means I can't afford it, so I won't buy it."
    - "I buy on credit whenever I can because credit increases sales and is good for businesses."
    - "You should use credit sometimes; it helps you establish a credit rating, which may be useful in case of emergency."

Communication

15. What advantages to buying on credit do you think are most important? Arrange your list of advantages from the most to least important. Compare your list with a partner. Discuss any differences.

16. With a partner, discuss the advantages and disadvantages of credit from the viewpoint of a small business owner. How might credit benefit the business? How might credit hurt it?

17. Do you think that teenagers should be given credit cards? Debate this issue with a partner.

18. Using a library, the Internet, newspapers, magazines, or local business resources, collect information on credit, consumer debt, credit bureaus, and credit ratings. Place your articles in a scrapbook, highlighting the key passages. Write one or two sentences explaining each article and its message.

Application

19. The following table represents the loan terms of one of Canada's financial institutions. The first column represents the size of the loan. Answer the questions listed under the table.

continued on next page

Amount of Loan	Monthly Payments	
	12-Month Term	36-Month Term
$2500	$222	$82
5000	443	165
7500	670	254

For each of the following loans, calculate the total amount that the monthly payments will be, and the total credit cost of each.

a) A $2500 loan for 12 months, for 36 months.

b) A $5000 loan for 12 months, for 36 months.

c) A $7500 loan for 12 months, for 36 months.

20. Using the Internet, research credit card interest rates. Find the rates for at least four retail cards and two universal cards. Create a chart of the interest rates. Calculate the interest paid for each card on a $1000 purchase if the payment is (a) one month late, and (b) one year late.

21. Find out what types of mortgage loans a local financial institution offers. What are the advantages and disadvantages of each type?

22. As a small business owner, you need to set up an office in your house. You estimate it will cost $6000 to buy furniture and supplies. Calculate the simple interest for one year if you used the following methods of credit to make these purchases: (a) retail credit card 24 percent, (b) universal credit card 17 percent, and (c) term loan 8 percent.

Team Activity

Team Goal: Buying a new computer system

Team Assignment: Using Credit to Finance Purchase

The team will gather information on credit costs from at least three different creditors.

Each credit plan should be detailed showing the amount borrowed and the cost of borrowing that money for one year.

Members of the team should generate a report that compares the credit plans and recommends which creditor to use for financing the purchase and why that creditor is the team's choice.

The team that finds the cheapest source for financing wins the competition.

Portfolio

Using a company within your industry sector as an example, illustrate how credit is involved in all aspects of the business. Be sure to include

- bank loans
- accounts payable
- accounts receivable
- other

Try to gather items such as annual reports, credit card request forms, loan application forms, etc. that will visually explain the role of credit in this industry. Interview retailers who use the products your selected company sells, and ask about payment terms. Include anything else that is related to the use of credit in this business.

Reflect on Your Learning

Is credit good or bad? Have your ideas changed now that you have read the chapter?

Should your parent or guardian provide you with a credit card? Explain what it will be used for. Explain how you meet the three Cs of credit.

Visa

Visa is everywhere you want to be, including the Olympics, FIFA World Cup events, and other major sporting events. With 1.5 billion Visa cards issued worldwide and more than 10 million transactions a day, Visa is one of the biggest credit companies in the world. More than 24 million merchants accept Visa in 160 countries, and a Visa card was used in making purchases in excess of $3.5 trillion in 2005.

In 1958, the idea of cashless purchases came about. Until that point, all purchases were typically made with cash or a personal cheque, which was seen as an inconvenience and a risk to both customers and retailers. Visa was launched officially in 1976, although it previously went by other names. In 1968, CHARGEX Ltd. came to Canada through BankAmeriCard, making Canada the second Visa region in the world. In 1977, the Visa brand made its Canadian debut on the CHARGEX Card. To date, there are 26.6 million Visa cards issued in Canada—including customers with credit cards, debit cards, and prepaid cash cards.

Visa has significantly evolved over the years in order to meet its customers' changing needs. Of particular importance in recent years has been credit card security. Credit card and identity theft is one

The Visa logo is stamped on all its credit cards.

of the fastest growing crimes. In fact, approximately one in 20 credit card users are thought to be a target of credit card fraud. This creates a significant problem for Visa. If credit card fraud continues to rise, it may discourage customers from using their credit card for purchases. Therefore, Visa has made security a priority.

Although Visa and its major competitors do not often agree on many things, they do agree that security is a high priority. The five major credit card players in the world—American Express, Discover Financial Services, JCB (a Japanese company), MasterCard Worldwide, and Visa International—have all teamed up to create a new credit standard organization. This represents the first time that all these companies have actually agreed on one standard, acknowledging that credit card fraud represents the greatest threat to their industry.

Visa has developed many security initiatives on its own. *Verified by Visa*, an online authenticity program, is used to verify identity with participating merchants using personal passwords. This helps to curb credit card theft online. Similarly, Visa has instituted the use of a personal identification number (PIN) for some clients when making purchases. The *Visa* chip card contains a microcomputer that is difficult to replicate, again helping to detect credit card fraud. All of these security measures help to ensure that people continue to choose Visa whenever they need to make a purchase.

QUESTIONS

1. Do you think that it is risky that Visa and its competitors have come together to create a security standard? Why would this be considered a risky thing to do in the business world?

2. How might Visa encourage customers to continue to use their credit cards in light of recent credit card fraud? List some strategies or ideas.

GLOSSARY

account statement A monthly record of all transactions in a bank account.

accounting The process of recording, analyzing, and interpreting the financial or economic activities of a business.

accounting scandal A publicly exposed crime involving accountants or senior executives who alter accounting records for personal benefit.

accounts payable Money that a business owes.

accounts receivable Money owed to a business.

acquisition A process or transaction in which one company takes over control of another company; also known as a takeover.

advertising The paid use of various types of media (such as television, radio, newspapers, and magazines) to try to convince consumers to buy a particular product or service.

advertising research Research that provides information on how to get a product message to potential consumers effectively.

agri-foods Farm-produced foods and services associated with primary agriculture.

annual report A publication that presents a company's financial statements for the year to shareholders and potential investors.

Asia–Pacific Economic Cooperation (APEC) An economic development organization based on consensus and voluntary participation that was formed in 1989.

Asia–Pacific market The region that includes all nations (other than the former Soviet Union) on the continents of Asia and Australia that have a Pacific Ocean shoreline.

ask price The lowest price that any shareholder is currently willing to accept for a particular stock.

assets Things of value that a business or a person owns.

auditor An accountant from outside the company who checks the financial records.

autocratic leader A leader who makes all the decisions and expects employees to do as they are told.

automated Work done by machine.

automated banking machine (ABM) A computer terminal that allows customers to withdraw, deposit, and transfer money with a coded access card.

automatic call distributor A computer that automatically dials phone numbers.

balance of trade The relationship between a country's imports and exports.

balance sheet A financial statement that shows the financial position of a business on a specific date.

balance sheet equation An equation expressed in two ways, depending on which part of the equation is known.

bank notes Paper money issued by the Bank of Canada and accepted as legal tender.

Bank of Canada A bank operated by the federal government that is Canada's central bank; it controls the money supply.

bank rate The minimum rate of interest charged by the Bank of Canada for loans made to the chartered banks; also called the prime lending rate.

barriers to entry Factors that prevent competition from being profitable in a given market.

barter To trade one thing for another without using money.

bear market A period of falling prices in the stock market.

bid price The highest price anyone is currently prepared to pay for a particular stock.

big-box store A large retail store that sells a wide range of products at low prices.

bilateral Involving two parties or countries.

blank cheque A cheque with no details filled in.

blue chip company A company with a long record of good earnings, regular dividend payments, stable growth patterns, and an active market for its shares.

board of directors A group of individuals who run a corporation or co-operative and make decisions on behalf of the shareholders.

bond A long-term loan made to a government or a large business on which interest is paid to the lender (the purchaser of the bond); a definite promise to repay borrowed money on a certain date, along with interest.

bonus A reward for good performance.

bookkeeping The method of recording all transactions for a business in a specific format.

branch banking A banking system in which there is a head office and interconnected branches or outlets providing financial services in different parts of the country.

brand equity The value of the brand in the marketplace.

brand management Grouping all the activities related to a particular brand into one department.

brand name A word or group of words chosen by a manufacturer or retailer to distinguish its products from its competitors.

brand trial Encouragement to consumers, through advertising, to try a product in its early stages.

budget A plan for how income will be spent.

bull market A period of rising prices in the stock market.

business The production and/or sale of goods and/or services to satisfy the needs, wants, and demands of consumers with the purpose of making a profit; an organization set up to do this.

business form A method of describing a business by its ownership, such as a sole proprietorship, partnership, corporation, or co-operative form of business.

business plan A document that describes the objectives of a business and summarizes the strategies and resources needed to achieve these objectives. Also referred to as a venture plan.

business type A method of describing a business by its function, such as a merchandising, manufacturing, or service type of business.

caisse populaire A type of credit union, located mainly in Quebec.

Canada Savings Bond (CSB) A loan from the purchaser to the Government of Canada, in return for a promise that the purchaser will receive the face value of the bond, plus interest, on or before the maturity date.

Canada–U.S. Free Trade Agreement (FTA) A trade agreement that came into effect in January of 1989, and was replaced by NAFTA in 1994.

cancelled cheque A cheque that has been cashed and paid by the financial institution.

capacity A borrower's ability to carry a debt and pay the debt when it is due (one of the three Cs of credit).

capital The value of a borrower's assets that could be used to repay a debt (one of the three Cs of credit).

capital assets Assets that businesses keep for a long time and that last longer than a year. Sometimes referred to as fixed assets.

capital resource A resource such as equipment, a building, or money, that is used to produce goods and services.

career A goal in life that is fulfilled through an occupation or a series of occupations.

career planning The process of studying career options, assessing one's career skills, and making decisions about a future career.

carpal tunnel syndrome A serious and painful injury to nerves in the hand, often caused or made worse by repeated use of a keyboard.

cash cow A mature product that generates high profits for a business.

cash flow The movement of cash in and out of a business, or cash that is available to the owner for the purpose of running the business on a daily basis and is used to pay for costs and expenses.

cash-flow statement A summary of the cash-in and cash-out transactions of a business in order to predict whether the business will have enough cash to meet its obligations.

chamber of commerce An agency that is supported by its chamber members from the business community. It takes responsibility for promotional activities, providing leadership opportunities, and helping its members to network with one another.

channels of distribution See distribution channels.

character A borrower's reliability and willingness to repay a debt when it is due (one of the three Cs of credit).

charge account A contract between a consumer and a retailer for sales in its own stores.

chartered bank A financial institution that has received a charter or licence from the federal government to operate in Canada; operates under the federal *Bank Act*; entitled to use the word "bank."

cheque clearing The processing of cheques and the settling of account balances among financial institutions.

choice The opportunity to select from several alternatives.

clearance sale A sale in which seasonal goods are sold below their regular prices to clear the shelves for stock that will sell best during the new season; also called end-of-season sale.

closed-ended question A question for which respondents must select an answer from two or more choices they are given.

code of ethics A document that describes specifically how a company's employees should respond to different situations.

collateral Something of value offered as security for a loan, which the lender can take and sell if the loan is not repaid on time.

collectible Any item of personal interest to a collector that can increase in value over time; for example, sports cards, stamps, and coins.

combination account An account that offers both savings and chequing features and that may pay interest on deposits.

commission A form of pay based on the amount of sales generated by the employee.

common stock Stock that represents general ownership in a corporation, carries voting privileges, and includes a right to share in its profits, but with no stated or fixed dividend rate.

comparison shopping Comparing the price, quality, and services of one product or store with those of another.

compensation The money and other benefits received by employees in exchange for their work.

competition A situation in which two or more businesses try to sell the same type of product or service to the same customer.

Competition Act A federal law governing business conduct in Canada.

competitive edge An obvious advantage over the competition.

competitive market Specific types of products as well as the companies that produce them.

competitive research Research into all the similar products on the market.

compound interest Interest calculated on the amount saved or borrowed plus any interest already accumulated.

comptroller The manager of the financial department of a business.

consolidation Centralizing work in one major site.

consolidation loan A consumer loan that combines all of a borrower's debts into one more manageable loan.

conspicuous consumption The purchase of products or services with the primary purpose of impressing others.

consumer A person who buys goods and services. Also referred to as a customer.

consumer market All the potential users of a product or service.

consumer price index (CPI) A figure calculated monthly by Statistics Canada and used to measure purchasing power.

consumer purchasing power When consumers have the power to choose where they will buy goods and services, and how much they will pay for them.

consumer research Research whose purpose is to discover possible products consumers would purchase and to predict overall sales potential.

convenience store A neighbourhood store that sells a limited number of items but has long operating hours.

co-operative A business owned by members who utilize the goods and services offered.

copyright The exclusive right to publish, produce, sell, or distribute an original work of literature, art, music, software, design, etc.

corporate citizen A business in the context of its relationship with its community.

corporate social responsibility (CSR) Conducting business in a way that is in line with society's values.

corporation A business owned by, but existing separately from, its shareholders.

corrective interview An interview with an employee who is having difficulties, in which problems are discussed openly and a plan for improvement is made.

co-sign A second person signs a repayment contract as a guarantee that payments will be made.

cost The amount of money that is required for each stage of production.

cost cutting A method of controlling expenses and making more profit.

cost of goods sold The cost of inventory that was sold to generate business revenue for a specific period of time.

cost principle The accounting practice of always recording an asset at the actual amount it cost the business.

counterfeiting The production of fake money.

creative strategy A plan for an advertising or promotional campaign that outlines how the target consumer will be persuaded to buy the product or service.

credit The borrowing capacity of an individual or company; also, a situation in which someone receives something of value now and agrees to pay for it later.

credit application An information form that a borrower must complete to help a lender make a decision about granting credit or approving a loan.

credit bureau A business that gathers credit information on borrowers.

credit counselling service A not-for-profit consumer debt counselling service that provides unbiased assistance for individuals and families experiencing money and credit problems.

credit rating An indication of the level of risk that a consumer, business, or government will pose if credit is granted.

credit union A financial institution organized, owned, and controlled by people with a common bond, such as employees of a private business or government organization.

creditor A person or business that is owed money; one who lends money or sells on credit.

credit worthiness A person's ability to take on and repay a debt.

crown corporation A business owned and operated by the provincial or federal government.

culture The sum of a country's way of life, beliefs, and customs.

current account An account in a financial institution for business, not personal, use.

custom A habit, routine, or accepted way of doing things.

customer loyalty cards Cards that are stamped with each purchase and, when full, entitle the customer to a discount or a free product.

customers Patrons of a particular store or business.

customs duty An amount added by a country to the cost of an imported product. The duty is usually a percent of the price of the product, depending on the tariff of the country.

data mining A research process used to look for unknown relationships and patterns among collected data.

database A list of information organized by category.

debit card Another name for a bank card that allows customers to access their accounts electronically at ABMs or at retailers using the Interac direct payment service.

debt financing Borrowing money to finance operations of the business.

debtor Any person or business that buys on credit or receives a loan.

decision-making model A five-step procedure that assists in making the most appropriate choice among competing alternatives.

demand The quantity of a good or service that consumers are willing and able to buy.

demand loan A loan, usually for a short term, for which repayment of the entire sum owing can be demanded by the lender at any time.

democratic leader A leader who encourages employees to participate in the decision-making process.

demographics The study of obvious characteristics that categorize human beings.

department store A store that offers a wide variety of goods and services; also called a full-service store.

deposit A sum of money placed in an account at a financial institution.

depreciation When an asset loses value over time.

dilemma A situation where a difficult choice must be made between two or more options. An ethical dilemma is a moral problem with a choice between potential right and wrong answers.

direct channel of distribution A direct connection between the consumer and the producer of a good or service; also known as a maker-user relationship.

direct competition Competition between products that are very similar.

direct deposit A banking service that allows funds such as wages or government payments to be transferred directly into a specific account.

direct exporting Exporting a product directly to an importer, without using an intermediary.

direct-to-home advertisement An advertising message that comes directly to a person's residence.

discount store A store that sells name brand products at prices usually lower than its competitors.

discretionary income The portion of one's disposable income that is not already committed to paying for necessities and can be used to buy things for pleasure, satisfaction, and comfort.

discrimination Denying a qualified individual an interview, a job, or a promotion because of religion, gender, or physical disability.

disposable income The amount of income that is left after taxes have been paid. This income can be used to pay for the basic necessities such as, food, clothing, and shelter.

distribution chain See distribution channels.

distribution channels The paths of ownership or control that goods follow as they pass from the producer or manufacturer to the consumer.

diversify Spreading out the risk of investment by choosing several different types.

dividend The part of a corporation's profit after taxes that each shareholder receives.

domain name The name given to a website; a web address.

domestic business The producing, distributing, or selling of goods and/or services within a country.

domestic transaction A transaction in which the production and sale of an item occur within the same country.

double-entry bookkeeping A bookkeeping system based on the principle that each transaction involves two entries.

downsize To reduce the size of a labour force or other aspect of a business.

draft A secure method of sending a large amount of money.

drawee The financial institution on which a cheque is drawn.

drawer The person or business from whose chequing account money will be taken.

duty to accommodate An employer's obligation to take appropriate steps to eliminate discrimination against employees.

duty to report An obligation to disclose all important information.

early adopter A marketing term for a consumer who likes to be one of the first to try a new product.

e-cash A form of money equivalent to cash that can be used in an electronic transaction.

e-commerce A method of direct distribution that uses the Internet to sell products directly to consumers.

economic resource The means through which goods and services are made available to consumers; natural resources, human resources, and capital resources are considered to be the three kinds of economic resources. Also known as factors of production.

economic system The way business and government work together to provide goods and services to consumers.

electronic funds transfer system (EFTS) A computerized system of electronic deposit and withdrawal of funds that reduces need for written cheques.

embargo A complete stoppage of the importing or exporting of a good or service.

embezzlement A type of accounting fraud in which an accountant or senior executive invents phony accounts and redirects money into them for personal gain.

empathy The ability to understand what other people think and feel.

employee layoff Dismissing staff to reduce expenses.

employee referral program An incentive program that pays employees a bonus if they find qualified applicants for new positions with the company.

employee turnover The rate at which employees leave a company voluntarily.

entrepreneur A person who takes risks and starts a venture to solve a problem or to take advantage of an opportunity; a person who provides an innovative product or service to meet a consumer want or need.

environmental degradation The consumption of natural resources faster than nature can replenish them.

equity The net value of property or assets after subtracting any mortgage or liabilities.

equity financing Raising money using the owner's resources or money from investors.

essential good An item that can be seen and touched and is necessary for survival.

essential service A service that is essential for survival, such as lighting, heating, and water.

ethical dilemma A moral problem with a choice between potential right and wrong answers.

ethics The principles of morality and proper conduct that people or businesses use to guide their behaviour.

euro The name of the single common currency for the European Union.

European Free Trade Association (EFTA) Britain engineered the formation of this association in 1960 and was joined by other European nations that did not belong to the Common Market. The current members are Norway, Switzerland, Iceland, and Liechtenstein.

European Union (EU) In 1993, the European Union united its 12 member states (Belgium, Denmark, France, Germany, Greece, Ireland, Italy, Luxembourg, the Netherlands, Portugal, Spain, and the United Kingdom) into a true single market, not simply an area of free trade. Today the EU is composed of 15 independent states (Austria, Finland, Sweden joined after 1993) with a total population of more than 370 million people.

exchange rate The value of one currency compared to the value of another currency.

excise tax A tax on the manufacture, sale, or consumption of a product within a country.

exit interview An interview with a departing employee.

expenses Expenditures that help a business generate revenue; assets that are consumed in the process of generating revenue.

export A product or service produced in one country and sold in another.

face value The value of a bond that appears on the face or front of the bond. It is the amount the issuer promises to pay the purchaser on the maturity date.

factor of production Another name for economic resource.

factory outlet A store that sells goods directly from the manufacturer's factory.

fad A product that is extremely popular for a very short period of time.

fair trade The practice of helping producers in developing countries bypass middlemen so they can sell their products for a fair profit.

feasible Having the potential to succeed.

feasible venture A venture that has the potential to succeed.

financial institution A bank, trust company, credit union, or other organization that accepts money from depositors and lends it to borrowers.

fiscal year Business year; the 12-month period used for financial calculations and comparisons by a business.

fixed cost An expense that does not change depending on the quantity produced.

fixed expenses Expenses that occur regularly and for the same amount each time; for example, rent or mortgage payments.

flow of funds The process of paying for imported and exported goods and services; the movement of funds in international investment transactions.

focus group A company-arranged meeting of potential consumers that the marketer observes during an organized discussion.

forecasting Predicting future conditions.

foreign direct investment (FDI) Foreign money invested in Canada.

foreign trade See international business.

forensic accountant An accountant who investigates legal and financial documents looking for evidence of tampering.

four Ps of marketing The four elements of a good marketing campaign: product, price, place, and promotion. When all four are present it is called the marketing mix.

franchise agreement An arrangement for one business to license the rights to its name and procedures to another business or person.

franchisee A person who runs a franchise operation and is under contract, or licensing agreement, with the franchiser.

franchiser The parent company who grants the franchise and provides goods and/or services to the franchisees.

fraud The crime of lying or pretending.

Free Trade Area of the Americas (FTAA) A proposed trade agreement that would extend NAFTA to all the democratic countries in the Western Hemisphere.

free trade zone A designated area, usually around a seaport or airport, where products can be imported duty-free and then stored, assembled, and/or used in manufacturing.

FTA See Canada–U.S. Free Trade Agreement.

FTAA See Free Trade Area of the Americas.

fundraising Collecting money to support an identifiable cause.

gatekeeper A person who makes buying decisions for others.

gender discrimination An employee being treated differently based on gender.

General Agreement on Tariffs and Trade (GATT) A trade agreement that was originally signed by 23 nations after World War II. It was designed to encourage economic growth through international trade and grew to 115 member states before it was replaced by the World Trade Organization in 1995.

General Agreement on Trade in Services (GATS) A WTO agreement that came into effect in 1995 and that set guidelines for the trade of services across international borders.

general partnership The most common form of partnership, in which the partners share in responsibility, decision making, and profits. However, the partners have unlimited liability for the debts of the business.

generic brand A product packaged in a very plain container; also called a no-name brand.

glass ceiling The invisible barriers said to be faced by women, the disabled, or people from visible minorities as they approach senior leadership positions in companies.

global dependency The phenomenon that occurs when many items consumers need and want are created in countries other than their own.

global economy The exchange of goods and services among people in different countries throughout the world.

globalization A term used to describe the process of doing business all over the world.

global product A standardized item offered in the same form in all the countries in which it is sold.

goal An objective; something that one works to achieve or attain.

good An item that can be seen and touched.

grading Checking products for size and quality against fixed standards for the product category.

grassroots movement A movement that develops from the bottom up.

gross domestic product (GDP) The total value of all goods and services produced in a country during a specific period of time (including items produced by foreign-owned companies).

gross income The total amount of money received from one's employer, before any deductions.

gross profit All the money left over after deducting the cost of goods sold from revenue, but before deducting the business expenses that helped generate the revenue.

Group of Eight (G8) An association of the world's most powerful industrialized nations: Britain, France, Germany, Italy, Canada, the United States, Japan, and Russia.

growth company A company that directs its profits back into the company's operations instead of paying dividends, and has prospects for above-average future growth.

guarantee A promise by a manufacturer or retailer, usually in writing, about the performance or quality of a product; also called a warranty.

guaranteed investment certificate (GIC) A savings plan similar to a term deposit, but usually involving a larger sum of money invested for a longer period of time.

harassment Making a particular person or group feel uncomfortable in a work situation because of race, religion, gender, etc.

headhunter A recruitment agency or executive search company.

hold A delay in clearing a cheque, imposed by a financial institution.

human resources People who work to produce goods and services in a business; also known as workforce or labour.

human resources department Department responsible for coordinating all activities involving the company's employees.

Human Resources Development Canada (HRDC) The department of the federal government responsible for workforce issues and programs.

idea-driven enterprise A venture that begins as the result of an invention or innovation.

image The consumer's perception of a business or its products.

import A good or service brought into a country for sale.

importer Someone who seeks out foreign products to bring into his or her own country.

impulse buying Purchasing an item on the spur of the moment without considering whether it is a wise purchase.

incentive Something added to the pay of an employee to encourage harder work or particular types of work.

income The money that an individual or business receives from various sources, such as wages or sales, interest, and dividends.

income statement A financial statement that shows a business's profit (or loss) over a stated period of time.

independent call centre A service business that makes telemarketing telephone calls for other businesses.

indirect channel of distribution The presence of one or more intermediaries between the producer and the consumer.

indirect competition Competition between products or services that are not directly related to each other.

indirect exporting Exporting a product to an intermediary, who then conveys the product to the importer.

inflation The reduction in purchasing power of a given amount of money when wages and prices increase.

ingredients The raw materials that go into a product.

innovation Using new technology, materials, or processes to improve on existing products, or on how they are produced and distributed.

insider trading Illegal buying or selling of shares of a company based on confidential information that isn't available to the public.

installment sales credit A credit plan that requires a down payment and fixed regular payments, with finance charges added to the purchase price.

insurance company Financial institution that insures risks.

intellectual property A business's trade secrets or the ideas or talent of its workforce.

Interac Direct Payment (IDP) A method of paying for goods and services electronically that uses customers' banking cards to immediately and directly transfer funds from their bank accounts to those of merchants or other service providers.

interdependent Mutually dependent; relying on others who also rely on you.

interest The money paid for the use of borrowed or loaned money over a period of time.

intermediary A business that takes possession of the goods before the consumer does.

international business All the business transactions necessary for creating, shipping, and selling goods and services across national borders. Also referred to as international trade or foreign trade.

international investment Investing that occurs across national borders.

International Labour Organization The UN specialized agency that seeks the promotion of social justice and internationally recognized human and labour rights.

international trade See international business.

international transaction A transaction in which the production and sale of an item take place in different countries.

invention A product or process that does something that has never been done before.

inventory Goods and materials kept on hand.

inventory management Balancing product quantity with sales; having merchandise when it is needed and not having merchandise when it is no longer needed.

investing Using savings to earn extra income.

invoice A bill for goods and services either bought by or sold to the business.

joint account A financial institution account shared by two or more people.

joint venture A business project that matches the skills of two individuals or businesses for mutual benefit.

just in time (JIT) A process by which required items are delivered immediately before they are needed, rather than kept on hand.

knock-off A cheaper version of a product that is experiencing a fad.

Kyoto Protocol An agreement reached in 1997 on targets to reduce greenhouse gases in the atmosphere.

labour All the physical and mental work needed to produce goods or services.

labour market The way connections are established between buyers of skills (employers) and sellers of skills (employees).

laissez-faire leader A leader who leaves employees alone to do their job.

landed costs The actual cost for an imported purchased item, composed of the vendor cost, transportation charges, duties, taxes, broker fees, and any other charges.

launch The introduction of a product.

law of demand The economic principle that demand goes up when prices come down, and comes down when prices go up.

law of supply The economic principle that supply goes up when prices go up, and comes down when prices come down.

lease An agreement to rent something for a period of time at an agreed price.

legal tender Coins and paper money, as defined by the Government of Canada, that must be accepted as payment for goods and services.

liability A debt of the business.

licensee Someone who has obtained a licence.

licensing Permission from the inventor of a product that allows another business to use his or her invention for a fee.

licensing fee Money paid to obtain a licence.

lifestyle The way people live, including their values, beliefs, and motivations.

lifestyle advertising Advertising that implies that using the product or service being promoted will improve one's lifestyle.

limited liability A restriction on the extent to which the shareholders (owners) of a corporation are personally responsible for its debts, limiting their liability to the amount they originally invested.

limited partnership A partnership in which the liability of each partner is limited to the amount of his or her investment.

line of credit A form of borrowing that allows access to credit up to a maximum amount agreed on between the borrower and the financial institution.

liquid Easily turned into cash.

liquidity The ability to convert an asset or investment into cash quickly and easily.

listserv A kind of e-mailing list that distributes queries and information to all the people who belong or subscribe to it.

loans payable Debt acquired by borrowing money from investors, banks, or other financial institutions; also called notes payable.

logo A special symbol that is associated with a product or company.

long-term assets See capital assets.

long-term goal A plan intended to be achieved within a long period, such as a year or more.

long-term liability A debt that takes longer than a year to pay in full.

luxury good An item which can be seen and touched but is not necessary for survival.

luxury service A service that is not necessary for survival.

magnetic ink character recognition (MICR) Special coded characters printed across the bottom of cheques and read by cheque-sorting machines.

maker-user relationship See direct channel of distribution.

management Those who decide how best to use an organization's human, financial, and material resources.

managers People who get things done by directing others.

manufacturing business A business that produces goods for sale.

margin The difference between the cost of the product and the selling price of the product.

market-driven enterprise A venture that begins with an idea about the market rather than about a product.

marketing All the activities involved in getting goods and services from the businesses that produce them to the consumers who wish to purchase them.

marketing mix See four Ps of marketing.

marketing research The collection and analysis of information relevant to the marketing strategy or process.

marketplace Any location where producers and consumers come together to engage in the buying or selling of goods and services.

market research Research used to identify specific groups of consumers who would use a particular product or service.

market segment Any part of an overall market that has common characteristics.

market share The amount spent on one company's product, expressed as a percent of the total amount spent by consumers on all products of that type.

market value The price at which a share of stock or a bond can be bought or sold; the amount people pay for a good or a service.

matching principle The principle that accurate profit reporting can be done only if all the costs of doing business in a particular period are matched with the revenue generated during that period.

maturity date The date on which a bond or loan becomes due and must be repaid.

merger A process whereby one company combines with or takes over the ownership of one or more other companies.

minimum wage The lowest hourly wage an employer can pay an employee.

minted Manufactured, as in the minting of coins by the Royal Canadian Mint.

money management Daily financial activities aimed at satisfying one's needs and wants within a limited income.

money order A form of payment, like a cheque, in which the issuing institution guarantees to pay the amount shown on the form to a payee.

money supply The total amount of money in circulation in Canada, including cash and deposits and savings in financial institutions.

moral A rule used to decide what is good or bad.

mortgage The legal document in which the borrower of a mortgage loan gives the lender a claim against the property purchased if the loan is not repaid as agreed.

mortgage loan A long-term credit plan for purchasing real estate.

mortgage payable The debt owed on a building.

motivation research Psychological research into the behaviour of consumers.

multinational corporation A business operating in or involving several nations. Also known as a transnational.

municipal corporation The formal name for a city or town.

mutual fund A pool of money from many investors set up and managed by an investment company to buy and sell securities from other corporations.

name brand A well-known brand that is advertised nationally and available in most communities; also called a national brand.

national brand See name brand.

natural resource Those raw materials that we get from the earth, the water, and the air.

need An item necessary for survival such as food, clothing, or shelter.

net income See net profit.

net pay The amount of money received from one's employer after deductions such as those for income tax, Canada Pension Plan contributions, and employment insurance.

net profit The money left over once operating expenses have been deducted from the gross profit.

networking The process of meeting new people and establishing business relationships with them.

net worth See personal equity.

niche A section of the market in which a product dominates and into which few competitors enter; a place or position particularly suitable to the person or thing.

night depository A secure, locked deposit facility at a financial institution that lets business clients make deposits at any time, especially after hours.

no-name brand See generic brand.

non-profit organization A charitable organization or charity that does not seek profit from the operations of the business and raises funds for a specific goal.

non-tariff barriers Controls, other than tariff barriers, to restrict or deter the importing of goods and services.

not-for-profit organization An organization, often a charitable organization, that does not seek to make a profit from the operations of the business.

North American Free Trade Agreement (NAFTA) An agreement among Canada, the United States, and Mexico to allow freer trade among the three countries, which came into effect on January 1, 1994.

notes payable See loans payable.

NSF cheque A cheque for an amount that is greater than the amount of funds in the account from which it is drawn.

observation The collection of information by recording a person's actions without interacting or communicating with that person.

obsolete A product or service that consumers no longer want because it has become outdated or outmoded or has been replaced by a new or improved product.

occupation Something one does to provide a good or a service; a job.

occupational forecasts Predictions about jobs.

offshore outsourcing The relocation of some of a company's operations to another country.

online Linked electronically, especially over the Internet. To "go online" is to establish oneself on the Internet.

online banking A service that allows customers to conduct banking activities from their personal computers through their financial institution's website.

online investing Buying and selling stocks on the Internet.

open-ended question A question that allows respondents to develop their own answers.

operating budget A type of budgeting done on a monthly, yearly, or project basis that clearly sets out the on-going revenues and expenses of the business.

operating expenses The cost of doing business for a particular period.

organization A method of combining people, finances, and physical resources.

organization chart A graphic representation of the structure of an organization or business.

orientation A familiarization period for new employees.

out-of-home advertising An advertising message that the consumer is supposed to receive while not at home.

outplacement counselling Assistance given to laid off or terminated employees in finding a new job.

outsourcing The practice of subcontracting work to other companies.

outstanding cheque A cheque that has not been cashed and deducted from your bank statement balance.

overdraft A temporary loan from a financial institution that results when the institution pays a cheque written for more money than is in the drawer's account.

overtime A higher hourly rate for working longer than the regular scheduled time or on holidays.

owner's equity The owner's investment in the business or the financial portion of the business that actually belongs to the owner.

partnership A business with two or more owners who share the responsibilities and profits/losses.

partnership agreement The legal document that establishes a partnership and each partner's responsibilities.

passbook A customer's record of transactions for accounts in financial institutions.

patent The registration of an inventor's legal right of ownership of his or her invention, preventing others from using the invention without permission.

patent pending A warning that an application for a patent has been filed, giving the patent owner legal protection for his or her invention.

payables See accounts payable.

payee The person or business to whom a cheque is made payable.

peer pressure The strong influence of people from one's own social group.

pension Income paid to an employee who has retired from a company.

periodical index A list of all articles published about specific topics over a particular period of time.

perk A special benefit beyond ordinary compensation.

personal equity A person's assets after all their liabilities are deducted.

personal identification number (PIN) A special customer code number or electronic signature used with a coded card to operate an ABM.

piecework A form of pay based on the amount of a particular product a person can make.

portfolio investment An investment made solely to earn interest or dividends.

postdating Putting a future date on a cheque.

preauthorized debit A regular, automatic withdrawal from a bank account.

preauthorized payment The process of paying regular monthly bills like loans, car and home insurance, and utilities automatically from one's account on specified dates.

preferred stock Stock that has priority over common stock in the payment of fixed rate dividends and gives its holders certain additional privileges.

premium Something a consumer gets free with the purchase of a product.

price The value of a product or service expressed in dollars and cents.

price fixing An illegal action by companies who agree on the quantity of a product they will supply and the prices they will charge their customers, in order to reduce competition.

pricing power When businesses are in control and can charge high prices and raise prices when costs go up.

pricing research Research into the possible price to charge for a business's product.

primary data Current information collected and analyzed for a specific purpose.

primary industry The six natural resource industries: agriculture, fishing and trapping, mining, water, fuel and energy, and logging and industry. Also called extractive industries.

prime lending rate See bank rate.

principal The original amount of money deposited or borrowed.

private brand A product that is manufactured by another company but is sold with a store's brand name; also called a store brand or private label.

private corporation A corporation owned by a small number of shareholders.

private label See private brand.

private sector The economic sector represented by individually owned and operated businesses rather than government.

processing Converting raw materials into a product.

producer An individual or business that makes a product.

product life cycle The changes in the popularity of a product over time.

product mapping An activity that allows the entrepreneur to visualize all the products or services that are available in a particular segment and to group them by specific features.

product research The examination of each detail of a product or service and the analysis of its potential impact on the market.

productivity A comparison of the resources used with the products or services that result. If fewer resources are used per unit produced, productivity increases.

professional labour Highly trained people in specific occupations such as accountants and electricians.

profit The reward that an owner receives for taking risks. It is the money left over from sales after the costs and expenses of operating a business have been paid.

profit equation Selling Price − Cost of Goods Sold − Expenses.

promotional sale A sale in which goods are sold below their regular price, for example, to build acceptance for a new product or to publicize the opening of a new store.

protected grounds Characteristics of an employee that, by law, cannot lead to harassment or discrimination.

protectionist Tending to protect one's own economic interests by imposing trade barriers.

provincial securities commission A provincial governmental agency responsible for regulating the securities industry and prosecuting crimes such as insider trading.

psychographics The study of lifestyles.

public corporation A corporation with many shareholders, whose shares can be bought and sold on a stock exchange.

publicity Information about a business, either positive or negative, that appears in the media and is not paid for by the business.

public relations firm A business that is hired to manage the publicity of another company.

public sector The sector of the economy consisting of agencies or departments controlled by the different levels of government.

purchasing power The amount and quality of goods and services that money will buy.

quality control Ensuring that the product a company makes meets certain standards.

quota A specified quantity that cannot be exceeded, such as a limit on the number of items to be imported or their dollar value.

random Without bias; offering an equal chance for anyone in a population to be selected as a representative of that population.

rate of return Interest expressed as a percent of the original investment; also called yield.

rate of return on average owner's equity A figure calculated in order to determine the success of a business. Rate of Return on Average Owner's Equity = (Net Profit ÷ Average Owner's Equity) × 100. See owner's equity.

rate of return on net sales Net profit divided by total revenue in order to show the portion of business sales that are kept as profit.

raw materials Ingredients that are transformed into another product.

real estate Land and anything attached to it.

receivables See accounts receivable.

reconciliation In relation to financial institutions, checking bank statements against personal records to ensure that they agree.

redemption rate The percentage of coupons issued in a sales promotion that are used by consumers.

refining A processing step that converts a raw material into a finished product.

regional relating to a geographic area or to a group of countries.

registered education savings plan (RESP) A long-term, tax-sheltered savings plan to finance a child's post-secondary education.

registered retirement savings plan (RRSP) A long-term savings plan that builds up a savings fund for a person's retirement. Tax is deferred on money earned in the plan until it is withdrawn.

retail business A business that buys goods and resells them to consumers.

return on sales Profit expressed as a percent of sales.

revenue The money a business receives for the products and/or services it sells or from its investments.

royalty The fee paid to the owner of a patent or copyright by someone who used it.

Rule of 72 A formula to determine how many years it will take to double your money if you let your investment compound. If you divide 72 by the interest rate being earned, the result is the number of years until your principal doubles.

safety deposit box A box located in a financial institution's vault that is rented by an individual or business to store important documents and valuables.

salary A fixed amount of money paid to an employee on a regular schedule.

sales pitch A scripted sales presentation that anticipates all possible consumer responses.

sales promotion Any attempt to sell a product.

sales quota A performance goal an employee is expected to achieve.

saving Putting money aside for future use; the opposite of consuming; the difference between the money you earn and the money you spend.

savings plan Putting money aside in a regular way to reach a financial goal.

secondary data Information collected by others.

second-hand shopping Purchasing goods that have already been owned by someone else.

securities A general term for stocks and bonds that are sold by corporations and governments to raise large sums of money.

semiskilled labour Labour required for a job that needs some instruction. Employees will be productive after a few days of training.

seniority Length of service with a company.

service Assistance provided, usually in return for payment, that satisfies needs and wants of people or businesses but that does not result in a product that can be touched.

service business A business that provides a service to satisfy the needs or wants of consumers.

service charge A fee charged for a service provided; a processing fee.

service sector The part of the economy composed of businesses that provide mainly services.

set of books Accurate accounting records of each transaction the business makes.

severance package Final compensation paid to a laid-off or terminated employee.

share A unit of ownership in a corporation.

shareholder A person who owns shares in a corporation; also called a stockholder.

shareholders' equity The shareholders' investment in a corporation or the financial portion of the corporation that actually belongs to the shareholders

short-term goal A plan intended to be achieved within a short time, usually less than one year.

sick pay Wages paid to an employee who is absent from work due to illness.

signature card A financial institution's official record of a customer's handwritten name, used to verify a customer's identity.

simple interest Interest calculated only on the principal amount loaned or deposited.

skill The ability to do something specific or to translate knowledge into action.

skilled labour Labour required for positions that need training from an educational institution and/or previous employment.

slogan A short, catchy advertising phrase associated with a company or product.

small- or medium-sized business (SMB) Any business that employs fewer than 500 people.

smart card A plastic card with a computer chip that stores information.

social costs Hidden costs of doing business that have a negative impact on people or the environment.

SOHO Short for "small office, home office," SOHO are home-based businesses.

sole proprietorship A business directly owned by one person who receives all profits and is responsible for all liabilities.

solvent Having the ability to pay all debts and other obligations.

specialty channel of distribution Any indirect channel of distribution that does not involve a retail store.

specialty store A store that carries a specific type or line of products.

stakeholder Someone affected by or with an interest in a decision or activity.

staledated cheque A cheque with a date more than six months in the past.

standard of living The way one lives, as measured by the kinds and quality of goods and services one can afford.

standard of value A function of money that determines the worth or value of goods and services.

start-up budget A budget that shows the costs needed to open a business.

statement In relation to financial institutions, a computer printout that lists all transactions in an account each month.

statement of cash flow See cash-flow statement.

stock See share.

stockbroker A licensed financial expert who advises buyers on which stocks to buy and sell and when.

stock exchange A trading market in which investors buy and sell shares and other investments through stockbrokers.

stockholder See shareholder.

stock options Company shares offered at a lower-than-market price to employees of the company.

stop payment An order requesting a financial institution not to pay a particular cheque.

store brand See private brand.

straight transaction account A basic account meant for paying personal and household bills.

strategic alliance An agreement between businesses to commit resources to achieve a common set of objectives.

strategy A plan for achieving goals.

style curve A graphic representation of a product's success in the market, illustrating the volume of sales over time.

supermarket A large full-service food store that carries a wide variety of name brand, private brand, and generic products.

supplies The raw materials used in the running of a business that do not go into the product.

supply The quantity of a good or service that producers can provide, determined by the costs of producing it and by the price people are willing to pay for it.

supply quota The amount of a product that producers agree to make available to consumers.

survey A planned set of questions used to gather data that can be analyzed to help solve problems.

sustainable development A process of developing land, cities, businesses, and communities that meets the needs of the present without compromising the needs of future generations.

sweatshop A piecework factory with low wages and unsafe or unhealthy working conditions.

takeover See acquisition.

tariff A list or schedule of the percent of the product price to be charged as customs duty.

tariff barrier An effort by a country to protect its domestic industry by increasing the cost of imported goods.

term The period of time over which a loan is to be repaid.

term deposit A savings plan in which a fixed sum of money is deposited for a specific length of time, paying a fixed rate of interest higher than that paid on regular savings accounts.

term loan A form of borrowing in which the borrower agrees to make fixed payments over a set period of time.

third-party guarantee A loan guaranteed by someone other than the borrower who has collateral.

three Cs of credit The three qualities of a potential borrower that a lender considers when making a decision about credit worthiness: character, capacity, and capital.

trade agreement An agreement between countries to allow goods and services to flow more freely across their borders.

trade deficit A situation in which a country pays more for its imports than it earns from its exports.

trademark A word, symbol, or design, or a combination of these, used to distinguish one company's goods or services from other goods or services.

tradeoff Something one gives up in order to have something more important.

trade show An exhibition where a large number of manufacturers and distributors show their goods.

trade surplus A situation in which a country pays less for its imports than it earns from its exports.

trading bloc A group of countries that share the same trade interests.

transaction The process of exchanging something of value for something else that has value.

transaction account A type of account in a financial institution used to deposit money needed for everyday use, such as paying bills, rather than for savings.

transaction register A record similar to a passbook, used with a transaction account.

TransFair Canada A non-profit organization that assures consumers that goods bearing their logo are fair trade.

transnational See multinational.

traveller's cheques A cheque-like form that can be purchased at financial institutions and used in place of cash to pay for items in most countries of the world; similar to a cheque but accepted like cash around the world.

treasury bill A short-term government bond issued in a large denomination.

trust company A financial institution that manages estates, acts as a trustee in business transactions, and provides a number of financial services similar to those provided by banks.

two Cs of marketing The two major external factors in marketing: the competition and the consumer.

unlimited liability Responsibility for claims against the business that goes beyond the amount invested in the business and extends to one's personal assets.

unskilled labour Labour required for a job that almost anyone could do because it requires very little training.

value A personal or corporate belief about what is important.

value-added service An extra service added to attract or retain customers.

variable cost An expense that changes depending on the quantity produced.

variable expense An expense that differs each time and is usually difficult to estimate in advance; for example, food, clothing, and entertainment.

venture A business enterprise involving some risk, established with the expectation of gain or profit.

venture capital market A market that brings together inventors and financial investors who are interested in developing new ideas.

virtual bank See online banking.

want An item not necessary for survival but that adds pleasure and comfort to life.

warehouse club A no-frills retail outlet that offers bulk quantities of products at prices lower than those of most supermarkets. Shoppers often pay a membership fee to join the club.

warranty The manufacturer's or dealer's promise, usually in writing, that a product is of a certain quality.

web page A portion of the information posted on a website.

website A place, or site, on the Internet where a business can be established and accessed by consumers. A website consists of one or more web pages designed to provide information about the business and display goods or services offered for sale.

website hit A visit to a website by someone using the Internet. The number of hits indicates the popularity or usefulness of the site.

wellness program A program that promotes and encourages the physical and emotional health of employees.

whistle-blowing The decision of an employee to inform officials or the public about a legal or ethical violation.

wholesaler Someone who buys goods from producers or importers and resells them to retailers.

wide selection A large number of different brands or types of merchandise.

withdrawal The act of taking money out of an account at a financial institution.

working capital The funds a business uses to pay its short-term debts (working capital = current assets − current liabilities).

work team A group of qualified people brought together for a specific task.

World Trade Organization (WTO) The principal international organization that deals with the rules of trade between nations. It was created in 1995 and replaced the General Agreement on Tariffs and Trade (GATT).

yield See rate of return.

CREDITS

Every reasonable effort to trace the copyright holders of materials appearing in this book has been made. Information that will enable the publisher to rectify any error or omission will be welcomed.

Cover
© 2007 JupiterImages and its Licensors. All Rights Reserved.

Table of Contents
xi Sherman Hines/Masterfile; xii Swerve/Alamy; xiii LWA/The Image Bank/ Getty Images; xv David Young-Wolff/Photo Edit.

Unit 1
2–3 Dale Sanders/Masterfile

Chapter 1 4 Steve Satushek/Photographer's Choice/Getty Images; 5 Dick Hemingway Editorial Photographs; 7 CP PHOTO/Steve Russell-Toronto Star; 9 Robert W Ginn/Photo Edit; 12 Don Mason/Corbis Canada; 13 Hemera Technologies/Alamy; 15 Poppy Berry/zefa/Corbis Canada; 19 Tony Freeman/ Photo Edit; 23 Brian Sytnyk/Masterfile; 24 Wally Bauman/Alamy; 25 top left Chris Cheadle/British Columbia Photos; top right Gunter Marx Photography; centre left James Hardy/PhotoAlto/Getty Images; bottom left Keith Douglas/ British Columbia Photos; bottom right Keith Douglas/British Columbia Photos; 30 © 2004 Thaves; 36 Megapress/Alamy

Chapter 2 38 Ed Gifford/Masterfile; 40 Dick Hemingway Editorial Photographs; 42 Derek Capitaine Photography; 44 W Geiersperger/Corbis Canada; 45 Al Harvey/The Slide Farm, www.slidefarm.com; 49 both Dick Hemingway Editorial Photographs; 50 © 2003 Thaves; 53 Ron Elmy/firstlight. ca; 54 Michael Keller/Corbis Canada; 56 Justin Sullivan/Getty Images News; 57 Public Works and Government Services Canada; 59 Rachel Epstein/Photo Edit; 60 Bob Daemmrich/Photo Edit; 62 Adam Woolfitt/Corbis Canada; 63 Dale Wilson/Masterfile; 64 Jochen Tack/Alamy; 67 Fredrik Renander/ Alamy; 71 Peter Titmuss/Alamy

Chapter 3 72 Al Harvey/The Slide Farm, www.slidefarm.com; 74 © 2003–2007 Kicking Horse Coffee, www.kickinghorse.coffee.com; 76 Kayte M Deioma/ Photo Edit; 78 © 2005 Thaves; 79 Jim Craigmyle/Corbis Canada; 80 Richard Hutchings/Photoresearchers/firstlight.ca; 82 © Paramount Pictures 2007. All rights reserved; 85 top AP Photo/Gatra Magazine; bottom DREAMWORKS/ The Kobal Collection; 87 Reuters/Landov; 89 Spencer Platt/Getty Images; 90 Jeff Greenberg/Photo Edit; 92 blphoto/Alamy; 93 Todd Korol/Reuters/ Corbis Canada; 94 Creasource/Corbis Canada; 96 Spencer Grant/Photo Edit; 97 Jose Luis Pelaez, Inc./Corbis Canada; 100 Reuters/Corbis Canada; 101 Christinne Muschi/Reuters/Corbis Canada; 104 Per-Anders Pettersson/Getty Images News/Getty Images; 105 © 2007 TransFair Canada; 108 CP Photos/PA Photos Limited (2002), all rights reserved

Chapter 4 110 Ron Watts/British Columbia Photos; 112 Chris Farina/Corbis Sygma; 113 Motoring Picture Library/Alamy; 114 La Belle Aurore/Alamy;

118 © 1997 Thaves; 119 Arindam Mukherjee/Landov; 122 Dick Loek/The Toronto Star/firstlight.ca; 125 M Stock/Alamy; 131 Shutterstock; 135 Antonio Scorza/AFP/Getty Images; 139 Paul J Richards/AFP/Getty Images; 141 Dick Hemingway Editorial Photographs; 143 Michael Newman/Photo Edit; 145 GUANG NIU/Reuters/Corbis Canada; 148 Boris Roessler/epa/Corbis Canada.

Unit 2
150–151 Mark Segal/Stone/Getty Images

Chapter 5 152 Gunter Marx Photography; 153 Copyright © Ganong Chocolates; 155 Paul A. Souders/Corbis Canada; 156 top left David A Northcott/Corbis Canada; 156 © 2006 Thaves; 157 top Derek Capitaine Photography; bottom left Bill Brooks/Alamy; bottom centre JA Kraulis/Masterfile; bottom right Raymond Gehman/Corbis Canada; 158 top Dick Hemingway Editorial Photographs; bottom Steve Skjold/Alamy; 159 © 2001–2006 Ubisoft Entertainment. All Rights Reserved; 160 Courtesy of D-Code, www.d-code.com; 162 Envision/Corbis Canada; 163 David Young-Wolff/Photo Edit; 164 Science Photo Library; 167 John Sturrock/Alamy; 168 John Springer Collection/Corbis Canada; 170 Benelux Press/Taxi/Getty Images; 174 Frederic J Brown/AFP/Getty Images; 175 Scott Olson/Getty Images News/Getty Images

Chapter 6 176 Jeremy Maude/Masterfile; 177 Courtesy of Robert Notman, KWA Partners; 178 Stewart Cohen/Foodpix/firstlight.ca; 179 Steve Neidorf Photography/The Image Bank/Getty Images; 180 Ariel Skelley/Blend Images/Corbis Canada; 182 Mark Karrass/Corbis Canada; 184 © 2004 Thaves; 185 Kayte M Deioma/Photo Edit; 186 David Young-Wolff/Alamy; 190 Edward Parker/Alamy; 191 Jose Luis Pelaez, Inc./Corbis Canada; 198 top Gary Conner/Photo Edit; bottom; 199 top Robert Brenner/Photo Edit; bottom Comstock Select/Corbis Canada; 201 Gail Mooney/Masterfile; 206 Matt Stroshane/epa/Corbis Canada

Chapter 7 208 Jon Feingarsh/Iconica/Getty Images; 209 Dick Hemingway Editorial Photographs; 210 © 1998 Thaves; 213 Sebastian/Alamy; 214 Andersen Ross/BrandX/Corbis Canada; 215 Marnie Burkhart/Masterfile; 216 Krause, Johansen/Archivo Iconografico, SA/Corbis Canada; 218 Peter Ryan/Science Photo Library; 219 © The New Yorker Collection 1975 Dana Fradon from cartoonbank.com. All Rights Reserved; 221 Fabio Cardoso/Corbis Canada; 224 Stephen Hilger/Bloomberg News /Landov

Chapter 8 226 LHB Photo/Alamy; 227 Patti Sapone/Star Ledger/Corbis Canada; 229 David Young-Wolff/PhotoEdit; 230 Dennis MacDonald/Photo Edit; 231 top Courtesy of IBM; centre © 3M 1995-2007; bottom © 2006 Kellogg; 232 © 2001 Thaves; 233 Worldwide Picture Library/Alamy; 234 Dick Hemingway Editorial Photographs; 234 Amy Etra/Photo Edit; 236 top James Nesterwitz/Alamy; bottom Brooks Kraft/Corbis Canada; 238 Steve Terrill/Corbis Canada; 240 Michael Newman/Photo Edit; 241 © AriZona Beverage Company; 244 Chris Smith/British Columbia Photos; 245 top Kathy deWitt/Alamy; bottom © 1998–2007 by Lee Valley Tools Ltd. and Veritas®Tools Inc.; 247 top Copyright © 1995-2007 eBay Inc.; bottom © 2006 Tim Hortons; 248 Michael Newman/Photo Edit; 249 Jeff Greenberg/Photo Edit; 250 David Young-Wolff/Photo Edit; 251 Derek

Capitaine Photography; 253 left Myrleen Ferguson Cate/Photo Edit; right David Young-Wolff/Photo Edit; 253 © Orbitz, Inc.; 258 Michael Newman/Photo Edit; 263 David Young-Wolff/Photo Edit; 265 Michael Newman/Photo Edit; 268 David Young-Wolff/Photo Edit

Chapter 9 270 Jose Luis Pelaez, Inc./Corbis Canada; 271 © 2007 Liquidation World; 273 Chris Cheadle/British Columbia Photos; 275 David Young-Wolff/Photo Edit; 276 Susan Van Etten/Photo Edit; 278 Cindy Charles/Photo Edit; 281 Lon C. Diehl/Photo Edit; 290 The Photolibrary Wales/Alamy; 293 Catherine Karnow/Corbis Canada; 295 top © 2005 Thaves; bottom Bonnie Kamin/Photo Edit; 297 Sandy Huffaker/Bloomberg News/Landov; 304 Susan Goldman/Bloomberg News/Landov.

Unit 3
306–307 Corbis Canada

Chapter 10 308 Herman Agopian/Taxi/Getty Images; 309 Copyright © 2002–2007 Rumba Marketing Inc; 312 top David Crausby/Alamy; bottom Bettmann/Corbis Canada; 313 top CP PHOTO/Paul Chiasson; *The Little Engine That Could*, © 1954 Platt & Munk; 314 Aviation Image Management / Alamy; 317 Radius Images/Alamy; 318 © Public Works and Government Services Canada; 319 Copyright © 2002–2006 Auction Transportation; 320 Sue Cunningham Photographic/Alamy; 324 © 2003 Thaves; 325 CP Photo/Chuck Stoody; 327 Derek Capitaine Photography; 328 Wally Bauman/Alamy; 330 Copyright © 2005–2007—Matrix Productions Inc; 332 BENOIT TESSIER/Reuters/Corbis Canada

Chapter 11 334 Victor Habbick Visions/Science Photo Library; 335 Justin Kase/Alamy; 337 Jim Craigmyle/Corbis Canada; 338 © 2002 Thaves; 339 Rick Fischer/Masterfile; 340 Lon C. Diehl/Photo Edit; 343 DigitalVues/Alamy; 344 Eric Nathan/Alamy; 346 Jim Arbogast/Digital Vision/Getty Images; 350 Frances Roberts/Alamy; 351 Michael Newman/Photo Edit; 355 top Bob Daemmrich/Photo Edit; bottom imagebroker/Alamy; 356 top Car Culture/Corbis Canada; bottom Bo Zaunders/Corbis Canada; 358 YURIKO NAKAO/Reuters/Corbis Canada.

Unit 4
360–361 Barrett & Mackay/All Canada Photos
Chapter 12 362 Tony Freeman/Photo Edit; 363 Bob Pardue/Alamy; 365 Lee Snider/Photo Images/Corbis Canada; 366 Courtesy of Bank of Canada; 367 © 2004 Thaves; 368 CP PHOTO/Troy Fleece; 371 Spencer Grant/Photo Edit; 372 David Young-Wolff/Photo Edit; 373 Bill Aron/Photo Edit; CP PHOTO/Steve White; 376 Derek Capitaine Photography; 379 David Young-Wolff/Photo Edit; 392 Kathy deWitt/Alamy
Chapter 13 394 Keith Levit/Alamy; 395 Ian Crysler/Bloomberg News/Landov; 397 Library & Archives Canada/A031686; 399 from top to bottom Courtesy of Bank of Montreal; Courtesy of CIBC; Courtesy of ScotiaBank; © Royal Bank of Canada 2001 – 2007; TD Group Financial Services © TD; © National Bank of Canada; © Canadian Tire Financial Services; © Copyright 2007 Citizens Financial Group; © Pacific & Western Bank of Canada; © Canadian Western Bank Group; Courtesy of Alterna; © Laurentian Bank of Canada, 2006; © 2006 Dundee Wealth Management Inc.; 401 Derek Capitaine Photography;